A Banqu
Consequences

Satyajit Das is a globally respected former banker and consultant with over forty years' experience in financial markets. In 2014 *Bloomberg* nominated him as one of the fifty most influential financial thinkers in the world.

Das anticipated, as early as 2006, the Global Financial Crisis. Subsequently, he accurately described the evolution of the post-crisis world, especially sluggish growth, disinflation, the increasing ineffectiveness of policy measures and retrenchment from globalisation. He identified the increasing political and social dimensions of the crisis, especially the growing democracy deficit and the end of trust. In 2016, in the context of the SARS and Ebola epidemics, he drew attention to the risk of disease and the lack of preparedness to deal with a global health crisis.

In his writings and public talks, he highlighted the linkages between the economic challenges and environmental, resource and socio-political constraints, such as inequality and intergenerational tensions. The extend-and-pretend model, he argued, had reached the end of its utility, and rising complacency combined with the reluctance to make difficult choices made a serious future crisis inevitable.

Das is the author of two international bestsellers, *Traders, Guns & Money: Knowns and Unknowns in the Dazzling World of Derivatives* (2006) and *Extreme Money: The Masters of the Universe and the Cult of Risk* (2011). He was featured in Charles Ferguson's 2010 Oscar-winning documentary *Inside Job*, the 2012 PBS Frontline series *Money, Power & Wall Street*, the 2009 BBC TV documentary *Tricks with Risk*, and the 2015 German film *Who's Saving Whom*.

ALSO BY SATYAJIT DAS

Traders, Guns & Money: Knowns and Unknowns
in the Dazzling World of Derivatives

Extreme Money: The Masters of the
Universe and the Cult of Risk

A Banquet of
Consequences

Satyajit Das

VIKING
an imprint of
PENGUIN BOOKS

VIKING

UK | USA | Canada | Ireland | Australia
India | New Zealand | South Africa | China

Penguin Books is part of the Penguin Random House group of companies
whose addresses can be found at global.penguinrandomhouse.com.

Penguin
Random House
Australia

First published by Penguin Group (Australia), 2015
This revised edition published in 2021

Text copyright © Satyajit Das 2015, 2021

The moral right of the author has been asserted.

All rights reserved. Without limiting the rights under copyright reserved above,
no part of this publication may be reproduced, stored in or introduced into a retrieval
system, or transmitted, in any form or by any means (electronic, mechanical, photocopying,
recording or otherwise), without the prior written permission of both the copyright
owner and the above publisher of this book.

Typeset in 11.5/17 Adobe Caslon Pro

Printed and bound in Australia by Griffin Press, an accredited ISO AS/NZS 14001
Environmental Management Systems printer.

 A catalogue record for this
book is available from the
National Library of Australia

ISBN 978 1 76104 192 1

penguin.com.au

for Jade Novakovic
to whom I owe a debt
that I can never repay

*The truth is sometimes a poor competitor
in the market place of ideas — complicated,
unsatisfying, full of dilemmas, always
vulnerable to misinterpretation and abuse.*

GEORGE F. KENNAN

*In a time of universal deceit, telling the
truth is a revolutionary act.*

GEORGE ORWELL

CONTENTS

Neither a Borrower Nor a Lender Be / Visits from Alien
Economists / Buy the F**king Dip / Washing Hands While
Singing 'Happy Birthday' (Twice) / Hamsterkauf / A Future
More Uncertain / The Road to Nowhere / A Date with the
Finite

PREFACE TO THE 2021 EDITION

A Banquet of Consequences (retitled *The Age of Stagnation* for American and Indian audiences to avoid confusion with a cookbook) was published globally in 2015. It sold modestly well but did not receive the coverage or interest that it perhaps deserved.

The disappointing reception and lack of engagement with the concerns it raised was puzzling. Critics and media, at least the few who showed interest, were hostile. The litany of facts and evidence was confronting. Energy and intelligence were deployed to deflect unwelcome questioning of the status quo. Things would surely continue as they were or improve. There was no cause for alarm, was there?

A Banquet of Consequences was before its time. It appeared during a period of optimism, no matter that it was propped up by deceptions and crumbling structures. The book predictably suffered Cassandra's fate in Greek mythology: its cautions were ignored. Unfortunately, the fears expressed proved well founded. The world's stored-up troubles have come to the fore. Events have made the work a cipher for reading the past, present and future.

A Banquet of Consequences is based around an observation, incorrectly attributed to Robert Louis Stevenson, that, 'Sooner or later, everybody has to sit down to a banquet of consequences.' It outlined several factors likely to affect future prosperity and progress:

- A deeply flawed economic model, over-burdened by debt and age and healthcare commitments, which was now incapable of delivering rising living standards that people assumed were their entitlement.
- Existential environmental problems that, at a minimum, required expensive realignment of societies but ultimately threatened the survival of significant sections of the global population.
- Resource – food, water – constraints that limited the ability to meet the demands of a rising population and improving lifestyles.
- Rising inequality that jeopardised social cohesion.
- A 'democracy deficit' whereby existing political systems and leaders would be unable to resolve the challenges, leading to the risk of collapse.

The book's concerns have been borne out:

- Economic policies that emphasise magical thinking have failed to restore conditions to those that existed prior to 2007/08. Prioritising national objectives, countries have retreated from globalisation and an international trading order that was pivotal to the post-World War II expansion.
- Environmental problems have accelerated at an alarming rate. Food and water shortages globally have manifested themselves in a variety of ways: draconian water rationing in Cape Town,

massive 'beggar-thy-neighbour' water diversion projects in China and Africa, as well as increasing risks of wars over water.

- Concern about inequality has spawned protest movements globally, frequently turning violent.
- The political system is on the verge of collapse as leaders fail to find easy and costless answers to the challenges. This has prompted the rise of populism and authoritarian leaders undermining democracies and free societies.

The 2020 pandemic brought these issues into even sharper focus. The public health emergency, which was unsurprising, revealed unpreparedness in many countries. The flawed response highlighted deep fractures in the underlying polity. The ensuing financial setbacks, brought on by measures implemented to control the virus, exposed the vulnerabilities of a structurally unsound economic system.

With the simultaneous collapse of the real and financial economy, this was more serious than the Global Financial Crisis of 2008/09. The only comparison may be the Great Depression. Having ignored earlier lessons, households, businesses and governments have few buffers and limited capacity to manage this new mess.

The COVID-19 episode, which will probably be much longer than forecast, will eventually pass. But our fragile systems will take longer to recover. Future crises will compound matters. Pandemics may become more frequent. Severe weather events, driven by climate change, resource shortages and financial problems will become a regular part of our history.

This revised edition, which was under discussion before the pandemic, updates the content, covering events since 2015 around each of the identified issues. There is also extensive coverage of the COVID-19 disaster. To avoid the temptations of hindsight, the primary text remains unchanged. The new material is placed in an extended postscript, 'The End of the Game'. The references and index have been updated.

At the time of its initial publication, the thesis might have felt theoretical and far-fetched. Today, the ideas are real and immediate.

Events have now created a perfect storm of consequences that will continue to be felt across the world in every aspect of our lives for a long time. It may recalibrate private and public discussions around the themes *Banquet* sought to highlight. Perhaps people may now have an appetite for the hard truth, and the courage to face their – and the world's – predicament. The need to transcend narrow self-interest and denial of the truth has never been greater.

As Winston Churchill warned when facing another existential crisis, 'The era of procrastination, of half-measures, of soothing and baffling expedients, of delays, is coming to its close . . . We are entering a period of consequences.' Time is very short.

Satyajit Das
Sydney, Australia

Reality Bites

The world is entering a period of stagnation, the new mediocre. The end of growth and fragile, volatile economic conditions are now the sometimes silent background to all social and political debates. For individuals, this is about the destruction of human hopes and dreams.

After the end of World War II, much of the world came to believe in limitless growth and the possibility of perpetual improvement. There was an unbridled optimism that all economic and social problems could be solved. The increasingly unsound foundations of prosperity and improved living standards were ignored. As Ayn Rand knew, 'you can avoid reality but not the consequences of reality'.[1]

*

A confluence of influences is behind the ignominious end of an era of unprecedented economic expansion. Since the early 1980s, economic activity and growth have been increasingly driven by financialisation – the replacement of industrial activity with financial trading, and increased levels of borrowing to finance consumption and investment. By 2007, US$5 of new debt was necessary to create an additional US$1 of American economic activity, a fivefold increase from the 1950s. Debt levels had risen beyond the repayment capacity of borrowers, triggering the 2008 Global Financial Crisis (GFC) and the Great Recession that followed. But the world shows little sign of shaking off its addiction to borrowing. Ever-increasing amounts of debt now act as a brake on growth.

These financial problems are compounded by lower population growth and ageing populations; slower increases in productivity and innovation; looming shortages of critical resources, such as water, food and energy; and man-made climate change and extreme weather conditions. Slower growth in international trade and capital flows is another retardant. Emerging markets that have benefited from and, in recent times, supported growth are slowing. Rising inequality has an impact on economic activity.

The official response to the GFC was a policy of 'extend and pretend', whereby authorities chose to ignore the underlying problem, cover it up, or devise deferral strategies to 'kick the can down the road'. The assumption was that government spending, lower interest rates, and the supply of liquidity (or cash) to money markets would create growth. It would also increase inflation to help reduce the level of debt, by decreasing its value. But activity did not respond to these traditional measures. Inflation for the most part remains stubbornly low. Authorities have been forced to resort to untested policies, stretching the limits of economic logic and understanding in an attempt to buy time, to let economies achieve a self-sustaining recovery, as they had done before. Unfortunately the policies have not succeeded. The expensively purchased time has been wasted. The necessary changes have not been made.

In countries that have recovered, financial markets are, in many cases, at or above pre-crisis prices. But conditions in the real economy have not returned to normal. Must-have latest electronic gadgets cannot obscure the fact that living standards for most people are stagnant. Job insecurity has risen. Wages are static, where they are not falling. Accepted perquisites of life in developed countries, such as education, houses, health services, aged care, savings and retirement, are increasingly unattainable. Future generations may have fewer opportunities and lower living standards than their parents.

In the US, which has recovered better than its peers, the middle classes are increasingly vulnerable. American families in the middle 20 percent of the income scale now earn less money and have a lower net worth than before the GFC. In 2014, 44 percent of Americans considered themselves to be middle class, compared to 53 percent in 2008. In 2014, 49 percent of 18–29-year-old Americans considered themselves to be lower class, compared to 25 percent in 2008. The experience of Germany, UK, Canada, Australia and New Zealand is similar.

In more severely affected countries, conditions are worse. Despite talk of a return to growth, the Greek economy has shrunk by a quarter. Spending by Greeks has fallen by 40 percent, reflecting reduced wages and pensions. Reported unemployment is 26 percent of the labour force. Youth unemployment is over 50 percent. One commentator observed that the government could save money on education, as it was unnecessary to prepare people for jobs that did not exist.

A 2013 Pew Research Center survey conducted in thirty-nine countries asked whether people believed that their children would enjoy better living standards: 33 percent of Americans believed so, as did 28 percent of Germans, 17 percent of British and 14 percent of Italians. Just 9 percent of French people thought their children would be better off than previous generations.

*

Global debt has increased, not decreased, in response to low rates and government spending. Banks, considered dangerously large after the events of 2008, have increased in size and market power since then. In the US the six largest banks now control nearly 70 percent of all the assets in the US financial system, having increased their share by around 40 percent. The largest US bank, J.P. Morgan, with over US$2.4 trillion in assets, is larger than most countries. Banks continue to be regarded as too big to fail by governments.

Individual countries have sought to export their troubles, abandoning international cooperation for beggar-thy-neighbour strategies. Destructive retaliation, in the form of tit-for-tat interest rate cuts, currency wars, and restrictions on trade, limits the ability of any nation to gain a decisive advantage.

The policies have also set the stage for a new financial crisis. Easy money has artificially boosted prices of financial assets beyond their real value. A significant amount of this capital has flowed into and destabilised emerging markets. Addicted to government and central bank support, the world economy may not be able to survive without low rates and excessive liquidity. Authorities increasingly find themselves trapped, with little room for manoeuvre and unable to easily discontinue support for the economy.

Unsatisfactory and complex trade-offs complicate dealing with interrelated challenges. Lower growth assists in reducing environmental damage and conserving resources, but it dictates lower living standards and increasing debt repayment problems. The alternative, faster growth, lifts living standards; however, this would, where the expansion is mainly debt-driven, add to already high borrowing levels and increase environmental and resource pressures.

Lower commodity prices would also help boost consumption and growth. But again, this encourages greater use of non-renewable resources and accelerates environmental damage. Low commodity prices also cause disinflation or deflation – falling prices. The resulting lack of growth in incomes, or the shrinking of them, makes the task of managing high debt levels more difficult. It also reduces the revenue of those heavily indebted businesses and countries that are reliant on selling commodities, affecting both their growth and their ability to meet debt commitments. On the other hand, inflation reduces debt levels but penalises savers and adversely affects the vulnerable in poorer nations.

Reducing the free movement of goods and capital assists an individual country, but the resulting economic wars between nations impoverish everyone.

*

While the changes that are necessary are actually simple, they're painful, and require courage and sacrifice. Living standards will decline in real terms. Citizens will have to save more and consume less. Working lives will lengthen. For many, retirement will revert to being a luxury. Taxes and charges for government services will rise to match the cost of providing them. There has to be greater emphasis on the real economy – the creation and sale of goods and services. Financial institutions need to return to their actual role of supporting economic activity, rather than engaging in or facilitating speculation.

Within nations, inequality may rise still further as different groups battle for their share of what is produced and available. Between countries, there will be increased competition to gain an advantage, by fair means or foul. In the short term, the thrifty will see the value of their savings diminish as they are appropriated to meet the costs of the crisis. Future generations will have to pay for the errors and profligacy of their forebears.

The magnitude of the adjustment required is unknown. Its exact trajectory and timescale are also uncertain. Denial of the problems is common. Refusal to recognise the lack of painless solutions is widespread. Governments preach and sometimes practise austerity, while assuring the population that their living standards can be maintained. Politicians refuse to accept that popular demand for public services is irreconcilable with lower taxes. During summits, national leaders regularly espouse internationalism, which is contradicted by fierce nationalism in their actual policies.

Conscious that the social compact requires growth and prosperity, politicians and policymakers, irrespective of ideology, are unwilling to openly discuss a decline in living standards. They claim crisis fatigue, arguing that the problems are too far into the future to require immediate action. Fearing electoral oblivion, they have succumbed to populist demands for faux certainty and placebo policies. But in so doing they are merely piling up the problems.

It is not in the interest of bankers and financial advisers to tell their clients about the real outlook. Bad news is bad for business. The media and commentariat, for the most part, accentuate the positive. Facts, they argue, are too depressing. The priority is to maintain the appearance of normality, to engender confidence.

Ordinary people refuse to acknowledge that maybe you cannot have it all. But there is increasingly a visceral unease about the present and a fear of the future. Everyone senses that the ultimate cost of the inevitable adjustments will be large. It is not simply the threat of economic hardship; it is fear of a loss of dignity and pride. It is a pervasive sense of powerlessness.

For the moment, the world hopes for the best of times but is afraid of the worst. People everywhere resemble Dory, the Royal Blue Tang fish in the animated film *Finding Nemo*. Suffering from short-term memory loss, she just tells herself to keep on swimming. Her direction is entirely random and without purpose.

*

It was C. S. Lewis who advised, 'If you look for truth, you may find comfort in the end; if you look for comfort you will not get either comfort or truth, only . . . wishful thinking to begin, and in the end, despair.'[2] Knowledge is the key to change. The world has to first face up to the unalloyed reality of its current predicament.

GREAT EXPECTATIONS

Postwar Booms
and Busts

'Most of our people have never had it so good,' British Prime Minister
Harold Macmillan told his fellow citizens at a political rally in July
1957.[1] He painted an optimistic picture of the postwar English economy, predicting an era of unparalleled prosperity. The phrase today is
used to deride political promises. At the time, it was accurate. The output of steel, coal and motor cars was increasing; export earnings and
investment were rising; wages and living standards were improving.

Across the Atlantic, the United States was enjoying even more
rapid growth and improvement in living standards. In 1960 John F.
Kennedy, the first American president born in the twentieth century,
in his speech accepting the Democratic nomination, spoke of con-
quering new frontiers, code for his administration's ambitious policy
agenda. After his assassination, the Kennedy agenda was subsumed
into the Great Society programs of his successor, Lyndon B. Johnson.

The ambition of these programs was unbounded. They targeted

poverty, unemployment, incomes, agriculture, education, aged care, healthcare, housing, transportation, urban problems, culture, the environment, racial injustice, international disarmament, arms control and the space program. They were the most comprehensive in scope since Franklin D. Roosevelt's 1930s New Deal agenda, designed to address the Great Depression. A new America would be built by legislators, technocrats and citizens using government funds.

Seen through the lens of nostalgia, it was the best of economic times, a period of unprecedented optimism and great expectations. Today, ordinary people long for this lost idyll of good jobs for life, rising prosperity, social mobility and egalitarianism.

Over the postwar decades, the emphasis would shift from industrial and social to economic and financial agendas, creating a succession of boom-ier booms and bigger busts, culminating in the GFC.

*

The initial phase of postwar expansion – known variously as the Long Boom, the Golden Age of Capitalism, or the New Gilded Age – spanned a period from around 1950 to the early 1970s. In France the thirty years of economic expansion from 1945–75 is known as *Les Trente Glorieuses* (the Glorious Thirty), rivalling *La Belle Époque* (the Beautiful Era, which covered the period from 1871 to the beginning of World War I). Its hallmarks were economic prosperity, low unemployment, rising incomes, growing wealth, increased availability of social services, and greater affordability of household items, leisure activities and holidays.

There had been fears at the end of the war that the reduction in military spending would result in a return to prewar stagnation. Instead, pent-up demand and the postwar baby boom drove rapid growth. Men and women simply wanted to get on with their lives. Rationing and a lack of consumer goods during the war years had tripled household holdings of cash and liquid assets. In America there was US$200 billion in maturing war bonds alone. This money helped finance the spending.

Industries such as car manufacturing, now freed of wartime demands and raw material shortages, resumed production. New industries, such as aerospace and electronics, established themselves. There was also a shift from agriculture and manufacturing to services. The movement of low-income farm workers into better-paying urban jobs assisted growth. Agricultural productivity itself was improved by the use of new high-yield crop varieties, chemical fertilisers, pesticides and heavy farm equipment. In manufacturing, rates of production were lifted by increased automation, better machinery and advanced control systems. Government investment in infrastructure, such as transport and communications, improved logistics and distribution, increasing productivity.

The migration from cities to the suburbs and into less populated regions, where land was cheaper and opportunities greater, also increased economic activity. Good jobs were plentiful. Rising incomes underpinned the rise of the middle classes. Falling prices, driven by mass production, put houses, cars, televisions and other possessions within the reach of a larger group of people than ever before. There was a housing boom, assisted by the availability of subsidised mortgages for returning servicemen.

Productivity gains were driven by a more skilled workforce, the result of wartime training and increased educational access. The US GI Bill provided generous benefits for ex-servicemen, including payment of tuition fees and living expenses while studying, one year of unemployment compensation, and low-interest loans to start a business. Productivity was also assisted by technological improvements, some of which were derived from the war effort: nuclear energy, pressurised and jet aircraft, rocketry, radio navigation, radar, synthetic materials, computers, and medical therapies.

In Britain too such improvements played a part in growth. Addressing the Labour Party conference on 1 October 1963, leader Harold Wilson called for a new Britain, forged in the 'white heat' of the technological and scientific revolution. But the postwar recovery in that country, and to a greater degree in Europe and Russia, was different to the US, due to the effects of the war. Parts of Germany, Italy and Japan were completely destroyed and needed reconstruction. The scale of the damage is evident from the fact that at the end of World War II the US accounted for well over 50 percent of the world's GDP (Gross Domestic Product), the value of all goods and services produced.

The Allied powers, anxious to avoid the mistakes of the Treaty of Versailles following World War I and the Great Depression, sought to normalise relations with the vanquished Axis nations as quickly as possible, and one of the means for this in Europe was the Marshall Plan. From 1948 this provided over US$12 billion in economic aid for postwar reconstruction and modernisation. The plan was not altruistic; it created markets for US exports and opportunities for investment.

In 1951 Belgium, France, West Germany, Italy, the Netherlands and Luxembourg created the European Coal and Steel Community, which ultimately evolved into the European Union (EU). Conceived by French Foreign Minister Robert Schuman, it was designed to create a common market for coal and steel. It would foster regional integration, making war both less likely and more difficult.

The war-damaged economies of Europe recovered, being transformed, modernised and internationalised in the process. Britain and France grew prosperous as activity expanded and incomes and productivity improved. Under Chancellor Konrad Adenauer and Economic Minister Ludwig Erhard, Germany's rebirth was dubbed the *Wirtschaftswunder* (an economic miracle). A far-reaching compact between business and labour unions allowed the rapid rebuilding of industry and strong growth, creating the foundations of an economic powerhouse. Italy also experienced rapid growth, enjoying its own *miracolo economico*.

Japan too recovered, commencing an expansion that would continue with few interruptions until the end of the 1980s. Like Germany, it successfully rebuilt its industrial base, emerging as a leader in steel, ship building and manufacturing, especially of automobiles and electronic products.

Not everything was the same, however; World War II had weakened the Western colonial powers. The Atlantic Charter of August 1941 recognised the right to self-determination and the restoration of self-government in those countries deprived of it. Between 1945 and 1960 a large number of countries, mainly in Asia and Africa, achieved autonomy or outright independence from their colonial rulers, peacefully or through armed revolution. Previously exploited for their natural resources, labour and markets, these countries now became part of the global trading system. Their efforts to develop and to improve living standards provided further impetus for global expansion, but despite their new freedom, most initially found themselves continuing to provide raw materials, investment outlets, markets and cheap labour for the industrialised countries of the West.

*

The international monetary order and infrastructure of postwar economic expansion was provided by the Bretton Woods Agreement of July 1944. Bretton Woods sought to ensure that there would be no return to the conditions of the Great Depression, especially the collapse of growth, employment and international trade, and the rise of protectionism that accompanied it. The focus was on establishing free trade based on the convertibility of currencies with stable exchange rates. In the past this problem had been solved through the gold standard, whereby the government or central bank of a country guaranteed to redeem notes upon demand for a fixed amount of gold.

The gold standard was not feasible for the postwar economy. There was insufficient supply to meet the requirements of growing international trade and investment. The West moreover did not want to confer any advantage on the communist Soviet Union, which controlled a sizeable proportion of known gold reserves and had emerged as a geopolitical rival to the US. Bretton Woods therefore established a system of fixed exchange rates using the US dollar as a reserve currency. The dollar was to have a set relationship to gold, at US$35 an ounce, and the US government committed to converting dollars into gold at that price. Other countries would peg their currencies to it, giving the US an unprecedented influence in the global economy that exists to this day. Supreme as the world's currency, the dollar was now as good as gold.

Bretton Woods also established the International Bank for Reconstruction and Development (better known as the World Bank) and the International Monetary Fund (IMF). Together with the 1947 General Agreement on Tariffs and Trade (or GATT), which evolved into the World Trade Organization, and the United Nations, which in 1945 succeeded the League of Nations, these institutions promoted relative stability in the world economy.

But the economic expansion had to coexist with the political uncertainty and confrontations of the Cold War. The need for the US and the Soviet Union to invest in weapons systems and maintain large defence establishments ironically helped growth. In his farewell address on 17 January 1961 President Eisenhower warned about the military-industrial complex – the relationship between politicians, the military and defence industries that gave these players great power.

During the Cold War, the US sought to limit the perceived communist threat to democracy and capitalism from what came to be known as the domino theory. In turn, the Soviet Union and China sought influence in international relations, especially over newly independent nations. The Korean War boosted the position of Japan, which was welcomed into the Western alliance, becoming a military base and major supplier to UN forces. Germany benefited similarly from the Soviet threat to Europe. Aid and technical assistance, linked to each side's strategic priorities, helped the development of many nations, even non-aligned countries that resisted pressure to take sides in the Cold War. It also laid the foundations for the Vietnam War.

Socially, the 1950s was a period of stultifying conformity and order. The postwar dream was a good job, marriage, children, a house in the suburbs and a growing number of possessions. Books like David Riesman's *The Lonely Crowd*, William Whyte's *The Organization Man* and C. Wright Mills's *White Collar: The American Middle Classes* recorded the narrowness of life where consumption and material abundance coexisted with a profound absence of self-knowledge and the denial of human potential. In *The Man in the Gray Flannel Suit*, Sloan Wilson's bestselling novel of the period, Betsy Rath complains to her husband, Tom: 'I don't know what's the matter with us . . . We shouldn't be so discontented all the time.'[2]

*

In the sixties the US stock market entered its go-go years, even as the postwar economic boom slowed. From its low in 1962 of 536, the Dow Jones Industrial Average rose, reaching the 1000 mark in 1966. Stock trading also grew quickly. In 1960 a busy day at the New York Stock Exchange entailed trading about 4 million shares. By 1966 it meant around 10 million shares. As in the 1920s, the conversation of ordinary people was once more about the stock market. In May 1967 Harris Upham, a stock brokerage, even sent out a letter linking stock prices and skirt hemlines, attributing the rise of share prices to the miniskirt.

The dominant figures were star mutual fund managers, who gained ascendancy over conservative investment professionals, aggressively chasing growth with rapid purchases and sales of stocks to take advantage of market momentum. In a pattern that was to be repeated in the 1980s, 1990s and 2000s, the boom was driven by a mixture of glamorous technology stocks, speculation and financial engineering. Conglomerates such as Ling-Temco-Vought, International Telephone & Telegraph, and Gulf & Western anticipated future private equity firms, buying and selling disparate businesses in sectors such as missiles, hotels, real estate, car rentals, golf equipment and film studios. Low interest rates and cheap financing costs helped fuel the rapid increase in stock and asset prices.

The sixties was also the decade in which the counterculture gained traction. Coalescing around the black, women's and gay rights movements, it sought greater social equality and mobility, and opposed war, particularly nuclear war and the Vietnam War with its associated conscription. Mainly white, middle- and upper-class youth and campus rebels, primarily in developed countries, challenged existing social norms and their parents' values.

The political agenda was unclear. Activist Tom Hayden found the values and aspirations of the poor, who wanted better lives rather than revolution, to be similar to those of the middle class, which he personally found vacuous. Sixties political activists concluded that people needed to have their real interests explained to them. The focus was, in reality, less political than personal, centred on the sexual (assisted by the availability of the contraceptive pill), the spiritual, new styles of dress and appearance. It found its clearest expression in drugs and music, culminating in Woodstock in August 1969. The festival marked an end, not a beginning, as many of its stars would die shortly and the counterculture movement fade away.

In August 1967 Abbie Hoffman and Jerry Rubin led a group of fellow Yippies onto the visitors' balcony of the New York Stock Exchange to denounce greed and the Vietnam War. In a piece of political theatre, they threw dollar bills onto the trading floor below. In the 1980s Rubin re-emerged as a businessman, arguing that the market system was a means of achieving meaningful change in the world, and actor Jane Fonda, who once campaigned for radical causes, starred in bestselling fitness videos. The generation who argued that no one over thirty could be trusted had changed their minds on reaching that age. The legacy of the sixties was not social change, but an intense self-absorption, selfishness, and a disengagement from social responsibility, setting the stage for the age of greed and speculation that would follow.

The real threat at the end of the sixties was increasing violence, which evolved out of the social unrest and protests in inner cities and on college campuses. Radical-left groups like the Weather Underground sought to overthrow the government and conducted a campaign of bombings. In Europe the Baader-Meinhof group and the Italian Red Brigades engaged in armed resistance, carrying out sophisticated assassinations of political, business and military figures, including Deutsche Bank chairman Alfred Herrhausen and former Italian prime minister Aldo Moro. Japan too had a radical group known as the Red Army.

The 1969 film *Easy Rider* provided the coda for the period, symbolising the confused dissent of a generation. Wyatt (played by Peter Fonda, Jane's brother) admits in the film's climax that they had failed, blown it.

*

The seventies was the decade of oil shocks, which occurred in 1973 and 1979 and ended a period of low prices. In the US this was compounded by oil production peaking.

In October 1973 Arab members of the Organization of the Petroleum Exporting Countries (OPEC) proclaimed an oil embargo, in response to US backing for Israel during the Yom Kippur War and in support of the Palestinians. The price of oil rose from us$3 per barrel to nearly us$12. In 1979, in the wake of the Iranian revolution, oil output fell and the price rose to nearly us$40 per barrel. This resulted in higher inflation and a sharp global economic slowdown.

This decade saw the collapse of the Bretton Woods international monetary system. The cost to the US of the Vietnam War and the Great Society programs had spurred sharp increases in prices, along with large budget deficits and increased dollar outflows to pay for the expenditures. Fearing devaluation of the US currency relative to the German Deutsche Mark and the Japanese yen, traders sought to change dollars into gold. By the early 1970s, dollar holders had lost faith in the ability of the US to back its currency with gold, as the ratio of gold available to dollars deteriorated from 55 percent to 22 percent. On 15 August 1971 President Richard Nixon unilaterally closed the gold window, making the dollar inconvertible. In February 1973 the world moved to the era of floating currencies, abandoning any link between the dollar and gold. The resulting uncertainty regarding currency values and rising interest rates undermined economic confidence.

Also in 1973 the US stock market fell to levels from which it would not recover for nearly a decade. The economy slipped into a recession. Corporate profits fell. As with all market booms and busts, much that was recently fashionable proved unsustainable, with mutual funds and conglomerates becoming discredited.

The UK too was in decline, with low growth, high unemployment and high inflation. The 1973 oil crisis and the subsequent energy shortages forced a three-day working week. Britain's trade with the Commonwealth fell. Attempts to offset this decline by improving economic relations with Europe were limited by Britain's exclusion from the EU (then known as the European Economic Community), with France vetoing British entry in 1963 and again in 1967. British industry, much of it government owned or controlled, lacked the ability to compete globally. There were growing industrial problems. Under the conservative government of Edward Heath, more than 9 million working days were lost to strikes. In 1976 the UK was forced to apply to the IMF for a £2.3 billion loan. Britain had become the sick man of Europe.

Germany, now a major economic power, relied on the *Magisches Viereck* (the magic rectangle) of currency stability, economic growth, strong employment and a positive trade balance. Under Economics Minister Karl Schiller, the government provided *Globalsteuerung* (global guidance) to foster noninflationary, continuous growth. But in the 1970s Germany too slowed, reflecting the rise in energy prices, a weakening global economy and the rising value of the Deutsche Mark, which reduced the country's international competitiveness.

The communist economies also slowed, due to failures of the centrally planned system, high defence spending, higher energy prices (for countries reliant on oil imports), and growing dependence on food imports, amongst other factors.

Some countries benefited and some suffered from the growing international trade in manufactured goods such as automobiles and electronics. The North American Rust Belt and the West German Ruhr area, both centres of mining and heavy industry, decayed as steel demand declined and Western producers faced competition from newly industrialised countries. In contrast, Asian economies such as Japan, South Korea, Taiwan, Hong Kong and Singapore continued to expand and prosper due to increased exports of these same goods, a result of lower labour costs, improving productivity, better quality and more innovative products.

Developed economies were forced to adjust, focusing on high-end manufacturing and controlling intellectual property. They expanded their service economy – information technology, financial services, retail, distribution and transportation logistics, health and aged care, education, hospitality, leisure and entertainment.

Economic management in the postwar era had focused on NAIRU, the non-accelerating inflation rate of unemployment, which refers to maintaining a level of unemployment consistent with low inflation. It was now the era of stagflation, a combination of high inflation and high unemployment. According to economic theory, the phenomenon was impossible, as availability of surplus workers should force prices down. Yet in the US, where the average annual inflation rate for the period 1900–70 was approximately 2.5 percent, the 1970s saw the rate rise to around 6 percent, peaking at over 13 percent in 1979. Slowing growth increased unemployment, to high single figures. The pattern was similar in much of the developed world.

In political language, stagflation is the misery index, the simple addition of the inflation rate to the unemployment rate. During the 1970s the US misery index hovered around the mid to high teens, peaking at around 22 percent by 1980. But soon political change, different economics, innovation and luck would usher in 'morning in America', and elsewhere. The economy would recover, giving the postwar boom new impetus.

*

In 1979 Margaret Thatcher became the first woman prime minister of the UK. In 1980 Ronald Reagan was elected US president. They were to preside over a significant shift in how economies were run.

There was increasing scepticism about government programs and intervention in the economy. The existing model of a mixed economy, with significant state involvement, had been unable to deal with stagflation. The Watergate scandal, which ended President Nixon's reign, and the conduct of the Vietnam War engendered suspicion of authority and the political process. It was one of the world's periodic mood swings between a Calvinistic urge to control and the impulse for greater freedom. Western developed countries now placed faith in markets to solve economic and social problems.

The successful 1984 Los Angeles Olympics, staged without public support and featuring the McDonald's Olympic Swim Stadium, was the new model. Nobel Prize-winning economist Milton Friedman, the unlikely star of 1980's ten-part Public Broadcasting Service series *Free to Choose*, provided the script for a new era of free markets.

The focus was on structural reform. Taxes were cut, price controls removed. Telecommunications, banking, airlines, transport, electricity, gas and water were deregulated to increase competition. Labour markets were also deregulated. Organised labour power was reduced in brutal confrontations, such as the strikes by the US air traffic controllers and the UK miners. The UK privatised many state-owned companies, reversing decades of nationalisation and government ownership. In France, and other European countries where the *dirigiste* tradition was the ruling orthodoxy, state control over the economy was reduced as they were forced to embrace markets.

Lower interest rates, lower energy costs, rapid technological change, increasing financialisation, and a surge of global integration were crucial in restarting growth. Paul Volcker, chairman of the US Federal Reserve ('the Fed'), brought inflation under control and restored sound money. The Fed forced interest rates up to brutal levels (the US prime rate went beyond 21 percent per annum) to reduce inflationary expectations. Volcker received death threats written on bricks and two-by-fours as the economy slowed and unemployment and bankruptcies increased. But inflation eventually fell, ushering in a period of low interest rates.

The oil price also fell, driven by a surplus of crude, falling demand due to slower economic activity, and energy conservation spurred by high prices. Commencing in 1980, oil prices declined over the next six years, culminating in a 46 percent price drop in 1986. After adjustment for inflation, the oil price was to remain low until the early 2000s, helping growth.

Rapid development of computing and telecommunications technology boosted productivity and created new industries. The exponential rise in the 1980s in computing power, and the availability of personal computers at ever-decreasing prices, revolutionised business. In the 1990s the expansion of the internet and fibre-optics-based communications changed it further, also dramatically changing media and entertainment.

In the preceding decades, developed economies had shifted through agricultural, manufacturing and service phases. The mid-1980s saw the rise of the finance economy. This was driven by the deregulation of the financial sector; a rising appetite for debt and risk; growing wealth and savings that needed to be invested; the requirement to manage exposure to the increasing volatility of interest rates, currencies and commodity prices in a deregulated environment; and, most importantly, the collapse of the Bretton Woods monetary system. The fact that states and their central banks now controlled the supply of money, and through it the economy, was crucial in the evolution of the finance economy.

Under the influence of financialisation, debt levels increased rapidly. The range of financial instruments and services expanded; the sector became large relative to the size of the real economy, and a major contributor to growth. In previous eras the creation, production and sale of goods and services were the means to success. Now, the structuring and trading of financial products representing claims on businesses and underlying activities was the path to wealth. Financial engineering was to ultimately become more important than real engineering.

*

Commencing in the 1980s, there was unprecedented expansion in cross-border trade and flow of capital. The large US deficits resulting from the Vietnam War and Great Society programs had created significant overseas holdings of US dollars. The need to lend these out led to a nascent international money market centred in London – the euro market.

The oil shocks had created petrodollars, US dollars paid to oil-exporting countries. Saudi Arabia, Kuwait and others amassed large surpluses of petrodollars, which they could not immediately use because of their small populations and lack of industrialisation. The surpluses were deposited in the euro market and lent out, mainly to less developed countries. Between 1973 and 1977 the foreign debts of these countries increased by 150 percent, ending in a debt crisis.

Countries borrowed huge sums of money from international creditors to pay for oil imports. Others borrowed to finance massive infrastructure programs and rapid industrialisation. Some oil exporters borrowed heavily against future revenues, assuming continued high prices. Borrowing from US commercial banks and other creditors by Latin America, led by Brazil, Argentina and Mexico, increased from US$29 billion in 1970 to US$327 billion in 1982. When countries found themselves unable to repay, especially as US dollar interest rates rose, sixteen Latin American nations and eleven developing countries in other parts of the world were forced to reschedule their debts.

Citibank chairman Walter Wriston had argued that countries could not go bankrupt. Now the bank was forced to write off US$3.3 billion in debts, wiping out a substantial part of its shareholders' capital. Other banks followed suit. The countries themselves slipped into deep recessions, suffering a lost decade, but the system of international capital flow and global trade survived.

Further trade expansion came with the fall of the communist governments of Eastern Europe. While President Nixon's policy of détente in the 1970s had helped ease Cold War tensions, ultimately it was internal economic problems and declining living standards that proved the catalyst for the abandonment of centrally controlled economies. In November 1989 the Berlin Wall fell, followed by the collapse of the Soviet Union. This paved the way for the reintegration of these economies into Western Europe and the global trading system, although former German chancellor Willy Brandt feared that the mental barriers would outlast the concrete wall.[3]

In a parallel development, China cautiously embraced market-based reforms. The objective was to improve the living standards of ordinary Chinese, some of whom remained desperately poor as the result of Mao Zedong's failed Great Leap Forward and Cultural Revolution of the late fifties and sixties. Deng Xiaoping, China's 'Paramount Leader', embraced a change in philosophy: 'Poverty is not socialism. To be rich is glorious.'

India too embarked on economic reforms in the nineties. Countries affected by the 1980s debt crisis gradually recovered, assisted by debt forgiveness and the recovery of the global economy. A reintegrated China, India, Russia, Eastern Europe and Latin America now helped drive growth. These nations represented new markets for goods and services and investment. A significant number of additional workers, whose labour was much cheaper than those in developed economies, joined the global labour force. Over time, this aided further expansion in the supply of cheaper goods, keeping inflation in check and interest rates low.

The end of the Cold War also provided a peace dividend, in the form of a significant drop in defence spending that freed up money for other purposes. Reduced funding for military research, the cancellation of the Superconducting Super Collider project, and the scaling down of Bell Laboratories meant that a large number of scientists, some from Eastern Europe and China, drifted into finance. These

POWs – physicists on Wall Street, a term coined by Goldman Sachs's Emanuel Derman – helped drive the trading of complex instruments, which were now an established part of the finance economy.

These events and their influences were central to the continuation of postwar expansion.

*

The period commencing in the 1990s became known as the Great Moderation, an era of strong economic growth, high production and employment, low inflation, reduced volatility in the business cycle, and self-adulation amongst politicians, central bankers and academic economists.

UK Prime Minister Gordon Brown boasted that under New Labour's stewardship the boom–bust cycles of the domestic economy had been banished. University of Chicago's Professor Robert Lucas claimed that macroeconomics had 'solved, for all practical purposes' the problem of economic depression.[4] US Federal Reserve chairman Ben Bernanke argued that improvements in monetary policy helped create the Great Moderation. In 2007 Bank of England governor Sir Mervyn King concluded that greater economic stability was not solely the result of good fortune.

In 1999 the magazine *Wired* outlined a vision of ultra-prosperity in which average household income in the US would triple to US$150,000 by 2020 and families would be served by their own household chefs. The Dow Jones Industrial Average would be at least 50,000, probably on its way to 100,000. A utopian future of endless expansion beckoned, where the economy doubled every dozen years, bringing prosperity to billions. Growth would help resolve poverty and political tensions, without damaging the environment.[5] The power and mobility of capital, free trade, and a globally integrated economy were now articles of faith. Political scientist Francis Fukuyama, in his 1992 book

The End of History and the Last Man, made the case for the triumph of Western liberal democracy and market systems as the end point of ideological evolution.

In reality, though, the period was punctuated by a series of rolling bubbles and crises: the 1987 stock market crash, the 1990 collapse of the junk bond market, the 1994 great bond market massacre, the 1994 Tequila economic crisis in Mexico, the 1997 Asian financial crisis, the 1998 collapse of the hedge fund Long-Term Capital Management, the 1998 default of Russia, and the 2000 dot-com crash. These one-in-ten-thousand-years events seemed to occur every year or so.

In 1989 Japan, considered an economic poster child, fell into a pro-longed recession following the collapse of a credit-fuelled real estate and stock boom. Apologists for the new economic model argued that the experience of Japan confirmed the superiority of the more flexible, competitive and dynamic market models of the US, and others like them, for delivering growth.

The Great Moderation was really a Goldilocks economy, reliant on a massive expansion in debt and financial speculation, underwritten by the Greenspan Put. This referred to a practice originated by US Fed chairman Alan Greenspan, and adopted widely, whereby in a finan-cial crisis central banks lowered interest rates sharply and flooded the system with money, to prevent asset prices from falling and to avert potential deterioration in economic activity. The severing of the link between money and gold allowed central banks greater flexibility to adjust the supply of money. Over time this led to the perception that central banks would underwrite risk-taking, thus creating increasing incentives for more and more risky behaviour.

The final phase of the postwar boom unfolded after 2001. Following the collapse of the internet bubble and a US slowdown after the 9/11 attacks, Greenspan dropped interest rates sharply. In his book about the period, Greenspan proudly quoted an economist's assessment of his policy: 'The housing boom saved the economy . . . Americans went on a real estate orgy. [They] traded up, tore down and added on.'[6] It was to end, of course, in disaster.

In 2008, in a deliberate rejoinder to *The End of History*, Robert Kagan titled his new book *The Return of History and the End of Dreams*, an appropriate description of the events that unfolded.

*

The financial crisis in the US subprime mortgage market commenced in 2007. It spawned jokes about loans made to NINJAs (no income, no job or asset), NINAs (no income, no asset) and to unemployed men in string vests buying houses with no money.

In truth, subprime loans to people with poor or no credit records, whether due to unemployment, bad health, disability or family problems, had always been a part of the US financial system. These loans carried higher interest rates to compensate for the additional risk and lack of collateral. But by 2006, driven in part by low interest rates, the volume of these loans had risen sharply to around 20 percent of all mortgages, up from around 8 percent historically. The artificially low initial interest rates allowed more people to borrow ever larger amounts using variable-rate mortgages. In general, US households had become increasingly indebted. Many borrowers lacked the income to meet their mortgage commitments and were dependent on increases in the value of houses in order to refinance the loan.

In 2005 interest rates increased from 1 percent per annum to 5.25 percent per annum, in response to higher inflation driven by higher oil and food prices. US house prices stalled and then fell. Borrowers began to default, especially on subprime mortgages. Given the modest size of the US subprime market (around US$1 trillion) relative to that of the global financial market, experts assumed the problem would be minor, dismissing the risk of broader contagion. But they were wrong, and the trend spread rapidly and far, to banks and investors in Europe and Asia. In fact, the subprime crisis exposed the weaknesses of the global banking system, with its complex connections, unsustainably high debt levels, and exotic financial instruments.

US private debt had increased to 290 percent of GDP in 2008, up from 123 percent in 1981. The ratio of household debt to disposable personal income rose to 127 percent at the end of 2007, up from 77 per-cent in 1990. Consumers had become over-leveraged as they saved less and borrowed more to finance consumption. Between 2001 and 2007 households borrowed around US$5 trillion against their homes as they rose in value. Mortgage debt in 2008 was 73 percent of GDP, up from an average of 46 percent during the 1990s. The debt was made even riskier because of looser credit conditions, weak creditworthiness of borrowers, and predatory lending practices. The same phenomenon was observable in the UK, Canada, Australia and some European countries.

While debt-fuelled consumption had contributed significantly to economic growth worldwide, high levels of risky debt made the global economy vulnerable to a downturn. If the rate of increase in borrow-ings decreased, then growth would slow and asset values, inflated by low rates and abundant credit, would fall. In turn, the inability to repay debt would trigger a financial crisis that would reduce the supply of credit, deepening the economic downturn. The process would repeat in a series of negative feedback loops.

Complex instruments allowing risky loans to be repackaged into higher quality securities – a form of financial magic – compounded the problem. As the value of these securities fell sharply, investors who had borrowed against them were forced to sell, triggering ever larger losses. Risk turned out to have been egregiously underpriced; the potential problems of complex financial innovations had not been understood. Everyone, it seemed, including international bond-rating agencies and bank regulators, had relied on someone else to analyse the risk.

The aggressive deregulation of the 1980s had left the banking system with low levels of capital and reserves with which to absorb rising losses, something that mathematical models had dismissed as highly improbable. Banks had become excessively reliant on funding from professional money markets rather than from depositors. The shadow banking system, a network of bank-like financing vehicles and investment funds created by banks to circumvent regulation, added to the problem. In a version of the financial shell game, banks shuffled assets to these vehicles so as to reduce capital and boost returns. In theory, banks were not exposed to potential losses from these transactions. In practice, the risk returned to the banks under certain conditions, especially if the ability of the vehicles to raise money was impaired, exposing banks to large losses.

Further adding to the problem was the conflict of interest between: banks and rating agencies; investment managers and their institutional clients; bonus-driven traders and the managers and shareholders of banks. The incestuous relationship between financial institutions and their regulators had led to inadequate and insufficient oversight.

The world's financial system, which had grown increasingly interconnected since the birth of international money markets, proved a perfect mechanism for the transmission of shocks and losses. Through ownership of securities that fell in value, through links to other banks or investors who owned these securities, most of the global financial system gradually became infected with the deadly virus. Fearing that everyone else was insolvent, institutions were reluctant to lend money: its availability fell sharply; its cost rose. Liquidity evaporated. Easy credit had lubricated the engine of the financial system, driving the boom. Now the oil was draining out through a large crack and the system gradually seized up.

*

At the start of the crisis there was a sense of Schadenfreude in the rest of the world as storied US institutions like Bear Stearns, the government-sponsored mortgage providers Fannie Mae and Freddie Mac, Merrill Lynch, Lehman Brothers, and AIG were bought up or collapsed. But European and Asian self-satisfaction at the failure of Anglo-Saxon, especially American, red-in-tooth-and-claw capitalism was short-lived.

In 2009, as the US economy and financial system stabilised, Greece's finances were found to be parlous. The Hellenic state had unsustainable levels of debt, large budget deficits, profligate spending and a large government sector, and generous welfare systems, particularly for public servants. This was compounded by low productivity, an inadequate tax base, rampant corruption and successive poor governments. Investors belatedly discovered that other European countries had similar issues.

Ireland's problems arose from excessive dependence on the financial sector, poor lending and a property bubble. Portugal had slow growth, anaemic productivity, large budget deficits and poor domestic savings. Spain had low productivity, high unemployment, an inflexible labour market, and a banking system with large exposure to property and European sovereign debt. Italy suffered from low growth, poor productivity, and a close association with the other peripheral European economies. Collectively, the PIIGS (Portugal, Ireland, Italy, Greece, Spain) had around €4 trillion of debt.

There was also increased focus on the US, France, Britain and Japan. They all had high levels of public debt, unsustainable budget deficits, and in most cases unfavourable current account deficits (both in absolute terms and relative to GDP). The deterioration in public finances predated the crisis, but spending to cushion the economies from the worst effects of the downturn and to rescue embattled financial institutions now exacerbated the problem. All also had long-term issues of ageing populations and unfunded pension and health schemes.

The financial crisis that began in the US in 2007 came to be known as the GFC. Large financial institutions throughout the world collapsed or suffered near fatal losses. The value of houses and financial assets, like shares, fell sharply. In the real economy there was a major downturn in economic activity, rising unemployment, housing foreclosures and evictions, and business failures.

There was an unprecedented loss of wealth. In 2009 the IMF estimated the cost by that stage at around US$12 trillion, equivalent to some 20 percent of the annual world economic output. Another estimate that included lost output calculated the ultimate loss to be even higher, at between one and three times annual GDP and equivalent to between US$60 trillion and US$200 trillion. In 2013 Tyler Atkinson, David Luttrell and Harvey Rosenblum, three economists at the Federal Reserve Bank of Dallas, tentatively quantified the loss to the US economy alone as US$6–14 trillion, equivalent to US$50,000 to US$120,000 for every American household, or 40 to 90 percent of one year's economic output. Under certain assumptions, they found that the loss could be higher – US$25 trillion. We may never know the full cost.

*

The GFC and its aftermath, known as the Great Recession, was the most serious financial crisis since the Great Depression of the 1930s. On 18 September 2008, at the height of the crisis, Ben Bernanke, Alan Greenspan's successor at the Fed, made the case for a massive bank bailout to sceptical legislators: 'If we don't do this, we may not have an economy on Monday.'[7] Three years earlier, during an interview on financial news channel CNBC, Bernanke had stated: 'We've never had a decline in house prices on a nationwide basis ... house prices will slow, maybe stabilize, might slow consumption spending a bit. I don't think it's gonna drive the economy too far from its full employment path, though.'[8] He had repeatedly stated that housing prices reflected strong economic fundamentals.

Back in 2001 IMF economist Prakash Loungani had concluded after a study that economists' forecasts were generally grossly inaccurate. Following the GFC, Loungani and his colleague Hites Ahir found that no economist in 2008 had seen the recession coming – a remarkable outcome, given that the crisis had already commenced. It confirmed psychologist Philip Tetlock's work, which has found that political and geopolitical forecasts are not much better than guesswork.

Most commentators assumed that the GFC was merely a larger than normal correction. It too would pass and a new period of expansion would commence. Prosperity and strong economic growth would return. Governments and central banks committed vast sums of money, succeeding in stabilising the economy but failing to engineer a strong recovery. It was deliverance, not victory, to paraphrase Winston Churchill's observation about the British Expeditionary Force's escape from Dunkirk.

Spanish Prime Minister Mariano Rajoy in September 2013 summarised the post-GFC world. The Spanish economy, badly affected by the crisis, had finally registered modest growth. But the economy had shrunk by around 10 percent, unemployment was over 25 percent (more than 50 percent amongst the young), housing prices were 30–50 percent below pre-crisis levels, and public finances and the banking system were fragile. Prime Minister Rajoy ruefully observed that the recession was over but the crisis continued.

BORROWED TIMES

Causes of the Global Financial Crisis and the Great Recession

The GFC was not part of the normal boom and bust cycle, but a major inflection point in economic history. Billionaire investor George Soros called it the end of the super boom.[1] The postwar expansion collapsed under the weight of four main factors: high debt levels, large global imbalances, excessive financialisation, and a build-up of future entitlements that had not been properly provided for.

*

The first factor behind the crisis was the increasing reliance of the global economy on borrowings to create economic activity. A 2015 study covering twenty-two developed economies and twenty-five developing economies found that between 2000 and 2007 total global debt grew from US$87 trillion to US$142 trillion, an increase of 7.3 per cent per annum, double the growth in economic activity.[2] In many countries, debt reached levels not normally seen outside wartime.

Everybody, it seemed, agreed with Oscar Wilde that living within one's income merely showed a lack of imagination.

Households borrowed because real wage levels, especially in the US, had not kept pace with living costs. They borrowed more to buy houses, which kept rising in value. They borrowed to maintain lifestyles portrayed in the mass media. They borrowed to speculate in stocks and property so as to pay for healthcare, their children's education, retirement. They borrowed because they could.

The availability of finance and low interest rates allowed businesses to expand. Corporations substituted debt for equity, as it was cheaper and interest was tax-deductible. They borrowed to buy back their own shares. This boosted the returns for shareholders and the value of stocks and options granted to key employees.

Governments borrowed to build essential infrastructure and to provide additional services for their citizens – it was electorally more palatable than increasing taxes. Financial institutions borrowed to meet the rising demand for loans. As money was their stock-in-trade, lending more increased profits and dividends.

Borrowing must be financed by savings. The borrowed money came from increased savings driven by greater prosperity and the need to provide for retirement and healthcare. Global financial assets in the form of shares and debt securities grew from US$51 trillion in 1990 to US$294 trillion (some 3.8 times global GDP) by 2014, an annual growth rate of about 8 percent, again well above real economic growth.

Banks circulated these savings in a process known as reserve or fractional banking. Where the money was deposited with a bank, the original holder of, say, $100 still had their money, but the bank and whoever it lent to also had the $100. The money that was lent would come back to the bank or go to another bank as a deposit. The money could then be re-lent and recirculated in a continuous process, expanding the supply of both money and debt. The only limitation was the requirement for banks to keep a small fraction of deposits in reserve to be available to meet withdrawals.

Banks became adept at speeding up the circulation of money, further increasing the supply of credit. Central to this was the shadow banking system, estimated to be between US$25 trillion and US$100 trillion in size (40–160 percent of global GDP). Other devices included derivative contracts – leveraged financial instruments that allowed risks to be transferred and investors to place bets on the prices of loans, bonds, interest rates, currencies, shares or commodities. As at 2014, total outstanding derivatives globally were around US$700 trillion (more than ten times global GDP). The actual value, profit or loss, of the contracts at any given time was much lower, but typically a still significant US$30 trillion (50 percent of global GDP).

Debt now drove economic growth, allowing immediate consumption or investment against the promise of paying back the borrowing in the future. Spending that would normally have taken place over a period of years was accelerated because of the availability of debt.

Some economists downplayed the problems. Debt, the argument went, cannot increase aggregate demand. The reduced spending resulting from one person's saving is offset by increased spending by the borrower, leaving expenditure unchanged. For every debtor there is a creditor, so one party merely relinquishes their current purchasing power to another, with the transaction being reversed when the loan is repaid with interest. If money represents a claim on income or resources, then borrowed money is merely a transfer of claims to future resources. Debtors need not repay, but simply re-borrow to cover maturing debts, or default on the loan.

Not all agreed. Writing in 1946, American business journalist Henry Hazlitt argued that, other than things that were available for free in nature, everything has to be paid for. In effect, you cannot get something for nothing. You cannot increase borrowing without limit.

He dismissed the idea that debt can be ignored, because as a society we owe the money to ourselves.[3]

Debt can be beneficial, where the economic activity generated is sufficient to repay the borrowing, but the build-up of debt since the late 1980s was excessive, beyond repayment capacity. A significant proportion of this debt financed activities that did not generate sufficient income or value to repay the principal and interest.

Only around 15–20 percent of the borrowed money went into investment projects. The remaining 80–85 percent financed existing corporate assets, real estate, or unsecured personal finance to 'facilitate life cycle consumption smoothing'.[4] In the US, Ireland, Spain and Portugal, construction and GDP was boosted by debt-fuelled housing investment for which there was no demand. Many other countries also increased their public and private debt levels to increase living standards and social welfare provisions. Borrowings were frequently used to purchase existing assets in anticipation of price rises, and these assets would then be used as the source of repayment. A slowdown in borrowing, which leads to a fall in asset prices below the outstanding debt, would create repayment difficulties.

Debt also must be repaid on a fixed date. Deteriorating asset values or creditworthiness can reduce the ability to re-borrow in order to repay the original borrowing, triggering financial crises, as illustrated by European sovereign debt problems. Debt requires regular payments. The claim on future income and wealth reduces the money available for other purposes, and can become a drag on economic activity.

Fractional banking, as well as the shadow banking system and derivatives, can amplify the risk within an economy. Debt is intermediated by banks, which by design are leveraged with each dollar of shareholders' capital supporting anywhere up to 30 dollars in borrowings. Losses can quickly threaten the solvency of financial institutions, increasing the risk of failure of the payment system crucial to modern economies. Weakness in the banking system can reduce the supply of credit to successful businesses, hampering activity.

As investors, directly or indirectly through the banking system, hold the borrowers' IOUs, the value and security of savings are inextricably linked to borrowing. Default, debt forgiveness or inflation wipe out savings designed to finance future needs, such as retirement. This results in additional claims on the state to cover the shortfall. Alternatively, it reduces the future expenditure of the saver, which crimps consumption.

Ultimately, excessive debt resembles a Ponzi scheme. Nations, businesses and individuals need to borrow ever-increasing amounts to repay existing borrowings and maintain economic growth. In the half-century leading up to 2008, the amount of debt needed to create US$1 of GDP in the US increased from US$1–2 to US$4–5. This rapid rise is unsustainable, given an ageing population, slower growth and low inflation.

American economist Hyman Minsky identified three phases of finance. In the early stages of a business cycle, money is only available to creditworthy borrowers whose income can meet the principal and interest on the debt, a phase known as hedge finance. As the cycle develops, competing lenders extend money to marginal borrowers, whose income can cover interest payments but not the principal, requiring the debt to be continually refinanced, a phase known as speculative finance. Finally, lenders finance borrowers whose income will cover neither the principal nor interest repayments, relying on increasing asset values to service the debt, a phase known as Ponzi finance. The cycle ends when the supply of money slows or stops. Borrowers unable to meet financial obligations try to sell assets, leading to a collapse in prices that triggers a financial and economic crisis. The GFC was such a Minsky moment.

With debt and savings being two sides of the same coin, when the liabilities cannot be repaid the phantom assets become worthless. The system collapses.

*

The second factor in the events of 2008 was a large global imbalance in consumption, investment and savings. Some countries overconsumed or overinvested relative to income, running up large foreign debts. Other countries consumed less and saved more, financing the shortfall.

America was the world's consumer of last resort. With the US economy growing strongly, Americans bought more goods and services than anyone else, fuelling demand for other nations' products and keeping the world economy expanding. This process had operated since the 1960s but it accelerated after the 1997–98 Asian crisis when the US stepped in to support global demand.

American consumers initially reduced savings to finance consumption. Then they increased borrowings. With many of the goods they bought being imported, the US ran large trade deficits, exporting less than they imported. The US borrowed from overseas to finance the difference.

During this period, China emerged as a large exporter, importing raw materials and parts that were then processed or assembled and shipped out again as finished goods. Exporting more than it imported, China created large foreign reserves, totalling over US$4 trillion. Dollars received from exports and foreign investment had to be changed into renminbi. In order to maintain the competitiveness of its exporters and avoid the renminbi appreciating, China invested its foreign currency overseas. Over 60 percent of its reserves were invested in dollar-denominated securities, mainly US government bonds. This reflected America's high credit rating and large, liquid money markets.

Like the petrodollars of the 1970s, the recycled dollars flowed back, helping finance America's large trade and budget deficits and maintaining demand for Chinese products.

The Asian crisis of 1997–98 encouraged China to build even larger surpluses, as protection against the destabilising volatility of short-term foreign capital flows that almost destroyed many Asian countries. Japan, South Korea, Taiwan and others used similar strategies to boost growth.

In the nineteenth century China exported more to England than it imported. The British East India Company sought to correct this imbalance by forcing China to buy opium. It ended in China's humiliating defeat in the Opium Wars, after it restricted imports of the narcotic. There are parallels between the current imbalances between China and the rest of the world, especially America, and this history.

The imbalances are not confined to Asia. With the introduction in 1999 of a single European currency, the euro, weaker members of the Eurozone benefited from currency stability and significantly lower interest rates. This enabled them to grow rapidly, buying more imports from countries like Germany. The result was a large increase in German trade surpluses and foreign exchange reserves. Germany lent these reserves and its large pool of domestic savings to France, Italy, Spain, Portugal, Ireland and Greece, which would otherwise not have been able to pay for the imported products.

High levels of savings and foreign exchange reserves in Germany, Japan, China and other Asian economies were driven by traditional values of thrift, a lack of social welfare, or undervalued currencies. Sometimes, reserves were designed to protect against uncertainty in the availability of finance. Commodity producers frequently invested surplus export proceeds for a future when mineral resources were exhausted. Irrespective of the rationale, the reserves and savings became a giant lending scheme that allowed countries with surpluses to finance and boost trade, accelerating global growth.

Beginning in the 1990s, these imbalances grew rapidly, facilitated by increased capital mobility and highly integrated financial markets. By 2007 the US was absorbing up to 85 percent of total global capital flows (US$500 billion each year). Asia and Europe were the world's largest net suppliers of capital, followed by Russia and the Middle East. Cross-border debt flows funded the US government and a rapid expansion in US private debt. This global imbalance reduced interest rates, encouraging increased borrowing in some countries. Ready availability of underpriced capital lessened the need for countries to save or live within their means.

An economic order where some nations save money and others borrow it to fund consumption is inherently unstable. The seller of goods is not paid until the debt financing the purchase is repaid. During the GFC the financial linkages helped transmit the problems across economies.

*

The third factor was financialisation, which manifested itself in a large financial sector and reliance on financial engineering.

As debt levels rose, banks increased in size, especially relative to the size of economies. By 2007, bank assets in many developed countries were in excess of 100 percent of GDP. Those in the US were around 78 percent of GDP. In Japan the figure was around 160 percent. In Germany it was around 270 percent. In Italy and Spain it was 213 and 269 percent respectively. It was over 500 percent in the UK, 700 percent in Ireland, and over 600 percent in Switzerland, reflecting in part the role of these nations as major financial centres channelling capital between countries.

The banks fed domestic credit, financing asset purchases, investment and consumption, as well as cross-border lending. As banking became more international, cross-border capital flows increased, peaking in 2007 at around US$12 trillion, up from US$500 billion in 1980, growth of around 12 percent per annum.

In the US, at its peak, the finance industry generated 40 percent of corporate profits and represented 30 percent of the market value of stocks. A large banking system is not necessarily problematic. In the UK, financial and insurance services contributed £125 billion in gross value added (GVA) to the UK economy, or 9 percent of the total GVA, around 46 percent of it from London alone. Financial services contribute significantly to the UK's trade surplus. The sector provided around 4 percent of the UK's jobs, and in 2010–11 contributed £21 billion to UK tax receipts.

But a large banking system does create problems when its role expands beyond support for the real economy – facilitating payments, providing a safe place for savings, financing real activity, and managing risk. The drive for growth and higher profitability leads banks to take greater risks. It encourages a higher volume of loans by lowering the lending standards, as exemplified by the US subprime loans, so that credit is extended against inadequate collateral or without acceptable legal protection. The focus shifts to channelling funds into speculative activities and trading for profit unrelated to client needs. These are frequently zero-sum games, entailing transfers of wealth between the parties to a transaction and adding little to overall economic activity. One problem is the global financial system's intricate linkages, which in 2008 became a conduit for transmitting contagion. This led to sharp falls in cross-border capital flows, which today remain well below the pre-crisis levels.

Financial innovations create new risks, both for individual institutions and systemically. Financiers profit from and exploit the asymmetry of information between sellers and buyers of complex products. Bank managers, directors and regulators are unable to keep up with new developments or provide adequate supervision. Few people before the GFC understood the potential problems of riskier mortgages or loans, complex securities, derivatives and the shadow banking system.

In the past twenty years, capital ratios and liquidity reserves of banks have fallen sharply. Leverage increasingly drove higher and more volatile returns on equity. During the GFC, the high leverage, both on and off balance sheets, amplified the problems.

The risk associated with the increase in size and complexity of the banking system is implicitly underwritten by the state, a fact recognised by rating agencies. It typically takes the form of protection of depositors' money, liquidity insurance, and implied capital support. Given the central role of banks in payments and credit provisions, it is difficult for governments to allow them to fail. During the GFC governments in the US, UK, Ireland and Europe were forced to step in and support their banks. Other countries indirectly supported theirs by increasing the scope of deposit guarantees. This led to higher government debt, or increased the potential financial commitments.

The Bank of England's Andrew Haldane identified in 2009 'a progressive rise in banking risk and an accompanying widening and deepening of the state safety net'. This was the equivalent of *Through the Looking-Glass*'s Red Queen's race, with the system running to stand still while governments raced to make finance safer and bankers created more risk.[5]

*

Businesses increasingly relied on financial engineering not linked to the provision of goods and services to improve earnings or increase their share price.

Companies increased the use of lower-cost debt financing. In private equity transactions the level of debt is especially high. Complex securities frequently exploit discrepancies in ratings and tax rules to lower the cost of capital. Mergers and acquisitions, as well as various types of corporate restructurings (spin-offs, carve-outs etc.), were used to create value. Given the indifferent results of such transactions, the major benefits accrued to insiders, bankers and consultants. Share buy-backs and capital returns supported share prices. In January 2008 US companies were using almost 40 percent of their cashflow to repurchase their own shares.

In a *Dilbert* cartoon, Scott Adams depicted a company that abandons making good products in favour of a strategy of random reorganisations – mergers, acquisitions, spin-offs of parts of the business, partnerships, joint ventures, and a program of paying the good employees to leave. The stock price goes up.

Companies traded in financial instruments for profit. Oil companies could make money irrespective of whether the oil business was good or bad, the price high or low, profiting from uncertainty and volatility. It was not necessary to actually produce, refine or consume oil to benefit from price fluctuations.

Legendary investor Warren Buffett's Berkshire Hathaway used financial engineering extensively, including leverage and derivative contracts. The company received the insurance premiums in cash, which could then be used to finance investments. It sold long-dated options (a form of insurance) on international stock indices and corporate default risks. The option fees received augmented its investment capital. In both strategies employed by Berkshire Hathaway, the leverage derived from the receipt of cash up-front against a promise to make a contingent payment in the future. The risk is back-ended and the company only has to make payments when the contracts are unwound or expire, allowing them the use of the cash received.

Financialisation interferes ultimately with market mechanisms, creating an artificial economy with manipulated and unsustainable values. Stock markets are designed to facilitate capital raisings for investment projects. They allow savers to invest, and provide existing investors with the ability to liquidate their investments when circumstances require. Financialisation undermines these functions.

Stock markets have increasingly decoupled from the real economy. Despite the fact that shares represent claims on the real economy, equity prices now do not correlate to fundamental economic factors, such as GDP growth, or, sometimes, earnings.

High frequency trading (HFT), which entails super-fast computers rapidly trading stocks, usually with other computers, constitutes up to 70 percent of the trading volume in some markets. The average holding period of HFT is around ten seconds. The investment horizon of portfolio investors has also shortened. In 1940 the average investment period was seven years. In the 1960s it was five years. In the 1980s it fell to two years. By 2014 it was around seven months. Momentum trading, rather than investing for the long run, now dominates. It increases volatility and the risk of large short-term price changes, discouraging genuine investors.

The nature of stock markets has been changed by alternative sources of risk capital; the high cost of a stock market listing, particularly increasing compliance costs; increased public disclosure and scrutiny of activities, including management remuneration; and a shift to different forms of business ownership, such as private equity. New capital raisings are used by private investors or insiders to realise accreted gains, subtly changing the function of the market.

Longer term, these developments threaten the market's viability as a source of capital for businesses and also as an investment, damaging the real economy. The fictitious cover boy of *Mad* magazine, Alfred E. Neuman, captured the surreal world of modern finance: 'We are living in a world today where lemonade is made from artificial flavors and furniture polish is made from real lemons.'

*

The fourth and final factor was entitlement programs, designed to protect and promote the economic and social wellbeing of citizens, especially the vulnerable and disadvantaged. Although these programs grew prominently in the postwar economy, they're not new. The Roman Empire provided grain for those unable to afford food. The sixteenth-century English Poor Law introduced rudimentary care for the impoverished. Churches and other religious and benevolent organisations provided for the poor, the elderly, orphans, widows and the disabled. One of Islam's five pillars is the obligatory zakat (a charity tax), collected to ease economic hardship and eliminate inequality.

In the nineteenth century German Chancellor Otto von Bismarck introduced the first state welfare systems for working classes, including provisions for old age, sickness, accident and disability. The Great Depression of the 1930s resulted in large falls in economic activity; high levels of unemployment (between a quarter and a third of the workforce); bank failures, with loss of savings; declines in income, tax revenue, profits, and prices for crops and commodities; a halving of international trade; and lower share prices. In response, President Franklin D. Roosevelt's New Deal introduced basic social insurance policies, principally focused on work programs and stimulating the economy through public spending on infrastructure.

The most ambitious programs were in the UK, and grew out of the 1942 Beveridge Report, named after its chairman Sir William Beveridge, who wanted to create a better world. Building on earlier twentieth-century initiatives, including old-age pensions, unemployment and health benefits, and free school meals, the report proposed a series of measures to deal with 'the five giants' – want, disease, ignorance, squalor and idleness. It recommended action to provide adequate levels of employment, income, housing, healthcare and education, subject to testing of an individual's private means.

Similar programs became common elsewhere, especially in developed countries. In some, additional services such as income supplements, and benefits for those with young children, were provided. These programs were based on notions of equality of opportunity and wealth distribution, enfranchisement, and public responsibility for the less privileged. They were made possible by strong postwar economic growth and rising prosperity.

Employer-supported pension and healthcare schemes emerged to complement the universal but modest public welfare arrangements. Senior management and public servants initially acquired occupational retirement plans. During World War II, businesses offered retirement plans to get around a US government pay freeze and excess profits tax on corporate profits. The plans were eventually extended to lower ranks, in part to obtain favourable tax treatment, which required the plans to be open to at least 70 percent of employees. In a competitive postwar labour market, businesses increasingly offered benefits to retain skilled workers and to incentivise employees.

Welfare systems involve the redistribution of income and wealth, a transfer of funds from one group to another in the form of cash benefits or subsidised services. They have to be financed – from taxation, earnings, or contributions by the beneficiaries – but businesses and governments frequently did not properly provide for promised retirement pensions and healthcare benefits. Both entail deferred costs, paid when an individual retires or needs medical care, the requirement for which increases with age. Employers can trade off lower wages against the assurance of future benefits, thereby avoiding costs in the present and boosting profits. Politicians can promise their constituencies generous future entitlements which do not need to be paid out of current tax revenues and which, when they do become payable, can be funded by borrowing.

Retirement benefits or pensions are of two types, the first being defined benefit schemes, where beneficiaries enjoy a fixed entitlement, usually a percentage of their final salary irrespective of their contribution, which is indexed for inflation (sometimes known as cost-of-living adjustments). Alternatively, they are defined contribution schemes, where beneficiaries receive the contributions made by them or the sponsor, such as the employer or government, along with returns earned on the funds. Upon retirement, the benefit can be paid as a single lump sum or as an income stream.

Entitlement schemes covering retirement or healthcare are either pay-as-you-go or fully funded. In a pay-as-you-go arrangement, benefits are met out of the fund or sponsor's current income, which for governments is tax revenue or borrowings. In funded schemes, over time, the worker, employer, or government makes specific agreed contributions that are invested. Where a scheme is fully funded, the expected liabilities of the fund are completely covered by the value of investments at any given point in time.

Initially, retirement and healthcare schemes were defined benefit schemes funded on a pay-as-you-go basis. There were exceptions, mainly in the US, which feared welfare socialism more than it feared Russian communism. The US social security system is theoretically a fully funded defined benefit arrangement. Taxes from employers and employees are collected by the Internal Revenue Service and are formally entrusted to the social security trust funds and invested to meet the specified benefits.

Pay-as-you-go schemes are sustainable where the benefits payable remain modest relative to contributions. They require the membership to keep increasing, so that new inflows are maintained to provide adequate cash to meet payments. In fully funded schemes, if the assumed rates of return on investment or the expected future liabilities are incorrect, then there is a risk that fund resources may be inadequate.

Increasing life expectancies and ageing populations ultimately threaten the sustainability of retirement and healthcare benefits. By the early twenty-first century, average life expectancy worldwide was around 65–70 years, having risen from around 30–40 years at the start of the twentieth century. In developed countries it was higher still, at eighty or more years. This was the result of improved economic circumstances, safer workplaces, clean drinking water, sanitation, better nutrition, improved public and personal hygiene, and better medical care.

Longevity increased the cost of retirement benefits, which had to be paid for longer periods. Higher healthcare costs reflected more expensive medical procedures, such as joint replacements and cancer therapies, as well as new drugs. It also reflected expenditure targeting early detection, prophylactic procedures and long-term treatments for formerly terminal diseases, which had been converted into chronic conditions. Declining birthrates and an ageing population meant that inflows into funds and growth in tax revenues declined at the same time.

In 1889, under Chancellor Bismarck, the retirement age in Germany was seventy years, and average life expectancy around forty-five. In 1908, under Prime Minister Lloyd George, the British retirement age was seventy, at a time when few survived past fifty. In 1935 America's official pensionable age for social security was sixty-five, when the average lifespan of Americans was around sixty-eight. By the year 2000, workers in developed countries could expect to retire at 55–67. With life expectancy approaching 80-plus years, retirees could potentially draw retirement and healthcare benefits for 25-plus years. The schemes were never meant to cover workers for ever-lengthening lives after retirement, with fewer workers and taxpayers to support them.

*

General Motors (GM), once a symbol of America's industrial might, is now a token of the problems of entitlement programs. Shaped by chairman Alfred P. Sloan, who ironically was indifferent to cars, GM once produced more vehicles than all its competitors combined. In 1955 the company made unprecedented profits of us$1 billion. In the apocryphal words of their chief executive, Charlie 'Engine' Wilson, what was good for America was good for GM, and probably vice versa.

Between the late 1940s and the 1960s, GM and the United Automobile Workers, led by Walter Reuther, negotiated increased employee benefits. These included guaranteed wage increases tied to increases in the cost of living and to improved productivity, more paid vacations, pension benefits (adjusted for government-sponsored social security entitlements), disability benefits, and medical benefits for both workers and retirees. GM provided job security, guaranteeing payments to supplement unemployment benefits for workers made idle by plant shutdowns. In 1973 the United Automobile Workers negotiated the infamous thirty-and-out arrangements, enabling any employee with thirty years' service to retire with full pension and healthcare benefits.

The steel, railroad and airline industries negotiated similar arrangements for their workforces. By the late 1960s, around 45–50 percent of US workers were entitled to company pensions.

With demand buoyant, GM wanted to avoid labour unrest and lengthy disruptive strikes that would reduce profits. The firm reasoned that higher costs could be easily passed on to buyers. In the 1970s and 1980s a weaker GM continued to increase benefits, preferring deferred payments to immediate cost increases so as to remain competitive, and obtaining agreement to changed work practices. Critics expressed concern about these future obligations, questioning whether companies could finance the payments. A young management consultant, Peter Drucker, doubted that a company could forecast its ability to meet such obligations decades into the future.[6]

In the 1950s and early 1960s the immense profitability of GM and favourable economics supported the schemes. In the late 1960s GM's profitability declined. With car ownership having reached very high levels, the market was saturated. In 1965 Ralph Nader's bestselling *Unsafe At Any Speed* drew unwelcome attention to the auto industry's safety issues, mechanical defects and quality problems, placing additional pressure on earnings.

Then came the oil shocks of the 1970s and an increased demand for compact, fuel-efficient vehicles, which US car makers had shunned in favour of ever larger, more powerful dream machines. Foreign carmakers captured market share. The quality and features of Japanese cars, once the object of jokes, improved. Sophisticated buyers came to prefer European luxury marquee brands, such as Mercedes-Benz, BMW, Porsche and Ferrari.

Foreign carmakers also enjoyed significant cost advantages. By the early 1980s, lower labour costs meant that Japanese cars, even after transportation costs, could be produced for around US$1500 less than the American equivalent. Pensions and healthcare contributed to this cost difference. Healthcare alone added around US$400 to the cost of an American-made car. In Japan and Europe, pension and healthcare costs were borne by the state, not individual companies. Even when foreign manufacturers established production facilities in the US, they were not always unionised. They did not always provide retirement benefits, and when they did, they had no older workers and therefore no legacy retirement obligations.

At GM, pioneers of employee benefits, legacy responsibilities grew as its workforce began to shrink and the bulge of workers hired in the middle of the century retired and started drawing pensions. Productivity improvements and cost pressures meant that the company was making more vehicles than in the early 1960s but with about

a third of the employees. In 1963 GM had 405,000 workers, supporting its 31,000 retirees (a ratio of thirteen workers for each retiree). By
the early 2000s it had 141,000 workers and paid benefits to 453,000
retirees (a ratio of one worker for three retirees). In the 1950s and 1960s
GM's large profits had been paid out in dividends to shareholders,
but by the end of the twentieth century the company was being run
to meet its pension and healthcare obligations, with a sideline in car
manufacturing.

GM and other companies belatedly closed their defined benefit
plans to new employees, and tried to convert existing retirement plans
into defined contribution schemes. Despite spinning off and restructuring operations, buying out healthcare entitlements, and borrowing
to fund its pension plans, GM was forced to file for Chapter 11 reor-
ganisation in 2009, triggering the biggest industrial bankruptcy in
history. It would result in important concessions on compensation and
retiree healthcare from the union.

*

Governments in developed countries faced similar problems. They
were providing increasingly generous benefits and broadening eligibility, including reducing the retirement age. This was supported by a
belief in continuing prosperity and the idea of the leisure society.

English economist John Maynard Keynes in 1930 predicted that
capitalism would eventually deliver a fifteen-hour working week for
the masses. Improved technology would allow goods and services
to be produced more quickly, efficiently and cheaply. Wages would
rise. The challenge would be occupying the extra leisure time, not the
struggle for existence.

Government welfare obligations were generally defined benefit
schemes, financed on a pay-as-you-go basis out of general revenue.
Even for those schemes constituted as funded, governments rarely

fully set aside money for future liabilities. Unlike businesses, governments had the advantage of being able to meet unfunded welfare obligations by increasing taxes or borrowing. But, as it was for businesses, the ability to meet future payments was increasingly threatened by inadequate funding, an ageing population and rapid increases in obligations due to longevity and rising healthcare costs.

Beginning in the 1970s and 1980s, governments offered generous tax incentives to encourage personal savings for retirement, preserving the universal system as a social safety net only for the needy. Contributions could be made from pre-tax incomes, avoiding normal income tax. Investment earnings on contributions were either not taxed or taxed at concessional rates. Drawings on retirement savings in old age also received favourable tax treatment, especially where taken over time as an annuity.

The new pension schemes were defined contribution plans, with employees being forced to contribute to a fund, and relied on the savings and returns to finance retirement. In the 1970s, citing pressures in the social security system and low saving rates, the US government introduced individual retirement accounts and, later, Clause 401(k) plans, a tax-efficient, defined contribution pension account. Other countries, such as the UK, Australia and New Zealand, implemented similar arrangements.

By 2010 the proportion of workers enjoying defined benefit retirement plans had fallen from around 60 percent to 10 percent of the workforce in developed countries. The proportion of workers with defined contribution plans was around 60–70 percent, if they had pension coverage at all. The shift was particularly marked outside the US.

Individual retirement portfolios created vast pools of money that had to be invested. As of 2014 US 401(k) accounts alone held over US$4.4 trillion, while Australian retirement savings totalled over US$1.5 trillion, disproportionately large relative to the size of its economy. Globally, over US$40 trillion is held by pension funds.

The schemes were presented as offering people greater choice and portability, with the ability to change jobs without affecting pension entitlements, but the real objective was to transfer the risk from governments and companies to the individual. The level of retirement savings now depended upon the employee's contribution and investment results.

Contributions and investment earnings are not guaranteed to provide sufficient funding for retirement. Given that globally around half or more of retirement savings are invested in stocks, a significant fall in the equity market close to retirement date could have a disproportionately large impact. In periods of low returns, savers are forced to take excessive risks to generate returns that would meet targets. In some cases the resultant losses may wipe out or significantly reduce their savings. For governments, it is a Pyrrhic victory. The cost of the tax incentives increases over time. Where savings are inadequate, retirees revert to public welfare, adding to the claims on state resources.

In 2014 the US government had outstanding debt of around US$18 trillion. In addition, it needed around US$36 trillion to ensure the ability of programs like social security and Medicare to meet its future obligations. This means that total federal government liabilities, debt as well as future commitments, were over three times the GDP. In addition, US state and local government had debt of around US$1 trillion and potential commitments to underfunded pension plans of around US$3 trillion.

The average EU country would need investments equal to over four times current annual GDP to fund its obligations. Alternatively, it would have to set aside around 8 percent of GDP each year for about half a century. Failing this, major reforms to retirement, health and social welfare programs would be needed, or taxes would have to increase significantly.[7]

The vast majority of government pension and healthcare schemes in other developed countries, especially those for public employees, are similarly underfunded. British Prime Minister Winston Churchill proved to have been prescient in his scepticism about the Beveridge Report's dangerous optimism about what was possible.

Speaking in 2012, nearly 150 years after Bismarck, German Chancellor Angela Merkel summed up the problem: 'If Europe today accounts for just over 7 percent of the world's population, produces around 25 percent of global GDP, and has to finance 50 percent of global social spending, then it's obvious that it will have to work very hard to maintain its prosperity and way of life.'[8]

*

Addressing the GFC and minimising the risk of a future recurrence required a coordinated, consistent plan dealing with the individual causes. It required reducing debt, correcting imbalances, reversing financialisation, and controlling the growth of entitlements, by scaling back welfare programs and covering future obligations. But fearing economic collapse and electoral defeat, governments eschewed these essential changes, refusing, like Errol Flynn, to reconcile their net income with their gross habits.

They preferred expediency, lowering interest rates and public spending – which was financed by issuing government debt or borrowing from central banks – to boost demand. The very policies that created the crisis had become the solution, echoing Viennese critic Karl Kraus's observation about psychiatry being the disease that masquerades as the cure. Politicians and central bankers gambled that growth and increased inflation would over time correct the problems.

Total public and private debt in major economies increased, rather than decreased. The table below sets out the changes in debt levels in the global economy.

Global Stock of Debt Outstanding

(US$ trillion, constant 2013 exchange rates)

TYPE OF DEBT	2000	2007	2014	COMPOUND ANNUAL GROWTH RATE (%) 2000–07	2007–14
Household	19	33	40	8.5%	2.8%
Corporate	26	38	56	5.7%	5.9%
Government	22	33	58	5.8%	9.3%
Financial	20	37	45	9.4%	2.9%
Total Debt	87	142	199	7.3%	5.3%
Total Debt (as % of GDP)	246%	269%	286%		

Source: Richard Dobbs, Susan Lund, Jonathan Woetzel and Mina Mutafchieva (2015), *Debt and (not much) deleveraging*, McKinsey Global Institute: 1

Since 2007, global debt has grown by US$57 trillion, or 17 percent of GDP. As at mid-2014, global debt was US$199 trillion, or 286 percent of the world's GDP. In comparison, global debt was US$142 trillion (269 percent of GDP) in 2007 and US$87 trillion (246 percent of GDP) in 2000.

During this period, no major economies and only five developing economies have reduced the ratio of debt to GDP in the real economy (households, corporations and governments). In contrast, fourteen countries have increased their total debt-to-GDP ratios by more than 50 percentage points. Over twenty countries now have debt-to-GDP ratios above 200 percent, led by Japan (400 percent). The US, Canada, UK, Germany, France, Italy and Australia have ratios of 233, 221, 252, 188, 280, 259 and 213 percent respectively. China, India, Brazil, Russia, South Africa and South Korea have ratios of 217, 120, 128, 65, 133 and 231 percent respectively.

In the period since 2007, developing economies have accounted for roughly half of the increase in debt. China's debt levels have risen rapidly, quadrupling between 2007 and 2014 from US$7 trillion to US$28 trillion.

Business, household and government debt have all grown. Only the financial sector in developed markets has reduced leverage. Businesses have borrowed not to invest, but to repurchase their own shares or buy other companies. Household borrowing, around 74 percent of which is mortgage debt, has increased in 80 percent of countries. Based on risk measures, such as debt-to-income ratios, debt service ratios, and house price changes, households in Canada, the Netherlands, Sweden, Australia, Malaysia and Thailand are potentially vulnerable.

Since 2007, government debt has grown globally by US$25 trillion, to US$58 trillion. It exceeds 100 percent of GDP in ten countries, including Japan and a number of European nations. Japanese government debt is over 240 percent of GDP. Given slow growth, low inflation rates, and the imbalance between tax revenues and expenditure, government debt-to-GDP ratios are forecast to rise for the foreseeable future in the US, Japan and many European countries. In a lot of these countries, government debt has reached unsustainable levels, and it is unclear how or when it is to be reduced.

Debt hangs like the sword of Damocles over the global economy.

*

Global imbalances in trade and capital flows persist. Modest initial reductions were the result of lower growth and large decreases in private and public investment, rather than reform. Germany, Japan and China remain reluctant to alter an economic model reliant on exports and large current account surpluses.

But the flaws in the strategy of financing the buyer of your exports are clear. Creditors find themselves forced to lend more to the beleaguered borrowers in order to protect the value of existing investments, and to prevent falls in the value of the debtor's currency or securities.

After the GFC, countries like China found themselves exposed to a deteriorating US economy, the US government's falling debt rating, and decreases in the value of Treasury bonds and the US dollar. Premier Wen Jiabao expressed China's concern in 2008: 'If anything goes wrong in the US financial sector, we are anxious about the safety and security of Chinese capital.'[9] German, French, Dutch, Spanish and UK banks and investors found themselves similarly exposed on their lending to the increasingly risky PIIGS. They angrily rejected calls for debt forgiveness, characterising the borrowers as immoral beggars wanting to repudiate their contracts. The lenders refused to admit that they had lent unwisely, without concern about the borrowers' ability to meet their obligations.

The supposed generosity of the EU in providing new loans to rescue borrowers was false. These new loans went overwhelmingly to the banks and investors who had lent the original funds, rather than to the borrower. In the case of Greece, only around 11 percent of more than €200 billion in new loans (about 125 percent of GDP) directly financed the Greek government. German, French, Dutch and Spanish participation in bailouts for Greece, Ireland, Portugal, Spain and Cyprus were driven by the need to protect their own banks and investments, increasing the nations' exposure to future losses.

By early 2015, American debt-fuelled consumption had resumed, making the largest contribution to growth since 2006, before the GFC. American imports were rising again, with the trade deficit approaching 3 percent of GDP and heading towards its pre-recession peak of 6 percent, despite the much lower prices of imported energy. Germany and China continued to run ever-larger trade surpluses and to export capital. The imbalances remained unbalanced.

*

In the years since the GFC, too-big-to-fail banks have become larger, not smaller, increasing in both size and concentration. This is the result of forced consolidation (shotgun mergers), regulations that favour larger banks, and promotion of them internationally by governments as national champions. A flight by customers to the perceived safety of large banks, a reduction in alternative funding sources, and less competition from smaller institutions have also enhanced the position of these entities.

Banks, which had to be bailed out, now were crucial in financing governments, often with the assistance of central banks. By 2014 Italian, Spanish and German banks held around 24 percent (over €400 billion), 41 percent (around €300 billion) and 15 percent (around €240 billion) of their assets in government bonds respectively.

Instead of fundamental reform, policymakers introduced labyrinthine capital, liquidity and trading controls of dubious efficacy. Some initiatives, such as new regulations governing derivatives and large banks, introduced complex interconnections and new systemic risks.

In June 2013 Bank of England governor Sir Mervyn King stated: 'It is not in our national interest to have banks that are too big to fail, too big to jail, or simply too big.'[10] But the combination of government support (which protects depositors and creditors), limited liability (which protects shareholders), profit maximisation, and incentive pay for financiers continued to encourage a culture amongst large banks of 'rational carelessness'.[11]

Too-big-to-fail banks have been increasingly joined by too-big-to-fail fund managers, who are responsible for investing over US$87 trillion in retirement and other savings, around three-quarters of the size of the global banking system and 150 percent of global GDP. The ten biggest fund managers control over US$25 trillion in assets, with the largest,

Blackrock, alone responsible for over US$4 trillion, more than any bank. A January 2015 paper by the Financial Stability Board, an international forum set up to prevent future financial crises, argued that large fund managers may pose systemic risks and require greater regulation. The industry's lobbyists reacted angrily, insisting that, unlike banks, asset managers had not been a major factor in the GFC. But, as fund managers customarily state in their solicitations to invest, the past is no guarantee of future performance.

*

Financial engineering continues to be used to mask the true performance and real position of enterprises and nations. To maintain or increase earnings in a difficult environment, businesses have re-engineered their structure and finances rather than their operations. They have merged with or acquired companies. Since 2009, US share buybacks totalling nearly US$2 trillion, frequently financed by low-cost debt, have boosted share prices and now make up an increasing proportion of the value of stocks traded.

Since the crisis, governments too have resorted to financial engineering to deal with economic problems. The EU experimented with complex finance techniques, originally used for repackaging residential mortgages, to finance bailouts of troubled member countries and ambitious infrastructure investment programs. The aim was to overcome the lack of available funds.

Governments use creative accounting. In the period prior to the introduction of the euro, Italy and Spain used derivative transactions, allegedly to understate their debt levels. Now, governments use off-balance sheet structures and often delayed payments to massage the level of borrowings. Governments have consistently understated liabilities, such as unfinanced commitments for future healthcare, aged care and retirement benefits. In order to overcome the lack of available money to recapitalise its banks, the Spanish government used accounting instead, agreeing that €30 billion worth of tax losses could be used to bolster their regulatory capital. While the EU was seeking to improve the solvency of banks by increasing capital reserves, Spain adopted a strategy of financial manipulation that did little to improve the real loss-absorption capacity of its banks.

European governments have sought to avoid recognising that some bailout loans to beleaguered Eurozone members are unrecoverable. In November 2012 Chancellor Angela Merkel was able to honour her promise that Germans would not suffer any losses from the Greek bailout by agreeing to the debt being restructured so as to have minimal interest rates and the repayments deferred well into the future, to maintain the fiction that it would be repaid. Consideration was even given to a zero-interest loan with no fixed maturity, to avoid immediate losses.

In the aftermath of the GFC, governments borrowed from and paid interest to central banks. The income received by the central bank was accounted for as profit, which was then paid as dividends back to the government. Recorded as income, these payments enhanced government revenue, improving public finances. It was all financial pettifoggery.

Periodic jeremiads about welfare cheats and middle-class welfare notwithstanding, reform of entitlements has proved difficult. Greece, Portugal, Ireland and Spain were forced by the EU to reduce entitlements as a condition of their bailouts. France and Germany tried to increase the age of retirement, but were forced to water down changes or reverse course due to public resistance. Even if adopted, this modest measure would take decades to become effective. Forcing workers to remain in employment longer assumes their fitness to continue and the availability of jobs. In reality, the measures would result in older workers going onto unemployment or disability benefits.

If they stay in the workforce, then they would reduce employment opportunities for younger workers.

The policies adopted to deal with the GFC actually worsened the problems of unfunded pensions and entitlement. Low or zero interest rates reduced the return on savings, exacerbating shortfalls. Miniscule returns on safe investments, such as government bonds, forced pension funds and retirees into riskier investments, increasing their vulnerability to loss. Politicians everywhere refused to tell voters that they had come to the end of the 'providential allotment of inexhaustible plenty'.[12]

*

Governments now lie to their electorates about the magnitude of economic problems, the lack of painless solutions, and the cost of possible corrective actions. In a moment of unusual candour, the then prime minister of Luxembourg and head of the Eurogroup, Jean-Claude Juncker, stated, 'We all know what to do, we just don't know how to get re-elected after we've done it.'[13]

Irish literary critic Vivian Mercier observed that in Samuel Beckett's play *Waiting for Godot*, nothing happens, twice! Vladimir and Estragon while away time with distractions waiting in vain for Godot to arrive. Policymakers too await an elusive recovery. Like the two characters in the play, they pretend they are in control but do not know what happens or why. Their ability to influence events is limited. The global economy in the aftermath of the GFC resembles Beckett's absurdist plot.

ESCAPE VELOCITY

The Power and
Impotence of
Economic Policies

In the age of capital there was no longer a society, just the economy and the mirages of personal wealth – the value of your home, and the stock market, which affected your savings and investments. Presiding over it all were economic officials and central bankers.

The influence of economic policymakers was directly related to postwar prosperity, which they claimed was the result of their prudent stewardship. Alan Greenspan, a master of politics and public relations, succeeded in making the US Fed chairman the second most powerful person on the planet, after PotUS (President of the United States). Feted as rock stars at the annual Davos World Economic Forum, their every gnomic utterance was reported reverently in the media and meticulously parsed by analysts.

But the GFC and the Great Recession posed the supreme challenge to policymakers and their theories.

*

Many economists modestly consider economics the most important social science, applicable to all human behaviour as well as to financial and social problems.[1] The appearance of rigour and science relies on statistics and complex mathematics used to model and forecast outcomes. John Maynard Keynes, in considering this phenomenon, concluded: 'too large a proportion of recent "mathematical" economics are mere concoctions, as imprecise as the initial assumptions they rest on, which allow the author to lose sight of the complexities and interdependencies of the real world in a maze of pretentious and unhelpful symbols'.[2] In reality, economics is religion, with different sects. Governments profess faith in whichever prophet is fashionable, as long as it is consistent with their ideological framework and delivers growth and rising living standards.

Clannish economists rarely agree on anything. A feud between prominent economists prompted a 2013 article entitled 'The Paranoid Style in Economics'.[3] There are disagreements on fundamental issues like the role of money and banks. Key assumptions about rational maximisation behaviour, efficient markets, stable preferences and equilibriums are unrealistic. Model forecasts are unreliable. Economists and central bankers with little experience of business or markets move mainly in each other's company, confusing wisdom with knowledge, knowledge with data, and data with noise.

Unfortunately, complex phenomena seldom conform exactly to economic models when removed from their fuzzy sociological, political and historical contexts. In 2008 economists were caught out by what G. K. Chesterton feared: 'the real trouble with this world of ours is ... it looks just a little more mathematical and regular than it is; its exactitude is obvious, but its inexactitude is hidden; its wildness lies in wait.'[4]

Central bankers and economists struggled to frame a response to the crisis. There are two major instruments available to policymakers:

fiscal, or budgetary, policy; and monetary, or interest rate, policy. They can also act directly, regulating key sectors like banking, or prescribing the pattern of economic activity. After the events of 2008, policymakers deployed all available measures, contradicting the long-asserted view that intervention was unnecessary in self-regulating and automatically correcting free markets. To paraphrase Voltaire's observation on doctors, they now prescribed medicines of which they knew little, to cure diseases of which they knew less, in economic systems of which they knew nothing.

*

Governments ran significant budget deficits, spending in excess of tax revenues to boost demand or recapitalise the weakened financial system. Where a government borrows by mobilising unused funds from domestic or foreign investors, it adds to aggregate demand, as long as it does not crowd out other borrowers.

But fiscal stimulus does not always work. In a globalised world it can, in the absence of coordinated national policies, increase imports, creating or exacerbating trade imbalances rather than boosting domestic activity.

If additional spending finances consumption, then it needs to be ongoing to remain effective. If it finances investment, such as infrastructure, then the long-term effect depends on the project. If the investments produce low returns, then the effect on the economy can be negative, with capital tied up in poorly performing assets. Politically or ideologically driven misallocation of capital diminishes benefits. In investment matters, governments are no more or less incompetent or inefficient than private businesses. Once completed, investment projects require ongoing maintenance, which absorbs scarce financial resources, compounding the problem of low-returning investments.

Ghost cities, empty buildings and airports, roads and bridges to nowhere in Japan, China and Europe highlight this problem. A 2014 report by China's state planning agency concluded that around half the total investment in the economy since 2009 (US$6.8 trillion) was ineffective – that is, wasted. The investment, which formed part of government stimulus measures, was funnelled into real estate and suppliers of steel, glass and cement, creating overcapacity. A significant portion of the funds was also stolen by corrupt officials.

Keynes famously argued for the employment of workers to dig holes and then fill them in – in effect, seeking to restore economic health by creating activity even where it has no value other than to provide employment. The consumption spending by the newly employed workers is assumed to trigger a virtuous cycle of economic growth, increasing income and employment.

This relies on the fiscal multiplier effect, the increase in economic activity resulting from each additional dollar of government spending. If the multiplier is greater than one, then it creates a self-sustaining recovery. If below one, it may have social benefits but will detract from growth, especially in the longer run.

But multipliers are difficult to estimate. IMF chief economist Olivier Blanchard and his colleague Daniel Leigh controversially found that the multiplier was considerably larger (up to 1.7) than expected (0.5) when governments reduced public spending or increased taxes as part of austerity programs after the crisis. The simultaneous reduction of debt by governments as well as the financial sector, corporations and individuals led to a sharper contraction than expected. Similarly, expansionary fiscal policy in an environment of contracting private sector demand and reduction in debt can result in lower multipliers, as the government cannot fully offset the fall in private economic activity.

*

Budget deficits must be financed, requiring governments to borrow. By 2009 there was increasing unease about rising government debt.

Based on data from hundreds of years of financial crises, economists Carmen Reinhart and Kenneth Rogoff argued that sovereign debt levels above 60–90 percent of GDP affected growth.[5] In 2013, in the academic equivalent of *Fight Club*, three economists from the University of Massachusetts in Amherst published a paper alleging that Reinhart and Rogoff had exaggerated the decline in growth at higher debt levels, due to unorthodox statistical choices and a spreadsheet error. Critics, whose concerns about the original research had been ignored, now pounced.

With their membership of the club of celebrity economists threatened, Reinhart and Rogoff mounted a desperate defence: they had not stressed any single number in their analysis; they had not implied causality; recalculation still supported their thesis. But in previous opinion pieces, speeches and interviews, they had not mentioned these caveats, suggesting instead that the relationship held, and favouring cutting debt levels aggressively. Kenneth Rogoff darkly accused his critics of orchestrating a 1950s McCarthyist witch-hunt.[6]

Pressure for grant funding, the lure of lucrative commercial opportunities, and vanity have corrupted academic standards and reduced professional accountability. In his 2010 film *Inside Job*, Charles Ferguson interviewed former Federal Reserve vice-chairman Frederic Mishkin, who was paid US$124,000 for a study on Iceland. The study was originally titled 'Financial Stability in Iceland' but after the GFC had decimated the country, it was included in Mishkin's CV as 'Financial Instability in Iceland'. Mishkin dismissed the difference as a typo and argued that the film made too much of it.[7]

Empirical studies show a negative association between debt and growth, although a definitive threshold is not supported. Politicians and policymakers used the Reinhart-Rogoff proposition to justify austerity policies, especially in Europe. It is unlikely that they ever read the original research, being content to rely on any support of pre-conceived, politically motivated policies.

In reality, government debt rarely ever gets repaid. It is a matter of servicing the debt and maintaining investor confidence, allowing maturing debt to be refinanced. The level of tolerable sovereign debt depends on a multitude of factors.

Where it borrows in its own currency, a sovereign's debt capacity is only constrained by its ability to convince investors to purchase its securities or by its willingness to print money. Where a country's currency is also used in global trade or is popular with central banks as an investment of their reserves, the scope for borrowing is higher, something that enables the US to continue to borrow large amounts to finance its budget and trade deficits.

A large domestic savings pool, like Japan's, enhances the ability of the government to borrow. Low interest rates enable higher levels of borrowing. While short-term debt creates vulnerability to market disruptions, long maturities and a low concentration of maturing debt in an individual period increases debt capacity.

Sustainable debt levels also depend on the size and economic structure of the country, as well as its expected economic growth. A dynamic economy capable of high levels of growth, with the attendant ability to generate additional tax revenues and provide attractive investment opportunities, can maintain a higher level of debt than one with lower growth prospects. As British Prime Minister Lloyd George recognised: 'Success means credit. Financiers never hesitate to lend to a prosperous concern.'[8]

*

In response to the GFC, central banks reduced official rates to historical lows, often to zero (known as ZIRP, or zero interest rate policy).

When the ability to change the price of money (that is, the interest rate) became restricted as the rate went to zero, central banks increased the quantity of money, in a process known as quantitative easing (QE).

If an economy is cash-based, this means printing money. In Weimar Germany the government took over newspaper presses to print money to meet demand for banknotes. In modern economies, the process requires central banks to purchase securities, primarily government bonds, to inject liquidity into the financial system.

The balance sheets of major central banks expanded from around US$5–6 trillion prior to 2007/08 to over US$18 trillion. The quantum of money injected into the financial system was sufficient to purchase a large flat-screen TV for every single human being on the planet. By 2015, in many developed countries, central bank assets constituted 20–30 percent of GDP. In Japan it was headed for 80 percent.

The basic strategy was elementary economics: boost growth and inflation so as to make the existing high debt levels manageable. Budget deficits financed by QE would support economic activity and growth. Artificially low interest rates would help stimulate demand, and manage debt by reducing its cost. It would also create inflation, boosting nominal growth and reducing the ratio of debt to GDP by increasing the latter.

The sustainable level of borrowing depends on the existing level of public debt (percent of GDP), the current budget position (percent of GDP), nominal interest rates and nominal growth rates:

Changes in Government Debt = Budget Deficit + [(Interest Rate ×
Debt) – GDP Growth]

Assuming borrowing costs of 3 percent and a debt-to-GDP ratio of 90 percent, a nation needs to grow at a minimum of 2.7 percent to avoid increasing its debt burden, provided the budget is balanced.

Following the GFC, despite governments expanding their

borrowing, a global chronic deficiency of demand meant growth has not recovered to the level needed. High levels of debt, structural budget deficits, low growth rates and increasing borrowing costs now make the public finances of many countries unsustainable. It is not a problem of debt, but of growth. Current levels of government debt are only sustainable if growth returns quickly to high levels. Given that recent economic growth has been debt-fuelled, reduction in credit growth slows economic activity, making the borrowings unsustainable, feeding a deadly negative-feedback loop.

As the global economy stagnated, weak countries were targeted by bond vigilantes, making it difficult to finance and forcing up their financing costs. Nations were forced to implement austerity programs, cutting spending and increasing taxes to stabilise public finances and reduce debt, trapping them in recessions or low growth, which only aggravated the problems.

With the basic strategy ineffective, the focus shifted to keeping interest rates near zero and creating inflation to increase nominal GDP, that is, unadjusted for price increases. If the budget could be kept in check, then debt levels would not rise and perhaps begin to fall.

It wasn't ever much of a plan, although there was no alternative. It was the old Kerryman joke: If you want to go there, then I wouldn't start from here.

*

The policies, especially QE, helped stabilise conditions by lowering borrowing costs and allowing high debt levels to be managed, but did not restore growth or create sufficient inflation. The predictable failures were reminiscent of the observation of Helmuth von Moltke, a nineteenth-century head of the Prussian army: 'No battle plan ever survives first contact with the enemy.'

In practice, the relationship between lower rates and economic activity is tenuous. With demand weak and an excess of capacity, low interest rates did not encourage new investment. Larger companies took advantage of low rates to raise long-term debt to refinance existing borrowings, repurchase shares or return capital to shareholders, and undertake mergers and acquisitions. In the US, Europe and UK, investment declined significantly, falling below pre-2007 levels. Illinois Tool Works' CEO David Speer spoke for businesses: 'I could borrow $2 billion tomorrow for 3.5 percent. But what am I going to do with it?'[9]

The borrowing costs of small and medium-sized enterprises reliant on banks did not decrease significantly. Banks in many countries increased credit margins, offsetting the fall in overall interest rates.

In the housing market, demand depends on many factors – the level of required deposit, existing home equity (the price of your house less outstanding debt), the ability to sell a current property, income levels and employment security. Households crippled by high levels of debt, uncertain employment prospects or stagnant income, as well as falling house prices (in some countries), reduced rather than increased borrowings. In their 2014 book *House of Debt*, economists Atif Mian and Amir Sufi found that since 2009 poor demand from over-indebted consumers who markedly reduced their spending, rather than credit availability, was a major constraint on growth. Low rates are unlikely to be effective in these circumstances.

The policies increased the value of financial assets but did little for the real economy. US Fed chairman Ben Bernanke argued that low rates and QE worked via the wealth effect: higher house and asset prices would encourage additional consumption and riskier investments. Empirical evidence suggests a weak link between higher stock prices and increased consumption. The slightly stronger link between housing prices and consumption may reflect the effects of the historically unique period in the late 1990s and early 2000s, when homeowners borrowed against home equity built up over decades so as to finance consumption.

Since 2009, American household wealth has increased by more than US$25 trillion, primarily from higher house and equity prices. Only around 1–2 percent of this gain has flowed through into added consumption, below the 3–4 percent average between 1952 and 2009. The increase in wealth also accrued to better-off sections of the population, with a lower propensity to spend. In the Eurozone and UK, the effect of higher asset prices on consumption was also low.

Successive rounds of central bank bond-buying have had a minimal impact on real activity. US Fed purchases of US$600 billion worth of long-term government bonds in the second QE program of November 2010 may have only added about 0.13 percent to real GDP growth in late 2010, and 0.03 percent to inflation. The improvement in US economic conditions may have less to do with Fed policy than with natural factors: 'As long as people have babies, capital depreciates, technology evolves, and tastes and preferences change, there is a powerful underlying (and under-appreciated) impetus for growth . . .'[10]

*

Although asset prices increased sharply after 2009, there was little evidence of inflation, other than for some commodities affected by structural factors, such as a weak US dollar. Inflation was needed to reduce debt levels by increasing nominal growth rates above interest cost. Inflation would also decrease debt by reducing purchasing power, and via currency depreciation where the debt was held by foreign investors. Consumers anticipating higher prices in the future may accelerate purchases, generating growth.

Policymakers also fear the destructive effects of deflation, when tax revenues stagnate, or even fall, and consumption and investment may be deferred. Declines in asset prices and appreciation in the real value of debt make existing high borrowings difficult to service, creating problems for banking systems. The shrinking economy increases the debt-to-GDP ratio. Deflation would also reduce the effectiveness of low or zero rates.

Quantity theory sets out the relationship between money and prices:

$Q \times P = M \times V$

Where:

> *Real Economy = Quantity (Q) x Price of goods and services produced (P)*
>
> *Financial Economy = Money supply (M) x the Velocity (or circulation) of that money (V)*

Milton Friedman, spiritual patron of monetarist economists, believed that, based on this connection, increasing money supply creates inflation, as higher monetary claims on real goods and services create higher prices. Fellow economist Robert Solow observed that everything reminded Friedman of money supply. He added that while everything reminded him, Solow, of sex, he thought it wise to keep it out of the media.

The relationship between the monetary base, credit creation, nominal income and economic activity is unstable: 'Governments can no more control stocks of either bank money or cash than a gardener can control the direction of a hosepipe by grabbing at the water jet.'[11]

In practice, increased money supply was offset by reduced velocity, or circulation, of money. The liquidity supplied to banks did not flow into the economy in the form of loans. Instead the money was redeposited as excess reserves with central banks, reflecting weak credit demand and an unwillingness to lend. In the US, for a time after the GFC, bank holdings of cash and government securities exceeded the outstanding volume of commercial and industrial loans. The circulation of funds was affected by higher bank capital levels, reductions in permitted banking leverage, onerous liquidity controls, and post-crisis constraints on transferring loans and risk. The transmission system was broken, limiting the impact on economic activity.

Even where the money flowed into the wider economy, companies frequently did not spend it, preferring to hold surplus cash. This reflected a lack of investment opportunities and caution about future business and financial market conditions. By 2014, total cash balances worldwide were as much as US$7 trillion, roughly double the level of ten years earlier. American corporations held over US$1.7 trillion in cash. The five largest hoarders alone held around half a billion dollars in cash. Technology firms held around US$690 billion in cash, roughly double the levels of five years ago. Apple alone held over US$170 billion. Over 60 percent of this cash was held abroad. Interestingly, the large cash balances coexisted with elevated overall corporate debt levels. Many corporations borrowed at home to fund their spending, taking advantage of low interest rates and avoiding paying taxes on repatriated overseas profits.

Inflation requires imbalances between demand and supply. Many developed economies had a significant output gap – the amount by which the economy's potential to produce exceeds total demand – reflecting lower demand and excess capacity, though the extent was uncertain due to lower labour participation, which reduced the theoretical output.

Low demand and lower costs also reduced price pressures. Corporations took advantage of record low interest rates, substituting machinery for labour to improve output. High unemployment levels kept wage pressures low. Lower energy prices reduced costs. In the US this was the result of increased production of shale gas and oil. The more than 50 percent fall in the oil price in 2014 reduced energy costs globally.

Emerging economies suffering weak demand for exports transmitted deflation by cutting prices. Fearful of losing market share, businesses everywhere lacked pricing power, contributing to low inflation.

In November 2012 IMF chief economist Olivier Blanchard admitted that the impact of the unconventional monetary measures was both limited and uncertain. He acknowledged the minimal effect of the policies on business and consumer confidence, consumption, employment, and growth in incomes or credit.[12] It was Keynes's liquidity trap, where policy is largely ineffective, analogous to pushing on a string.

But central banks continued with the failed policies. In January 2015 the European Central Bank announced its own version of QE after over two years of prevarication. No one was convinced that it would create growth or inflation. Board members felt that they had to do something. Launching their umpteenth round of ineffective monetary stimuli, Japanese central bankers resorted to marketing, rebranding QE as QQE (qualitative and quantitative expansion).

Fyodor Dostoyevsky knew that 'the man who lies to himself and listens to his own lie comes to such a pass that he cannot distinguish the truth within him or around him'.[13] Decision-makers deluded themselves about the efficacy of their policies.

*

The real effects of the policies were different. Low rates made high debt levels manageable. QE also allowed central banks to finance governments. Between 2009 and 2014 the US Fed purchased over 50 percent of bonds issued by the US government. At one stage it was purchasing around 70 percent of all new issues. The Fed now holds 12 percent (more than US$2 trillion) of all US Treasury bonds outstanding.

In 2013 the Bank of Japan announced plans to purchase 70 percent of its government's debt issuance, doubling the monetary base from

29 percent to 56 percent of GDP. Faced with a slowing economy and low inflation, in 2014 the Bank of Japan increased purchases of Japanese government bonds to an annual rate of ¥80 trillion (US$705 billion), equivalent to 16 percent of GDP. The planned purchases were larger than the amount the government planned to issue.

Theoretically prohibited from financing governments directly, the European Central Bank initially channelled liquidity to Eurozone banks, either directly or via member central banks, to purchase government bonds that were then pledged as collateral for the loans. Government bond holdings total around 10 percent of the banking system's total assets. Eventually, in January 2015, the European Central Bank and Eurozone central banks announced plans to purchase government bonds directly.

Low interest rates provide an artificial subsidy to financial institutions, allowing them to borrow cheaply and then invest in higher yielding governments bonds. US banks received US$6 billion in interest on the US$2.4 trillion in excess reserves that resulted from the central bank's QE programs. Financial institutions benefited from higher asset prices driven by low rates, thereby reducing losses on investments that had fallen sharply in value in the GFC. The value of collateral acting as security for bank loans also increased. The policy justification was that higher profits improved the bank's capital and reserves, enabling increased lending and bad loans to be written off. In fact, banks paid higher bonuses to staff, increased dividends, or returned surplus capital to shareholders through share buybacks.

Low interest rates and QE policies also weaken a currency. The US, UK, Japan, Europe, China and Switzerland have used direct intervention, by way of artificially low interest rates and QE, to try to devalue their currency. Devaluation makes exports more competitive and assists individual countries to capture a greater share of global trade, boosting growth. It also reduces real debt levels, decreasing the purchasing power of foreign investors holding a nation's debt. The competition to devalue came to be known as the currency wars, a term used in 2010 by Brazilian Finance Minister Guido Mantega.

Low rates reduce incentives for overextended borrowers to reduce debt, and decrease the income of retirees living off savings, thus decreasing demand. Vladimir Lenin's fulminations about idle, parasitic capitalists living off interest were now irrelevant. There were no interest coupons from bonds to collect with rates at or near zero, completing what John Maynard Keynes termed the euthanasia of the rentier.

Low rates also discourage savings. But sometimes, in a complex cycle of cause and effect, they may perversely reduce consumption, as lower returns force people to save more for future needs. And low rates increase the funding gap for defined benefit pension funds. In the US, for every 1 percent fall in rates, pension fund liabilities increase by around us$180 billion.

Citigroup equity strategist Robert Buckland has argued that low rates and QE reduce employment and economic activity, rather than increasing them. These policies encourage a shift from bonds into equities. As investors are looking for income rather than capital growth, they force companies to increase dividends and undertake share buybacks. To meet these pressures, companies must boost cash flow and earnings, by shedding workers and reducing investment to cut costs. The process increases share prices and returns for shareholders of the company, but is bad for the overall economy.

Stimulus from low interest rates is temporary. Demand reverts to normal levels when rates are normalised. Once this happens, high debt levels are harder to service, requiring the diversion of income to meet larger interest bills, which reduces economic activity. A 1 percent rise in rates would increase the interest cost to the US government by around us$180 billion. A rise of 1 percent in the interest rates of the Group of 7 industrial countries would increase their expense by around us$1.4 trillion. A 2013 McKinsey Global Institute Study found that a 1 percent increase in interest rates would result in US household debt payments going up by about 7 percent, from us$822 billion to us$876 billion. Similarly, 1 percent higher interest rates would increase UK household debt payments by about 19 percent, from £96 billion to £113 billion.

In reality, low rates create zombie economies. Weak businesses survive, directing cash flow to cover interest on loans that cannot be repaid but that banks will not write off. With capital tied up, banks reduce lending to productive enterprises, especially small and medium-sized ones, which account for a large portion of economic activity and employment. Firms do not dispose of or restructure underproductive investments. The creative destruction and reallocation of resources necessary to restore the economy does not occur. As French playwright Molière noted, 'More men die of their remedies than of their illnesses.'[14]

*

Low interest returns and central bank monetary methamphetamine encouraged asset price bubbles, which in turn created conditions for a future financial crisis. It drove a desperate dash for trash, where investors chased riskier, increasingly expensive investments to generate some return in an environment when safe assets were yielding nothing.

By 2013 stock markets in many developed countries, led by the US, exceeded their pre-crisis levels. Investors bought up dividend-paying shares. Seeking capital appreciation, investors sought technology and biotechnology stocks, which promised higher rates of earnings and revenue growth than the overall market.

Property prices rose, supported by low financing costs and rental income. In the US and UK property prices recovered, in some cases exceeding 2008 levels. In Germany, Switzerland, Canada, Australia, New Zealand, and a number of emerging markets, especially in Asia, property prices reached record levels. In October 2013 former regulator Lord Adair Turner complained about the hair-of-the-dog remedy: 'We had a fantastic party, we got a whacking great hangover, and we've decided that the best cure is a really stiff drink … Which is the same all over again – get the housing market going …'[15]

Money flowed into bonds, looking for income. Sovereign bond interest rates fell to historic lows, fuelled by central bank buying. Over 50 percent of government bonds now returned less than 1 percent. Even rates for beleaguered countries like Greece, Ireland, Portugal and Spain fell, in some cases returning to pre-crisis levels.

In April 2014, rivalling Lazarus's rise from the dead, Greece issued €3 billion worth of five-year bonds at a yield of 4.95 percent. Investor demand was over €20 billion. Greece had defaulted on its debt two years previously. The economy was fragile. Debt levels remained unsustainably high, even without adjusting for unpaid government bills or the potential recapitalisation needs of the banking sector. A further debt restructuring could not be ruled out. Investors bet that Greece was too big to fail, and that Germany and the EU would continue to support it and the euro. But the election in January 2015 of a Syriza government, opposed to austerity and seeking a further writedown of Greek debt, saw interest rates rise to over 15 percent, inflicting large losses on holders.

Non-investment grade bonds, or junk bonds, globally increased from us$82 billion in 2000 to us$556 billion in 2013, rising from 4 percent to 18 percent of all corporate bond issues. Since 2010 the number of US companies issuing non-investment grade bonds has exceeded the number issuing investment grade bonds. In Europe non-investment grade bonds, which were relatively uncommon previously, accounted for about 12 percent of issuance by 2013. The strongest increase was in the speculative categories rated B and CCC, only just above the D rating that signalled default. Leveraged loans (a riskier form of lending) reached US$455 billion, up from US$389 billion in 2007.

Interest rates on A-rated investment grade debt fell to around 2.4 percent, well below the levels of 7–8 percent in 2008/09, and below the historical average of 5.1 percent since 2000. Interest rates on B-rated non-investment grade debt were 6 percent per annum, well below the levels of 15–20 percent in 2008/09, and below the historical average of around 10 percent since 2000. Bond investors desperate for yield moved beyond emerging markets to frontier markets, embracing ever more exotic African and Asian borrowers.

Loans with minimal creditor protection, loans which paid interest in the form of new debt, and borrowing to return share capital to investors re-emerged. Even subprime loans, now used to buy automobiles and commercial real estate, and 125 percent business loans (whereby a bank lent 125 percent of collateral) recommenced.

Investors priced for perfection, assuming that nothing could, or would be allowed to, go wrong. In the worst case, they assumed they could sell out before the problems emerged. But failures, industry consolidation, reduction in trading, and new regulations meant that the number of dealers and inventory levels had fallen, by as much as 70 percent. In the US, historically, investment funds held around three times the volume of bonds as dealers. By 2015 the level had increased to twenty times. Between 2007 and 2015 the amount of capital available to support trading in government bonds fell from US$2.7 trillion to US$1.7 trillion, coinciding with a doubling in the value of outstanding US debt. The position in Europe was worse, with a greater increase in government debt and a more significant retrenchment in dealer capacity. The ability of investors to exit without creating sharp price falls and volatility was now heavily constrained.

Wherever you looked, the pattern was the same in the credit casino.

Desperate for return, investors took more risks, buying overvalued financial assets, forcing the price ever higher. Low rates again threatened financial stability.

*

Increasingly, there was focus on the limits of official support. Governments are not like households. Backed by taxing powers and the resources and wealth of the country and citizens, they have greater freedom in their financial actions. But there are still limits. The ability of governments to borrow is constrained by private-sector domestic savings and the willingness of foreign investors to lend.

Ultimately, reliance shifts to the ability of central banks to monetise debt, creating money to finance governments. And central banks also have practical constraints on their actions. They can operate without conventional capital, creating reserves and printing money, but a large loss may affect their credibility, and their ability to perform functions and implement policies.

Central banks earn the difference between interest received on government securities acquired and the near-zero cost of money (notes and reserves) created to pay for these purchases. As long as the current value of this future seigniorage income is greater than its liabilities, a central bank is considered solvent.

Like the banks they regulate, central banks are leveraged. The US Federal Reserve has US$54 billion in capital, supporting assets of around US$4 trillion. The European Central Bank has €10 billion in capital, supporting assets of around €3 trillion. The Bank of Japan has around ¥2.7 trillion in capital, supporting assets of ¥160 trillion. The Bank of England has £3.3 billion in capital supporting assets of £397 billion.

Balance-sheet expansion under QE programs has increased the risk of insolvency for central banks. They are exposed to losses on holdings of securities from defaults or higher yields. According to the Bank for International Settlements, a normalisation in government bond rates, say a 3 percent increase, would result in a change in the value of outstanding government bonds, ranging from a loss of around 8 percent of GDP for the US to around 35 percent for Japan. Ironically this exposure increases if the easy money policies are successful and the economy recovers, causing rate rises.

Debt monetisation by central banks theoretically can create inflation in excess of politically, economically and socially acceptable levels. It may damage, perhaps irreparably, the status of the currency as a medium of exchange or accepted store of value, as in Zimbabwe, where printing money led to hyperinflation and extraordinary currency debasement. Before the Zimbabwe dollar was replaced with the US dollar, notes with a face value of 100 trillion were needed. One cheque for the purchase of a car was made out for one quadrillion, seventy-two trillion, four hundred and eighteen billion and three million Zimbabwe dollars only (z$1,072,418,003,000,000.00). The Victoria Falls Hotel erected signs asking guests not to put Zimbabwe dollars used for personal hygiene into the toilets.

*

The post-GFC policies cannot be reversed easily. Withdrawing fiscal stimulus would result in a slowdown in economic activity. Reducing government spending and higher taxes would decrease disposable incomes, resulting in a contraction in consumption, especially in an environment of stagnant incomes and uncertain employment. Slower growth makes it harder to correct budget deficits and control government debt levels. The difficulty in reversing an expansionary fiscal policy corroborates Milton Friedman's sarcastic observation: 'There is nothing so permanent as a temporary government program.'[16]

The normalisation of interest rates, stopping government bond purchases, and reducing central bank holdings of securities all risk disruption through higher rates. With global debt at the highest levels ever recorded, borrowing encouraged by low rates will become rapidly unsustainable at higher rates, triggering business failures and losses. Asset values supported by low rates would fall, setting off a chain reaction of financial instability. The reduction in liquidity and supply of credit would destabilise a fragile financial system.

The policies have compounded existing issues, especially rising debt levels, making the problems more intractable. Former Bank of England governor Sir Mervyn King put it bluntly: 'Printing money is not . . . simply manna from heaven.'[17]

In May 2013 US Fed chairman Bernanke proposed the taper, a gradual reduction in new bond purchases. It was a valedictory gesture, with an eye to his place in history as the end of his term approached. The ten-year US Treasury bond rate increased by 1 percent, causing losses of around US$40–50 billion on bank holdings of US Treasury bonds. The US Fed suffered losses of around US$190 billion, reversing its cumulative gains. Higher mortgage rates slowed the refinancing of existing mortgages and the recovery of the housing market. Stock and asset prices also fell sharply. Price falls reduced the value of financial assets used as collateral for loans, triggering margin calls and leading to a withdrawal of liquidity from markets.

Higher US rates drove a rise in rates across the world, with the exception of Japan, which had launched a new QE program. In emerging markets there were large outflows, exposing their reliance on foreign capital, and currencies fell, resulting in losses on foreign currency debt. The taper tantrum forced Bernanke to furiously back-pedal.

In December 2013 the US Fed finally began reducing bond purchases, stopping its QE program completely in November 2014. In order to avoid any repeat of the earlier volatility, the Fed committed to keeping policy rates low for an extended period and maintain existing holdings of securities. The effect of the end of Fed purchases of Treasury bonds was ameliorated by reduced government funding needs. The US budget deficit was lower, reflecting an improved economy and higher tax revenues. Additional liquidity injections from the European Central Bank and the Bank of Japan also helped decrease the pressure caused in global money markets by the US's ending of QE.

*

But withdrawing support has risks.

In September 2011 the Swiss National Bank (SNB) set a ceiling on the Swiss currency at 1.20 Swiss francs to the euro, to discourage large inflows of capital seeking a safe haven following the 2008 crisis and, especially, the Eurozone debt problems. The value of the Swiss franc had increased by around 20 percent relative to its major European trading partners, making Swiss exporters uncompetitive, damaging growth, and importing disinflation or deflation.

In order to stabilise the Swiss currency's value, the SNB bought euros, funding them by creating Swiss francs. This resulted in the accumulation of record foreign currency reserves. The SNB's balance sheet expanded to around US$500 billion, equivalent to around 80 percent of Swiss GDP. Relative to the size of its economy, the SNB's balance sheet was about three times larger than that of the US Federal Reserve and the Bank of England. Switzerland's monetary base quintupled to Swiss franc 400 billion. Bank lending increased by 25 percent to around 170 percent of GDP, resulting in sharp rises in property prices and rents.

On 15 January 2015, without warning, the SNB abandoned the ceiling. Large inflows, driven by European Central Bank actions to weaken the euro as well as money from Russia, Greece and the Middle East fleeing political and economic turmoil, were making the policy unsustainable. Continuation of the currency ceiling would have required a commitment to expanding the money supply without constraint, which would have heightened the risk of financial instability, given the already rapid increases in asset prices. The size of the SNB's balance sheet and the currency mismatch would have created exposure to large losses if the Swiss franc appreciated. Its ability to exit would have become increasingly compromised. Confronted with these risks, the SNB reversed its policy.

Following the announcement, the Swiss franc rose by around 40 percent against the euro and dollar, ending the day about 20 percent higher. The rise, which caught financial markets by surprise, resulted in immediate large losses to holders of short positions and borrowers of the Swiss franc. The losers included Polish and Hungarian home buyers who had taken out Swiss franc mortgages at low interest rates. The SNB itself suffered losses of around us$50–60 billion, equating to 10–15 percent of GDP.

The most important ramifications of the abandonment of the ceiling were outside Switzerland. The decision forced other countries to reduce interest rates and seek to devalue their currency so as to preserve competitiveness and limit unstable capital movements. These measures exacerbated existing asset price bubbles and the risk of future problems in the financial system in these nations.

The abandonment also drew attention to the ability of central banks to intervene in and control market prices, as well as the risks of continued expansion of balance sheets. For conservative, orthodox economies, such as Germany, the experience of the SNB reinforced fears about the potential costs and risks of unconventional policies.

It further highlighted the fact that the relative stability of financial markets and the recovery in financial assets since 2009 was heavily reliant on central banks. Additional risk-taking was based on artificially decreasing the availability of and returns on low-risk investments, such as cash or government bonds. This had increased the prices of risky assets without adequate additional compensation for possible losses, based on the assumption that central banks can suppress volatility and support prices as necessary. The Swiss franc episode foreshadowed potential problems if and when central bank activism ends, or disappointed markets cease to rely on it.

The authorities now may have no option but to maintain low rates and abundant liquidity in the face of low growth and the risk of disinflation or deflation. Some 50–60 percent of global growth since 2009 has been the result of these policies. Nor can central bankers risk a sharp fall in asset prices in the current fragile conditions. The value of as much as 80 percent of stocks have benefited to some degree from current monetary policies.

Many economies in the world today have debt-to-GDP ratios of 300 percent. If the average interest rate is 3 percent, then to meet interest payments the economy would need to grow at 9 percent (300 percent [debt] times 3 percent [interest rate]), an unlikely nominal rate of expansion. Disposal of assets to pay down borrowings is difficult. Sales at real value, below the exaggerated prices driven by abundant and low-cost finance, may incur significant losses. In effect the loans cannot be repaid but must be continuously refinanced to avoid default. Lenders need funding to maintain the loans to the borrower, and also to continue supplying credit to the broader economy. If such funding is commercially unavailable from depositors or investors, then central banks have to inject money into the financial system to reduce the risk of decline in asset prices and default by borrowers. In 2014 Citibank economists estimated that liquidity injections of around US$200 billion per quarter (around 1.3 percent of global GDP) are needed simply to maintain financial asset prices at their current levels.

In a letter to the *Financial Times* in January 2015 Jeff Frank, a professor of economics at the University of London, argued: 'It isn't bold to print money. It will be bold to withdraw it later.'[18]

*

With policy measures increasingly ineffective, there was concern about the economic trajectory. The world was turning Japanese.

In the postwar period, Japan's export-driven economic model thrived on low costs, manufacturing competence and an under-valued yen. It generated strong growth, around 9.5 percent per annum between 1955 and 1970 and around 3.8 percent per annum between 1971 and 1990.

In September 1985 the Plaza Accord saw the US dollar devalued against the Japanese and German currencies. The shift from an era of *enyasu* (inexpensive yen) to a period of *endaka* (expensive yen) or *endaka fukyo* (recession caused by an expensive yen) affected Japanese exports and growth. Japanese authorities cut interest rates from 5 per-cent to 2.5 percent to revive economic activity, fuelling debt-funded real estate and stock price increases. At the height of the bubble econ-omy, the Tokyo Imperial Palace (3.4 square kilometres, or 1.3 square miles) was theoretically more valuable than all the real estate in the state of California. The bubble economy collapsed around 1989 when interest rates rose.

Japan has been mired in an environment of low growth and dis-inflation, or deflation, for over two decades. Growth has averaged around 0.8 percent per annum. Nominal GDP has been largely stag-nant since 1992. Japan's economy operates far below capacity, with the output gap around 5–7 percent. The Japanese stock market is more than 50 percent below its peak, with the Nikkei index falling from 38,957 at the end of 1989 to a low of 7607 in 2003. It now trades at around 19,000. Japanese real estate prices are, for the most part, at the same levels as the early 1980s.

Public finances deteriorated as chronic budget deficits resulted in government debt increasing to 240 percent of GDP. Japan now spends more than ¥200 for every ¥100 of tax revenue received. In effect, the country borrows more each year than it raises in taxes, paralleling the German Weimar government of 1919–33. Even at current near-zero interest rates, Japan spends around a quarter of its tax revenues on interest payments. Its total debt, over 500 percent of GDP, is higher today than at the onset of the crisis in 1989/90.

In early 2013 second-time Prime Minister Shinzō Abe initiated the ambitious Three Arrows plan, dubbed 'Abenomics' or 'electrifying the corpse' by sceptics. New initiatives combined fiscal expansion, QE and structural reforms to encourage consumption, investment, borrowing and higher inflation, so as to create a virtuous cycle of growth. The scale of the program exceeded anything attempted elsewhere. The Bank of Japan committed to purchasing more than double the amount of government bonds that the US Fed purchased at the peak of its QE program. It was four times larger as a percentage of GDP.

The policies were not new, having been tried repeatedly before. Since 1990, Japan has had more than fifteen stimulus packages. The Bank of Japan has maintained a zero interest rate policy for over fifteen years and implemented nine rounds of QE. Given that short-term rates were near zero and ten-year rates around 0.5 percent before the announcement of Prime Minister Abe's plan, the effects of the new fiscal and monetary initiatives on real economic activity are not likely to be significant or long-lasting.

Enthusiastically received, the program weakened the yen, boosted exports, and increased stock and property prices. But by 2014/15, Abenomics was struggling, increasingly resembling kamikaze economics.

There are similarities and differences between the collapse of Japan's bubble economy and the current global position. In both cases, low interest rates and excessive debt build-ups financed booms to drive the economy out of recession. Both ultimately collapsed. Both were characterised by the overvaluation of financial assets and weaknesses in the banking system. The curative policies pursued – government spending to support economic activity, debt monetisation and zero interest rates – are similar.

At the onset of its crisis, Japan had low levels of government debt, high domestic savings, and an abnormally high home bias in investment. This allowed the government to finance its spending domestically, assisted by an accommodative central bank. Around 90 percent of Japanese government bonds are held by compliant domestic investors. Many of the world's problem economies have low domestic savings and are reliant on foreign capital.

Japan's problems occurred against a background of external economic growth. Strong exports and a current account surplus partially offset the lack of domestic demand, buffering the effects of its economic slowdown. In contrast, individual countries today will find it more difficult to rely on their external account to support their economies, due to the global nature of the present problems.

An ageing population has increasingly compounded the downturn, but Japanese demographics at the commencement of the crisis were helpful. Its older population had considerable wealth, and low population growth meant that fewer new entrants had to be absorbed into the workforce during a period of slow economic growth, alleviating problems of rising unemployment.

Japan is an insular, homogenous society, whose citizens have a strong national consciousness and a stoicism shaped by the experiences of World War II and the postwar period. Citizens were accepting of the sacrifices necessitated by the economic problems. Savers accepted the net transfer of wealth to borrowers through low interest rates. The social structure of many troubled economies may not accommodate the measures required to manage the crisis without significant break-downs in order.

Japan highlights the difficulty of engineering a recovery from the collapse of a debt-fuelled asset bubble. It reveals the limitations of traditional policy options – fiscal stimulus, low interest rates and debt monetisation. The lesson from Japan's experience may be that the only safe option is to avoid debt-fuelled bubbles and the subsequent build-up of public borrowing in the first place.

*

In 2014 the new governor of the Bank of England and former head of the Bank of Canada, Mark Carney, spoke of the global economy achieving 'escape velocity', the speed needed to break free from a grav-itational force field without further propulsion.[19] He was referring to a sufficient rate of growth and inflation to slip free of the prevalent economic torpor.

But this self-sustaining recovery has proved elusive. In 2014 the Group of 20 countries committed to growth targets and actions to boost economies by a collective US$2 trillion by 2018. If it was so easy, why hadn't they acted sooner? Within twenty-four hours of the communiqué, Japan announced that its economy had unexpectedly shrunk by 1.6 percent. Europe and emerging markets were facing major slowdowns in economic activity.

Apart from well-worn homilies about fiscal sustainability and other economic shibboleths, policymakers provided little detail on how high debt levels, weak public finances, continuing global imbalances, deflationary pressures, exchange rate instability and other vulnerabilities would be managed. There were only vague references to exits from current policies and normalisation of rates. Complex jargon, obscure mathematics and tired ideologies disguised the policies' failures and limitations.

But growth and prosperity would magically return. Ben Bernanke's successor, Janet Yellen, offered a 'don't worry, be happy' message. Low growth was attributable to the weather, not weak investment and exports. People had dropped out of the workforce, reducing labour participation to 1978 levels, due not to lack of jobs, but retirement and lifestyle choices. There were no concerns about deflation, inflation or asset bubbles. European leaders talked about 'expansionary austerity'. In an interview on 19 December 2012 Australia's central bank governor Glenn Stevens channelled Charles Dickens' Mr Micawber in responding to a question about future growth. He was confident that something would turn up: 'most of the time it comes'.[20] George Bernard Shaw was correct in his judgement that all professions are a conspiracy against the laity.

In March 2014 William White, a Canadian economist who had warned about increasing risks before the GFC, pointed out that the analytical foundations of the economic theory underlying the policies being followed were weak.[21] Fiscal and monetary policy could not address deep-seated structural problems within the real economy – debt levels, demographics, declining productivity, slowing industrial innovation – and the actual economic model. By 2015 Dr White was alarmed at the mispricing of assets, currency wars and reliance on failed policies. He saw the global economy as dangerously unanchored, admitting that he had no idea how this was going to end. In January 2015, after retiring from the Bank of England, former governor Mervyn King candidly admitted that the biggest monetary stimulus the world had ever seen had not solved the problems. He now did not think that even more was the answer.

After leaving the Fed, Ben Bernanke launched himself on the lecture circuit with a haste unrivalled since Hamlet's widowed mother wed her brother-in-law. In one week in March 2014 he spoke in Abu Dhabi, Johannesburg and Houston. His reputed fee of US$250,000 for each speech compared to his annual salary as Fed chairman of around US$200,000. Bernanke's forecasting record was indifferent – championing the Great Moderation 1.0, missing the subprime and housing bubble, rejecting the risk of a Japan-like stagnation. Attending investors probably believed that his closeness to his successor might provide valuable insights into the Fed's future policy. The sixty-year-old Bernanke gave the impression that he did not expect official rates to increase to their long-term average of around 4 percent in his lifetime.

There is in fact little agreement on the appropriate policy response. As Russian playwright and doctor Anton Chekhov wrote in *The Cherry Orchard*, 'If many remedies are prescribed for an illness, you may be certain that the illness has no cure.'[22] Policymakers are making it up as they go along. The measures are basically of limited use, but presented to a credulous public as sound policy.

*

At the start of the GFC the choice was always pain now or agony later. Policymakers have consciously or unconsciously chosen the latter, engineering a long period of stagnation or a managed depression. Some developed economies will not be back to their pre-2008 output levels until at least 2018. Optimists point to low volatility, christening it the Great Moderation 2.0. Critics point to the lack of growth, calling it more moderate than great.

Vindicating Edmund Burke's mistrust of the utopian promises of professors, more extreme policy measures are probable. Extension of the forms of QE can be expected, encompassing purchases of a wider range of assets, including shares, as in Japan. The US is considering cancelling Treasury bonds held by the Fed to reduce debt, ignoring the loss to the central bank from the writedown of its holdings. In the UK one idea considered was for the Bank of England to exchange holdings of government securities for zero coupon bonds, which pay no interest and have no maturity or fixed repayment date, and which were to be valued at face value to avoid loss.

The global economy risks becoming trapped in a QE-forever cycle. A weak economy forces policymakers to implement expansionary fiscal measures and QE. If the economy responds, then increased economic activity and the side effects of QE will encourage a withdrawal of the stimulus. Higher interest rates slow the economy and trigger financial crises, setting off a new round of the cycle. If the economy does not respond to expansionary policies, then there is pressure for additional stimuli, as policymakers seek to maintain their aura of economic control. There may be no alternative to monetary morphine. As celebrity and former drug addict Russell Brand put it: 'The priority of any addict is to anaesthetise the pain of living to ease the passage of day with some purchased relief.'[23]

The position of the global economy is akin to a black hole, from which gravity prevents anything, including light, escaping. Excessive levels of debt and deep-seated fundamental imbalances now prevent escape from stagnation or worse. Black holes form when massive stars collapse at the end of their life cycle, an appropriate metaphor for the recent period of economic history.

The Factors Driving Secular Stagnation and the New Mediocre

The playwright Arthur Miller thought that 'an era can be said to end when its basic illusions are exhausted'.[1] The central illusion of the age of capital – endless economic growth – is ending.

Historically, financial crises and recessions have been followed by strong recoveries, with GDP growth rebounding to around 6 percent per year. But the recovery from the GFC was abnormally weak, with growth of around 2–3 percent. The US, one of the strongest performers amongst developed countries, was further below its economic potential than even Japan was at an equivalent time following the collapse of its bubble economy.

*

In late 2013 Harvard economist and former US Treasury Secretary Lawrence Summers argued that the US economy may be suffering from secular stagnation, a concept introduced by economist Alvin

Hansen in the 1930s. Changes in the economy's structure made growth at previous rates unattainable, with little prospect of recovery to pre-crisis output levels. The situation was global, not confined to the US. IMF president Christine Lagarde termed it the new mediocre.

Slow growth reflected weak demand as households and businesses reduced debt, and governments cut spending and raised taxes, responding to debt concerns. Post-GFC uncertainty and lack of confidence increased global savings, which drove strong demand for safe liquid assets. Higher overall savings rates created a capital glut and lower spending, which slowed growth. Along with low inflation rates, this reduced interest rates. The combination of these factors diminished the effectiveness of current policies, such as QE.

Reduced consumption reflected increasing inequality. In the last 15–20 years the incomes of 99 percent of the population in developed economies have been stagnant or fallen, by as much as 8–10 percent. Most income gains have accrued to a small group, who are wealthy and save perhaps 20–30 percent of their income, around ten times the 2–3 percent on average saved by the rest.

Corporate profits have increased as a share of GDP relative to wages. The profits are distributed to shareholders, who also tend to be wealthier, with a lower marginal propensity to consume, further increasing available savings. Businesses today are reluctant to invest available cash, reflecting the lack of demand, and overcapacity. Advances in technology have changed industrial structure, with many new ventures no longer needing the large investments once required by heavy industry or manufacturing. The shift in developed countries from manufacturing to services has accelerated this trend. The undistributed corporate cash further boosts savings.

Some countries, like China and Germany, continue to accumulate large trade surpluses and foreign exchange reserves. These savings, which must be invested, further exacerbate the capital glut, and where used to artificially lower exchange rates, they reallocate demand between countries.

Economic activity globally was affected by slower growth in populations and workforces, as well as declining improvements in productivity.

Lawrence Summers argued that the problem was not the result of the GFC itself, having emerged slowly over the previous twenty years. Critics claimed there was no direct evidence of secular stagnation. Some disputed the existence of a savings glut. Others thought that government intervention had distorted the economy. Many pointed out that Alvin Hansen's thesis proved incorrect. World War II, the postwar baby boom, rising consumption, investment, and technological innovation had revived economic growth.

Channelling Keynes, Summers argued that greater public investment, rather than monetary policy, was the key to recovery. The ability of over-indebted governments to finance proposed investments was unclear. Problems in economics are always the same; it's the answers that are different.

*

Measuring growth is not easy. GDP is the main tool, calculating the market value of all recognised final goods and services produced in a country in a year. GDP per capita is the country's GDP divided by its population.

There are several approaches to measuring GDP. The production approach seeks to calculate the output of enterprises to arrive at the total. The income approach uses the incomes, which should logically equal the value of their products. The expenditure approach uses total expenditure, assuming that the goods and services that are produced must be purchased. All are flawed.

In 2014 Americans awoke to discover that China was about to

become the world's largest economy by GDP, assuming the mantle held by the US since 1872. The change reflected adjustments for differences in purchasing power, effectively the lower cost of living in China. US GDP itself had been boosted by around 3 percent in 2013, when statisticians included intellectual-property products, in effect the value of research and development expected to generate future income.

In April 2014 Nigeria, notorious for exporting monetary scams, increased its GDP by 89 percent, making it the largest economy in Africa, surpassing South Africa. It replaced a redundant 1990 view of the Nigerian economy with a new 2010 model, incorporating rapidly growing industries such as telecommunications and filmmaking that did not previously exist. The average Chinese or Nigerian did not become richer because of the adjustments.

GDP calculation is arbitrary. The value of non-traded goods and services must be estimated using the cost of production or the available value of a similar item. The value of a home may be the imputed rent that could be charged. During the GFC, the financial sector's output mysteriously rose even as it struggled to survive, reflecting the increase in the margin between bank lending and deposit rates.

GDP generally excludes non-market transactions such as household work, much of it done by women, and volunteer or unpaid services. It focuses on income generated, excluding the economic value of leisure. It also excludes the underground economy, such as illegal or unreported activities, the informal economy and subsistence production. In India around half of economic activity and 90 percent of employment are informal, making accurate GDP calculations difficult.

Depreciation of the means of income generation, such as equipment or capital, is excluded. GDP can be overstated where technological investment is recorded as investment, or understated where it is written off as a cost incurred. GDP does not accurately capture new products, improvements in quality, or innovation. It does not discriminate between defence spending, consumption, healthcare and aged care. Expenditure following war or a natural disaster may increase GDP but it produces no real net change, only rebuilding what was destroyed. Nor does it take into account depletion of natural resources, especially non-renewable elements. It incorrectly accounts for environmental despoliation, with the cost of causing and correcting the damage both recorded as economic activity.

GDP ignores the distribution of wealth. It measures output in a particular country, even where the ultimate profits may accrue to owners in another jurisdiction.

Nations can boost growth by misallocating investment, excessive borrowing, or misuse of natural resources. A significant part of China's recent rapid growth may have been an illusion. In a 2007 conversation disclosed by WikiLeaks, Chinese Premier Li Keqiang told the US ambassador that GDP statistics were 'for reference only'. Li preferred to focus on electricity consumption, the volume of rail cargo, and the amount of loans disbursed (promptly dubbed the Li Keqiang Index).[2]

Since 2008, China's headline growth of around 8 percent has been driven by investment funded by new bank lending, from state-controlled banks, averaging around 30–40 percent of GDP. Some 10–20 percent of these loans may prove incapable of being repaid, amounting to losses of 3–8 percent of GDP. If these losses are correctly accounted for by writing them off against income, Chinese growth is much lower.

Economist Simon Kuznets, who formulated the concept of GDP, cautioned against an over-simplified quantitative measurement providing a misleading illusion of precision. Senator Robert Kennedy gave the most eloquent criticism of GDP, highlighting distinctions between quantity and quality of growth:

Our gross national product ... if we should judge America by that – counts air pollution and cigarette advertising, and ambulances to clear our highways of carnage. It counts special locks for our doors and the jails for those who break them. It counts the destruction of our redwoods and the loss of our natural wonder in chaotic sprawl. It counts napalm and the cost of a nuclear warhead, and armoured cars for police who fight riots in our streets. It counts Whitman's rifle and Speck's knife, and the television programs which glorify violence in order to sell toys to our children.

Yet the gross national product does not allow for the health of our children, the quality of their education, or the joy of their play. It does not include the beauty of our poetry or the strength of our marriages; the intelligence of our public debate or the integrity of our public officials. It measures neither our wit nor our courage; neither our wisdom nor our learning; neither our compassion nor our devotion to our country; it measures everything, in short, except that which makes life worthwhile.[3]

As the European debt crisis gathered momentum, French President Nicolas Sarkozy lamented GDP fetishism, lashing out at 'a cult of figures'. He commissioned Nobel Prize-winning economists Joseph Stiglitz and Amartya Sen to develop a new measure, the gross national happiness championed by Bhutan, which would take into account the quality of health services, welfare systems, leisure and intergenerational issues. But like GDP, gross national happiness is difficult to measure. The enthusiasm for it was, in reality, based on the president's desire to boost France's moribund economic performance, especially relative to the US.

In 2014 Europeans started to include drugs, prostitution, and other unreported businesses in GDP calculations. This increased Italian GDP by around 2 percent, allowing the government to produce the required budget surplus before financing costs of 3 percent of GDP and reduce its debt-to-GDP ratio, at the time over 130 percent, well above the agreed 60 percent limit. Statisticians even considered incorporating bribes, estimated globally at around US$1 trillion per annum, in GDP. The UK Office for National Statistics based the GDP contribution of prostitution on approximately 58,000 sex workers serving an average of twenty-five clients each week. The field research on which these estimates were based is unknown.

*

Irrespective of measurement problems, the focus of economic management is GDP growth. All brands of politics and economics are rooted in the idea of growth, of keeping the economy operating at near-full capacity and increasing living standards. This is combined with the belief that governments and central bankers can exert substantial control over the economy to bring this about.

Historically, economic growth was needed, in part, to absorb the rising supply of goods and services as technology and global trade rapidly increased production capacity. In *Das Kapital* Karl Marx identified this inherent tendency of capitalism towards overproduction. Theologians, like Reinhold Niebuhr, saw society as enslaved to its productive process, reversing the normal process of producing to satisfy consumption needs. Economists dismiss the notion of overproduction, arguing that supply creates its own demand (known as Say's Law). They view consumer needs as essentially unlimited, with people wanting more and better goods.

Building on Thorstein Veblen's idea of conspicuous consumption, American journalist Vance Packard showed how people's desire for goods was cultivated through advertising. His 1957 book *The Hidden Persuaders* detailed the use of (often subliminal) psychological techniques, especially hedonism, fashion, status, and fear of its loss, to manipulate expectations and induce desire for products. Advertising converted shopping and consumption into an essential part of leisure.

Planned obsolescence and disposability also increased demand. Instead of allowing for replacement based on failure or innovation, products were designed with a limited useful life so as to increase consumption. With the US car market approaching saturation, GM chairman Alfred Sloan initiated annual design changes to encourage drivers to replace their vehicles frequently. In his 1960 book *The Waste Makers*, Vance Packard coined the term 'obsolescence of desirability': marketing designed to wear out a product in the owner's mind.

New technologies were promoted as superior or modern, creating demand. Gramophone records were replaced successively by cassette tapes, CDs, MP3s, and digital media such as iTunes and live streaming. Some thirty years after it was displaced, analog vinyl re-emerged as an expensive, fashionable niche product, completing the cycle. Although it made minimal difference to their enjoyment, people owned the same music in several different media, together with the associated paraphernalia, creating a peculiar form of economic activity.

Manufacturers used notions of hygiene, cleanliness and convenience to promote disposable items. Re-use gave way to disposability in baby nappies, paper napkins and towels, and plastic and Styrofoam cups, bottles and containers. Kimberly-Clark promoted disposable Kleenex as a replacement for germ-filled handkerchiefs that apparently threatened public health. In a world of abundance, prolonging the useful life of products to save money was now unfashionable, confined to the poor and undeveloped societies.

Increasing availability of debt, from a deregulated banking industry, ensured that consumers could borrow to pay for their new and ever-changing got-to-haves. Credit cards, which allowed individuals to buy now and pay later, took the waiting out of wanting. The have-nots could become haves because they did not have to pay immediately for what they had to have. Debt-fuelled consumption supported demand and production.

Economic growth subtly softened the impact of increasing inequality. Greater economic activity helped improve living standards, reducing pressure for wealth redistribution. The democratisation of credit allowed lower income groups to borrow and spend despite stagnant real incomes.

Global economic growth improved the wealth of emerging nations, increasing the living standards of their citizens. This avoided awkward issues of colonial exploitation and reparations.

Growth was perceived to benefit poorer members of society by improving the economy as a whole. Henry Wallich, a former governor of the US Federal Reserve, summed it up: 'So long as there is growth there is hope, and that makes large income differentials tolerable.'[4]

*

But while growth has been the focus of economic management, it is a relatively recent phenomenon.

Historian J.R. McNeill has found that up until 1500 AD the world economy grew minimally. Between 1500 and 1820, global GDP increased from US$240 billion to US$695 billion (in 1990 dollars), a growth rate of 0.3 percent per annum, driven mainly by increases in population and improvements in agriculture. Between 1820 and 1900, global GDP almost tripled from US$695 billion to US$1.98 trillion, a growth rate of 1.32 percent per annum, driven by the Industrial Revolution and colonial expansion. Between 1900 and 1992, global GDP grew from US$1.98 trillion to around US$28 trillion, a growth rate of just under 3 percent per annum. Between 1992 and 2014, it doubled again to US$60 trillion, a growth rate of around 3.5 percent per annum. The average human being today has about nine times and four times the income per head of their predecessors in 1500 and 1900 respectively.[5]

Northwestern University economist Robert Gordon confirmed McNeill's results. Using British data, he found minimal growth in real output per capita, 0.2 percent per annum, between 1300 and 1700. By 1906 British growth reached around 1 percent per annum. According to later US data, growth reached around 2.5 percent per annum by 1950, then declined. Professor Gordon found that living standards took five centuries, between 1300 and 1800, to double. They then doubled again in the century between 1800 and 1900, and again in the twenty-eight years between 1929 and 1957, and again in the thirty-one years between 1957 and 1988.[6] The strongest growth was concentrated in two periods: 1873–1914 and post-World War II. The progress and improvements made over the past 150 years, especially the last half a century, may well be unique.

Economic growth is partly a function of demographics – rising population and increased participation in the labour force. It is affected by opening up new markets, and by the availability of low-cost natural resources, such as water, food and energy. It requires innovation and productivity improvements. In recent years it has also been driven by financialisation, especially the use of debt.

The global economy now faces a number of headwinds. An ageing population in developed countries limits growth. The integration of China, India, Russia and their satellites provided a one-off boost to global economic activity. Since 1989 most economies, with the exception of North Korea, have been integrated into the global trading system, and gains from globalisation may reverse. The global economy faces increasing resource constraints. The pace of innovation and productivity increase has slowed. Dealing with high debt levels will slow future growth.

*

Of the identified factors affecting future growth, demographics may be crucial.

For much of recorded history, human mortality has been high and lifespans short, with births matching deaths. Following the Industrial Revolution, life expectancy steadily improved, leading to growing populations, but since then, global demographics have reached a turning point. The synchronised increases in population, innovation and productivity are slowing and, in some countries, reversing.

World population today is around 7.3 billion. Most of the growth in it has come in the period since the Industrial Revolution. In 1804 world population was 1 billion. In 1900 it was 1.6 billion. The global workforce increased as a result of population growth, and greater participation in organised work by women and by rural citizens who moved into urban centres. But the rate of growth has slowed. During the twentieth century the global population doubled twice. It will not double even once in the twenty-first century. The current growth rate is just over 1 percent, well below the peak rate of around 2 percent in the early 1960s. Between 1994 and 2008, the forecast for the world's population in 2050 declined from about 10 billion to 9 billion. But even this lower projected growth may be unsustainable, placing huge pressures on resources and the environment.

Future population growth will be uneven, with major increases in South Asia and Africa because of high fertility rates. But the increase will slow in these regions too, and will not offset the declines in many developed countries and some emerging countries, such as China.

Sometime during the twenty-first century, global population will peak and then decline. In Japan, Germany, Spain, Portugal, Greece and Eastern Europe population is already falling. This overall slowdown and then reversal will adversely affect economic growth. The growth in population in poorer parts of South Asia and Africa will not generate a commensurate rise in economic growth because those countries will require support from richer donor nations for the essentials of survival.

The world will also be older in the future. By 2035 more than 1.1 billion people, 13 percent of the total population, will be above sixty-five years of age, a doubling of this age group from current levels. The ratio of old people to those of working age (old-age dependency ratio) will grow. By 2035 there will be one person aged over sixty-five for every 3.85 workers aged 25–64, down from 6.25 in 2010. In developed countries the proportion of older people will be higher still. The dependency ratio (per person over sixty-five) in Japan, Germany and the US will be 1.45, 1.52 and 2.27 respectively, an increase of 50–100 percent. Emerging countries will see the rate double to 4.55 by 2035. In China and Latin America it will be 2.78 and 3.70.

Population ageing reflects declining fertility rates and longer life expectancy. A stable population requires a fertility rate of 2.1 children per woman, allowing for the possibility of death before adulthood. Global average fertility is currently 2.5 and falling. The decline is driven by the higher opportunity costs of taking time out of the workforce for childbearing, better education, the availability of contraception, the cost of bringing up children, familial instability, urbanisation, specific government initiatives such as China's one child policy, and the changed role of women in many societies.

In 1800 no country had an average life expectancy greater than forty years. The current average life expectancy for a girl and boy born in 2012 is around seventy-three and sixty-eight years respectively, an increase of six years since 1990. People born in high-income, developed countries can expect to live 15–20 years longer than average. Longer life expectancy reflects changes in the type of work done, occupational safety, medical advances and the availability of healthcare.

In developed countries the baby boom after World War II substantially altered the population's ageing structure. A large cohort of these boomers will reach retirement age at or about the same time, causing a jump in dependency ratios.

*

Demographic changes affect the workforce, productivity, spending, savings and public finances. As the workforce increases, the economy can produce more, and consumption by the employed increases growth.

The economic needs of people vary over their life cycle. Consumption increases with age, peaking around the mid-forties. In younger years, consumption is constrained by income, as individuals undertake education or training. Following entry into the workforce, spending on cars, housing, furniture, appliances and children progressively increases with income. The pattern of consumption changes as offspring reach adulthood, when there is greater emphasis on leisure, health and aged care. In retirement, as in youth, spending falls, constrained by reduced income and physical capacity.

The US census bureau estimates that average annual expenditure per individual peaks at around US$50,000 at age forty-six. In contrast, expenditure in old age is 50–60 percent lower, around US$20,000. An ageing population drives lower consumption, with an exaggerated reduction where retirement income or savings are inadequate.

Savings are higher amongst working-age adults than for the young and elderly. Ageing reduces available savings, decreases the capital available for investment and increases its cost. All other things being equal, a country with large cohorts of aged citizens will experience slower growth than one with a high proportion of working-age people.

An ageing population reduces tax revenue, decreasing the ability of governments to meet the increasing demand for pensions, aged care and health services. Many previously terminal illnesses are now chronic conditions that can be managed with expensive care, medication and procedures. However, the impact of ageing on healthcare and aged care costs is unclear. James Fries, professor of medicine at Stanford University, argues that the age of onset of the first chronic infirmity has been partially or wholly delayed, a phenomenon termed compression of morbidity. The burden of serious illness occurs in a shorter period before death, which may reduce costs.

In the future, public services will have to be supported by a dwindling number of workers. This need not be a problem where adequate provisions exist, through taxes paid during working lives, or personal savings. Unfortunately, entitlements are not generally fully funded. Even in countries where compulsory retirement schemes exist, the savings are frequently insufficient. The state must contribute towards services for the aged. In most countries the majority of citizens will need some retirement income support as well as subsidised aged and healthcare services. An ageing population places pressure on public finances, constraining growth.

The effects of an ageing population can be mitigated by increasing the retirement age and reducing entitlements. But an extension of working-life spans will be more difficult for workers with lower skills and those engaged in physically demanding work. The cost of workplace safety and retraining must be balanced against the contribution from a longer working life.

Immigration, effectively redistributing available workers, offers an option. But other than for limited humanitarian reasons, most immigration focuses on the wealthy and skilled workers. Individuals with money from politically unstable countries can buy residency in a more desirable location. The island of Malta at one stage proposed selling EU passports for €650,000, allowing buyers immediate right of residency in all member states. Weak economic conditions and a lack of employment opportunities have driven emigration from Spain, Ireland, Portugal and Greece, especially of skilled workers. The home nation loses the investment in education of the individual and also future tax revenues, contributing to further economic weakness.

Immigrants bring different cultures as well as their labour, skills and wealth. Integration problems can create social disharmony and resentment in the host country. Over recent years, resistance to immigration has grown throughout the world.

*

Japan's demographics exacerbated its economic decline. The population is forecast to decrease from its current level of 128 million to around 90 million by 2050, and to 50 million by 2100. The proportion of the population above the age of sixty-five will rise from 12 percent to around 23 percent by the middle of the twenty-first century. The workforce is expected to fall from its current 70 percent of the population to around 55 percent over the next twenty years. For every two retirees there will be around three working people, down from six in 1990. According to one forecast, by 2050 Japan will have a median age of fifty-two, the oldest society ever known.

Sales of adult nappies now exceed those for babies. It's popularly joked that, based on the present rate of decline, in 600 years there will be 480 Japanese left.

Japan's postwar economic growth benefited from positive demographics, by as much as 3 percent per annum at the peak. Between 2000 and 2013, shrinkage in the Japanese workforce reduced growth by around 1 percent, and will reduce growth ultimately by 2 percent. This reversal represents a large drop in nominal GDP. Using similar assumptions, shrinking workforces could reduce growth in Germany and the US by 0.5–1 percent per annum.

Demographics also contribute to deflation. Falling prices have helped maintain the purchasing power and consumption of the Japanese, compensating for stagnant and falling incomes and very low investment returns on retirement savings.

There are no simple answers to the problems of an ageing world and its impact on economic growth. In Japan, immigration would provide one way of stabilising a declining population. But a survey found that elderly Japanese would rather be looked after by a robot than an immigrant. In 2013 Finance Minister Tarō Asō helpfully suggested that older Japanese 'hurry up and die' to reduce pressure on the state to pay for their medical and aged care.[7]

*

Increasing productivity and innovation have been crucial catalysts of growth over the last two centuries. Productivity measures the ratio of output to input in production. Rising productivity allows growth to be maintained irrespective of demographics. It increases income, living standards and business profitability. But rises in productivity have slowed.

In the US, despite considerable volatility, productivity increases between the late nineteenth and late twentieth century averaged around 2–2.5 percent per annum. Productivity rises were high, 3–4 percent, in the first three decades after World War II. In recent years it has slowed to around 1 percent. The decline in other developed countries, especially Europe, has been greater. Emerging nations have higher but declining rates of productivity increases. Improvements in labour productivity, which measures output produced per unit of labour, and total factor productivity, which takes into account the combined input of labour and capital, have both declined, with the latter declining more sharply.

Even recent modest gains in productivity may be overstated. Increased output in sectors like financial services, education, hospitality, healthcare, aged care or government may not equate to real improvements. In mid-2014 economists rationalised a fall in the US GDP of 2.9 percent, the worst performance in five years, on the grounds that it resulted from a fall in healthcare spending. It is unclear why a us$500 visit to a doctor is any better or more productive than one costing us$200. Statistics showed that productivity in the finance sector grew strongly in the period before the GFC, but the industry created many products of dubious economic value. The subsequent cost of reversing the damage caused by the failure of these instruments was high.

Lower productivity growth reflects the fact that major gains from mechanisation, automation, mass production, and improvement in workforce skills are not repeatable. Increased investment in these areas has limited marginal effect on productivity. The benefits of reducing workforce levels, outsourcing production to lower-cost jurisdictions, and improved logistics may have been substantially extracted.

Shifts in industrial structure, especially in developed economies, also affect productivity. Manufacturing and heavy industry are particularly suited to mechanisation and automation as a means of increasing productivity. In contrast, service industries like aged care and health-care may not lend themselves to similar strategies. The inherently labour-intensive nature of the activities, even with advances in robotics, and the often variable environment and non-routine work mean that large-scale productivity gains are difficult to achieve.

Changing demographics and slower productivity improvements threaten growth. In 2015 the McKinsey Global Institute estimated that, without labour productivity increases to offset the effects of age-ing populations and declining birthrates, it is conceivable that there will be a 40 percent drop in GDP growth rates and a 20 percent drop in the growth rate of per capita income globally.[8]

*

Innovation too may be flagging. Economist Robert Gordon identified three phases of innovation.[9] Industrial revolution 1 (1750–1830) focused on coal, steam engines, railroads and textiles. Industrial revolution 2

(1870–1900) saw five key innovations: electricity; the internal combustion engine; running water, indoor plumbing, and central heating; rearranging molecules central to petroleum, chemicals, plastics, and pharmaceuticals; and communication and entertainment devices such as the telephone, the phonograph, popular photography, radio and motion pictures. Industrial revolution 3 (1960 to the present) has been concentrated around computing and telecommunications.

Innovation entails a series of discontinuous, highly significant technological jumps, followed by gradual adoption and modest incremental improvements. For industrial revolutions 1 and 2, the follow-on period lasted in excess of a hundred years, as the full potential of the innovations were realised. Professor Gordon found that industrial revolution 2 had the most impact on productivity and living standards.

Electricity and the internal combustion engine illustrate the scale of the change. Electricity became commercially viable around 1880, and since then has been the preferred source of energy, unmatched in terms of conversion efficiency, the ability to employ different fuels, productivity, transportability, precise control of delivery, and flexibility of use. Internal combustion engines and the availability of oil revolutionised transport and industry. By replacing animals or humans, it increased power and speed, reduced cost, improved efficiency, as well as removed the problem of dealing with unsanitary animal waste.

Over the next hundred years the inventions of industrial revolution 2 evolved through derivative technologies like television, air conditioning, and road and transport networks to fully exploit their potential. The large-scale changes of this phase were a one-off event. Improved sanitation, longer life expectancy, the freeing of women from their role as household slaves, better transport and communications, and the inhabitation of more climatically extreme regions drove unrepeatable increases in living standards.

The impact becomes evident by comparing changes in ordinary

life between 1870–1970, by which time the innovations of industrial revolution 2 had been fully exploited, and 1970 to today. A modern individual would find the world of 1970 familiar, though perhaps more basic in terms of work, houses, sanitation, energy sources, transport, entertainment and household appliances. In contrast, a 1970 individual would not recognise the world of 1870.

Transport speeds highlight the magnitude of change. Until industrial revolution 2, transport was by hoof and sail. Subsequently, speed increased steadily, culminating in jet-engine-powered travel from 1958. But speed has not increased greatly in the last fifty years, with aircraft actually travelling slower than in the 1960s to conserve fuel.

*

Industrial revolution 3 was less important, creating only short-lived improvements in productivity. This prompted economist Robert Solow in 1987 to question why 'we can see the computers everywhere except in the productivity statistics'.[10]

Commencing in the 1960s, industrial revolution 3 focused on computers, evolving through mainframes, minis and ultimately into laptops, tablets, smart phones and wearable devices. Computers automated repetitive, routine and low-value work. Increasingly sophisticated software improved automation and efficiency in offices and industry, including word-processing and numerical-analysis in the former, and control and design software in the latter.

Once the established base of computers and applications was sufficient, the emphasis was on linking users through sophisticated telecommunications, such as high-speed broadband and wireless. By 2014 more than one-third of the world was using the internet. One billion individuals were on Facebook, nearly the population of India or China. Around 9 billion text messages and 500 million tweets were sent each day worldwide.

The major impact on productivity occurred between 1970 and the mid-1990s. Innovations since that time do not seem to have been as significant, only improving existing technologies, enhancing efficiency, speed, capability and power. Many recent innovations are centred on entertainment and communication devices, with marginal impact on productivity. Venture capitalists Founders Fund have lamented that instead of the promised flying car, all they've got is the ability to send a 140-character message via Twitter.[11]

While it may simply be too early for the full impact to become evident, industrial revolution 3 does not appear to be causing the epochal change that electricity or the internal combustion engine did.

The internet boom of the 1990s, which culminated in the crash of 2000, was based on email, search engines, e-commerce and online retailing seeking to replace existing bricks-and-mortar businesses. While some online retailers, like Amazon and travel agencies, survived, the majority of ventures failed. Even Amazon changed its virtual model, investing heavily in warehouses, logistics and computing facilities.

The post-2000 internet boom has focused on social networking, instant messaging, online gaming, and new media; there's also been resurgent interest in e-tailing. One commentator wryly dismissed social networking sites as 'just places for people to express their narcissism cheaply'.[12]

In June 2014 Amazon announced its latest innovation, a smart phone that uses image-recognition technology to allow customers to purchase products by pointing it at more than 70 million objects in its online store. Designed to minimise barriers to spending, it exemplifies the instantaneous gratification that passes for innovation in the new economy. Critics have branded it a weapon of mass consumption that allows you to point and shoot yourself in the foot.[13]

Many new technologies displace existing industries, limiting the effect on growth and productivity. Recent innovations have focused on marketing and distributing existing goods and services, rather than on creating entirely new industries. Smart phones and tablets have cannibalised desktop and laptop computers. Apple's iPhones have replaced BlackBerrys, portable music players such as Sony's CD Walkman, and personal digital assistants like the once ubiquitous PalmPilot. Google and blogs divert revenue from newspapers, publishing and libraries. Digital advertising diverts revenue from newspaper, magazine and TV advertising.

Technological innovation increasingly relies on lowering costs, which is achieved by reducing the quality of the product as well using untrained individuals or personal assets. Airbnb allows people to rent out their own home for accommodation. Uber, a ride-sharing application, allows individuals to use their own cars to provide transport services. Wikipedia and other online media or entertainment services rely on unpaid labour.

This kind of innovation also focuses on creating free platforms or services in order to build a sufficiently large user community from which stealth revenues can be extracted, either directly or by selling user data to allow targeted marketing, or worse. The economic contribution of many recent innovations, in terms of revenue, profits and employment, is difficult to gauge. Whatever their cultural impact, Facebook, Twitter and their successors may not have viable long-term economic models. Further underlying the nature of modern innovation, in 2015 Ashley Madison, an online site for people seeking extramarital affairs, announced plans to raise US$200 million to expand the market for adultery.

Industrial revolution 3 emphasises disruptive technologies, a term associated with Harvard professor Clayton Christensen and his influential 1997 book *The Innovator's Dilemma*. It differentiated between sustainable innovations, which improve products and make

valuable changes for a firm's current customers, and disruptive innovations – cheaper, poorer-quality products that initially target less
profitable customers so as to undercut existing businesses, with the
object of eventually dominating the industry.

In a vituperative exchange characteristic of academic cloisters,
historian Jill Lepore criticised Christensen's heavily marketed and
promoted thesis, arguing that his hand-picked case studies did not
support the theory. She also pointed to its poor predictive quality. The
Disruptive Growth Fund, launched by Christensen, lost around two-
thirds of its money within a year when Nasdaq collapsed. Lepore also
drew attention to Christensen's 2007 prediction that Apple's iPhone
would fail.[14]

Businesses now pursue disruptive technologies with limited
long-term growth and productivity potential. Entrepreneurs, backed
by venture capital, focus on this type of innovation hoping to
extract short-term monetary value by selling out to an incumbent
or through an initial public offering of shares. The few successful
businesses and individuals that emerge then engage in a destructive process, investing high-margin profits from their original
products into risky, low-margin speculative projects, sometimes
with very large investment needs. Google has used the profits from
its monopolistic search business in this way, looking for a second
profitable product. It is like investing one lucky large lottery win
in more games of chance, ignoring the statistically infinitesimal
chance of a second success.

The process creates a perpetual cycle of technology booms and
busts. But it is unclear whether it creates the significant long-term and
economy-wide impact on growth and productivity of previous industrial revolutions.

*

Educational levels and funding for research affect innovation, but the contribution from these, and the proportion of the workforce labouring in idea-generating industries, may have reached a plateau. Education standards may have stabilised and even be declining, especially in developed countries.

Although talented students remain, the evidence points to a reduction in average reading, writing and numeracy skills, driven by excessive use of computers as well as changes in teaching approaches. Curriculums now place less focus on mathematics and sciences. Business, cultural and social biases that favour narrow specialists and extroverts may be inconsistent with creativity.

Resistance to accurate performance evaluation encourages mediocre work. Almost half of US college students need more than six years to complete four-year degrees. Educators talk of teacup students, so fragile that they shatter easily.

Proliferation of universities and colleges also contributes to mediocrity. Places of higher learning have succumbed to commercial pressures. Well-funded institutions staffed by well-credentialed scholars with adequate facilities to teach and research have given way to a pragmatic, market-oriented approach to selling degrees and acquiring paying students.

Social activist Jane Jacobs identified the shift from educating to credentialing, where the emphasis is on preparing students for employment. In some countries the increasing cost of education has placed it beyond the reach of many, or forced graduates to start their working lives with significant debts. The decreasing income advantage of some higher qualifications, after deducting costs, has reduced their attraction.

Scientific research funding has declined in real terms in many nations. This has affected the amount of as well as the approach to research, shifting the focus to safer proposals likely to receive funding, and away from uncertain but potentially groundbreaking areas. Corporate co-investment or sponsorship of research accentuates the focus on applied rather than pure research. Crucial fundamental knowledge is now neglected. But it was quantum physics that made silicon chips possible, and Einstein's theory of relativity underlies satellite navigation systems. Abstract mathematics allows computers and telecommunications.

Large-scale investment in pure research and development, such as that undertaken by the Bell Labs, Xerox's Palo Alto Research Center (PARC), and Lockheed's famed Skunk Works, is less prevalent today. Researchers at Bell Labs helped develop radio astronomy, the transistor, the laser, the charge-coupled device, information theory, the UNIX operating system, and the C and C++ programming languages. PARC contributed such innovations as the personal computer, the laser printer and the graphical user interface.

Historically, government funding for research has been important. Public money funnelled through the Pentagon helped develop the internet. A National Science Foundation grant seeded development of Google's algorithmic search engine. Publicly funded venture capital provided great societal benefits as well as large profits for private businesses. But increasing pressures on public finance have reduced government funding, and the lack of such investment may limit the scope for future quantum leaps in innovation.

*

Techno-optimists dismiss fears about slowing innovation, typecasting nonbelievers as Luddites. The impact of recent technological changes, they believe, will be realised over time. They point to the potential of Big Data, robotics, 3D manufacturing and new wonder drugs. Techno-optimists believe that progress is near a singularity, the hypothetical moment when artificial intelligence will have progressed to the point of greater-than-human intelligence, with radical implications for human beings and society.

Big Data uses inductive statistics and nonlinear system tools on large data sets to measure and establish relationships and dependencies and to identify trends. The technology remains unproven. Its predictive powers are highly variable, based on assumptions about data properties that in practice are not well understood. To date, it has been used mainly in epidemiology and targeted marketing. Big Data requires big money and big assumptions, and entails big judgemental risks. It has the same problems as all analysis, with more data merely creating new problems rather than providing solutions.

Robotic technology is already extensively used in manufacturing, especially of motor vehicles. Robots designed for aged and healthcare are attracting interest. Despite advances, they remain restricted in terms of power source, locomotion, manipulation, and sensory perception, limiting their use for non-routine tasks. Robots have had difficulty completing simple human tasks such as sorting washing.

First suggested twenty years ago, 3D or additive manufacturing is a process in which successive layers of material are placed under computer control to create three-dimensional objects. It may prove to be a valuable niche industry, reducing the cost of manufacturing single or small-run items where there are no economies of scale.

Technology is also a source of problems. Bot fraud, where computer programs artificially create page views of online advertising, costs advertisers over US$6 billion annually and constitutes up to 25 percent of all hits. Sophisticated cyber attacks, malware and computer viruses cause chaos, disruption, data loss, financial damage, and personally or politically humiliating public disclosures. Security, trust and privacy are compromised. The cost of preventing these attacks is considerable.

Long life expectancies and higher productivity in the postwar period relied in part on improved medical therapies, including antibiotics such as penicillin. But overuse has increased drug-resistant infections, which a 2014 British study found may cause 10 million deaths a year worldwide by 2050. The potential cost is us$100 trillion, reducing GDP by 3.5 percent.

Ultimately, genius and innovation cannot be engineered on demand. The rate of technological change of the nineteenth century, when the 'method of invention' was developed, may be impossible to rediscover.[15]

There may be scientific and economic limits to technology. The number of new patents is not commensurate with the billions of research dollars spent. Gains in life expectancy have slowed. Medical advances have disappointed, with cures to many diseases, such as cancer, proving elusive. One model suggests that the rate of innovation per capita peaked in 1873 and has declined subsequently. It estimates that 85 percent of the economic limit of technology has been reached, a figure projected to reach 95 percent by 2038.[16]

Opportunities for important and game-changing innovation do remain: better crop yields to feed the planet; cheap, sustainable sources of energy; the conservation of scarce commodities, and improved logistics and distribution techniques so as to use existing resources more efficiently. But no innovations on the scale of industrial revolution 2 are on the horizon. Scientists have a saying: nuclear fusion is thirty years away and always will be.

While a few creators might capture large benefits, innovation now has limited effects on economic growth, failing to increase employment and income levels. Identifying a productivity feast, former Fed chairman Alan Greenspan mistakenly believed that reducing the number of workers to zero gives you infinite productivity. Given that consumption makes up 60–70 percent of economic activity in developed economies, a continuous reduction in employment and incomes limits the benefit to the wider economy.

In 1955, showing off a new, automatically operated plant, a Ford company executive asked United Automobile Workers head Walter Reuther, 'How are you going to collect union dues from [the robots]?' Reuther countered, 'And how are you going to get them to buy Fords?'[17]

*

Economic expansion is not a continuous process that can persist forever. Growth and improvements in living standards will slow significantly. For 'shock value', economist Robert Gordon speculates that future US growth rates, adjusted for his six headwinds (demographics, declining educational attainments, rising inequality, the effects of globalisation, environmental costs, and the debt overhang) may be 0.2 percent, well below even the modest 1.8 percent of 1987–2007.

Low or no growth is not necessarily a problem. In nature, growth is only a temporary phase, which ceases at maturity. Low economic growth may have positive effects on the environment and the conservation of scarce resources. But the current economic, political and social system is predicated on endless economic expansion and related improvements in living standards. Strong growth is also needed now to resolve the problem of high levels of government and private debt. In his novel about the Depression, *The Grapes of Wrath*, John Steinbeck identified this tendency: 'When the monster stops growing, it dies. It can't stay one size.'[18]

RUNNING ON EMPTY

The Resource and Environmental Constraints on Growth

English economist John Hicks defined true growth as the amount that can be withdrawn without affecting the ability to produce the same the next year.[1] In recent years, economic growth has been at the expense of the future. The world has chosen to ignore author Edward Abbey's warning: 'growth for the sake of growth is the ideology of a cancer cell'.[2]

The global economy is increasingly constrained by the scarcity of water, food and energy, as well as a changing climate. At a minimum, dealing with resource availability will require increased investment to supply essential needs as low-cost reserves are depleted. The additional cost will affect growth and living standards. In more extreme scenarios, the exhaustion of crucial resources will limit human activity.

*

The idea of scarcity is not new. In his 1798 essay *An Essay on the Principle of Population*, Reverend Thomas Robert Malthus argued that limited available resources restricted growth, and that population would ultimately be checked by famine and disease. Malthus's position was anti-utopian, opposing the eighteenth-century European view informed by the Enlightenment, which saw society as continually improving and perfectible.

Malthus's predictions proved unfounded. Developments in science, technology and productivity, along with economic freedom, allowed production to increase to meet demand. 'Malthusian' became a pejorative adjective.

In 1972 the Club of Rome, a think tank, revisited Malthus's thesis in their report *The Limits to Growth*. Against the background of rising oil prices and 1970s stagflation, it concluded that economic growth could not continue indefinitely because of the limited availability of natural resources, particularly oil. Subsequently, two academics at Case Western Reserve University, Eduard Pestel and Mihajlo Mesarovic, used a more elaborate model to test the predictions. Published in 1974, *Mankind at the Turning Point: The Second Report to the Club of Rome* was more optimistic, arguing that society had the ability to improve or control resource use, making environmental and economic catastrophe avoidable.

Governments, businesses, scientists and economists dismissed the idea of any limit to economic expansion as alarmist, pessimistic, ill-informed and nonsensical. The commitment to high levels of growth remained, combined with a belief that all constraints could be solved by technology or policy measures. Capitalists argued that the market would solve the problem of growth and resource scarcity. Communists relied on Marxist dogma that technology was capable of solving any problem.

Return to strong growth in the 1980s reinforced the belief that the forecasts were erroneous. But a 2008 study reviewed the 1972 *Limits to Growth* forecasts, finding that the subsequent thirty years of historical data was consistent with a scenario of continued business as usual, resulting in the collapse of the global system midway through the twenty-first century.[3]

Essential resources *are* finite. New discoveries and improved methods of extraction defer the date of exhaustion. American anthropologist and historian Joseph Tainter argued that science has diminishing marginal returns, making technological progress more difficult and expensive.[4] Ultimately, this limits the ability to expand the amount of available resources. At the same time, demand continues to rise, due to increases in population and the rapid development of emerging countries. As nations grow and living standards rise, the amount of resources used and the pressure on the environment increases. Andrew Sheng, chief adviser to the China Banking Regulatory Commission, argues that 'the planet simply cannot support 3 billion people in Asia living European lifestyles'.[5]

*

One constraint on economic growth is water, which all life on earth requires. About sixty-five percent of the human body is water. Depending on conditions, humans can survive for two to three weeks without food but only two to three days without water.

The amount of water on earth is finite. Only 2.5 percent is freshwater, the remaining 97.5 percent is saltwater. Of the available freshwater, two-thirds is locked in glaciers and the polar ice caps. Life depends on less than 1 percent of the available water on the planet.

The system is governed by the hydrological cycle, where seawater is converted by sunlight into vapour and returned to land in the form of rain and snow to renew freshwater supplies, which then run into the sea again. All non-marine life and activity depend on surface water in rivers, lakes and freshwater wetlands. They also depend on groundwater, usually freshwater, which has seeped into the pore space of soil and rocks or flows within aquifers below the watertable – this is known as fossil water, in recognition of its age.

Freshwater is unevenly distributed on the globe. Around 4 billion people, 60 percent of the world's population, live in areas that receive only a quarter of the world's annual rainfall. In Africa, the Congo River basin accounts for about 30 percent of the continent's water but contains only 10 percent of its population. In many parts of the world, seasonal rains run off too quickly for efficient use. India receives 90 percent of its annual rainfall during the summer monsoon, getting little rain for the other eight months.

Personal use, for drinking, cooking, bathing and sanitation, accounts for around 8 percent of water demand. Basic household water consumption is around 50 litres per person per day, ranging from a minimum requirement of 20 litres to the 100 litres or more used routinely in developed countries.

Industrial use accounts for 22 percent of demand. Water is used to generate electricity, either directly using hydroelectric power plants, or indirectly through heat exchange in coal, nuclear or geothermal power processes. Energy production accounts for around two-thirds of industrial consumption, with water required for coal mining; hydraulic fracturing (fracking), to extract gas and oil from shale formations; and the cooling of gas, coal and nuclear power plants. Water is used in the production of foodstuffs, fuels and chemicals. Textiles, paper production and mining are especially water-intensive.

Agriculture accounts for 70 percent of demand. Professor John Anthony Allan from King's College, London introduced the concept of virtual or embedded water, the volume of freshwater used to produce a product. A single espresso requires 140 litres of water; a slice of toast 40 litres; a serving of bacon 480 litres. Depending on living standards, climatic conditions and agricultural practices, the food requirements of a single person use 2000–5000 litres of water per day. This compares to around 2–3 litres of water required for drinking.

*

The rise in population from around 6 billion in 2000 to around 9 billion in 2050 will increase water demand. The annual increase in global population requires an additional 64 billion cubic metres of water a year, equivalent to the annual water flow through Germany's Rhine River. Much of the population increase is in developing countries that lack adequate water infrastructure, and therefore suffer water stress.

Water use is increasing at double the rate of population growth, exacerbating demand. During the last century, per capita water demand rose due to higher living standards and a shift from cereals to more meat and vegetables.

Use of water in energy extraction has grown rapidly. Demand from tourism (golf courses in arid climates) and entertainment has increased pressure on water resources.

Urbanisation, a driver of economic growth, increases water stress. High population density leads to the depletion of groundwater. It also increases pollution and contamination risks. Large investments in water infrastructure are needed, as simpler, cheaper wells and septic tanks, which are suitable for low population densities, become unworkable.

Water engineering, such as dams, reservoirs, canals, pipelines, treatment plants and centralised sewers, is required for water storage and supply management, and improved hygiene. The cost is altered natural water flows, pollution and environmental degradation.

India's first prime minister, Jawaharlal Nehru, saw dams as temples of modernity. Morarji Desai, as India's interior minister, once threatened to release reservoir waters to drown villagers opposed to one particular project. But there is increasing recognition that large dams are the problem rather than the solution. Aid agencies, once keen supporters, are increasingly reluctant to finance such projects.

Dams exacerbate water loss from evaporation. Changed flow from intermittent releases can damage rivers, increase erosion and degrade agricultural land. Trapped silt and suspended sediment remove fertile alluvial soil and reduce hydroelectric output, increasing maintenance costs. Large dams change water loads and tables, and contribute to seismic activity. They destroy ecosystems, reducing fish stocks by changing breeding cycles or blocking migration paths. Their reservoirs are a source of greenhouse gases like methane, produced by the decay of organic matter such as aquatic vegetation and flooded soil.

Egypt's Aswan Dam has reduced the risk of flood, expanded farmland, generated electricity and facilitated tourism. It has also resulted in an increased dependence on rainfall for power, and polluted irrigation channels. It has led to high rates of bilharzia (an infection caused by parasites that live in freshwater), an explosion of water hyacinth due to the unnatural enrichment of reservoirs with plant nutrients, and coastal erosion from Egypt to Lebanon. Dams in the American south-west divert water to agriculture and industry. They have turned the delta of the Colorado River, where it once flowed into the Gulf of California, into a saline dead zone. Diversion of water for agriculture has seriously damaged Australia's Murray–Darling river system.

Pollution compromises water resources. The discharge of garbage, sewage, industrial waste and agricultural run-off into natural waters is widespread.

Around 450 million Indians depend on the 2500-kilometre Ganges for water. But the Ganges is highly polluted, by the burning of more than 30,000 human corpses each year at the holy city of Varanasi, untreated sewage, toxic chemicals, and the industrial waste produced by India's large population and rapidly developing economy. Faecal contamination of the Ganges has led to dangerous levels of a bacterial gene known as NDM-1, which creates several life-threatening, highly antibiotic-resistant infections that are spreading in South Asia and beyond. India's government and medical authorities deny the problem, fearing it will affect a growing medical tourism industry.

Every day, thousands of Hindus attend the Ghats of Varanasi for spiritual purification. Devotees regard it as sacrilegious to consider the sacred Ganges as anything other than pure. They do not accept the warnings of scientists or their own eyes, considering the river to be beyond harm and resisting remediation actions.

*

Water consumption has tripled over the last fifty years. The world's annual requirement is around half that contained in rivers, lakes and underground aquifers. By 2025 it is expected to be 90 percent. Major aquifers are becoming depleted, with annual drops of 10–50 metres in water levels becoming common. With groundwater supplies decreasing, it is unclear whether natural renewal can meet rising human needs.

In 2014 over 2 billion people, 30 percent of the global population, lacked access to clean drinking water. By 2025 two-thirds of the world population will face significant water stress. In 2015 shortages forced California to introduce mandatory water restrictions requiring a 25 percent reduction in usage. Sao Paulo in Brazil, one of the largest cities in the world, with a population of 20 million, faces a chronic, crippling water crisis, in part due to changes brought about by global warming and an increase in deforested areas in the Amazon basin. Scarcity will push up the cost of water, driving higher prices for food and industrial products, and retarding economic growth. If not managed, this may cause social and geopolitical conflict.

The diversion of water for human use adversely affects marshes, rivers, coastal wetlands, and the millions of species of animals, birds and fish that depend on them. Declining fish species and stocks and damage to ecosystems essential in regulating water quality and quantity add to the cost of scarcity.

With water supply limited, large-scale investment will be needed in desalination and purification technologies, storage and delivery

infrastructure, measures to reduce water intensity in industry and agriculture, recycling and conservation. Water technologies are expensive
and energy-intensive. Desalination is only economically practical for
high-value uses in arid areas like the Persian Gulf. OECD nations
alone require more than us$200 billion each year merely to maintain
ageing water infrastructure.

In 1569 Emperor Akbar founded the Indian city of Fatehpur Sikri,
as the capital of his empire. The imperial complex, one of the finest
examples of Mughal architecture, had to be abandoned in 1585, shortly
after completion, due to paucity of water. The Aral Sea, formerly one
of the four largest lakes in the world, has almost totally dried up as a
result of the diversion of rivers by Soviet irrigation projects. The retreat
of the sea created public health problems and local climate change.
The once-prosperous fishing industry, which produced one-sixth of
the Soviet Union's entire fish catch, was destroyed. The fishing boats
stranded in a dry Aral Sea echo Salvador Dali's 1934 surrealist painting
Paranoiac-Astral Image, where oblivious inhabitants sit in a rowboat
resting on a dry lake or ocean. It is a reminder of the consequences of
humanity's voracious appetite for water.

*

Another constraint on economic growth is food resources. Agronomists
estimate that production will need to increase by 60–100 percent by
2050 to feed the world's population.

This growing demand is driven by rising populations and altered
diets. Since 1950, global meat consumption has increased by 500 percent. As the incomes of billions of people in developing countries rise,
so does demand for meat, dairy products and eggs. By 2050 the calories provided in developing countries by cereals are expected to fall
from 56 percent to 46 percent. The amount provided by meat, dairy and
vegetable oils will rise from 20 percent to 29 percent. Meat production

requires large amounts of grain, exceeding the additional calorie value it provides. Chicken, pork and beef need two, three and seven times the amount of grain respectively for each additional increment of weight gain, requiring the output of grain or legumes used as animal feed to more than double.

Food production is constrained by available farmland, eroding soil quality, a lack of improvement in crop yields, water shortages, over-exploitation of natural food sources, and the effects of climate change.

The amount of global arable land has remained relatively constant for the last decade, at around 3.4 billion acres. Soil quality has deteriorated, making farmlands increasingly vulnerable to wind and water erosion, with around one-third losing topsoil more quickly than it can be replenished.

Over-cultivation is rapidly reducing the productivity of farmland in parts of Africa, Asia, and the Middle East. Rising livestock numbers, which have increased by more than 1.2 billion since 1960, have resulted in over-grazing. Slash-and-burn agriculture and over-clearing have resulted in deforestation, which in turn has increased carbon dioxide emissions, soil erosion and land degradation. Globally, an area of 5.6 million hectares of forest – larger than Switzerland – is cut down each year.

In the US during the 1930s over-exploitation forced the abandonment of farmland, and hundreds of thousands of people had to move to avoid starvation. In the Soviet Union the ill-fated Virgin Lands project, which aimed to convert grassland to productive farmland, resulted in a dust bowl.

*

The Green Revolution of the twentieth century was based on rapid increases in agricultural productivity. Rising crop yields were driven by mechanisation, irrigation, improved seeds and artificial fertilisers. The ability to produce the fertiliser ammonium nitrate by synthesising nitrogen cheaply facilitated large increases in food production. Herbicides, fungicides and insecticides reduced loss from disease and predation. Better yields relied on the increased use of dwarf species with a higher plant density, and on artificially enhancing the edible parts of plants, such as seedpods, rather than stalks and leaves.

Average grain yields have tripled since 1950. But the rate of improvement has fallen from 2.2 percent between 1950 and 1990 to around 1.3 percent between 1990 and 2011. Wheat yields rose on average at 0.5 percent between 1990 and 2007, a fall from around 3 percent between 1961 and 1990. Rice yields halved over the same period.

Agricultural productivity may be approaching its technological and biological limits. One factor in improved productivity was seeds that enabled grains to absorb more fertiliser and water. Today, pressures on water availability make this more difficult. The use of fertilisers to boost yields may have already passed saturation point. Manufactured using energy-intensive processes, the costs have increased. Their use is also unsustainable because of environmental damage in the form of run-off, which is harmful to rivers and oceans.

The long-term side effects of genetically modified foods, nicknamed Frankenfoods by sceptics, remain unknown. There is concern that large multinational companies are creating dependence on expensive commercial seed products by forcing farmers to give up traditional seeds. Instead of 200–300 different crops, agriculture is focused on a few varieties of wheat, corn, rice, maize and soybean. Such monocultures are inherently dangerous: a lack of diversity makes crops less resilient to parasites and disease. In the 1840s potato crops in Ireland became blighted, causing famine. Collapses in the French wine industry and US corn production highlight the risk of reliance on a single strain. Moreover grain crops emphasise varieties that are designed for yield rather than nutritional content. The poor, whose diet consists primarily of grain, are deprived of nutrients and trace elements, creating health problems.

Food production depends on water, itself a scarce resource. Some 40 percent of grain crops need irrigation. With half the world's population extracting groundwater faster than it is replenished, shortages constrain food supplies.

Natural food resources, such as fish stocks, are stressed. Around 80 percent of oceanic fisheries are being fished at or beyond their sustainable yield. For many of these, recovery is now unlikely. Traditional sources of protein, such as wild cod and salmon, are becoming scarce. With most wild fisheries fully or over-exploited, demand is now met by fish farms, which require grain and soybeans as feed. Fishmeal is another source of feed, placing additional pressure on oceanic fisheries.

The revelations about Chicago's meatpacking industry in Upton Sinclair's 1906 novel *The Jungle* caused public outrage about industrial food production methods. Despite subsequent regulatory safeguards, modern large-scale food production, which emphasises efficiency and quantity over quality, has side effects. Liquid manure threatens water quality, contributing to rising nitrate levels in near-surface groundwater. The need for cheap feed drives deforestation in emerging countries, with forests being cut down to create farmland. Animal cruelty is routine.

Widespread use of antibiotics to keep livestock free of disease promotes the development of drug-resistant bacteria, which pose a threat to human health. Up to 20 percent of all hospital-acquired infections are now traceable to pathogens attributable to antibiotic use.

Malthus argued that population growth would be limited by the ability to find food. He did not anticipate the expansion of farmland as geographical frontiers expanded, or increased crop yields. But with the amount of arable land now relatively constant, and land quality and productivity improvements declining, Malthus's limits are less far-fetched.

Rising demand and tightening supply are likely to increase food prices and create shortages. In 2007–08 grain and soybean prices more than doubled, with additional price spikes in 2010–11 and 2012. The problem is compounded by a small and decreasing margin between grain consumption and production, as well as limited buffer stocks.

The permanent threat of severe food shortages places the poor at risk of malnutrition and starvation. Even if production can be increased to meet rising demand, the higher cost may make essential foodstuffs unaffordable for a growing portion of the world. As with water shortages, this undermines political stability, driving conflicts over resources and the potential failure of nations. With nearly a billion people on the planet still lacking sufficient food or essential nutrients, the risk of food-driven social unrest is high. The 2007–08 food riots and unrest in some sixty countries may be a sign of things to come.[6]

*

The threat to adequate cheap energy is another constraint on economic growth. Prior to the Industrial Revolution, the energy needed for life and industry was provided by humans and animals, and biomass fuels like wood, water and wind. In the nineteenth century the use of fossil fuels commenced.

In the first age of fossil fuel exploitation, coal-driven steam engines powered industry, ships and railroads, as well as generating electricity. Pollution from burning coal, over time, encouraged the use of oil and gas. Coal remains an important source of electricity, especially in China and India, where poor air quality and respiratory illnesses are reminiscent of nineteenth-century London and Manchester.

The second age of fossil fuel exploitation focused on hydrocarbons, beginning in 1859 with commercial oil production in the US. After

World War II, it became the predominant energy source because of superior portability and energy intensity (the amount of energy released per unit of volume). The rising use of oil is intertwined with the development of the internal combustion engine, crucial to modern transportation in the form of cars, trucks, trains and aeroplanes. Oil also became important in agriculture, chemical processes, and the manufacture of synthetic materials and fibres.

Increased oil use was facilitated by discoveries of large fields in the Middle East, Soviet Union, US, Canada, Mexico, the North Sea, and North and West Africa progressively from the 1920s. It was supported by investment in infrastructure – such as pipelines – tankers and improved refining technology.

In the twentieth century, natural gas emerged as a major fuel, driven by improved transportability using high-pressure pipelines, and the process of liquefaction and re-gasification. Technological developments allowed natural gas to be used for electricity generation, heating and cooking, as well as a raw material for the manufacture of ammonia or synthetic materials.

Today, coal, oil and gas provide 80–90 percent of all energy. They have allowed the development of modern economies, facilitating the production of food, goods and services, efficient transportation, climate control and improved living standards. Decoupling economic growth from the availability of cheap and efficient energy is difficult.

*

Since 1800, global energy consumption has increased by around twenty-five times. Since 1965, it has tripled, compared to a doubling of global population. The consumption of oil, coal and gas has increased by two and a half times, two times and three times respectively.

Energy consumption is driven by changes in population, urbanisation, industrialisation, economic growth, and energy efficiency (the

amount of energy needed per unit of GDP). Since 1990, energy consumption in developed economies has grown slowly. A significant
factor in this lower growth was the economic slowdown in 2008. In the
US and Europe energy consumption has increased by 20 percent and
7 percent respectively. But it is growing strongly in developing countries. In China it has increased by 146 percent, in India by 91 percent,
Latin America by 66 percent, Africa by 70 percent, and the Middle
East by 170 percent. Since 1990, the average energy use per person
globally has increased by around 10 percent.

The information- and communication-driven digital economy
consumes increasing amounts of energy. Billions of computers, note-
books and mobile devices, in aggregate, consume significant amounts
of energy in both manufacture and use. The data centres, digital warehouses and server farms that lie at the heart of the internet and cloud
computing that run the global economy and infrastructure are also
heavy power users. The digital economy consumes around 10 percent
of the world's electricity, which is the equivalent of the amount that
was used to light the planet in 1985.

The US Energy Information Administration estimates that
between 2010 and 2014, world energy use grew by over 50 percent.
Roughly half of the increase was in China and India. By 2040 China's
energy use, based on current trends, will be double that of the US.
Fossil fuels may not be able to meet this demand. In 2013 proven
reserves of oil were around 1.7 trillion barrels, sufficient to last for some
fifty years at current rates of extraction. Recoverable coal reserves are
sufficient for around 150 years. Proven gas reserves are sufficient for
around sixty years.

*

In 1956 Marion King Hubbert, a petroleum geologist working for the
Shell Development Company in Texas, created the concept of peak

oil, correctly predicting that US oil production would peak in 1970. The concept was based on the inevitable consequence of geological processes. Once a significant proportion of the oil in a reservoir is extracted, water, gas, or chemical insertion is required to artificially restore pressure and sustain production, eventually becoming uneconomic.

Hubbert estimated a forty-year lag between the year of peak discovery and that of peak production. Globally, oil discoveries peaked in the 1960s and 1970s. During the 2000s there have been only around seventy major field discoveries, compared to more than 1200 in the 1960s and 1970s. Consistent with the peak oil theory, conventional world oil production peaked around 2005 and has been relatively constant since.

Currently there are about 70,000 producing fields, with about twenty super-giant fields accounting for more than 25 percent of world production. Many large fields, such as Ghawar (Saudi Arabia), Cantarell (Mexico) and Burgan (Kuwait), are more than half a century old and past their production peak. Oil production in Saudi Arabia, which is historically the world's biggest producer and controls its production levels to stabilise supply and prices, peaked in 2005. Saudi producers have resorted to massive water injections in major wells to maintain production.

Conventional oil production is expected to decline at 7–9 percent annually. New reserves are needed to meet current and expected growth in demand. One of the new large fields discovered, the Lula (formerly known as Tupi) field in deep waters off Brazil's Atlantic coast, may contain 8 billion barrels. At the present rate of consumption, around 90 million barrels a day or 33 billion barrels each year, Lula can only meet global demand for three months.

Critics of the concept of peak oil or peak energy question the accuracy of such long-term forecasts, admitting no limits to the global supply of oil. Techno-dynamism, they argue, will create the third age of fossil fuels: unconventional oil. This relies on enhanced oil recovery – increased output from existing fields. It exploits reserves previously considered inaccessible or uneconomic, such as deep oceans or the Arctic, assisted by new techniques and a reduction in sea ice due to global warming. It focuses on heavy, complex, carbon-laden oils and gases locked up deep in the earth, tightly trapped between or bound to sand, tar and rock, especially shale formations.

Unconventional oil and gas discoveries have helped cover declining production and reserves of conventional equivalents, but their potential is overestimated. They frequently have lower energy density – energy per weight. Deepwater drilling, horizontal drilling and fracking to extract shale gas or liquids are less efficient than conventional production methods. Brazil's Lula field lies 3000 metres below the ocean surface, under thick layers of salt. Extraction is energy-intensive, meaning that the energy return on energy invested is deteriorating.

Unconventional oils and gases are more expensive than conventional fuels. They currently require higher prices to be economic: currently around US$80 per barrel for oil obtained using advanced recovery techniques, US$90 per barrel for tar sands and extra-heavy oil, US$60–100 or more for shale gas, kerogen oils and Arctic oil, and US$110 for coal-to-liquids and gas-to-liquids.

Reserves of unconventional oil and gas may not delay peak energy significantly. The true level of reserves and the depletion rates of shale gas reservoirs are uncertain. Maintaining production levels requires drilling thousands of new wells each year. The recent rapid growth of American shale gas extraction is a result of unsustainable and speculative financial investment. The success of the US in exploiting shale fuels is not matched in other countries. In Europe, high population densities and environmental concerns have slowed development.

Exploiting unconventional oils poses significant environmental risks. The 2010 Deepwater Horizon oil spill in the Gulf of Mexico, the world's largest accidental marine oil spill, highlighted the risk of deep-water drilling. BP has paid more than US$40 billion in criminal and civil settlements to date. Accessing Arctic fields, believed to contain 13 percent of the world's undiscovered oil and 30 percent of its natural gas, creates the risk of catastrophic spills. Fracking and tar sand oils require large quantities of water for extraction, transport and refining. There is a risk of groundwater and aquifer contamination, and storing and treating waste water is difficult. There are suspected connections between fracking and earthquakes. Unconventional fuels, especially heavy oils and tar sands, have a higher proportion of carbon to hydrogen, resulting in higher carbon dioxide emissions when used. Fracking also increases potential emissions of methane, a potent greenhouse gas.

*

Concern about future energy shortages and the long-term effects of climate change are driving interest in renewable energies. These include solar, wind, wave, tidal and geothermal power, as well as biofuels. Traditional renewables like hydro-electricity and biomass, such as wood from sustainable forestry, supply around 13 percent of global energy needs. Other renewable sources currently supply only around 3 percent. Increasing the proportion of renewable energy will be slow and difficult.

Only solar power may have the ability to replace fossil fuels, because it does not suffer from the problems of other renewable sources. An unlikely high level of wind energy capture would be required to make it a significant source. Other technologies are too geographically specific or too difficult to convert to make them economically viable in the near future.

One problem of renewable energy is intermittency, inconstant availability due to weather – lack of sunlight, wind, rain or the right tide conditions. This makes them unsuitable for base-load energy applications. The transfer of power within the electricity grid requires storage or long-distance interconnections. Power sources driven by fossil fuels can be located near users. In contrast, renewables must be in locations favourable to their generation, often significant distances from consumers; they require realignment of the existing energy infrastructure, including the transmission grid.

Renewables have lower energy density. Coal, depending on its quality, provides 50–100 percent more energy than the wood it replaced. Oil and gas provide 3–6 times more energy per weight than coal. In contrast, ethanol, a biofuel, has 30 percent less energy density than petrol and 12 percent less than diesel fuel. Lower energy density reduces the attraction of electric cars because a battery only has one-sixth the joules per kilogram compared to petrol, reducing the range between recharging.

Power density, the rate of energy production per unit of land area, is also low for renewable sources. The power densities of fossil fuel energy systems are two or three times higher than for wind- or water-driven electricity or biofuel production. They are also far higher than those for solar energy. This means that the spatial requirements for the extraction, capture and conversion of fossil fuels are modest. In contrast, renewable energy sources need a large amount of space, bringing them into conflict with other land uses, particularly food production.

Ethanol is increasingly used as a biofuel to meet mandated renewable fuel targets in developed countries. Around a third of US grain production is used to make ethanol. To fill one 95-litre (25-gallon) SUV tank requires the same amount of corn sufficient to feed a single person for a year. The grain needed to fuel all US cars is equivalent to an amount that could feed 400 million people. Yet the entire US grain harvest would only generate enough ethanol to meet around 20 percent of current American petrol demand.

World ethanol production targets require the diversion of

10 percent of global cereal output from food to fuels, or finding large tracts of extra arable land. If existing farmland were to be used, the effect would be an increase in food prices by as much as 40 percent.

The emission reduction potential of renewables is overstated, ignoring the true energy cost. Wind power requires steel towers made from metal smelted by coal-derived coke, or arc furnaces using coal- or gas-generated electricity. It also requires turbine blades manufactured from plastics synthesised from crude oils extracted using diesel or diesel-electric motors. New biofuel plantations require additional land clearing, resulting in deforestation. The emissions from this and from fertilisers and transportation may negate the benefit of biofuels.

Although costs are likely to come down with increased scale and experience, many renewable energy technologies are currently uneconomic without government subsidies.

*

Commencing in mid-2014, the price of crude oil has fallen by over 50 percent to 1979 levels, adjusted for inflation. This fall reflects weaker than expected demand due to slower economic growth and increased supply, in part from new sources such as shale gas and liquids, but also due to the refusal of OPEC, led by Saudi Arabia, to cut output for strategic and geopolitical reasons. The strategy was to allow prices to fall below the production costs of high-cost producers and non-traditional oil sources, especially shale, forcing them out of business and thus protecting Saudi's and OPEC's market share.

Some argued that oil prices had entered a new, permanent long-term range of US$20–60 per barrel. Others saw the fall as temporary. The consensus was that lower oil prices would assist the global economy. Quantitative greasing would augment quantitative easing, supporting economic activity. A US$40 fall in oil price equates to an income transfer of around US$1.3 trillion (around 2 percent of global

GDP) from oil producers to oil consumers. The 50 percent fall in 2014 was expected to boost global growth by around 1 percent.

The essential assumption is that a lower oil price increases GDP by shifting income from producers to consumers, making them more likely to spend. But many governments in oil-producing countries are now fiscally profligate, using strong revenues to finance ambitious public-spending programs, or heavily subsidise domestic energy costs. Lower oil prices will force these governments to curtail programs and subsidies or increase debt, which might reduce growth. It is also unclear whether the consumption multipliers assumed now hold. A significant overhang of debt, employment uncertainty, and weak income growth may result in the transfer being saved or used to pay off debt, decreasing the boost to consumption and growth.

Low oil prices reduce investment in energy exploration, development and production. One estimate puts the decrease in investment spending as a result of the price fall at almost US$1 trillion, which will adversely affect activity and growth. Lower oil prices may also create instability in financial markets. According to the Bank for International Settlements, the global oil and gas industry had debt of US$2.5 trillion in 2014, two and a half times that of eight years earlier. Heavily indebted energy companies, and sovereign or near-sovereign borrowers with large oil exposures now face an increased risk of financial distress from lower revenues.

Low oil prices may not be sustainable, given that demand is likely to grow and supplies of the non-renewable resource will fall because of depletion. Reduced investment in new sources of supply and in renewables may create future shortages. Low prices also decrease incentives for conservation. They risk increasing emissions and carbon intensity, and reducing energy efficiency.

Columbia University's Professor Jeffrey Sachs argues that low oil prices provide a historic opportunity to introduce carbon pricing schemes, to properly reflect the environmental cost of the emissions from fossil fuels. Low prices would mitigate the effects of the tax on the economy, with the carbon-tax-inclusive price still below the levels of the recent past. Over the longer term, the tax would provide an appropriate price signal, encouraging reduced investment in fossil fuel and greater focus on renewable energy. It would also provide much-needed revenue for governments, some of which could be invested in low-carbon energy. But progress on this initiative to date is negligible globally.

The world's supply of energy will not be exhausted any time soon. But the human race is on track to use up the energy content of hundreds of millions of years' worth of sunlight stored in the form of coal, oil and natural gas in a few hundred years. The precious nature of fuel is not generally appreciated. Around 10 tonnes of pre-historic buried plant and organic matter converted by pressure and heat over millennia is needed to create 4.5 litres (a single gallon) of petrol.

Other high-quality and low-cost resources, such as essential metals, are also being depleted. While unlikely in the near term, shortages are probable in the long term, constraining growth. There are already shortages of certain rare earth metals used in smart phones, computers, medical devices, weapons and hybrid vehicles. Unlike energy, where renewable sources are theoretically available, metals may prove harder to replace, requiring increasing reliance on expensive recycling.

*

The impact of human activity on the environment is the final constraint on future economic activity. The planet has entered a new geological period, the Anthropocene, wherein human activities are significantly altering the earth's ecosystems. Its central feature is anthropogenic global warming and the resulting climate change, caused by increasing atmospheric levels of carbon dioxide from fossil fuel combustion, ozone depletion, deforestation and animal agriculture. In 2014 the Intergovernmental Panel on Climate Change projected that the earth's average temperature would rise by 1.5°–4.8°C (2.7–8.6°F) during the twenty-first century, depending on assumptions about carbon emissions. The current trajectory is already outpacing projections.

The scientific evidence for global warming is based on several markers. Greenhouse gases in the atmosphere have increased. Current CO_2 concentrations, of over 400 parts per million, far exceed the 170–300 ppm recorded over the last 800,000 years. The concentrations have increased by 100 ppm over the last 200 years, and primarily in the last fifty. This compares to an increase of approximately 90 ppm over the previous 6000 years. The rise coincides with the release of 1.3 trillion tonnes of CO_2 into the atmosphere from burning fossil fuels.

Key temperature indicators have increased: air temperature over land, sea surface temperature, marine air temperature, ocean heat, temperature in the troposphere (the active-weather layer of the atmosphere, closest to the earth's surface), and humidity. Each of the last three decades was warmer on average than any other since 1850. According to the World Meteorological Organization, fourteen of the fifteen warmest years on record have occurred in the twenty-first century.

Ocean levels and acidification have also risen, altering marine ecosystems; this may further reduce already diminished fish stocks, an important food source. Sea levels have risen by about 20 centimetres on average over the past hundred years. Arctic sea ice, glaciers, Northern Hemisphere spring snow cover, and stratospheric temperatures have all declined. Summer Arctic sea ice was at record lows in 2002, 2005, 2007 and 2012. In 2007 the sea ice was 39 percent below the 1979–2000 average, resulting in the Northwest Passage being navigable for the first time in recorded history. Summer arctic sea ice may cease to exist sometime during the twenty-first century.

Climate change deniers challenge the evidence, lobbying to prevent action to reduce greenhouse gases. They argue that the evidence is unclear, computer models are flawed, forecasts are inconsistent with actual experience, and that there's a lack of sufficient long-term data to formulate definitive conclusions. They claim that the earth's temperature has been higher in the past, with the current rise merely part of a long-term cycle, and that increases in CO_2 levels follow rather than precede temperature increases. They believe economic growth should take precedence over dealing with climate change.

The campaign against global warming is financed by ideologically motivated supporters and industries that would be adversely affected by the actions necessary to reduce emissions. It is reminiscent of the efforts of the tobacco industry to undermine the scientific evidence on the dangers of smoking.

Although the modelling is not perfect, there is a strong, credible body of multidisciplinary scientific evidence, accepted by the vast majority of scientists, establishing anthropogenic climate change. The main uncertainties are the extent of the temperature increase, the timescale over which this may occur, and the exact sequence of events. In a 1957 paper, oceanographers Roger Revelle and Hans Suess noted: 'human beings are now carrying out a large scale geophysical experiment of a kind that could not have happened in the past nor be reproduced in the future'.[7]

*

Global warming and more frequent extreme weather events entail large economic costs. Higher premiums for insuring against them, along with the cost of their damage, will reduce global growth. Severe storms currently diminish the world's annual GDP growth by around 1 percent.

In 2013 there were record temperatures in India, Pakistan, Russia and Australia. North-east Brazil experienced its worst drought in fifty years. The worst recorded tornado hit El Reno, Oklahoma. The number and intensity of wildfires in North America, Europe and Australia increased. Hurricane Sandy, which affected the East Coast of the US and the Caribbean in October 2012, destroyed or damaged an estimated 1.8 million structures and homes, causing economic losses exceeding US$65 billion. In 2005 Hurricane Katrina resulted in losses exceeding US$100 billion. The 2011 floods in Thailand caused estimated losses of US$45 billion. Automobile and electronics factories were flooded and inoperable for months. Prices for items like hard drives, a large proportion of which are produced in Thailand, doubled worldwide.

Rising sea levels will flood low-lying areas that are currently used for human habitation and agriculture. The melting of the Greenland ice sheet, which is now widely expected but the exact timing is debated, will raise sea levels by up to 7 metres. An increase of just one metre would inundate half the rice-growing areas in Bangladesh. Around 600 million people live in areas less than 10 metres above sea level. Two-thirds of the world's cities with a population over 5 million are also located in these areas. The relocation of vulnerable populations, either permanently or temporarily, will be expensive and economically disruptive. The rise in environmental refugees will be costly to manage.

Retreating or melting glaciers will reduce available groundwater and unleash destructive floods. Higher temperatures are altering the hydrological cycle and rain patterns, and they also increase evaporation. Water shortages are likely to be exacerbated. Both droughts and floods are likely to become more frequent.

Higher temperatures, water scarcity and more severe droughts will affect food production and reduce crop yields. An increase of one degree Celsius in temperature above optimum levels reduces yields of wheat, rice and corn by around 10 percent. Traditionally, extreme weather events were anomalies. Farmers recovered when conditions normalised. Global warming may end the long period of relative climate stability in which modern agriculture developed, resulting in higher prices and food shortages.

The changed weather patterns will have a detrimental effect on human health. Greater incidence of tropical diseases like malaria and dengue fever will affect healthcare costs and work practices. The spread of plant and animal pests may also affect agricultural productivity. Climate change will result in financial losses on investments in real estate, agriculture, construction and tourism in affected locations. Current reserves of fossil fuels, if burnt without recapture of the CO_2 emissions, would release roughly three times the global carbon budget, pushing the average annual temperature up by more than $3°C$. If governments regulate emissions, then the capital tied up in fossil fuels may be lost, with businesses prevented from exploiting reserves.

The 2006 Stern Review, commissioned by the UK government, concluded that failure to address climate change would result in economic costs of up to 20 percent of GDP. Addressing climate change by reducing emissions would also have significant costs, in the form of more expensive energy and other affected products.

To date, the primary strategies for dealing with global warming have consisted of endless conferences, unenforceable treaties, disagreements between the major emitters, and investment in projects unlikely to accomplish anything significant or lasting. Germany has spent more than US$130 billion in subsidies for solar power, which would only postpone the timetable of global warming marginally. Despite commitments to renewable energy, fossil fuel's share of global energy has not declined materially.

Dealing with climate change requires a reduction in greenhouse gas emissions. This would be economically costly and entail a radical transformation in living standards. Instead, governments have placed their faith in human ingenuity. Geoengineering is one such scientific fantasy. One of its schemes aims to remove excess CO_2 from the atmosphere through photosynthesis, by fertilising the oceans with iron. Another scheme involves reducing the amount of sunlight reaching the earth by reflecting it back into space, thus increasing the albedo, or the fraction of solar energy reflected. The technology is currently unproven and uneconomic.

As part of its long-term strategic planning, Shell Oil developed a scenario, named Scramble, where the world continues to use fossil fuels without regard for emissions. Unwilling to curb energy demand because it would slow economic growth, countries do not reduce energy intensity but increase the use of coal, and unconventional oil and gas and biofuels.

The differences between developed and emerging nations prevent international consensus on reducing emissions. This situation may continue until energy supplies become tight and there are major climate shocks. By this time, climate change will be irreversible, with CO_2 concentrations around 550 ppm, 60 percent above the currently agreed maximum acceptable level. The world will be forced to adapt, with a decline in economic activity and living standards as the cost.

Current trends suggest that Scramble is the most likely trajectory. Humanity has decided to ignore Joseph Conrad's advice: 'any fool can carry on, but only the wise man knows how to shorten sail in time'.[8]

*

The need to secure access to water, food and energy, as well as manage the effects of global warming, will result in clashes of national interest and potential conflict, even outright war.

River systems transect political borders, complicating water management. In Africa the Congo, Niger, Nile and Zambezi rivers flow through some ten countries each. In Europe the Danube is an important resource for nineteen nations. The Rhine passes through or borders six countries. Aquifers also cross borders. US water policies affect Mexico. Turkish dam projects alter the flow of the Tigris–Euphrates river system, affecting Syria and other downstream countries. Conflict over the water of the Jordan River affects Jordan, Israel and Palestine. Agricultural projects in Sudan and Ethiopia, often promoted by foreign interests, change the flow of the Nile. There are tensions between India and Pakistan over sharing the flow of the Indus River system. Proposed Chinese dams on the Mekong affect countries downstream, such as Laos, Cambodia, Thailand and Vietnam. China's Great Western Extraction plan will transfer huge volumes of water from Tibet to the Yellow River, reducing the flow of the Brahmaputra River, which is vital to India and Bangladesh.

In the face of rising food prices in 2008, concern over food security led to Russia, Thailand and other grain-growing countries restricting or banning exports. China, India, Saudi Arabia, South Korea and the United Arab Emirates have purchased or leased tracts of agricultural land elsewhere, mainly in South-East Asia, Latin America, the former Soviet Union, and sub-Saharan Africa. Investors, such as pension funds, institutions and hedge funds, have also purchased land in anticipation of shortages, hoping to profit from expected price increases. Such investments are creating discontent amongst local people, who are frequently deprived of their livelihoods. Ensuring food security was one reason behind the Indian government's opposition in 2014, subsequently reversed, to the World Trade Organization's agreement to improve trade facilitation.

Germany has committed to lower emissions, planning to generate 80 percent of its electricity from clean sources by 2050. But rising geopolitical concerns following Russian involvement in the Ukrainian civil conflict forced Germany to increase the use of coal so as to reduce dependence on Russian natural gas. Coal was also needed to manage the intermittency of wind and solar generation, after Germany's decision to close its nuclear power stations by 2022. In 2014 Poland and Sweden unveiled plans to develop Europe's rich deposits of lignite (a highly polluting form of coal) along the German-Polish border, to meet increasing German demand. National interest also makes it difficult for China and India to reduce their reliance on coal-fired electricity generation, despite commitments to reducing carbon emissions.

India is building its own Great Wall, a 3360-kilometre (2100-mile) border fence surrounding Bangladesh. Designed to prevent illegal immigration, it will also provide protection from future Bangladeshi climate refugees.

*

Economics, according to economist Robert Heilbroner, entails the study of resourcing society. But resource limits require re-evaluating society's consumption of the present at the expense of the future. In 1954 German economist E.F. Schumacher recognised that human beings had begun living off capital: 'Mankind has existed for many thousands of years and has always lived off income. Only in the last hundred years has man forcibly broken into nature's larder and is now emptying it out at breathtaking speed which increases from year to year.'[9]

At a minimum, resource scarcity and global warming will constrain economic growth. Geographer Jared Diamond thought the effects may be more severe: 'population and environmental problems created by non-sustainable resource use will ultimately get solved one way or another: if not by pleasant means of our own choice, then by unpleasant and unchosen means, such as the ones that Malthus initially envisioned'.[10]

CIRCLING THE WAGONS

Globalisation
in Reverse

In the period after World War II, economic growth benefited from the remarkable expansion in global trade and capital flows. Similarly, in an interesting parallel, increases in trade, the free movement of capital, and travel also facilitated growth and prosperity before 1914.

John Maynard Keynes celebrated this earlier golden age: 'The inhabitant of London could order by telephone, sipping his morning tea in bed, the various products of the whole earth, in such quantity as he might see fit, and reasonably expect their early delivery upon his doorstep; he could at the same moment and by the same means adventure his wealth in the natural resources and new enterprises of any quarter of the world, and share, without exertion or even trouble, in their prospective fruits and advantages.'

Keynes's Londoner came to regard 'this state of affairs as normal, certain, and permanent, except in the direction of further improvement, and any deviation from it as aberrant, scandalous, and avoidable'.[1] World War I and the Great Depression ended this earlier period of globalisation.

In economics, autarky, derived from a Greek word meaning self-sufficiency, refers to a closed economy with limited international trade or capital flows. The Austro-Hungarian Empire, Edo period Japan, Nazi Germany, and Italy under Benito Mussolini all pursued national policies favouring autarky. More recently the Soviet Union, Afghanistan (under the Taliban), Cambodia (under the Khmer Rouge) and Myanmar operated largely as closed economies.

Unprecedented economic and financial pressures are now reversing the tide of post-World War II globalisation. The shift to closed economies is driven by national self-interest, what Swiss philosopher Henri-Frédéric Amiel described as the survival of the animal in us.

*

In 2011 the cross-border flow of goods, services and finance peaked at 61 percent of global GDP, up from 40 percent in 1990. In forty-nine of the fifty-eight years from 1951 to 2008, trade grew faster than the global economy. Between 1980 and 2011 it grew at nearly 7 percent annually on average, double global economic growth. Foreign direct investment, and cross-border investment and lending also increased faster than global output. Between 1980 and 2007 these global financial flows increased from 4 percent (US$470 billion) to a peak of 21 percent (US$12 trillion) of global GDP.

The GFC may signal the zenith of globalisation. After a partial recovery following the crisis, growth in trade in goods and services subsequently slowed to around 2–3 percent per annum, at or below economic growth, something not recorded in decades. Financial flows remain around 60 percent below their pre-crisis level, falling from 21 percent of global GDP to only 5 percent in 2012.[2]

Historically, sluggish growth in trade and capital flows has signalled impending recession. It is not clear whether the current trend reflects cyclical factors or a fundamental structural change. Expectations of a rapid return to pre-crisis conditions appear optimistic.

*

In recent decades, international integration has focused on the geographic separation of production and consumption. Economist David Ricardo's concept of comparative advantage, whereby countries produce more of those goods and services in which they enjoy a competitive edge, gained ascendancy. The manufacturing process itself was divided into discrete components. A pair of trousers could be made using yarn spun in Bangladesh that was then woven into fabric and dyed in India, China or Vietnam; the zip might be manufactured in Japan and the buttons in China; and the whole could be stitched together in Sri Lanka, Pakistan or Honduras. Each stage was undertaken in the most efficient location, with businesses and nations embracing a transnational system of production. Firms aggressively sought competitively priced raw materials, labour and locations. With the ubiquitous call centres and processing hubs, business process outsourcing and multinational manufacturing became the norm.

The reintegration of China, India, Russia and Eastern Europe into the world economy increased the global labour pool from approximately 1.5 billion workers to nearly 3 billion. Costs fell as businesses relocated production to the cheapest locations. Savings sought profitable investment opportunities worldwide, facilitated by investment and risk management instruments.

Consumers benefited from a greater range of products at lower prices. The rising buying power of emerging nations provided new markets for goods and services. But workers with low levels of education and limited skills in developed economies were forced to compete globally, suffering a fall in employment and stagnation of incomes.

The World Bank, the IMF, the World Trade Organization and economists preached globalisation, free trade and capital movements, which rapidly supplanted protectionism as the preferred policy of development. Living standards improved on average throughout the world, lifting large numbers of people out of poverty.

But globalisation was never complete. Trade was not free, but managed. Less obvious trade restrictions persisted. There was limited progress on the harmonisation of laws and regulations governing labour, safety, environmental protection and intellectual property rights. The lack of standardisation of power voltages and electric plugs highlights the practical limits to integration.

Nor did globalisation ever embrace the free movement of people. A few skilled individuals traded up to countries with greater opportunities and higher rewards, using training frequently paid for by the country of origin, but for most, there was little mobility. Some unskilled workers found temporary work in richer countries, where they were at risk of exploitation and mistreatment. Asked about US immigration policy, hedge fund manager Julian Robertson rejected the Statue of Liberty's call to 'give us your tired, your poor, your huddled masses yearning to breathe free'. He argued that 'they really couldn't get here because of the great oceans. And that was the safeguard of our immigration.' Robertson was not enthusiastic about 'a refugee from Bangladesh who has had no schooling and has had no interest in school'.[3]

Globalisation both created and relied on strong economic growth. Individual countries sacrificed their national interests as the benefits of integration outweighed the costs. Prosperity dulled enquiry into the drivers and assumptions of global integration, ignoring its essential fragility. G.K. Chesterton argued that it was unwise to take a fence down until you know why it was put up. It seemed to be regarded as a question for different times.

*

In the aftermath of the GFC, the advantages of economic and monetary integration are less obvious. Reduction in the direct benefits of global trade and capital movement dictates a withdrawal to more closed economies. A domestic focus, nations believe, can capture a greater share of available growth and deliver greater prosperity for their citizens.

Developed countries face a period of stagnation. Less affected by the crisis, emerging nations continue to grow, albeit more slowly than before. For them, the benefits of participation in the global economic system have now diminished and they are wary of having to pay for the problems of developed economies.

Emerging countries also resent the unequal distribution of income and wealth. Increasingly, profits depend on the control of intellectual property rather than production. The majority of the profit from Apple's iPhones, which are made in China and recorded as part of its exports, comes from high-tech components, intellectual property and branding, which accrues to non-Chinese firms. Developed nations and multinational businesses control vital logistics and supply chains for trade. They dominate international capital flows, generating substantial earnings from financing trade and managing investments. When growth rates were high, the unbalanced distribution of benefits was grudgingly tolerated. But lower growth rates and decreased benefits encourage nations to maximise their own position at the expense of others, reducing engagement in a global economic system.

International supply chains for goods and commodities are sensitive to changes in cost structures and currency values. Low oil prices throughout the 1980s and 1990s kept transport costs low, facilitating global production. Higher fuel and transportation costs would undermine extended global production and supply chains.

In the 1990s low-priced exports from China adversely affected Mexico, but now, increasing labour costs in China, changing currency values, and proximity to the US have made Mexico competitive in manufacturing. In 2001 the cost of Chinese labour was around 25 percent of Mexico's. In 2014 they were roughly the same. The appreciation of the Chinese renminbi against the Mexican peso has changed cost structures. Manufacturing closer to the final market and shorter delivery times are also an advantage.

International supply chains are vulnerable to disruption from climatic and environmental factors, as was highlighted by the 2011 Japanese tsunami and Thai floods. Shortages of minor but essential components halted production elsewhere.

There is increased concern too that globalisation undermines economic and political sovereignty. Governments reacted to the GFC by initiating large spending programs to support their economies. In many cases this boosted imports rather than promoting domestic demand, employment, income and investment. The effectiveness of a nation's economic policies is reduced in the absence of internationally coordinated action.

National taxation policy can also be neutered by globalisation. Countries offer lower tax rates or special concessions to attract investment. Ireland arguably benefits at the expense of other Eurozone members from its concessional tax treatment of multinational firms locating there. Until the rules were changed, American businesses took advantage of a technique called tax inversion to change their tax domicile and reduce corporate taxes. Higher personal tax rates in the UK resulted in fund managers and bank executives relocating to Switzerland, or having to be compensated by employers for loss of income. Proposals for higher taxes in France engendered fears that businesses would relocate to the UK.

Autarky, a reassertion of economic sovereignty, is a natural response to these pressures. Restrictions on trade, manipulation of the currency, control of capital flows, and predatory extraterritorial regulations that target foreign competitors now signal the retrenchment of globalisation. As one nation adopts such policies, it compels others to pursue similar strategies to protect their own interests.

Internationalists argue that the siren call of protectionism has been avoided, pointing to the recovery in global trade since 2008. They argue that global rather than national capitalism remains the dominant ideology, and is now institutionalised and irreversible. But faced with low growth, high unemployment, stagnant income levels, and threats to national industries and iconic businesses, countries are increasingly retreating from free trade, placing pressures on trading partners. Despite repeated statements at Group of 20 meetings about the importance of free trade and avoiding the mistakes of the 1930s, trade restrictions are increasing. Since 2008, the member economies have introduced more than 1500 protectionist measures.

Subtler measures are favoured over outright import restrictions, so as to avoid open trade warfare and disputes before the World Trade Organization. Subsidies, government procurement policies that favour national suppliers, 'buy local' campaigns, preferential financing, industry assistance policies, and differential tax regimes are all used to direct demand. Safety and environmental standards are used to prevent foreign products penetrating national markets. The collective effect is significant, though less immediately obvious than the 1930 Smoot-Hawley Act, which increased tariffs on thousands of imported goods into the US, deepening and lengthening the recession.

Protectionist measures and a slowdown in global trade will reduce growth and living standards, especially in emerging countries. Pascal Lamy, director-general of the WTO, called it 'a crisis which threatens to undo the economic development achieved by many countries and to erode people's faith in an open international trading system'.[4]

*

Global trade is affected by the currency wars. Between 2007 and 2012 the US government, its banks and non-financial corporations received a benefit of around US$1.36 trillion from low interest rates and QE policies, including US$480 billion from the rest of world. Over this period, the depreciation of the US dollar resulted in a loss of more than US$600 billion for foreign investors in US-dollar-denominated securities. In February 2013 Chile's finance minister warned that 'by seeking relief at the expense of other economies, [QE] is, in its essence, a globally counterproductive policy'.[5] At their 2013 Moscow summit, the Group of 20 made a facile announcement that leading nations would not target or devalue currencies to make them more competitive.

Such policies invite destructive and self-defeating retaliation. Every country cannot have the cheapest currency. Since 2013 Japan and China have launched programs to weaken their currencies in an effort to boost their economies. Concerned that a strengthening euro could damage prospects for a European recovery, the European Central Bank implemented measures in 2014 and 2015 designed to weaken the euro.

In 2014 the US dollar began to rise at its fastest rate in decades, increasing in value by over 20 percent in a year, including a jump of 10 percent in the first three months of 2015. With 40 percent of sales and around a quarter of profits coming from abroad, US exporters were affected, issuing warnings of lower revenues and earnings. US legislators now complained about the effect of overseas central bank actions on the currency, threatening to classify Europe, Japan and China as currency manipulators. The Fed indicated that the increase in the value of the dollar and its effects on the American economy were now impinging on their policies. The difference between legitimate policies of low or negative interest rates and unfair devaluation depends on one's point of view.

Despite the evidence, European Central Bank president Mario Draghi has repeatedly stated that talk of a currency war was 'really excessive', favouring denial: 'I urge all parties to exercise very, very strong verbal discipline. I think the less we talk about this the better.'[6] One central banker colourfully described a policy of devaluation as being like urinating in bed. While it feels good at first, it turns rapidly into a mess.

*

Since 2008, the growth in cross-border capital flows has slowed, with global financial assets increasing by just 1.9 percent annually, well below the 7.9 percent average growth of 1990–2007. The GFC losses and subsequent deleveraging reduced the amount of capital available. In a process of financial domestication, national regulators forced banks and investors to adopt patriotic balance sheets, purchasing national government bonds or prioritising lending to domestic borrowers.

Competing national and international interests now restrict the free movement of capital. A Spanish bank's German operation may have deposits surplus to its requirements, which the parent bank wishes to access. The Spanish regulators will want the money to be freely available within the group, while the German regulators prefer to have the surplus cash remain in Germany, to avoid risk or to bolster the liquidity of the local operation.

In 2013 the Bank for International Settlements reported that interbank credit had fallen in seven of the last nine quarters, driven by a reduction in cross-border lending, which was at 1999 levels. Since 2007, Eurozone banks' cross-border claims have declined by US$3.7 trillion. US, UK and Swiss banks have reduced cross-border loans, with only Japan increasing activity. Countries dependent on foreign investment for development have had to find new sources of finance and have seen their financial vulnerability increase.

Within the Eurozone itself the reduction in cross-border holdings of government and of corporate bonds by banks has slowed the integration of the common currency's debt markets. With its individual countries increasingly domestically focused, Eurozone bank investment in bonds of other member countries has fallen to around 22 percent, down from 40 percent in 2006. It is lower than when the euro was launched.

Since 2009, low interest rates and weak currencies in developed countries have encouraged over US$3 trillion to flow into emerging markets, with their higher rates and stronger growth prospects. Volatile and short-term capital flows threaten to destabilise the developing economies by driving up the value of currencies, creating inflationary pressures, artificially lowering borrowing costs, encouraging rapid increases in debt levels, and increasing asset prices, thus creating financial bubbles.

Brazil, South Korea, Switzerland and India all implemented some form of capital inflow controls. Hong Kong, once lauded by Milton Friedman as the ultimate free market, introduced a 15 percent tax on property purchases by foreigners, to limit the effects of money from mainland China, which was distorting real-estate prices and reducing home affordability for citizens. In a historical shift, the IMF accepted the use of targeted, transparent and generally temporary direct controls to limit volatile cross-border capital flows.

Periods of US dollar weakness also drive up the price of food and energy traded in that currency. In poorer countries, where spending on these items, including everyday essentials like cooking oil, accounts for a high proportion of income, this causes hardship. Higher commodity prices in combination with large flows of capital create inflationary pressures, forcing emerging countries to increase interest rates, thus slowing economic growth. These developments threaten to reverse progress in reducing poverty.

*

Regulations are increasingly a weapon in the battle between nations. After the 2008 banking crisis, new rules for financial institutions were developed to ensure more rigorous regulatory oversight. They were intended to be adopted globally, to ensure international consistency. Emerging countries argue that stringent regulations intended for complex multinational financial institutions in developed countries are inappropriate for their simpler financial systems, and that adoption of them would impede the ability of local banks to provide the credit necessary to support the local economy. These regulations would also pose significant compliance costs and erode their competitive position.

India, China, and even foreign-bank-friendly Singapore are moving to a policy known as subsidiarisation, requiring foreign institutions active locally to operate through separate legal entities incorporated in the relevant jurisdiction. The local entities must have adequate separate capital resources and be ring-fenced from the parent, allowing local regulators and investors access to their assets in case of financial difficulties. The US has proposed that foreign banks with large operations in America should be forced to maintain a local reservoir of capital and liquidity. Disagreements over bank regulation will result in a Balkanised global financial system.

Under the guise of strengthening the financial system, the US has implemented measures whose extraterritorial application advantages American banks and restricts foreign competitors. Foreign banks have responded by routing transactions to avoid being subject to these rules. In 2013 the EU proposed a financial-transactions tax to raise revenue and rein in speculative trading. The tax would have extraterritorial reach, applying to all major financial centres. The UK and the US sought to protect their large and globally important financial services firms, just as the European proposal sought, indirectly, to reduce their influence.

US regulators and the Department of Justice are increasingly an arm of American economic and foreign policy. In 2014, after a lengthy investigation, French bank BNP Paribas pleaded guilty to criminal charges of conspiracy and falsifying records in connection with transactions involving Cuba, Iran and Sudan, in contravention of US sanctions. While the bank's conduct may have been egregious, the transactions were not illegal under European law. The bank agreed to pay a US$9 billion fine, which was greater than a year's profit, and its right to clear certain US dollar transactions was suspended. Earlier, US bank regulators accused British-based Standard Chartered of not disclosing US$250 billion of transactions with Iran, resulting in the bank paying a US$327 million settlement. A Dutch bank paid US$619 million to settle similar charges concerning Iran and Cuba. HSBC, another British bank, has set aside US$700 million against potential fines payable to US authorities for similar offences. The transactions had no American nexus in many cases, other than US dollar payments made via New York.

The UK argues that allegations of banking misconduct are designed to tarnish the integrity of London and its status as one of the world's major financial centres. The US argues that the problems relate to the laxity of Britain's famous light-touch regulations, which have been a factor in the rise of London as a global finance hub. Europeans argue that the prosecution of BNP Paribas was related to US opposition to the French sale of two helicopter assault ships for €1.2 billion to Russia, or to General Electric's unsuccessful bid for Alstom, manufacturer of France's TGV high-speed train. The use of banking laws in this way does not improve the safety of the financial system or facilitate international cooperation.

Fears of prosecution under wide powers for laundering money or financing terrorism have forced banks to stop dealing with counter-parts in many emerging countries. One European banker joked that he feared there was an orange suit waiting for him in the US. The actions have made it difficult for immigrants or foreign workers to remit funds to the developing world, which provide critical support for families and communities.

Foreign nations increasingly resent the extraordinary power enjoyed by the US through the position of the dollar as the global reserve currency, central to international finance, trade and payments. In response, non-Americans are seeking to reduce the dominance of the US dollar. Retaliatory prosecutions of American businesses are possible. Negotiation of closer trade and financial relationships will be detrimentally affected. In 2015 the EU commenced action against Google relating to alleged abuse of its dominance of internet search engines. A Standard Chartered director caustically stated a commonly held view: 'You f***ing Americans. Who are you to tell us, the rest of the world, that we're not going to deal with Iranians.'[7]

Dutch academic Dirk Schoenmaker argues that it is impossible to simultaneously reconcile national sovereignty, international finance and financial stability. While big banks operating across national boundaries require a global system of regulation, national govern-ments seek flexibility to modify the rules and preserve sovereignty, resulting in instability.

*

Nations may take poet Robert Frost's advice that good fences make good neighbours. The US, Europe and China are all likely to find autarky a realistic policy option, although for different reasons.

Structurally, the US could function successfully as a closed econ-omy. It remains the world's largest economy, with around 25 percent of global GDP, and is almost twice the size of China, the second-largest economy. With its large domestic market, America is less exposed to trade (around 15 percent of GDP) than other big economies. If trading with Canada and Mexico under the North American Free Trade Agreement (NAFTA) is excluded, then the reliance is even lower.

Despite the inequality in its distribution of income, America remains relatively wealthy, with per capita GDP of around US$50,000. This is amongst the highest in the world, especially when low-population countries (such as Luxembourg, San Marino or Singapore) or those that are commodity-rich (Middle East oil producers) are excluded. In comparison, China's GDP per capita is around US$5000–6000. While it's highly concentrated amongst the affluent, the total net worth of American households is substantial, in excess of US$70 trillion, although this is down from a peak of over US$80 trillion before the GFC.

The US remains a major producer and net exporter of food, controlling almost half the world's grain exports. It is also rich in mineral resources. New technology has enabled access to oil and natural gas formations that were previously inaccessible. Increased production of shale gas and oil has allowed the US to reduce imports, decreasing its US$600 billion trade deficit and reliance on foreign suppliers. Lower energy costs have seen American manufacturing output increase by 3 percent between 2006 and 2014, and exports increase by 6 percent. Until the 2015 fall in oil prices, shale gas and oil projects also increased investment by 10 percent and jobs by 2 percent. While US energy independence is not likely in the near term, and the benefits from shale gas are overstated, increased domestic production provides America with a significant advantage in the form of competitive fuel and power costs.

With no clear replacement available, the US dollar is likely to continue as the world's reserve currency, with a dominant share of global trade and investments. The US borrows in its own currency, benefiting from a ready market for its securities, both domestically and internationally. Over US$6 trillion of Treasury bonds are held by foreign investors, mainly in China, Japan, elsewhere in Asia, and the Middle East.

The US has favourable demographics. It has a higher rate of population growth than other industrialised countries, which have below-replacement fertility rates. It has higher levels of immigration, remaining a magnet for foreigners and thus attracting talent and labour.

But the US also faces significant challenges. Its economic model, based on housing and consumption financed by borrowing, is broken. Growth, at around 2–3 percent, while above that for most developed countries, is well below potential. It is narrowly based, continuing to rely on consumers taking out more car and student loans, business investments in equipment and software, and residential construction. Unemployment remains higher than at equivalent stages of previous recoveries from a recession. If discouraged workers who have left the workforce and those working part-time because of the lack of full-time jobs are included, then the unemployment rate is well over 10 percent. The US economy also has an overhang of high levels of government and consumer borrowings.

A retreat from globalisation is central to dealing with America's economic issues, irrespective of its effect on other nations. Low interest rates reduce the cost of servicing debt, allowing high levels of borrowing to be sustained in the short term. Low rates and QE measures help devalue the US dollar, reducing the level of government debt, by decreasing its value in foreign currency terms.

A weaker US dollar boosts exports, which are assisted by cheaper prices and by American dominance of key industries, such as technology and software, pharmaceuticals, complex manufactured products (in aerospace, defence hardware, heavy machinery), entertainment and services. A weaker dollar also reduces the cost base of domestic production, encouraging the return of manufacturing and assembly work to the US, which should in turn reduce unemployment. Stronger growth and lower unemployment will assist in reducing the large US budget deficit, helping control government debt levels.

A more closed economy is consistent with America's economic self-interest, power and influence. It plays well to America's desire to stand apart, its instinctive exceptionalism. As William G. Hyland, Deputy National Security Advisor to President Gerald Ford, noted, 'protectionism is the ally of isolationism'.[8]

*

Europe too has many of the requirements of a closed economy. While individual European economies are modest in size, the EU constitutes over 25 percent of global GDP, making it the world's largest economic unit.

The EU is a more open economy than the US, being the world's largest exporter and importer of goods and services. But around 75 percent of its trade is amongst member nations, aided by the absence of trade barriers and a common currency. Germany, the EU's largest economy and one of the world's largest exporters, sells over 60 percent of its products within the Eurozone.

The EU is largely self-sufficient in food. Like the US, this is based in part on subsidies, minimum price schemes, and trade restrictions that favour European farmers. The EU is a net energy importer, primarily from Russia and other contiguous, energy-rich countries. Natural gas finds with significant potential in the eastern Mediterranean Sea may alter this.

The need to deal with Europe's debt problems may be one catalyst for the drift to autarky. As a single unit, the Eurozone has a current account that is nearly balanced, and a trade account that has a small surplus; the overall fiscal deficit is modest, and the aggregate level of public debt, while high, is manageable. But there are significant disparities between individual members of the Eurozone in terms of income and debt levels, public finances and external balances. Greater integration would help resolve some of these variations.

This would necessitate a net wealth transfer from richer to poorer member nations. Stronger, more creditworthy members would have to underwrite the borrowings of weaker nations. There is significant opposition, predictably from countries like Germany, Finland and the Netherlands, to Eurozone members guaranteeing each other's obligations. But even without agreement, de facto mutualisation of debt may occur over time. As weaker nations increase reliance on official institutions like the European Central Bank and bailout funds, the commitment of stronger countries, especially Germany and France, increases. They implicitly assume the liabilities of weaker members of the Eurozone because they stand behind the institutions financing them.

If richer member nations will not agree to net transfers and mutual responsibility for debt, then it is possible that the euro may have to be abandoned or restructured, in which case the union fragments. Under such a scenario, the Eurozone would morph into a smaller version of the original, probably consisting of stronger core nations and a number of smaller entities. Nursing large losses and a significant diminution of wealth as the peripheral nations default on their borrowings, survivors are likely to favour autarkical policies to restore economic health.

Irrespective of its policy choices, Europe faces a very long period of economic stagnation as it works off its debt burden and undertakes major structural changes to correct imbalances. During this transition it will be forced to focus internally, husbanding savings and wealth to absorb the required large debt write-offs. Explicit or implicit capital controls and trade restrictions are natural policy measures to assist in this adjustment, marking a shift to a more closed economy.

*

Weaknesses in China's recent mercantilist model are emerging as a result of the economic problems of its major trading partners. Given their lower level of growth, net exports can no longer drive Chinese activity. China will have to rely on domestic developments to generate the growth necessary to preserve social stability and the rule of the Communist Party. An internal focus would help rebalance the economy from one driven by exports and state-directed, debt-financed investment to one with higher private consumption.

China's economic redirection may be influenced by potentially enormous losses through engagement with the West. Before the GFC, the US purchased real goods and services from China, financing them with US-dollar-denominated IOUs with low rates of interest. China's US$4 trillion of foreign exchange reserves are invested primarily in government bonds and other high-quality securities denominated in US dollars, euros and yen. These investments have lost value, due to the declining quality of the debtors and falls in the value of foreign currencies against the renminbi. The size of the holdings dictates that China cannot sell these reserve assets, as it would result in sharp falls in the value of the securities and a rise in the renminbi, exacerbating losses.

China has become increasingly concerned about the security of its savings. Yu Yongding, a former adviser to the Chinese central bank, has castigated the US over its reckless policies. Chinese resentment at the reduction in value of its savings has risen following Western criticism of China's lack of response to the European debt crisis. Reducing international engagement would allow China to writedown its foreign currency investment over time. It would also minimise the need for further investment to protect the value of existing holdings, freeing up resources for internal requirements.

At the June 2012 Group of 20 meeting in Mexico, China made it clear that it would not initiate the type and scale of bank-lending blitz that it undertook after the GFC to boost domestic and global growth. With China unwilling to take steps to become the consumer of last resort, or open its markets fully to foreign businesses, developed countries are increasingly critical of Chinese policies.

China's economic disengagement is dictated, in part, by developing tensions in relationships with trading partners and fears of repeating historical humiliations like the Opium Wars. The government resents external pressure on its economic policies, currency value, trading practices, political system, foreign policy and human rights record. China sees diminishing gains from engagement with external parties other than on its own terms. There is also resentment towards developed nations for a perceived lack of respect in dealing with a great power. China has shifted its priorities to food and energy security, needed to sustain its development.

For China, a reversal of a policy of international engagement represents a return to traditional economic self-reliance with a limited interest in trade. In 1793 the Chinese emperor told British envoy Lord Macartney that China did not value 'ingenious articles' and 'had not the slightest need of [England's] manufactures'.[9] As Robert Hart, nineteenth-century British trade commissioner for China, wrote, '[The] Chinese have the best food in the world, rice; the best drink, tea; and the best clothing, cotton, silk, fur. Possessing these staples and their innumerable native adjuncts, they do not need to buy a penny's worth elsewhere.'[10] Engagement with *gweilos* (a Cantonese term meaning foreigners or foreign devils) is the exception, not the norm, in Chinese history.

*

For nations without a large domestic economy, adequate economic resources, or the need for export markets, a retreat from global integration poses different challenges. Unlike major powers, smaller nations cannot influence exchange rates. In February 2013 New Zealand Finance Minister Bill English ruled out intervening in currency markets to reduce the value of the New Zealand dollar and relieve pressure on exporters and manufacturers: 'To influence the exchange rate you need a couple of hundred billion US [dollars] in the bank so they take you seriously. We'd be out in the war zone with a peashooter.'[11]

Alternative trading blocs or relationships may evolve to counter the shift to closed economies. If they could overcome their historical animosity and territorial conflicts, then Japan and China could create a mutually beneficial strategic partnership. Japan is one of China's largest trading partners and one of its major foreign investors. Japan possesses advanced technology and needs markets for its exports. China is a huge potential market and its businesses would benefit from Japanese skills and intellectual property. Still the world's largest pool of savings, Japan is continually seeking investment opportunities.

Despite a history of intermittent political differences and border disputes, India would benefit from closer ties with China. Such an alliance would help India finance its current account and budget deficits and investment needs. For its part, China would have access to India's raw materials and large domestic market. 'Chindia' is not far-fetched as a concept, given the two countries have rich cultural links reaching back to ancient times, and increasing trade links in the present.

Resource-rich countries may ally themselves with major nations, such as the US, China and European countries, becoming preferred suppliers of food, energy or raw materials. In turn, they can become markets for products or services and investment. Some African countries are pursuing this policy, entering long-term supply agreements for agricultural or mineral products sought by China. In return China is expanding investment and trade preferentially with these nations, coordinating transactions by Chinese businesses and banks. China is also targeting development aid to these countries. Australia and New Zealand have emerged as important sources of raw materials for China. Russia has become an energy and commodity supplier to Europe and China. Within the framework of NAFTA, Canada has become an important source of energy for the US, while Mexico provides low-cost labour to American businesses.

Strategically located, smaller nations like Switzerland and Singapore can become important trading or financial centres, facilitating trade or providing transport, logistics, financial or investment services.

Fragmentation of the global trading system is possible. Multilateral global trade agreements brokered by the World Trade Organization are now less important. Recent rounds of global trade negotiations have been narrowly focused, concentrating on trade facilitation through reducing bureaucracy and limited reforms in agriculture and development. Countries increasingly favour bilateral or regional trade agreements. Between 1990 and 2010 the number of preferential trade treaties rose from seventy to 300. Today, half the exports of the top thirty exporters go to preferential trade partners. The US is seeking agreements with countries around the Pacific Rim via the Trans-Pacific Partnership (TPP), and with the European Union via the Transatlantic Trade and Investment Partnership (TTIP).

But bilateral and regional trade arrangements are less beneficial than global agreements. They encourage purchases from inefficient producers simply because they're party to the treaty, rather than the cheapest source worldwide. Less efficient producers also lobby for bilateral and regional agreements that better protect their interests, preventing progress to better global trade arrangements.

Nations now must trade off political status against economic prosperity and security, abandoning historical ties and biases as necessary. After World War II, when France and Germany sought to create a united Europe, Winston Churchill argued that imperial Britain did not need peacetime entanglement with its continental partners. American Secretary of State Edward Stettinius told President Roosevelt that Britain had emotional difficulties in adjusting to a reduced international role after the war. Having been a leading player, Britain regarded such a position as a national right, and took many years to recognise the benefits of the EU. Even today it remains equivocal, having chosen not to adopt the single currency. Britain plans to hold a referendum in 2017 on its continued membership of the EU.

In the British TV series *Downton Abbey*, Cora Crawley wants to know whether she and her mother-in-law are friends. The Dowager Countess would prefer that they be allies, which, she argues, is much more effective. In the evolving world order, a similarly pragmatic approach will be required for nations to prosper.

*

The shift in global trade and capital movements is also affected by changes in geopolitical relationships. Following the end of the Cold War, a relatively benign security environment aided the movement of goods, services and capital. The 9/11 attacks and the subsequent war on terror changed this, and developed countries now spend vast amounts on security as well as monitoring and controlling the flow of people, money, goods and services. US prosecutions of UK and European banks have alleged that their actions increased American vulnerability to terrorists, weapons dealers, drug traffickers and corrupt regimes.

Failed nation-building combined with deep-seated ethnic, tribal and religious enmities have turned the Middle East and Africa into a graveyard of Western ambition. The Arab Spring began in 2010 in

Tunisia when a man set himself on fire in protest against desperate poverty, corruption, the absence of representative government, and political repression. It ushered in a brief period of optimism, which predictably foundered on a lack of institutional infrastructure and the inability to rapidly improve living standards. The security outlook for the region is now deteriorating. Exploiting complex political cross-currents, ISIS, the Islamic State in Iraq and Syria, has supplanted Al-Qaeda. It has seized territory, declaring a caliphate as a base for propagating its interpretation of pure Islam. It exceeds its predecessor in financial strength, military capability, ruthless pursuit of its objectives, and threat to stability.

Over a third of India is affected by the Naxalites, members of a violent, fifty-year-old Maoist insurgency, and combating them ties up substantial government resources and prevents development of remote, resource-rich forested areas. Communal tension between India's Hindus and Muslims is ever-present. China faces ongoing unrest in Tibet and its western provinces, as well as Hong Kong. In Thailand the military executed a coup in 2014, supplanting a dysfunctional political system and a divided population.

Wary of North Atlantic Treaty Organization expansion to its borders, and facing Muslim insurgencies in the Caucasus, Russia is actively defending its areas of historical influence. The change in policy has altered its relationship with the West, and is seen by some as the start of a new cold war.

Feted as an economic superpower, China increasingly seeks commensurate political influence. Relying on the nine-dash line, a U-shaped series of markings on a map published in the then Republic of China on 1 December 1947, it is in dispute with the Philippines, Brunei, Malaysia, Taiwan and Vietnam over claims to large parts of the South China Sea and its mineral resources, including oil. There are also territorial disputes between China, South Korea and Japan over parts of the Yellow Sea and the Sea of Japan. Japan's extensive economic investments and interests in China, including its export markets, have been damaged by the disputes.

This instability reflects a power vacuum. In the post-Cold War era, America served as the 'indispensable nation', policing the world's conflicts.[12] Many developed countries spent too little on defence, preferring to piggyback off US capabilities. But America is increasingly wary of 'entangling alliances' and overseas adventures 'in search of monsters to destroy'.[13] Its political and economic interests dictate withdrawal from large-scale military engagements such as Iraq and Afghanistan.

The US has reduced its defence expenditure to control the budget deficit and its borrowing. This requires other nations to increase their defence spending, reducing funds available for other activities. Diminished reliance on foreign energy supplies allows the US to reduce commitments to guarding crucial sea lanes, such as the Strait of Hormuz and the Strait of Malacca, forcing other nations to bear a greater proportion of the cost.

Nationalism is resurgent. Politicians facing domestic economic disappointments are tempted to maintain popular support by refocusing voter attention on an external threat. Russian President Vladimir Putin and Indian Prime Minister Narendra Modi are avowed nationalists. With Japan mired in endless economic stagnation, Prime Minister Shinzō Abe, whose maternal grandfather was a member of the Tojo Cabinet during World War II, is seeking to increase defence spending and remove constitutional limitations on military action other than for self-defence, despite popular opposition. Mr Abe wants to recreate a nostalgic imperial idyll based on military and economic strength, causing unease in other Asian countries that remember Japan's wartime atrocities.

These tensions threaten trade and investment relationships.

Instability in the Middle East threatens energy supplies. Conflicts elsewhere affect supply chains, disrupting production, transhipment routes, foreign investment, and the ability of skilled foreign workers to work in certain locations. Russia's annexation of parts of Ukraine and its support for separatists have resulted in economic sanctions and reprisals. Russia has retaliated, focusing on markets in the Far East for its energy exports, which has implications for current European dependence on Russian gas and oil. Tensions even threaten access to space, due to reliance on Russian launch capabilities following the end of the US Space Shuttle program.

The peace dividend from the end of the Cold War may reverse with rising defence spending. The costs of humanitarian relief operations, as well as refugees and illegal immigration driven by instability, are increasing. The risk of armed conflict is ever-present. A 2012 report to US Secretary of State Hillary Clinton spoke of China and Japan being one error away from outright war over the Diaoyu, or Senkaku, Islands in the East China Sea. Any conflict over the disputed islands could involve the US, if Japan were to activate treaty commitments.

The rise of autarky and nationalism is a dangerous cocktail. Stewart Patrick from the US Council of Foreign Relations likened current conditions in East Asia to Europe just before World War I. In the lead-up to 1914 Sir Norman Angell famously argued that the complex trade and investment relationships between great European powers made armed conflict unthinkable. The war to end all wars, of course, signalled the end of the first great period of globalisation.

*

In 1946 Winston Churchill famously coined the term Iron Curtain to describe the Cold War division of the world, which shaped political and economic structures for over forty years of postwar history.[14] The dismantling of the Berlin Wall, its most vivid, visceral manifestation, marked a shift to greater global engagement and integration. Twenty-five years later the pressure towards autarky, driven by economic and geopolitical factors, may mark another significant change.

English politician Lord Palmerston's famous dictum states that nations have no permanent friends or allies, only permanent interests. A confluence of economic self-interest and necessity is reversing global integration, favouring closed economies with narrowly based strategic links between nations. The growth in trade and cross-border investment that underpinned prosperity and development is weaker, removing a key driver of economic growth.

BRIC(S) TO BIITS

The Rise and Fall of Emerging Markets

In 2001 Goldman Sachs's Jim O'Neill coined the term BRIC, for Brazil, Russia, India and China. He predicted that these nations would overtake the six largest Western economies by 2041 (later revised to 2039 then 2032), arguing that there would be a corresponding decline in the economic status and power of the developed world.

When he launched the idea of BRIC, O'Neill had little firsthand knowledge of these economies. He was looking for something big with which to establish himself as the newly appointed sole head of the investment bank's economics unit. Competitors branded it a marketing gimmick, arguing that beyond platitudes about these countries' population size, large land area and resources, the underlying logic and mathematics were vague. The four nations were geographically distant, and culturally and economically dissimilar. They did not form, or see themselves as, a trade, financial or political bloc. Even the neat acronym was derivative of earlier formulations: LDCs (less developed countries), NICs (newly industrialised countries), EM (emerging markets), and FM (frontier markets).

But O'Neill's forecast that the BRICs had potential for rapid growth captured attention. The glib term became synonymous with an economic future driven by emerging nations. Businesses rushed to develop their BRIC strategy. Even rivals capitulated, creating dedicated funds to invest in the BRICs. The countries themselves slowly embraced the idea, initiating regular summits. Invited by China, South Africa joined in 2010, converting the group into BRICS. In 2014 it announced plans for a new development bank, with US$50 billion in capital to finance infrastructure and a US$100 billion Contingent Reserve Arrangement to assist members in financial difficulties. One journalist speculated that BRICS-branded fashion items, such as handbags, might be next.

Goldman Sachs earned large fees from investors and companies seeking opportunities in the BRICS. O'Neill, now an economic rock star, became influential and wealthy, at one time being linked to a bid by supporters to buy Manchester United Football Club. Any association with the BRICS became auspicious. In India, when a fund management company was listed on the Mumbai Stock Exchange in 2007, its share price went up sharply because one of the management team had worked with O'Neill on BRIC research.

Between 2001 and 2013 the economic output of the BRIC countries increased from US$3 trillion a year to US$15 trillion. Between 2000 and 2008, the countries contributed almost 30 percent of global growth. Investors made money.

After 2008 these economies, less affected initially by the GFC, accounted for around half of global growth. The increased reliance of the world on these economies spawned the decoupling theory: insulated from the turmoil of developed markets, the BRICS would become safe havens, driving global prosperity.

*

The relationship between the developed and emerging worlds is long, complex and fraught with tension. Historically, the developing world was seen as a new frontier to be conquered. From the 1500s, the European powers expanded, acquiring land and new resources to complement the increasingly intensive exploitation of their home-lands. Voyages of exploration and discovery opened up trade routes. Trading relationships evolved into colonial empires.

Conquest of these often sophisticated countries was made possible by Europe's superior military power. This in turn was supported by superior industrial and scientific technologies, as well as highly evolved legal systems, property rights, politics and systems of government. It was also underpinned by cultural attitudes and work ethics, which rewarded individual skill, energy and dynamism. By the nineteenth century, England, Spain, Portugal, the Netherlands, Italy, France and Germany had established major colonies in Asia, Africa and the Americas, built upon what English naturalist Alfred Russel Wallace termed 'the unblushing selfishness of the greatest civilized nations'.[1]

The objective was to strengthen economic and political power by controlling key resources and strategic trading routes, and to deny these advantages to sovereign rivals. Over time, the colonies came to resemble modern global supply chains. In a thoroughly contemporary twist, Britain even outsourced the management of its colonies to private interests, the British East India Company.

Colonialism provided access to low-cost raw materials, fuelling the growth and prosperity of the Old World. It provided cheap labour, often in the form of slaves, and new markets for the products of the colonial powers. Portuguese explorer Vasco da Gama was exultant at being able to buy pepper from indigenous traders in the East Indies for 3 ducats a hundredweight, knowing it would fetch 80 ducats in

Venice. Silver from the Potosí mine in Bolivia and gold looted by the Conquistadors helped finance the Spanish empire.

Karl Marx approved: 'the question ... is not whether the English had a right to conquer India, but whether we are to prefer India conquered by the Turk, by the Persian, by the Russian, to India conquered by the Briton'.[2] While recognising that the East India Company was exploiting Indian markets and labour, Marx argued that capitalism would transform the subcontinent. India would benefit from the fruits of the Industrial Revolution. It was a sentiment worthy of George MacDonald Fraser, creator of the fictional illustrious Victorian soldier Sir Harry Paget Flashman, who regarded the British empire as the greatest thing that ever happened to an undeserving world.[3]

The link between earthly power and spiritual glory provided justification for colonial conquest: 'It amounted to a theory of cultural destiny – that the European maritime nations were destined to bring Christianity and civilisation to a pagan and savage world, and their reward was to be the wealth and riches which the indigenous populations themselves were incapable of appreciating and valuing.'[4]

After World War II, many colonies gained independence. In his landmark 'tryst with destiny' speech on 14 August 1947, the post-independence Indian prime minister, Jawaharlal Nehru, voiced the aspirations of all former colonies. He spoke of freedom and the hopes for a future shaped by an emancipated native population.[5] The reality would not live up to these lofty expectations. A combination of casual indifference and malicious design created nation states whose borders ignored important historical, ethnic, tribal, religious and economic differences. It set the stage for frequently violent sectarian conflicts in a number of countries in Asia, Africa and the Middle East, which continue to this day. This impeded development, as political and economic resources were diverted to resolving disputes.

Many newly independent nations did not have the infrastructure, political and social institutions, or skilled workers necessary to administer the new states, a situation that often reflected a lack of nation-building by the colonisers. Most liberated colonies remained dependent on foreign nations for capital, technology, skills, and markets for their products. Developed nations carefully controlled innovation and intellectual property, to capture a substantial share of any commerce. The colonisers did not offer recompense for what in some cases amounted to centuries of looting or exploitation.

*

In the 1980s, facing stagnation, developed countries deregulated domestically. They looked to emerging nations for new opportunities, liberalising trade and capital movement. The re-emergence of Russia, India and especially China, three of the BRICS countries, was central to the rise of developing markets.

The Soviet Union, 'Upper Volta with rockets', collapsed under the weight of the unsustainable cost of the Cold War and a corrupt, inefficient central planning system.[6] President Mikhail Gorbachev's policies of *glasnost* (openness), *perestroika* (restructuring), *demokratizatsiya* (democratisation), and *uskoreniye* (acceleration of economic development) failed. Praised by foreigners but unpopular at home, Gorbachev later confessed to having hugely underestimated the depth of the problems. Slowly and painfully, Russia emerged from the detritus, adopting a more market-based economy and elements of democratic government. Development of its immense energy and mineral resources helped its economic recovery.

A bankrupt India was forced to reform, and to alter the failed, half-baked socialist policies and Soviet central-planning models admired by Jawaharlal Nehru. The economy expanded at a feeble rate of 3–4 percent per annum, and income rises were 1–2 percent annually, jokingly referred to as the Hindu rate of growth. In 1991, with remaining reserves only sufficient to cover foreign exchange payments for less than two weeks, the Indian central bank was humiliatingly forced to airlift 47 tonnes of gold to the Bank of England as collateral for a loan, while awaiting assistance from the IMF. In July the minister of finance, Manmohan Singh, told parliament that India could not continue to live on borrowed money. It no longer had any time or room for manoeuvre.

India passed a reformist budget, devalued the rupee, and opened the door to limited foreign investment. These actions paved the way for the economy to quadruple in size, growing at an average rate of about 7 percent per annum and over 9 percent from 2005 to 2007. Mr Singh quoted French author Victor Hugo: 'No power on earth can stop an idea whose time has come.'[7] The emergence of India as a major economic power seemed within reach.

Under Deng Xiaoping, leader of the Communist Party from 1978, China implemented *Gaige Kaifang* (Reforms and Openness), a program of domestic social, political and economic policy changes combining socialism and elements of the market economy. It reversed the traditional policy of self-reliance and a lack of interest in trade. Over the next three decades, China emerged as a major global economy, with average annual growth rates of more than 9 percent. Chinese living standards doubled every decade for thirty years, a greater rate of growth than the US, whose living standards only doubled approximately every thirty years, when it was experiencing its fastest growth. Dazzled commentators saw China as a miracle.

Progress was not uniform or consistent. In 1997/98 the Asian monetary crisis struck. In 1998 Russia defaulted on its debt. But the economies recovered, entering what would prove to be a golden age for emerging markets.

*

The development model was based on Russian-born economic historian Alexander Gerschenkron's theories, which were the basis of Germany and Japan's postwar economic recovery. It relied on exports and investment financed by domestic savings. Resource-rich nations used revenues from mineral exports to accelerate development. Reform of the economy and deregulation of key sectors played a part.

Growth was made easier by the low starting point. Even after several decades of expansion, the GDP per capita for China, India, Brazil and Russia is around US$7000, US$1500, US$11,000 and US$15,000 respectively. In comparison, GDP per capita for the US, Japan, Germany, UK and Australia is in the range of US$40,000–$60,000.

Favourable demographics and a growing workforce also assisted growth. Urbanisation and industrialisation helped mobilise a previously unemployed or under-utilised workforce. Investment improved underdeveloped industrial capacity, infrastructure and capital stock, transforming the economy. Development was financed by high levels of domestic savings. From the 1990s, debt-fuelled growth in developed economies, based on low interest rates and low oil prices, created strong demand for exports from emerging markets. This, combined with the relocation and outsourcing of production to low-cost emerging nations, drove expanding activity.

In colonial times, raw materials generally moved from the colonies to the colonisers, with a balancing flow of manufactured products in the opposite direction. Now, this flow was reversed. Emerging nations combined their cheap labour and local or imported resources with foreign technology or capital to manufacture and export goods and services to developed countries. Improvements in technology, telecommunications and transport allowed cheaper emerging nations to compete with advanced economies. One-off events were important. The Y2K software problems fuelled the development of India's software industry.

The new economy was centred on China, now the world's factory, exporting around 50 percent of its output. It imported resources and parts that were then assembled or processed and shipped out again. Smaller emerging economies, especially in Asia, became integrated into new Sino-centric global supply chains. Consultant David Rothkopf highlighted the uneven balance of power within emerging markets: 'Without China, the BRICs are just the BRI, a bland, soft cheese that is primarily known for the whine [sic] that goes with it ...'[8]

China was now the largest purchaser of iron ore and other metals, and one of the biggest purchasers of cotton and soybeans. It produced more than half the world's steel and cement. Between 1990 and 2010 its share of world coal consumption increased from 24 percent to 50 percent, doubling coal prices. In the same period, China's share of world oil consumption increased from 3 percent to 10 percent, pressuring oil prices. Miners in Brazil, Russia, South Africa, Australia and Canada benefited from higher prices and volumes.

Chinese savings and foreign exchange reserves financed developed countries, especially their governments. China exported savings of around US$400 billion each year, helping reduce interest rates in the US by as much as 1 percent per annum. Its role as an exporter of capital was surprising because China was much poorer than the countries it financed. Its average income per capita was well below that of the US and Europe, and the latter possessed around five times more fixed capital, along with greater human capital and intellectual property wealth.

The strategy of attracting foreign investment with cheap labour benefited from competition between the emerging nations. Rising costs in Japan, South Korea, Taiwan, Hong Kong and Singapore led to businesses shifting to China. Higher costs in China led to relocation in Bangladesh, Sri Lanka, Cambodia, Vietnam and Myanmar.

Lower costs were also based on minimal regulation, frequently entailing inadequate protection of workers and the environment.

Even where regulations existed, they were rarely enforced. During the Cold War, West German businesses disposed of toxic waste in East Germany, where dumps were unregulated and cheap. After 1990, when West Germany's environmental laws were applied to the unified nation, repairing the environmental damage proved expensive. Emerging markets followed writer Bertolt Brecht's observation in *The Threepenny Opera* that eating takes precedence over morality.

Emerging market growth led to improved living standards, at least for some. As momentum increased, foreign businesses invested to take advantage of the growth and rising spending power of a nascent middle class. Opportunities encouraged nationals living, studying and working in advanced economies to return to their native lands, as Deng Xiaoping had predicted: 'When our thousands of Chinese students abroad return home, you will see how China will transform itself.'

Expansion brought hubris. An editorial in an official Chinese publication boasted: 'High-level figures from the Western political and economic spheres ... envy China's superb performance ... as well as "China's spirit" – the kind of solid, unbreakable "Great Wall" at heart ...'[9]

Much ink was spilt over culture, values, and the merits of different political systems. Just before the 1997/98 Asian crisis, one author saw the 88-storey Petronas Twin Towers in Kuala Lumpur as symbolic of Asia's emergence, but the building's height was uneconomic, being largely taken up by elevator shafts necessitated by its height. Foreigners were dazzled by Indonesian President Habibie's unrealised plans for the world's highest tower. Designed as a leaning building, it was impractical, as it would have been difficult to install elevators.

In Noël Coward's play *Private Lives*, when asked about China, the character Elyot Chase can only describe it as very big. Foreign understanding of emerging markets was more surface than depth.

*

The unprecedented synchronised recession in developed economies following the GFC triggered a sharp slowdown in emerging markets, contradicting the decoupling hypothesis. After 2009 emerging markets were forced to rely on double-digit annual increases in the supply of credit to restore growth.

Responding to lay-offs of 20–25 million internal migrant workers in export-oriented Guangdong province alone, and threats to social stability, China led the way with massive stimuli. The fiscal measures were modest, equating to a budget deficit of around 2.2 percent. The policy banks, which were majority government owned and controlled, were directed to extend credit and to finance infrastructure projects on a large scale. If additional credit growth over and above normal lending is taken into account, then the Chinese government's stimulus package totalled around 15 percent of GDP, amongst the largest in the world.

Domestic credit expansion was augmented by foreign capital inflows. Loose monetary policies in developed countries encouraged capital inflows into emerging markets in search of higher returns. Banks, awash with liquidity, lent to emerging markets; international pension funds, investment managers, central banks and sovereign wealth funds increased their investment in them. The effect of capital inflows was exacerbated by the small size of the local financial markets. A 1 percent increase in portfolio allocation by US pension funds and insurers equates to around us$500 billion, much more than emerging markets could absorb easily.

Foreign ownership of emerging market debt increased sharply. In Asia foreigners hold 30–50 percent of Indonesian-rupiah government bonds, up from less than 20 percent at the end of 2008 and approximately 40 percent of government debt in Malaysia and the Philippines. Capital inflows drove sharp falls in borrowing costs. Brazilian US-dollar-denominated bond yields fell from above 25 percent in 2002 to a record-low 2.5 percent in 2012. After averaging about 7 percent for the period 2003–11, Turkish US-dollar-denominated bond yields fell to a record-low 3.17 percent in November 2012. The rate on Indonesian US-dollar-denominated bonds fell to a record-low 2.84 percent. Local currency interest rates in most emerging markets also fell.

Desperate for yield, investors turned to debt issued by less well known emerging market borrowers. In 2013 Rwanda, a country remembered mainly for a horrific genocidal civil war, issued ten-year bonds to raise US$400 million, around 5 percent of its GDP. Attracted by the 6.875 percent coupon, investor demand was 9–10 times the issue size. Other African issuers included Nigeria, Zambia, Tanzania, Kenya and Mozambique. Asian borrowers from Sri Lanka and Bangladesh also raised cheap money, despite the often speculative nature of the issuer. Demand was helped by the fact that the performance of investment funds is generally assessed against specified benchmarks. Where a bond is included in a major bond index, investors must purchase the relevant securities to avoid the fund's returns varying markedly from that on their relevant benchmark. These index tourists generally did not understand the risk of what they were blithely buying with other people's money.

Prices of other assets, particularly real estate, also rose sharply. The attraction of emerging markets was higher growth rates and better prospects. Investors ignored many issuers' reliance on foreign aid, their volatile commodity export revenues, their political instability and poor governance.

*

In May 2013 improving American economic conditions raised the prospect of the 'taper' – in effect, winding back the US Fed's liquidity

injections. The effect on emerging markets was immediate, with interest rates rising in response to the 1 percent increase in US government
bond rates. As investors shifted money back into developed economies,
especially the US, the Brazilian real, Indian rupee, Russian rouble,
Turkish lira, Indonesia rupiah, Malaysian ringgit, Thai baht and South
African rand all fell by between 7 and 18 percent. The ability to raise
debt declined and borrowing costs increased. Brazilian, Turkish and
Indonesian US-dollar-denominated bond yields rose from record low
levels to around 5–6 percent. Emerging market central banks, excluding China's, saw outflows of reserves of around US$80 billion (around
2 percent of total reserves). Indonesia and Turkey lost around 14 percent of central bank reserves. India lost around 6 percent.

The capital outflows exacerbated concerns about slowing growth
in emerging markets. James Lord, a currency analyst at investment
bank Morgan Stanley, popularised the term 'fragile five' to describe
the major vulnerable emerging economies. The term BRICS was now
supplanted by BIITS, for the five most vulnerable economies: Brazil,
India, Indonesia, Turkey and South Africa.

Like an outgoing tide revealing the treacherous rocks that lie hidden when the water level is high, slowing growth and the withdrawal
of capital exposed deep-seated problems, especially high debt levels,
reliance on foreign financing, unacknowledged bad loans made by
banks, and external and internal imbalances.

*

Since 2008, new borrowing in emerging markets has risen significantly. By 2014 total Chinese debt was US$28 trillion (282 percent of
GDP), higher than comparable levels in the US, Canada, Germany
and Australia. In comparison, China's debt was US$7 trillion (158 per-
cent of GDP) in 2007, and US$2 trillion (121 percent of GDP) in 2000.
This increase in debt of US$21 trillion since 2007 is approximately

one-third of the total rise in global debt over the period. South Korea, Malaysia, Indonesia, India, Thailand, Brazil, South Africa, and a number of Eastern European nations, like Hungary and Poland, also showed significant increases in debt, which was at levels considered high for developing nations.

Belying the country's reputation for thrift, Chinese household debt has also risen sharply, nearly quadrupling since 2007, from US$1 trillion to US$3.8 trillion. Mortgage debt has grown by 21 percent per year, in parallel to a 60 percent rise in urban property prices since 2008.

During the same period, consumer credit grew strongly in Brazil and many Asian countries. Under Brazil's *parcelas* (instalments) culture, cars, consumer goods, holidays, plastic surgery and funerals were available on credit. In Malaysia and Thailand it increased to around 80 percent of GDP, up sharply from the levels in 2007. In Thailand debt payments were equivalent to over 33 percent of income, roughly double that of the US's before the GFC. While economic growth is strongly linked to rising consumer credit, higher borrowing by lower-income households adds vulnerability.

Many corporations in China, South Korea, India and Brazil are highly leveraged. Chinese corporate debt, at 125 percent of GDP (over US$12 trillion), is amongst the highest in the world. Many emerging market corporations are overextended, with inadequate cash flow to meet interest and principal payments, especially in a weak economic environment.

Other than China and India, government debt levels are not high in emerging markets. However, state involvement in banks and industry means that the effective level of government obligation is understated. Brazil's BNDES, a state-owned development bank, and Caixa Econômica Federal, a consumer bank, have rapidly increased lending, which has often been government-subsidised.

Several benchmarks are used to assess a country's indebtedness.

An increase in debt of around 30 percent of GDP in a period of five years or less is a harbinger of problems. Since 2009, China has experienced an expansion in debt well above these levels. Less rapid growth in credit in Japan in the late 1980s, South Korea in the 1990s, as well as the US and UK in the early 2000s, resulted in serious financial crises. A separate measure of debt sustainability is the credit gap – the difference between increases in private-sector credit growth and economic output. Countries with large credit gaps experience a subsequent rapid slowdown in growth. In China the credit gap since 2008 has been over 70 percent of GDP. A further measure of debt levels is the national debt servicing ratio – the amount of GDP needed to make payments on borrowings. A reading above 20–25 percent frequently indicates heightened risk. China's debt servicing ratio is 30 percent of GDP, with around 11 percent for interest payments and 19 percent to repay the principal.

Lending practices and risk assessment in emerging economies are frequently weak. Quasi-government bank officials finance grand vanity projects with dubious economics sponsored by politically connected businesses and elites. In Brazil the collapse of former billionaire Eike Batista, who was close to the government, resulted in large losses to lenders and investors.

Emerging market debt is often secured over land and property, whose values are dependent on the continued supply of credit and strong economic growth. Around 50 percent of the loans to corporations in China are real-estate-related. A high proportion of debt is short-term. As few borrowers have sufficient operating cash flow to repay loans, new borrowings are needed to retire old ones. With a significant proportion of the new debt needed to merely repay the existing one, the amount of borrowing needs to constantly increase, to maintain economic growth. The requirement for regular refinancing exacerbates the risk.

Historically, borrowers in emerging markets were forced to borrow in foreign currencies, due to the lack of local debt markets. However, development of new funding sources following previous emerging market crises means that companies can now borrow in the local currency, reducing exposure to foreign exchange movements. Nevertheless, emerging market borrowers still have significant foreign currency loans, usually to benefit from lower interest rates.

Loan losses are frequently hidden by an officially sanctioned policy of restructuring potential non-performing loans. In China, loans to various local-government financing vehicles and state owned or sponsored enterprises have been extended, despite doubt about the ability of the borrower to meet their obligations. Bad and restructured loans at Indian state banks have reached about 12 percent of total assets, doubling since 2009. Chinese and Indian authorities subscribe to the theory that a rolling loan gathers no loss.

*

Short-term foreign capital inflows have masked underlying problems in external accounts, such as the balance between exports and imports and the shortfall between earnings on foreign investments and payments made to foreign investors. India, Brazil, South Africa and Turkey are especially reliant on overseas financing.

The current account surplus of emerging economies has fallen to 1 percent of their combined GDP, from around 5 percent in 2006. The real deterioration is greater, as the large trade surpluses of China and energy exporters distort the overall result. The falls reflect slow growth in export markets, lower commodity prices, higher food and energy import costs, and domestic consumption driven by excessive credit growth.

Many emerging countries have poor public finances, with spending outstripping taxes. In recent years India's federal and state

governments have consistently run a combined public sector deficit of up to 9–10 percent of GDP, including off-balance-sheet items.
The problem of large budget deficits is compounded by poorly targeted subsidies for fertiliser, food and petroleum. Subsidies affect
long-term growth and distort consumption and production as well
as the distribution of resources. They divert funds from other government spending, such as infrastructure, education and healthcare. Weak
safety nets make it difficult to shield the poor from changes in subsidy
arrangements. Political sensitivities make reform difficult and slow.

Emerging countries require around us$1.5 trillion annually in
external funding to meet financing needs, including maturing debt.
A deteriorating financing environment combined with falling currency reserves, reduced cover for imports and short-term borrowings,
declining currencies and diminished economic prospects increases the
vulnerability of emerging nations.

The problems of debt are compounded by mal-investment. Many
projects funded with borrowed money are not viable, making it
unlikely that they will be able to meet repayments.

Investment is focused on large-scale infrastructure and property.
China has made substantial investments in super-fast trains, new airports, roads, heavy industries, such as steel, as well as residential and
commercial property. Stories, some apocryphal, about wasteful expenditure abound. The value of unfinished properties is more than 20 percent
of GDP. At one stage, the ghost city of Kangbashi in Inner Mongolia
had enough unoccupied apartments to shelter a million people, about
four times its population. Tianjin, about a half-hour by high-speed
train south-east of Beijing, has invested more than us$160 billion to
create a world financial centre, almost three times the amount spent
on China's Three Gorges Dam. Changde, a city of 6 million in Hunan
province in southern China, borrowed more than us$130 million to
finance, amongst other things, an international marathon course.

Sinophiles argue that China lacks necessary infrastructure. They dismiss the inadequate financial return on capital invested. They blame it on falling growth rates due to low global demand, assuming that the world economy will rebound strongly, increasing the returns. They argue that investment in infrastructure will produce long-term economic benefits from increased productivity. They point to the fact that few investment programs of social infrastructure are profitable. The mid-nineteenth-century boom in investment in railways in Western countries generated economic benefits, but few made an adequate financial return, with many going bankrupt.

But the specific projects may be inappropriate. China has six of the world's ten longest bridges and the world's fastest train, while 40 percent of villages lack paved roads to the nearest market town. High-speed rail lines in China may provide social returns, raising the quality of life for those who can afford to use them, and they may be appealing to politicians and demagogues advertising Chinese technical proficiency, but investment in improvements to ordinary train lines and rural roads, and a greater focus on safety and more flexible pricing structures may have yielded higher economic benefits.

Trophy projects, such as the 2008 Beijing Olympics (costing US$40 billion), Russia's 2014 Sochi Winter Olympics (US$51 billion), and Brazil's 2014 football World Cup (US$14 billion) and 2016 Olympics (budgeted at US$14 billion), absorb scarce resources at the expense of essential transport, health and education infrastructure.

China's investment boom also exacerbates industrial overcapacity, which averages around 20–30 percent for industries such as steel, aluminium, cement, chemicals, refining, and wind power. As at 2015, mainland car factories can build around 10 million more vehicles than will be sold domestically. In property, China has 70 million units under construction or in inventory, compared to 1.2 million new homes in the US at the height of its real-estate bubble.

It would take decades for China to absorb this excess capacity, which in many cases will become obsolete before it can be utilised. Yet China continues to add capacity to maintain growth. If it is unable to absorb this new capacity domestically, it might seek to increase exports to maintain production and growth. This would exacerbate global supply gluts and increase deflationary pressures in the global economy.

Credit intensity – the amount of debt needed to create additional economic activity – has risen. The incremental capital-output ratio (ICOR), calculated as annual investment divided by the annual increase in GDP, measures investment efficiency. China's ICOR has more than doubled since the 1980s, reflecting the marginal nature of new investment. China now needs around US$3–5 to generate US$1 of additional economic growth; some economists put it even higher at US$6–8. This is an increase from the US$1–2 needed for each dollar of growth 8–10 years ago, consistent with declining investment returns. Debt-fuelled investment in emerging markets created economic growth, but in the medium- to long-term it will result in rising bad debts and financial problems.

*

Unaddressed structural deficiencies now impede expansion in emerging economies, many of which are narrowly based, often depending on commodity exports. Arizona Senator John McCain called Russia 'a gas station masquerading as a country', highlighting its dependence on oil and gas.[10] South America's debt-fuelled, consumption-driven economies were underwritten by a small, productive natural resources sector and high commodity prices. Chinese demand for iron ore and soybeans hid Brazil's weaknesses.

While China has over-invested, other emerging countries lack essential infrastructure. In critical sectors like power, transport and utilities, India is plagued by significant shortages. In 2012 it suffered a loss of electrical power that affected over 600 million people. Political pressure to keep utility prices low impedes cost recovery and discourages investment. Structural problems and difficulties with previous projects have made foreign investors cautious, creating a shortage of foreign capital for investment in infrastructure.

Labour costs in emerging markets are rising, reducing their competitiveness. In 2013 South African miners commenced ongoing industrial action for a living wage, disrupting production and increasing costs.

While the workforce in emerging markets is young and growing, it is constrained by a lack of skills. A dysfunctional Indian public education system means that 40 percent of students do not complete school. Forty percent of the workforce is illiterate. India's overall adult literacy rate is 66 percent, compared to 93 percent for China. Some universities, especially the sixteen Indian institutes of technology, are world-class, but their limited capacity means there are significant shortages of graduates, increasing labour costs. And while university students in emerging economies are practised at passing examinations, employers have to invest heavily to make them job-ready. The best students travel overseas for foreign qualifications, frequently preferring to remain and work there, where the rewards are greater. There are also cultural issues. In 2010 India's *Business Today* published a story entitled 'Brats at Work', complaining about the attitude of young workers. China's one-child family policy has produced generations of spoilt princes and princesses.

Environmental damage and industrial pollution are particularly problematic in developing nations. In 2015, when US President Barack Obama spent three days in India's capital, New Delhi, one of the most polluted cities on the planet, medical experts calculated that inhaling the world's most toxic air could reduce his expected lifespan by roughly six hours, the equivalent of smoking eight cigarettes per day throughout his lifetime. Shortly after the visit, the Indian government announced a 25 percent reduction in spending on the environment.

For the 2014 Asia-Pacific Economic Cooperation summit in Beijing, the hosts shut factories and suspended the use of private cars to provide visiting leaders with autumn-blue skies instead of the city's customary toxic smog. The cost of air pollution in China is estimated at around 10 percent of GDP. Research into the effects of air pollution on lifespan shows that people in northern China and India live, respectively, over five and three years shorter on average. Poor air quality in China has led to the phenomenon of lung-washing tourism, where citizens drive for several hours so as to be able to breathe cleaner air.

There are 'governance issues' in these economies, a polite term covering endemic corruption, kleptocracy, misuse of funds and lack of institutional controls. In 2014 Petrobras, the partially government-owned Brazilian oil company and one the world's largest energy businesses, was involved in a vast corruption scandal. In 'Operation Car Wash', Brazil's ruling PT party was alleged to have diverted company funds to pay off politicians and businesses to maintain power. Petrobras was forced to book US$17 billion in losses arising from the allegations and impairment charges partly related to delays on corruption-affected refinery projects in 2014. Ironically, when Petrobras announced the discovery of the Lula oil field, the PT revived a 1953 nationalist slogan: 'The oil is ours'. The corruption scandal cast a different light on the exact meaning of that statement.

Some Indian businessmen resemble nineteenth-century American robber barons, using corrupt means to acquire influence over politicians. They have improperly secured rich natural resources, especially land and minerals, and ensured favourable regulations and restricted competition, especially foreign competition, wherever possible. The unauthorised biography of Dhirubhai Ambani, the founder of India's

Reliance Industries, euphemistically notes his skill at 'managing the environment'.

Bribery is commonplace, frequently justified by inadequate salaries of politicians and public officials. Historian Ramachandra Guha tells of the burglary of the prominent Indian politician in the 1960s, in which the miscreant got away with a gold sovereign and 800 rupees (about US$15). Today, the haul might be better.

In China, businesses are frequently forced to pay 10–25 percent of the value of contracts in 'commissions' to politicians and bureaucrats. President Xi Jinping's administration sought to tackle the problem. It published an infidelity map as part of the campaign to root out corrupt Chinese government officials, simultaneously disposing of political opponents and consolidating the new regime's power.

Income inequality, excessive concentration of economic power in heavily subsidised state corporations or business oligarchies, as well as political rigidities and instability increasingly compound economic problems. The population in developing countries is also ageing rapidly, as a result of declining fertility rates and specific measures, such as China's one-child policy. The population structure in China requires each child to support two parents and four grandparents. These countries will become old before they become rich.

*

Despite progress, incomes in emerging markets remain modest by developing-country standards. The World Bank defines middle-income economies as those where per capita income is between US$1095 and US$12,775, equivalent to US$3 and US$35 per day.

An entry-level employee in a state-owned Indian bank earns about US$1.70 an hour, or US$4200 a year. The chief executive earns about US$11–14 per hour, or US$32,000–$40,000 annually, excluding the car, the driver and free housing they also receive. The average employee in one of China's five largest state-controlled banks earns an average of US$27,200 in salary, bonuses and benefits. Private-sector counterparts in both countries earn more. In contrast, a US worker at a fast-food outlet in Los Angeles receives the minimum wage of US$11 an hour plus a mandatory US$5 for healthcare benefits, for a total of US$16. This equates to an annual income of around US$33,000.

Many emerging markets are caught in the middle-income trap, a phenomenon where countries experience a slowdown in economic growth when GDP per capita reaches around US$15,000. The necessary rebalancing to shift to the next level of development is difficult. China, which needs to move away from investment to greater consumption to drive economic activity, provides an example of the policy dilemmas. Chinese consumption totals around 35–40 percent of China's GDP, a decrease from over 50 percent in 1980. Even by the prudent standards of Asia, Chinese consumption is low. In contrast, Chinese fixed investment is around 46 percent of GDP, having increased from 34 percent over the last decade. At a comparable stage of their economic development, fixed investment in Japan and South Korea was around 10–20 percent lower than in China. While China's consumption has grown, it has increased slower than the overall economy and investment.

Low spending is driven by a high savings rate necessitated by weak welfare safety nets; poor public health, education, retirement and aged care systems; as well as policies suppressing consumption and restricting income growth. Ironically, the need to save is the result of earlier reforms whereby Chinese workers lost their 'iron rice bowl' – state-guaranteed job security, a steady income, and benefits, including healthcare and education.

Finding a way to increase consumption is difficult. Large increases in wages would reduce export competitiveness. Large-scale social programs would strain public finances, necessitating higher tax rates. Greater consumption would reduce the high saving levels, which provide state-owned banks with deposits that can be used, as required, by the central government to drive economic growth and avoid a banking crisis. The low interest rate paid on deposits, set well below inflation, allows banks to earn substantial profits from the large margin between the rate at which they borrow and lend. The resulting high profits are then available to absorb losses on poor quality loans that cannot be serviced or paid back. The low returns on savings equate to a transfer of wealth to banks and borrowers from households, amounting to as much as 5 percent of GDP each year.

In the short run, continued mal-investment and the deferring of bad debt write-offs provide the illusion of robust economic activity. Over time, increasing amounts of capital and resources are tied up in unproductive investments, locking the economy into a lower growth path with the risk of a destabilising crash. The purchasing power of household savings falls. Wealth levels are reduced by a decline in the prices of overvalued assets. Businesses and borrowers find that their earnings, and the value of their overpriced collateral, are below the levels required to meet outstanding liabilities.

*

Crisis-weary policymakers dismiss the risk of an emerging market crisis, echoing former US Secretary of State Henry Kissinger: 'There cannot be a crisis next week. My schedule is already full.'[11]

The taper shock of 2013 (which came to be known as the taper tantrum), when US Fed chairman Ben Bernanke mused about tightening monetary policy, proved short-lived. The fragile five recovered relatively quickly. But in 2014 a stronger dollar, rising borrowing costs, withdrawal of capital, and lower commodity prices, which adversely affected emerging market exporters of raw materials, triggered a new round of instability.

There are striking resemblances to the 1990s. Then, loose monetary

policies pursued by the US Fed and Bank of Japan led to large capital
inflows into emerging markets, especially Asia. In 1994 Fed chairman Alan Greenspan withdrew liquidity, resulting in a doubling of
US interest rates over twelve months, triggering crises in Mexico and
elsewhere in Latin America. It precipitated the 1997/98 Asian monetary crisis, requiring IMF bailouts for Indonesia, South Korea and
Thailand. Asia took over a decade to recover from the economic losses.
Many now fear a rerun.

The basic dynamics of an emerging market crisis are familiar.
Weaknesses in the real economy and financial vulnerabilities will rapidly feed each other. Even if the reduction of central bank injections of
money in developed economies is slow or deferred, the current account
deficits, weak public finances, inadequate investment returns and high
debt levels will prove problematic.

Capital withdrawals will cause currency weakness, which in turn
will drive falls in the prices of bonds, stocks and property. Decreased
availability of finance and higher funding costs will increase pressure
on overextended borrowers, triggering banking problems that feed
back into the real economy. Credit-rating and investment downgrades
will extend the cycle through repeated iterations.

Fundamental domestic weaknesses and a slow external environment limit policy options. Responses may compound the problems.
Central bank currency purchases, money market intervention or capital controls will reduce reserves or accelerate capital outflow. Higher
interest rates, if used to support the currency and counter imported
inflation, will reduce growth, exacerbating the problems of high debt.
In 2013 India, Indonesia, Thailand, Brazil, Peru and Turkey were
forced to implement some of these measures.

A weaker currency will affect the prices of staples – food, cooking oil and petrol. Subsidies to allow lower prices will weaken public
finances. Support of the financial system and the broader economy

will further pressure government balance sheets.

Some economists argue that there are differences between 1997 and 2015. Vulnerabilities, such as fixed exchange rates, low foreign exchange reserves, and foreign currency debt, have been addressed, reducing the risk of the familiar emerging market death spiral. But they may be overoptimistic.

While local currency debt has increased, levels of foreign currency debt are significant. Since 2008, the amount of US-dollar-denominated borrowing by entities, excluding financial institutions, outside America has increased by 50 percent and now stands above US$9 trillion. Emerging market borrowers constitute around half this amount, a significant increase over the period. Borrowings by Chinese firms have increased to more than US$1 trillion, a rise of over 500 percent. Brazil, India and Turkey also have significant outstanding US-dollar loans. Many borrowers are unhedged, with the currency of revenues and debts not being matched. Twenty-five percent of China's corporate debt is US-dollar-denominated, versus 9 percent of earnings. The problem is compounded for oil or commodity businesses by the fall in prices, which reduces revenue and cash flow. Weakness of the local currency as the US dollar strengthens will result in losses.

Where the debt is denominated in local currency, foreign ownership is significant, especially in Malaysia, Indonesia, Mexico, Poland, Turkey and South Africa. Currency weakness will cause foreign investors to exit, to avoid foreign exchange losses, increasing borrowing costs and decreasing funding availability.

Changes may slow the onset of the crisis, but real economy and financial fragility mean that the risks are still high. Speaking about the 1994 Mexican crisis, economist Rudiger Dornbusch identified the trajectory: 'the crisis takes a much longer time coming than you think, and then it happens much faster than you would have thought'.[12]

*

Western policymakers deny any role in the problems facing emerging markets, arguing that their policies were beneficial. But developed economies now face serious economic blowback. Since 2008, emerging markets have contributed up to 70 percent of global economic growth. A slowdown will rapidly affect developed economies. Demand for their exports, which have boosted economic activity, will decrease. Profits of multinational businesses will fall as revenue from overseas operations declines. Investment losses will affect pension funds, investment managers and individual investors. Loan defaults and trading losses will affect international banks active in emerging markets.

Emerging markets have over US$7 trillion in foreign exchange reserves, invested primarily in US, Japanese, European and UK government securities. If emerging market central banks move to sell holdings to support their weak currencies or domestic economies, then the rise in interest rates will result in immediate large losses to holders, compounding the result of the reduction of monetary stimulus. It will also increase financial stress, adversely affecting the fragile recovery in developed economies.

Emerging market currency weakness will place upward pressure on major currencies, especially the US dollar. This will erode improvements in cost structures, and competitiveness engineered through currency devaluation by low interest rates and QE, truncating any recovery.

In reality, developed economies have sought to export more than goods and services, shifting the burden of adjustment necessitated by the GFC onto emerging economies. Like two people who cannot swim, developed nations and emerging markets are clinging to each other for support, and may drown together.

*

By 2014 the BRICS' economic growth had slowed from its earlier stellar levels, though it remained above that of developed countries. As economic fortunes changed, the idea of global economic power shifting from America to emerging markets faded.

Predictions about American decline are not new. In 1961, before he became US Secretary of State, Henry Kissinger argued that the US 'cannot afford another decline like that which has characterized the past decade and a half ... [Only] self-delusion can keep us from admitting our decline to ourselves.'[13] In 1979 *Japan As Number One* was one of the year's bestselling books. Japan collapsed in 1989 and has never recovered. In the 1990s America was going to be replaced by the Asian Tigers, which crashed in 1997/98 and have only recently recovered to pre-crisis levels. Predictions of a Chinese or BRICS century may also be similarly premature.

In 2011 Michael Beckley, a former Harvard research fellow, concluded that, based on various indicators, far from declining in relative terms, America was economically, technologically and militarily more powerful compared to China than it was in 1991.[14] Like previous empires, such as the British, the US has crafted a unique position built on advantages in its economic power, global finance, military capability and its geopolitical role.

The US economy remains the largest in the world and Americans on a per capita basis remain relatively wealthy. American dominance of key industries makes it an indispensable monopolist. Half of the world's twenty largest listed companies are based in the US. The lack of substitute suppliers and high switching costs ensure markets for American products. Its economy is substantially self-contained, insulating the country from international volatility. Its debt levels, while high, are below that of many other developed countries. Increased energy independence and the dominance of the US dollar as the world's reserve currency provides America with great financial flexibility.

America remains a leader in science and technology. While the overall quality of its educational systems is far from exceptional, elite US universities are amongst the best in the world. The labour market is flexible, albeit at a high human cost. American entertainment, fashion and style remain influential. The US has favourable demographics and is still a magnet for immigration.

The country's pre-eminence is based on complex systems and processes that are difficult to replicate. A World Bank study estimated that 80 percent of its wealth derives from intangible assets, such as property rights, the judicial system, skills, and the knowledge and trust embedded within its society.

America's ability to reinvent itself and change is crucial. Faced with massive problems of low or slowing growth, a lack of competitiveness and excessive debt levels, Japan, Europe and many emerging nations have struggled to agree on and implement the required reforms. America's ability to tolerate failure is crucial. Few countries consider bankruptcy a normal step in the evolution of an entrepreneur or innovator.

The US also has the ability to export its attitudes and values, shaping global economic, financial and political agendas and choices. People throughout the world still aspire to an American way of life. In the 2004 documentary *Control Room* about the Arabic news channel Al Jazeera, a journalist is highly critical of US foreign policy as well as American ethics and morals. Yet, he confesses, if he had the chance to work in America, he would.

The GFC damaged America's economic position, but as an ageing Clint Eastwood gruffly stated in an advertisement for Chrysler cars shown during the US Super Bowl in 2011, 'It's half-time, America. And our second half is about to begin.'

*

In 2010 Jim O'Neill introduced a new acronym for favoured markets – CIVETS (Colombia, Indonesia, Vietnam, Egypt, Turkey and South Africa). A competitor coined the term MIST (Mexico, Indonesia, South Korea and Turkey). Online humorists manufactured other acronyms for attractive investment opportunities: one was ANARCHY (Albania, Nauru or North Korea, Afghanistan, Romania, Chad, Haiti and Yemen). In early 2011, as North Africa and the Middle East were rent apart by political uprisings, an anonymous blogger wrote that emerging market investors were hunting in the MIST for CIVETS with only BRICS.

Notwithstanding their long-term potential, emerging markets increasingly resembled Potemkin villages. In 2013 Goldman Sachs advised clients to reduce investments in these markets, arguing that the shift in global economic power had been overdramatised. Returns were less attractive and risks were higher than previously believed.

In 2014 slumping, oversupplied real-estate markets prompted embattled Chinese developers to try different approaches to entice buyers. These included attractive women dressed as imperial concubines, discounts for people who lost weight, and appeals to patriotism. The most novel involved the offer of 1000 free live chickens to prospective customers. After a desperate scramble by locals, only chicken feathers and a few lost shoes were left. It was an apt postscript to the latest instalment in the rise and fall of emerging markets.

ECONOMIC APARTHEID

The Impact of
Rising Inequality
on Growth

In 2014 Thomas Piketty, a French economics professor, had an unexpected bestseller with the English translation of *Capital in the Twenty-First Century*. Self-consciously evoking Karl Marx, the 700-page book analysed income and wealth distribution. Like *Casablanca*'s Captain Renault who was shocked to find that gambling was going on under his nose, the world appeared surprised that inequality was increasing and capitalism concentrates wealth over time.

Not everyone agreed with the conclusion. Two of the richest plutocrats on the planet, Bill and Melinda Gates, thought that conditions for the poor had improved, on the basis that they hardly saw any these days on their visits to big cities.[1]

*

Piketty's *Capital* traces historical changes in the distribution of income and wealth. It notes that in the eighteenth and nineteenth centuries, Western European society was highly unequal, with private wealth concentrated in the hands of a few rich families within a rigid class structure. In the period that followed, inequality was reduced by taxes, inflation, redistribution through the welfare state, and insolvencies resulting from the world wars and the Depression. But the trend has reversed in recent decades, ushering in the return of patrimonial capitalism. Based on his research, Professor Piketty derives his fundamental law of capitalism: where the rate of return to wealth (r) grows faster than economic output (g) (*r>g*), it leads to a concentration of wealth.

Echoing the controversy around Carmen Reinhart and Kenneth Rogoff, the *Financial Times* raised doubts about Piketty's data, suggesting errors and questionable selection and analysis. Corrected for these errors, they argued, the conclusions of rising wealth inequality were flawed. But irrespective of the accuracy of the data, interpreting and extrapolating from information spanning centuries, in countries with different economic and social structures, is inherently difficult.

The elegant *r>g* relationship does not withstand critical scrutiny. *Capital* is vague about the meaning of capital and the rate of return used. Despite some empirical support, Professor Piketty's claim that the annual rate of return on capital is a consistent 4–5 percent before tax is questionable. Increased accumulation of capital should reduce this return, as available money seeks investment opportunities. In 2015 a 26-year-old graduate, Matthew Rognlie, provided a damaging critique of Piketty's analysis. The assumed stability of return depends on the ability to replace labour with capital – the elasticity of substitution. If workers can be replaced by machines easily, then the return on capital remains stable. However, if substitutability is more difficult, then additional capital becomes harder to employ productively, with a resulting fall in return. Rognlie found that the concept of substitutability used by Piketty was flawed. Correctly calculated, Rognlie argued, labour cannot be substituted by capital to the extent assumed. Other than for housing, the share of national income flowing to owners of capital has remained relatively constant, rather than rising as implied by Piketty's work. Rising returns on housing may not increase inequality, as home ownership is more widespread than other investment.

Capital ignores why inequality matters, and the question of whether the cost of reducing it might outweigh any likely benefits. Professor Piketty proposed higher taxes, up to 80 percent on high incomes. He overlooked the fact that such policies in the 1960s and 1970s failed to correct inequality. Taxpayers simply relocated to lower tax jurisdictions, or avoided tax in other ways.

Notwithstanding the studied references to Jane Austen and Honoré de Balzac, the book's success is puzzling. The problems of rising inequality have been identified before, by economic historian Angus Maddison, World Bank economist Branko Milanović, James Galbraith and the University of Texas Inequality Project, and Richard Wilkinson and Kate Pickett in their book *The Spirit Level: Why Equality is Better for Everyone*. The French reaction to *Capital* was subdued. Its rapturous treatment in Anglo-Saxon territories has been less about the book than deep-seated anxiety about inequality. The book challenges the mythology central to liberal societies of an egalitarian meritocracy based on skill, hard work, entrepreneurship and competition.

*

As with GDP, measuring inequality is difficult. One measure is the Gini coefficient, developed by Italian statistician and sociologist Corrado Gini. A measure of zero represents perfect equality, with everyone having the same income, while a hundred represents perfect inequality, with one person receiving all the income. Another measure is concentration, which uses the percentage of income or wealth controlled by the top 1 percent of the population. Both measures indicate rising inequality.

The Gini coefficient for the world rose to 68 in 2005, from 49 in 1820. Based on the latest statistics, the US scored 41. Canada, Australia and New Zealand were measured at 34, 31 and 36 respectively. The UK, Germany, France and Italy scored 38, 31, 33 and 36. Japan came in at 38. Brazil, Russia, India, China and South Africa recorded 53, 40, 34, 37 and 65 respectively.[2]

The concentration of income indicates similar patterns of inequality to the Gini coefficient. In 2012 the top 1 percent of American households received around 19 percent of US income. The percentages for Canada, Australia and New Zealand were measured at 12, 9 and 8 respectively. The UK, Germany, France and Italy scored 13, 13, 8 and 9. Japan came in at 10.

Inequality increased significantly between 1980 and 2002. In the US since 1977, the top 1 percent of earners received 47 percent of all income growth. In Canada it was 37 percent. In Australia and Britain the top 1 percent received 20 percent of all income increases. In most developed countries the highest income earners are the only group to have enjoyed a rising share in incomes since the 1990s. In the US the concentration of income and wealth is at its highest level since the early twentieth century – the Gilded Age.

The ability of the affluent to avoid taxation, utilising offshore tax havens or other stratagems, may understate the true level of inequality. The 'Queen of Mean', wealthy hotel magnate Leona Helmsley, argued: 'Only the little people pay taxes.'[3]

Statistics are an imperfect guide to inequality. The new rich are the working rich – entrepreneurs, business executives, bankers, lawyers and technologists – rather than scions of landed gentry or rentiers living off accumulated wealth. At the other end of the scale, low-income families juggle cash to pay essential bills. They live precariously from payday to payday, with few savings, and rely on expensive borrowings to manage shortfalls.

In the 1980s playwright Arthur Miller staged his Pulitzer Prize-winning play *Death of a Salesman* in China. The local actors struggled to grasp the reasons for Willy Loman's dissatisfaction. After all he had a job, family, house, and the material trappings that ordinary Chinese could only dream of. Today, in developed countries, those living below the official poverty line have access not just to basic shelter and food, but stoves, refrigerators, microwaves, cars, TVs, telephones and the internet. Their lifespan, healthcare, education and choices of food and entertainment exceed those of the rich from a few centuries ago. In contrast, in underdeveloped countries, the poor have remained as wretched as those in antiquity.

*

The causes of inequality are many and varied. The conventional view is that strong economic growth reduces poverty and inequality. Between 1959 and 1973, US GDP per capita grew by 82 percent, halving the percentage of the population below the poverty line to 11 percent. A continuation of that relationship would have theoretically eliminated poverty in America by the late 1980s. Instead, despite growth of GDP per capita of 147 percent, the rate of poverty subsequently increased to around 12–15 percent. Globally, the experience was similar. Stagnant incomes, the changing labour market, debt, decreased economic mobility, and shifts in government policy all limited progress in reducing inequality.

There were minimal rises in average wages. After adjustment for inflation, the US minimum hourly wage, us\$5–11 depending on the state, has declined by nearly half over the last fifty years. UK wages have experienced similar stagnation. Real earnings everywhere have risen slowly. Income gains in countries like the US have come from working a greater number of hours, rather than improved rates of pay. In a weak labour market after the GFC, workers who lost a US$20 per hour job were forced to replace it with two or more US$7 per hour jobs.

The change reflected a shift in the proportion of wages to corporate profits. In developed countries over the last fifty years, labour's share of income decreased from 60–65 percent of GDP to around 50–60 percent. Globalisation, technological changes and reduced competition in many sectors helped increase corporations' share of income. Monopolistic innovations, oligopolistic market structures and industry influence over regulations and public policy allowed businesses to generate above-normal profits, known as economic rents. The highly concentrated US financial sector employs around 5 percent of the total workforce but earns around 15 percent of total corporate profits.

Income distribution within the workforce also changed. In 2007 the lowest 80 percent of the US workforce earned around 50 percent of total labour income, down from 60 percent in 1979. Globally, income was less evenly distributed in 2007 than in 1979. In a winner-take-all culture, a select group of superstar entertainers, athletes and celebrities earned astronomical incomes, exploiting technological innovations that gave them global reach. In a parallel development, superstar managers increased their earnings. Between 1979 and 2005, around 70 percent of increases in income accrued to the top 0.1 percent of workers.

In the 1950s the average US chief executive officer was paid around twenty times the typical employee. Currently, the pay ratio of a CEO to an average employee is in excess of 200 times. In 2011 Apple CEO Tim Cook was paid US$378 million in salary, stock, and other benefits, over 6000 times the earnings of an average Apple employee. At Walmart the CEO earned 900 times the earnings of a typical worker.

Deregulation, incentive-based remuneration, the use of equity options, managers' bargaining powers and their ability to convince remuneration committees of a shortage of talent all boosted compensation packages. Interlinked boards of directors (often former or current CEOs), consultants and other insiders approved each other's pay, in a display of corporate solidarity.

High executive compensation percolated down, with overpaid managers feeling obliged to engage equally overpaid bankers, lawyers and advisers. In the US and UK the rising earnings of financiers, especially in the period leading up to the GFC, contributed significantly to the increase in the share of income earned by the top 10 percent of the workforce. Financial sector employees were overpaid relative to skill by as much as 50 percent. The additional earnings were not related to the creation of genuine value or increased productivity. They were the result of greater risk-taking, underwritten by the government, in institutions that were seen as too big or too important to fail. In effect they were the beneficiaries of large, hidden transfers from other parts of society.

Increased international trade, improvements in transport and information technology, and the development of global supply chains further altered the structure of labour markets, increasing inequality. Businesses in developed economies lowered costs by outsourcing labour-intensive production to low-cost locations, retaining the more profitable operations requiring higher skills. This allowed the firms to increase their earnings at the expense of workers. Cheaper goods and services and increased consumer choice came at the cost of displaced workers in developed countries. While it helped improve living standards in emerging nations, the influx of around 1.5 billion additional workers into the global economy reduced the bargaining power of employees in developed markets, ushering in declines in real wages. Ironically, China's new socialism did not unite the workers of the world, but divided them, triggering 'the profoundest global reshuffle of people's economic positions since the Industrial Revolution'.[4]

Automation increased both corporate profits and income inequality. Apple's ubiquitous i-gadgets consist of components made in multiple countries and assembled in China, with the supply chain being managed in the US by Apple, which earns around 30–50 per-cent of the final price. The process favours skilled labour, reducing the share of revenue accruing to low-skilled workers. Similar complex and fragmented production processes apply to the products that constitute around 85 percent of global GDP.

This approach has created a rising wage premium for skilled labour and a growing number of poorly paid, insecure, low-skilled jobs. The process is exacerbated in developed economies by the shift from man-ufacturing to service industries, which are currently more difficult to relocate or automate. This has driven large declines in better paid manu-facturing and mid-level professional or service jobs. In 2012, amongst developed economies, the US had the highest share of relatively low-paying jobs, primarily in leisure, healthcare and hospitality. Over recent decades, these forces, combined with the decline in unionisation and the power of organised labour, increased income inequality.

*

The concentrated ownership of property, financial assets and invest-ments is linked to inequality. The share of passive income, such as interest, dividends, rents and profits, while volatile, has increased over time, relative to income from labour. In 2010 the wealthiest 10 percent of US households owned 70 percent of all wealth, while the top 1 per-cent owned 35 percent. The bottom 50 percent of households owned 5 percent. The richest eighty-five people in the world, which includes Bill Gates, Warren Buffett, Carlos Slim and Jack Ma, are wealthier than the poorest 3.5 billion people on the planet.

As *Capital* points out, marrying into money or being born to the right parents, thus ensuring a large inheritance, delivers greater wealth than a successful career. In a notable if probably fictitious exchange with fellow author F. Scott Fitzgerald, Ernest Hemingway succinctly captured this difference between the rich and poor: 'Yes, they have more money.'

Financialisation drove inequality. Trading in financial instruments allowed the affluent to further increase their wealth. Available collateral allows higher income households to borrow more easily. With the decline in interest rates since the mid-1980s, debt was used to boost the returns on stocks, bonds, property, and collectibles like art, owned primarily by the better off. In periods of high inflation, gains accrue where the assets purchased appreciate while the fixed debt is repaid with money that has fallen in purchasing power. In periods of minimal inflation, low interest rates allow leveraging of financial investments to enhance returns, where the asset's income is greater than the cost of borrowing.

In contrast, less well-off households used debt to survive or supplement disposable income. Journalist Robert Frank argues that consumption entails emulation. Purchases by the wealthy, such as bigger houses, foreign cars, electronic devices, fashionable clothing, exotic holidays and entertainment, are celebrated by the media, enticing the less well off to consume similarly, often financed by borrowing.

Higher debt levels amongst the less wealthy have increased inequality in subtle ways. They borrow at high rates of interest, reflecting the increased risk to the lender. The repayments become a fixed claim on available income, reallocating earnings via interest to higher income groups and increasing the financial vulnerability of lower income households to unexpected changes in circumstances, such as loss of income, illness or family breakdown. Debt slavery limits the ability of the less well off to improve their financial position. It also

entrenches financialisation, as access to debt for housing, cars or education becomes central. It enhances the power of the financial sector
and financiers, who can command higher incomes, further increasing
their wealth.

*

Healthcare, education and childcare are essential to increased participation in and the quality of the workforce. In developed countries, higher
skill levels are needed to escape low-skilled jobs and falling real wages.
Occupations requiring a university education currently offer salaries
two to three times higher than those requiring lesser qualifications.

While manufactured products such as cars and electronics have
decreased in price, healthcare, education and childcare costs have
risen more than general price levels and incomes. The eponymous
Baumol's cost disease (or the Baumol Effect) identifies that increases
in the cost of labour-intensive services reflect intrinsically lower
rates of productivity improvement than industrial processes such as
manufacturing.

In recent decades, major productivity gains and cost savings have
been made in those industries where the process can be automated or
easily outsourced to cheaper foreign workers. In contrast, services are
local, and not globally traded. It takes, for example, a similar amount of
time to learn to play a piece of classical music today as it did when it was
written centuries ago. This makes productivity gains in growing industries like medical services, looking after and teaching children, caring for
the aged, entertainment and leisure more difficult, keeping prices high.
The influence of healthcare and education industries over government
policy also creates unfavourable pricing and regulatory structures for
consumers, making them either unaffordable or unavailable for many.
The lack of public education facilities in many countries forces disadvantaged students to take out loans, leaving them deeply indebted.

Poor health and chronic illnesses affect employability and the ability to complete educational and training courses. Lack or the high cost of childcare prevents participation in the workforce and the improving of skills.

The digital divide exacerbates inequality. Lower income families frequently lack access to fast broadband connections, essential to participation in the knowledge economy. This deprives children of an essential educational tool.

The gap in educational achievements between the children of higher and lower income families, measured by college enrolment and graduation rates, has increased. In part this reflects the lower quality of public education in some countries. Another factor is the extra-curricular education that children from affluent families frequently receive, estimated at 6000 hours per child in the US over the period of primary and secondary schooling.

With children from lower income groups facing significant obstacles to development, good health and educational achievement, economic mobility decreases. The result is that children of poorer families are likely to remain poor, perpetuating the cycle of disadvantage.

*

Policy shifts affect inequality. While the strong economic growth and the focus on income and wealth redistribution in the period after World War II improved living standards and reduced poverty, they had limited lasting effects on inequality. Beginning in the 1970s, changes in the tax system, reduced emphasis on income redistribution, the privatisation of public enterprises, and the shift to more market-driven economies coincided with rising inequality. Support for social welfare programs diminished, reflecting the belief that they had not been effective in reducing inequality.

Fewer people now accepted the argument made by jurist Oliver

Wendell Holmes that taxation is how societies buy civilisation. High taxes, seen as discouraging effort and entrepreneurship, were cut to improve competitiveness and spur activity. Additional pressure came from a narrowing of the tax base.

Around 40–50 percent of American households do not pay tax, either due to low income or the availability of deductions that eliminate their liability. One percent of American taxpayers contribute around 45–50 percent of all tax collected, up from around 20 percent two decades ago. One percent of British taxpayers contribute around 30 percent of all tax collected, an increase of around 10 percent. Five American industries, which constitute around one-third of the total number of companies, contribute around 80 percent of the corporate tax collected. In Britain, around 800 businesses contribute around 50 percent of all corporate tax.

The reduction in the number of taxpayers has driven a worldwide shift from income taxes to indirect taxes, such as sales tax, value added tax (VAT), or goods and services tax (GST). These taxes are regressive, applying at the same rate to all taxpayers irrespective of income and thus imposing a greater burden on the poor than on the rich.

Tax anomalies and distortions favour the affluent. According to the Internal Revenue Service, the top 400 taxpayers in the US paid an average tax rate of 18 percent in 2010. Capital gains and investment income receive preferential treatment. Property and wealth taxes have been reduced or eliminated, or are avoided where they exist. Tax-deductible interest payments subsidise debt financing for businesses and investors. Excessive, complex exemptions and deductions allow tax minimisation. These are exacerbated by special provisions for specific industries, especially oil and mining, financial services and real estate, obtained through intensive lobbying.

Tax rules have not kept pace with international business practices. Increasingly, firms shift profits from high- to low-tax jurisdictions, using licensing of registered patents, copyrights or trademarks, or intra-group financing arrangements. Stateless and virtual, internet-based firms are masters of tax minimisation as well as information technology. Governments compound the problem, using tax rates and special concessions to entice businesses to locate in specific jurisdictions.

The cost falls disproportionately on the less affluent. They do not benefit as much from tax cuts, deductions or special allowances. They bear the brunt of the reduced ability of governments to provide social services or supplement income without borrowing.

The deregulation of energy, water, telecommunications, banking, insurance, healthcare and transport was designed to increase flexibility, lower costs, and encourage innovation. It had some success in this regard, but also facilitated concentration within industries, increasing market power for some and reducing competition. The privatisation of public assets assumes that state ownership is intrinsically inefficient and distorts competition. Many public assets, such as water, power, communications and transport, are natural monopolies. In private hands, inadequate controls and inordinate influence by the regulated over the regulators has allowed new owners to earn excessive profits at the expense of consumers. Without state-owned enterprises, the ability of governments to influence competition and correct market failures is reduced.

These public assets, once owned by everybody, were transferred, frequently at bargain prices, to higher income households who purchased the shares offered. Lower income households paid by way of higher prices or reduced availability of essential services.

Gains from privatisation have been unevenly distributed. In the 1980s the Thatcher government sold British council houses at advantageous prices to tenants, who benefited from subsequent rising prices. But those without a council property missed out on the windfall.

Lower government investment in public and low-rent housing disadvantaged lower income households.

In the postwar period the core constituency of conservative and social democratic political parties in most countries was relatively stable. Electoral success required wooing a crucial middle block of voters. Sophisticated polling and marketing techniques skilfully targeted this group with a mixture of middle-class welfare, specific initiatives, and rhetoric that appealed to their innate biases. Addressing inequality was not a priority.

During the 2012 US presidential campaign, unsuccessful Republican candidate Mitt Romney was secretly caught on tape arguing that 47 percent of people would never vote for the Republican Party. These welfare communists did not pay taxes and were dependent on the government for their care, including housing, food, education and healthcare. The Republicans should not, he argued, worry about these people, and should concentrate instead on convincing the 5–10 percent in the centre.[5]

*

Policies designed to deal with the GFC, such as investment in financial institutions to ensure their solvency, cuts in interest rates, and QE programs, further increased inequality. The cost of the bailouts was borne disproportionately by lower income groups. Insolvency would have inflicted greater losses on the wealthy, with their larger investments. Where there were deposit insurance schemes, whereby governments guarantee the safety of money held in a bank up to a nominated sum, the less wealthy would have been protected. The servicing of the increased government debt incurred to finance these bailouts was paid for, in part, by the poor. Austerity measures reduced programs such as pensions, unemployment and disability benefits, important to the less well off.

A 2014 United Nations Children's Fund report examined the effects of the GFC on children between 2008 and 2012. The wellbeing of children in twenty-three of the forty-one countries included in the report had deteriorated, due to the recession and austerity policies. Child poverty had nearly trebled in Iceland and doubled in Greece and Latvia, nations severely affected by the crisis. Greece lost the equivalent of fourteen years of income progress; Ireland, Luxembourg and Spain lost ten years; Iceland lost nine years; Italy, Hungary and Portugal lost eight years; and the UK lost six.

Low interest rates and QE benefited financiers. Banks increased profits by borrowing, essentially for nothing, from central banks and investing the funds in government bonds or lending it out. Given the prevailing net margin between US Treasury yields and deposit rates of 2 percent at the time, in 2013 J.P. Morgan would have earned around us$26 billion on its customer deposits of us$1.3 trillion, roughly equal to its actual pre-tax profits. In effect, the bank's earnings did not require undertaking any banking activities, relying instead on the subsidy provided by government policy. Around 97 percent, 138 percent and 60 percent of Citibank's, Bank of America's, and Wells Fargo's pre-tax 2013 earnings was derived similarly. The position of banks in many developed countries was identical. Assuming a similar spread between UK government bonds and deposit rates, Barclays would have earned around £8 billion on deposits of over £400 billion, more than its actual earnings in 2013.

The well-telegraphed central bank policies of low rates and purchases of securities provided financial institutions with the opportunity for low-risk trading profits. Higher volumes of bond issues and new share issues generated handsome fees for banks and dealers. Private equity firms benefited from the ability to borrow money cheaply, rescuing a number of ill-conceived transactions, which may otherwise have ended in bankruptcy. The artificially buoyant stock markets also helped private equity managers to sell off their stakes to the public, reaping large gains for wealthy investors and fees for themselves. Hedge funds and investment managers all benefited from the low rates and the desperate scramble for returns.

Central banks were indirectly paying the bankers, traders and fund managers seven-figure bonuses and higher. Showing its gratitude to the American taxpayers who had rescued them, Wall Street paid itself record bonuses in 2009 and 2010.

Low rates benefited borrowers with larger mortgages, who were generally higher-income households. The benefit to the less well off was limited, with financial institutions now less willing to finance lower income households wanting mortgages, or small businesses.

In 2010 Fed chairman Ben Bernanke argued that QE had worked because 'stock prices rose and long-term interest rates fell'.[6] But higher prices of real estate, stocks and other investments benefited mainly high income households, with limited flowthrough into the wider economy, thereby increasing inequality. Bank of England research showed that gains were skewed in favour of the top 5 percent of households, who held 40 percent of financial assets.

Low rates and QE reduced the incomes of retired individuals reliant on interest from bank deposits and bonds. In October 2014 an American retiree with us$1 million invested in secure, two-year US government bonds would have earned us$3900 in annual interest, 92 percent less than the us$48,000 they would have received in 2007. The retired and savers in advanced economies were forced to purchase riskier securities or invest in dividend-paying stocks to earn a return, often at a time when they could least afford losses of capital. Retirees and lower income groups argued that the post-GFC policies amounted to a significant tax increase on them and a tax cut for the wealthy, borrowers and banks.

Policymakers rejected suggestions that their actions were contributing to rising inequality, arguing that a robust recovery would benefit everybody. The poor had become 'human shields' for the affluent, with the less privileged now required to make the wealthy wealthier.[7] Former Bank of England deputy governor Sir Paul Tucker lost his central banking sangfroid, testily telling British parliamentarians that it was a necessary evil: 'if we were not, and had not been, running an easing monetary policy for the last three years or so now, this economy would have been destroyed'.[8]

*

Inequality in emerging markets is more complex. Rapid growth lifted the living standards of more than a billion people. The number of people living on below US$2 per day, the formal measure of poverty, dropped to 40 percent from 70 percent in 1980. Some 2.8 billion people, 40 percent of the world's population, now earn US$2–10 a day, a level regarded as middle income. But about 1.5 billion of this group, known as the fragile middle, earn around US$2–4 per day, making them vulnerable to any unexpected reversals in economic conditions.

The coefficient for inequality between countries has increased from a very low level of 16 in 1820 to 55 in 1950, remaining relatively constant subsequently. In 1820 Great Britain, then the world's richest economy, was around five times wealthier than the average poor nation. Today the US is around 20–25 times wealthier than the average poor nation. The reasons lie in the relationship between developed and emerging economies.

In April 2013 Rana Plaza, an eight-storey complex of clothing factories near Dhaka in Bangladesh, collapsed, killing more than 1100 people. It followed an earlier fire at Tazreen Fashions, another Dhaka factory, which killed more than a hundred. In 2010 a number of workers at a Foxconn electronics factory in China, a supplier to Apple, committed suicide. These incidents are only a miniscule part of the human cost of low-cost manufacturing in emerging markets.

The proximate cause of the Rana Plaza collapse was clear. The original 2006 approval was for a five-storey building, which was correctly designed and constructed. Subsequently, three more floors were added, with permission based on allegedly false documents. The extension overloaded the structure. Vibrations from heavy generators used to provide standby electricity, essential on the subcontinent where there are power shortages and frequent outages, contributed to the collapse. Warnings were disregarded. There was reluctance to suspend production to avoid losses.

But the fundamental causes are more complex. In a globalised world, businesses seek out competitively priced raw materials, labour and locations, to lower costs, enhance profitability and offer reduced prices to consumers. Production migrates to emerging markets. There is a race to the bottom in costs and working conditions, as manufacturers compete for the business of foreign purchasers.

Lower costs come primarily from lower wages. In Bangladesh the minimum wage is US$38 a month, with typical take-home pay of around US$65, amongst the lowest in the world. Benefits such as leave, retirement or healthcare are minimal, if they exist at all. Lower costs also come from less stringent regulations governing workplace safety, industrial pollution and waste disposal. Developed countries have outsourced the problems of fair wages, workers' rights and environmental degradation as well as production.

For workers in emerging markets, the choice is to die from starvation, unsafe work practices or pollution. They frequently face a cycle of nutritional deficit, where the calories expended on the job exceed the wages that allow them to replace the loss. The Bangladeshi women employed in the clothing industry would agree with Oscar Wilde's observation that capitalism lays upon some 'the sordid necessity of living for others'.[9]

Bangladesh is one of the fastest-growing economies in the world. It relies on its successful garment industry, which generates over US$24 billion in revenue, mainly in foreign currency, and employs about 3.5 million people, most of them young women. Bangladesh competes with Vietnam, Cambodia, Laos and Myanmar for foreign clients. Prices have decreased by around 10 percent over the last five years. Return on investment in the garment trade has decreased from 50 to 20 percent, which is close to the cost of debt in Bangladesh. In turn, this drives further cost-reduction measures.

The problems are compounded by weak government, corruption, rent-seeking and poor administration. Bangladeshi building regulations are not enforced. Trade unions are aggressively suppressed. The owner of Rana Plaza was linked with one of Bangladesh's major political parties and allegedly used his influence to obtain approvals from the authorities, even though the building extensions did not comply with standards.

The same pattern, repeated across countries and industries, relies on what Palestine-born writer Edward Said in 1978 termed Orientalism. This refers to the patronising attitude of Westerners towards Asian, Middle Eastern and African societies, which are seen as static and underdeveloped, and which a superior West can shape in accordance with its own requirements. This dehumanising view was recognised by George Orwell in 1939:

> When you walk through a town like this – two hundred thousand inhabitants, of whom at least twenty thousand own literally nothing except the rags they stand up in – when you see how the people live, and still more how easily they die, it is always difficult to believe that you are walking among human beings. All colonial

empires are in reality founded upon that fact ... They rise out of the earth, they sweat and starve for a few years, and then they sink back into the nameless mounds of the graveyard and nobody notices that they are gone. And even the graves themselves soon fade back into the soil.[10]

*

For emerging countries, escaping poverty and improving living standards required joining the capitalist caravan. In 1974 Deng Xiaoping discovered that China had only US$38,000 in foreign currency to pay for his delegation's trip to the UN. Deng subsequently drove change, masterminding China's oxymoronic socialist market economy.

The path followed the Washington Consensus – specific policy prescriptions considered necessary for the development of emerging countries. To foster economic growth, international aid agencies and NGOs advised macroeconomic stabilisation, opening up trade and foreign investment, deregulation and the adoption of free markets. This encouraged developed countries to relocate or set up production facilities in places with cheap local labour or resources.

The approach included the sale of government-owned businesses. Privatisations in Russia, Asia and Latin America were characterised by corruption, allowing foreigners and politically connected locals, sometimes in partnership, to acquire assets at bargain prices and advantageous terms. Journalist Chrystia Freeland's 2000 book on post-Soviet Russia's economic transformation was titled *Sale of the Century*, a reference to the disposition of state assets to a small group of oligarchs, in exchange for loans to the government. The sales, at a fraction of true market value, made the buyers very wealthy. Despite the unprecedented windfall, one oligarch complained that a rival had been given a bigger company.

A 2009 study in medical journal *The Lancet* estimated that the privatisations in the former Soviet Union and Eastern Europe may have contributed to the deaths of up to a million working men, as Russian male life expectancy fell precipitously. A friend remarked to Freeland, 'Everything Marx told us about communism was false ... everything he told us about capitalism was true.'[11]

Opening up to the global economy can exacerbate local problems. In post-Chávez Venezuela some women were forced to choose prostitution. US dollars from foreign clients could be sold on the black market at ten times the official exchange rate. A woman could earn around double the monthly wage from each dollar-paying client, enabling the purchase of essentials like rice, flour, sugar and cooking oil, which other Venezuelans had to line up for hours to buy at regulated prices, if they were available.

Initially, where the favoured development recipe is followed, living standards in emerging countries increase, especially for the fortunate and connected. But inequality rises, as there are only minimal improvements for the bulk of people. Deng Xiaoping initially rationalised: 'Let some people get rich first.' Later he would grouse: 'Young leading cadres have risen up by helicopter. They should really rise step by step.'

A small middle class then develops. Property and share prices rise quickly as capital flows are attracted by tales of success. Pockets of prosperity coexist with widespread poverty. The wealthy are sheltered from inequalities, insulated by gated communities and access to First World services and comforts. Internet and satellite access accompanied by regular international travel transforms local difficulties into occasional inconveniences.

Finally, local constraints, rising costs, and demands from the disadvantaged for a greater share of the gains of development alter the dynamics. Costs rise to levels that make the economies uncompetitive. The capitalist caravan becomes restless, seeking newer, cheaper locations. While talking up the nation's prospects, especially to foreigners, smart locals shift money to Switzerland, Luxembourg, Hong Kong or Singapore.

Governments talk bravely about 'moving up the value chain' by focusing on higher quality or technologically advanced products. Ambitious initiatives are launched – the world's tallest building, a new port in a country that has no sea access, bridges over rivers between two cities that do not yet exist, entire new cities. Eventually, the country becomes mired in seemingly intractable economic, financial and political problems. In extreme cases, it collapses or becomes totally dysfunctional.

Emerging nations, so the argument goes, can develop and rise out of their impoverishment through trade and foreign investment. But most of the trade involves supplying cheap resources and low-cost labour, and relies on poor environmental and workplace safeguards.

The cost of improving safety in Bangladesh's clothing factories is estimated at around US$3 billion over a number of years, equivalent to only a few cents per garment. Consumers, business managers and shareholders are unwilling to accept the higher cost or lower profits required to improve working conditions. The short attention span of the media and Western buyers means that ethical purchasing campaigns, except amongst the most dedicated, have lost momentum.

You cannot separate, as Edward Said observed, Mansfield Park from the slave trade that was the source of its wealth. But little has changed since the early nineteenth century when Jane Austen wrote her novel. George Orwell was prescient when he wrote that 'we all live by robbing Asiatic coolies, and those of us who are "enlightened" all maintain that those coolies ought to be set free; but our standard of living, and hence our "enlightenment", demands that the robbery shall continue'.[12]

*

Economic apartheid, in the shape of inequality, now threatens growth.[13] The new-found focus on inclusive capitalism highlights the exclusion of significant portions of the population from the benefits of economic expansion.

Greater income inequality increasingly constrains an already weak recovery. Empirical research suggests that an increase in income inequality by one Gini coefficient point decreases the annual growth in GDP per capita by around 0.2 percent.

Higher income households have a lower marginal propensity to consume, spending a lower portion of each incremental dollar of income than those with lower incomes. US households earning US$35,000 consume an amount from each additional dollar of income that is around three times that of a household with an income of US$200,000. Given that consumption constitutes around 60–70 percent of economic activity, concentration of income at the higher end limits growth in demand.

Long-term potential growth rates are also affected by inequality. Poor health reduces participation in the workforce and productivity. A less-educated and lower-skilled workforce reduces competitiveness, innovation and future growth levels.

Widening disparities in income level also impose direct costs. British Prime Minister David Cameron has acknowledged this relationship: 'Per capita GDP is much less significant for a country's life expectancy, crime levels, literacy and health than the size of the gap between the richest and poorest in the population.'[14]

Rising inequality is associated with higher crime rates, particularly violent and property offences, poorer health, as well as family breakdowns and drug use. Unequal societies are affected by diseases of poverty, such as TB, malaria, and gastrointestinal illnesses arising from poor nutrition and hygiene, inadequate housing, and a lack of sanitation and access to timely health services. Almost a third of the world's population, mainly in developed countries, are overweight, two-and-a-half times the number that are undernourished. Obesity and related illnesses now cost the global economy around US$2 trillion annually. Inequality also affects the health of the affluent, in the form of psychological complaints, including depression, anxiety and obsessive behaviour driven in part by fear of not being able to keep up with peers and concern about loss of wealth and status.

Inequality creates debt problems as less affluent households increase their borrowings to finance consumption, accentuating boom and bust economic cycles. Over-leveraged consumers were a significant factor in the 2008 financial crisis, with default rates around three times greater than higher income households.

Excessive indebtedness also has long-term implications for growth, especially the recovery of consumption levels. The GFC has left a legacy of large debts, forcing households to reduce spending so as to repay borrowings, with low-income households reducing spending by twice as much as richer households. The debt overhang and caution about borrowing have reduced the impact of low interest rates. Households are unwilling or unable to increase debt. The fall in house prices in some countries, and the resulting decline in household wealth, has made borrowing difficult; lending against home equity has decreased. Banks have also tightened lending standards, in response to loan losses. These factors mean that a consumption-based economic recovery is unlikely without income redistribution to households with a higher propensity to spend, or finding a new source of demand.

Inequality results in poor economic policies, discouraging initiatives that favour growth such as trade, movement of capital, and flexible labour markets. Raghuram Rajan, now governor of the Reserve Bank of India, argues in his 2010 book *Fault Lines* that the government response to inequality by easing the flow of credit to poorer households increases the risk of financial crises.

No society can be built on English poet Thomas Gray's 'short and simple annals of the poor'.[15] Gross inequality irretrievably damages social cohesion and democratic beliefs. In 2014 there was outrage in Singapore when a British banker, upon being reunited with his repaired Porsche, posted on Facebook his relief at being able to 'wash [off] the stench of public transport'. The increasing wealth of Silicon Valley employees has created tensions in San Francisco. The influx of these higher income groups has pushed up rents and house prices. Private buses used by Google and other technology companies to ferry their workers to and from their workplace some 65 kilometres away regularly use public stops, blocking city bus traffic. Local protesters have launched campaigns, blockading the buses.

Concentrated wealth allows higher income groups to acquire power and influence. Michael Bloomberg spent US$260 million of his estimated net worth of over US$30 billion on his campaigns for mayor of New York. The cost of each vote received in 2009 was around US$180. Billionaire Peter Lewis, whose leg was amputated, spent millions of his own money in support of the legalisation of marijuana, which helped manage his pain. Irrespective of the individual merits of a candidate or policy, the use of private wealth to pursue specific objectives undermines democracy.

But true equality may be impossible to achieve. Efforts to correct inequality through socialism or communism have failed, often disastrously. The failure is encapsulated in an apocryphal factory manager's observation that under the Soviet system workers pretended to work and the state pretended to pay them.

In their 1968 *Lessons of History*, historians Will and Ariel Durant concluded that increased concentration of income and wealth promotes social tensions, which are resolved by state action to drastically reduce wealth or by popular revolutions that end up redistributing dysfunction and poverty.

*

At its apogee, the Piketty craze included T-shirts bearing the equation $r>g$, and speculation about who would play him in the film version (Colin Firth and Stephen Fry were favourites). By the end of 2014 *Capital* was following a trajectory identified by journalist Robert Shrimsley. [16]

In stage one, economists discuss the idea, believing that their own standing and credibility require it. Reviews in serious media, opinion pieces, commentaries, blogs and the like multiply rapidly. In stage two, a wider audience feels the need for engagement. Policymakers and politicians use the idea to support existing positions. Intelligent people purchase the book, leaving it lying around to give the impression of being the kind of person who has read the work, while hoping to learn its contents by osmosis. (At the height of its success, a second-hand, well-thumbed copy of *Capital* commanded a much higher price than a pristine new copy – over US$300 versus US$40 on Amazon – presumably because it lent immediate credence to the notion that it had been thoroughly studied.)

In stage three, opponents question the idea, validating the work in the eyes of acolytes. Stage four quickly follows, with supporters accusing the critics of not having read the book. Stage five entails the critics alleging that the supporters have not read the book either. By stage six, boredom sets in and mention of the book regresses into the polite or mannered. In stage seven, people disassociate themselves from the idea, becoming embarrassed to refer to it directly. In stage eight, it becomes fashionable to admit that you never read the book in the first place. In stage nine, the book is moved from its prominent place in the library or living room to the guest toilet, joining other such notable works as *A Brief History of Time*, *The End of History*, *The Black Swan*, and *The Tipping Point*. There may be an additional stage when the author and the book are subsequently rediscovered, usually posthumously, and undergo a revival.

But inequality remains a serious issue, constraining economic recovery and improvements in living standards globally. In his November 2013 apostolic exhortation, Pope Francis, familiar with poverty and inequality in his native Argentina, criticised the 'idolatry of money': 'While the earnings of a minority are growing exponentially, so too is the gap separating the majority from the prosperity enjoyed by those happy few. This imbalance is the result of ideologies which defend the absolute autonomy of the marketplace and financial speculation.'[17] Chilean President Michelle Bachelet complained that 'in the end the same old people keep losing out, and the same old people keep winning'.[18]

THE END OF TRUST

How a Democracy Deficit Harms Economic Activity

Modern societies cannot escape a network of direct and indirect mutual bonds. Institutions and mechanisms, including money, rely on trust, which allows strangers to deal with each other for mutual benefit, safely, in an increasingly virtual world. In Jean Renoir's 1939 film *La Règle du Jeu* (*The Rules of the Game*), a character bemoans the fact that they live in a time when everyone lies. The same is true about the present. Today, policymakers' refusal to be truthful about economic conditions has undermined essential trust.

In 1923 a rising German politician named Adolf Hitler shrewdly understood the impact of massive government intervention in the form of printing money, and how its destructive effects on society would ultimately enable him to seize power: 'Believe me, our misery will increase. The scoundrel will get by. But the decent, solid businessman who doesn't speculate will be utterly crushed; first the little fellow on the bottom, but in the end the big fellow on top too. But the scoundrel and the swindler will remain, top and bottom. The reason: because the state itself has become the biggest swindler and crook. A robbers' state!"[1]

A democracy deficit is now as much a problem as budget and trade deficits.

*

Policies designed to facilitate economic recovery increasingly punish the vast majority of ordinary citizens. Problems of excessive debt can only be solved by growth, inflation, austerity or default. Growth following the crisis has been stubbornly low. Inflation is below target levels in many countries. Austerity is proving self-defeating. Default or restructuring of debt would wipe out savings and trigger another financial crisis. With policy options limited, governments have turned to financial repression: policies to channel savings and funds to the public sector, lower borrowing costs and avoid default on borrowings.

Financial repression entails higher taxes, in combination with reductions in the level of state benefits or public services provided. Wealth or estate taxes may be reintroduced. Government spending is decreased through means-testing or co-payment schemes for public services, user-pays surcharges and special levies. Retirement benefits are reduced by delaying the eligibility age for pensions, lower benefit levels, linking payments to the contributions made by individuals over their working life, and delaying or eliminating cost of living indexation. The policies are cast as economically necessary and socially responsible. The approach is that of Louis XIV's minister of finance, Jean-Baptiste Colbert: 'the art of taxation consists in so plucking the goose as to get the most feathers with the least hissing'.

Policymakers manipulate interest rates, keeping them below the true inflation rate to allow over-indebted borrowers to maintain unsustainably high levels of debt. Increasingly, zero interest rate policy has given way to negative interest rate policy, entailing an explicit transfer of wealth from savers to borrowers.

In October 2014, coinciding with World Savings Week, one German bank announced that savers would have to pay the bank to deposit money. German savers termed it 'punishment interest' or 'the wrath of Draghi', referring to the negative interest rates imposed by the European Central Bank. Other countries, such as Denmark, followed suit, introducing similar charges on deposits. Negative interest rate loans also followed. In effect, borrowers would be paid to take out a loan. By early 2015 over US$7 trillion of government debt in the Eurozone, Switzerland and Japan had negative yields.

In a 2013 study the McKinsey Global Institute found that between 2007 and 2012 low interest rates and QE resulted in a net transfer to governments in the US, UK and the Eurozone of US$1.6 trillion, through reduced debt service costs and increased central banking profits. In 2014 the US budget deficit fell to 2.8 percent of GDP. QE helped improve US government finances by around US$80 billion, or 0.5 percent of GDP. The Fed's larger balance sheet (up from US$800 billion pre-GFC to around US$4.4 trillion) increased central bank earnings from interest on its purchases of government bonds. This allowed it to increase remittances to the government from US$25 billion to US$60 billion. Total Fed remittances to the US government post-GFC total around US$500 billion.

The losses were borne by households, pension funds, insurers and foreign investors. Households, particularly older households, lost US$630 billion in net interest income. Non-financial corporations in these countries benefited by US$710 billion through lower interest costs.

The policies debased the value of the currency. Once an unquestioned store of wealth, government bonds now threaten investors with the risk of loss from sovereign default or destruction of purchasing power. US economic commentator Jim Grant joked that where once government bonds offered risk-free return, they now provided return-free risk.

Low rates and QE force investors to make investments that provide inadequate returns for the risk assumed; they must leverage or use strategies based on complex financial products to amplify return. The chief investment officer for Oppenheimer Funds, Arthur Steinmetz, lamented that 'people, out of fear, are getting poor slowly'.[2]

Currently, banks are large holders of government bonds, in part because of the lack of loan demand, but if required, governments can mandate minimum holdings of government securities for banks, pension funds and insurance companies. New regulations designed to ensure that banks and insurance companies increase holdings of government bonds as a liquidity buffer assist in ensuring a captive market for sovereign debt.

In Iceland and Cyprus, currency controls have restricted the ability to take money out of the country. In Cyprus and Portugal, the value of deposits was compulsorily written down by regulators in order to force customers to absorb the banks' losses. In the restructuring of Greek debt, official creditors were preferred under retrospective legislation, allowing them to avoid losses at the expense of other lenders.

Governments can seize private savings or pension fund assets. In 2013, under pressure to reduce its budget deficit, Spain drew €5 billion from the state's Social Security Reserve Fund, designed to guarantee pension payments in times of hardship. The government also had the fund increase holdings of Spanish government bonds to 97 percent of its assets, an increase from 55 percent five years previously. Argentina seized pension funds and central bank foreign exchange reserves, and renationalised the YPF oil company, allowing the government access to US$1.2 billion of annual profits. Bolivia nationalised the power-grid company Transportadora de Electricidad. Indian authorities retro-spectively clarified tax regulations, resulting in additional liabilities for foreign companies and investors.

Financial repression also entails more explicit standover tactics. Many beleaguered governments delay or refuse to pay overdue bills to businesses, in a shell game that gives the appearance of reducing budget deficits and debt levels.

In several countries, banks must report large cash transactions. Some require information on how the money withdrawn is to be used. National governments are increasingly trying to eliminate physical cash altogether. They justify the initiative on the basis of preventing tax avoidance, crime and terrorism, as well as increasing efficiency and lowering costs. One commentator even argued that it would improve hygiene and prevent the transmission of diseases. But eliminating the freedom, privacy and anonymity allowed by cash also enables con-trol over the lives and access to the savings of individuals. It facilitates potential financial repression on an unprecedented scale.

These measures damage the rule of law. In November 2011 Jens Weidmann, president of the German central bank, the Bundesbank, criticised the European Central Bank's decision to effectively finance governments in breach of EU treaties: 'I cannot see how you can ensure the stability of a monetary union by violating its legal provisions.'[3]

The policies also punish frugality and thrift, and reward borrow-ing, profligacy, excess and waste. Debt monetisation and the erosion of the purchasing power of savings is a tax on holders of money and sov-ereign debt; it redistributes wealth over time from savers to borrowers and to the issuer of the currency.

The political and social response to financial repression is unclear. Following the announcement of Abenomics, Japanese analyst Ryoji Musha was triumphant: 'Pessimists and sceptics have no ammunition. Surrendering is their only choice.'[4] John Maynard Keynes would have counselled circumspection: '[It] is not sufficient that the state of affairs which we seek to promote should be better than the state of affairs which preceded it; it must be sufficiently better to make up for the evils of the transition.'[5]

*

The GFC revealed numerous instances of financial institutions placing their own interests before that of clients.

Goldman Sachs is one of the world's most important and influential investment banks. It is known as 'Government Sachs' because several former staff members have held senior government positions. On 14 March 2012 a former employee, Greg Smith, published an opinion piece in the *New York Times* detailing his reasons for resigning from the firm.[6] The letter criticised Goldman's 'toxic and destructive' practices. Clients, known internally as 'muppets', were encouraged to invest in securities or products that Goldman wanted to dispose of at a profit. They frequently did not understand the risk of the complex transactions.

During a 2010 US Senate hearing on investment banking practices in the lead-up to the GFC, Goldman executives illustrated Upton Sinclair's observation: 'It is difficult to get a man to understand something, when his salary depends on his not understanding it.'[7] The following exchange occurred during the hearing:

Senator Levin: 'Don't you also have a duty to disclose an adverse interest to your client? Do you have that duty?'

Dan Sparks (head of Goldman Sach's mortgage trading): 'About?'

Senator Levin: 'If you have an adverse interest to your client, do you have the duty to disclose that to your client?'

Dan Sparks: 'The question about how the firm is positioned or our desk is positioned?'

Senator Levin: 'If you have an adverse interest to your client when you are selling something to them, do you have a responsibility to tell that client of your adverse interest?'

Dan Sparks: 'Mr Chairman, I am just trying to understand what the "adverse interest" means . . .'[8]

Rolling Stone magazine journalist Matt Taibbi called Goldman Sachs 'a great vampire squid wrapped around the face of humanity, relentlessly jamming its blood funnel into anything that smells like money'.[9] But the US investment bank was not alone.

In 2011 UK's biggest bank, HSBC, was fined for selling long-term investment bonds that might never pay out to customers as old as ninety-three. Towers Watson, a global consulting firm, found that fund managers were focused on short-term gains and insufficiently on improving investment returns. They ran funds for themselves and intermediaries, such as financial advisers, rather than for customers whose savings were being invested.

In 2012 the UK's Barclays bank was fined US$450 million for manipulating key money-market benchmark rates used in trillions of dollars of transactions. Evidence presented suggested that this was done to obtain financial benefit, or due to reputational concerns during the GFC. Bank of England governor Mervyn King lamented the loss of trust: 'the idea that "my word is my Libor" is now dead'.[10]

A who's who of financial institutions – J.P. Morgan, Citigroup, UBS, Credit Suisse, Deutsche Bank, Société Générale, RBS, and a number of brokers – were forced to pay fines totalling over US$2 billion in relation to manipulation of money-market rates. Evidence emerged about manipulation of currency, oil and gold prices. In November 2014 a group of banks agreed to pay over US$4 billion to settle allegations of fixing currency rates. The Bank of America paid US$16 billion to a collection of federal agencies and six state attorneys-general to settle infractions in the American mortgage market. In the UK, disputes related to the alleged mis-selling of payment-protection insurance are expected to cost banks over US$40 billion by the end of 2016.

In 2015 HSBC was forced to apologise for assisting clients to evade tax. The bank argued that it was being held to unreasonably high standards, as senior managers could not possibly be aware of everything done by the organisation's 257,000 employees. It did not help matters that the chief executive was forced to defend allegations of sheltering millions of dollars from tax in a Panamanian company, via HSBC's Swiss private bank.[11]

By the end of 2014 fines and restitution payments by financial institutions globally totalled over US$280 billion.

Regulators belatedly criticised this poor conduct and the damage caused to public trust. In reality, they may have known that banks were posting artificial rather than actual rates but did not object, fearing that the truth would destabilise already panicked markets. If they did not know what was happening, then their competence was questionable. If they did know, then they were complicit.

Several dealers accused of participating in the rate fixing were members of influential central bank committees, where concerns about this conduct had been discussed. Price fixing in currency markets was carried out openly, using electronic messaging by dealers calling themselves the Mafia, in an internet chat room called the Cartel. When these messages were published in the *Financial Times*, a reader was appalled at the poor punctuation, indifferent grammar and text-speak spelling. He argued that there was sufficient evidence for conviction for crimes against language, in addition to market manipulation.

The enforcement of regulations was lax. In 2014 Carmen Segarra, a banking examiner, sued the New York Fed for unfair dismissal. Ms Segarra was allegedly fired when she refused to revise her findings that Goldman Sachs's policies on conflict of interest did not meet the regulatory requirements. A 2014 report by the Fed's Office of the

Inspector General on a US$6 billion trading loss at J.P. Morgan found that supervisors identified risks but did not pursue them. The Bank of England's chief currency dealer was found to have failed to pass on concerns about collusive behaviour in the currency markets. In 2014 the bank commenced an investigation into whether its officials were aware or facilitated the manipulation of auctions designed to inject money into the credit markets during the GFC.

Little appears to have changed since Ferdinand Pecora conducted the 1932 commission examining Wall Street practices prior to the 1929 crash. His observation remains true today: 'Legal chicanery and pitch darkness were the banker's stoutest allies.'[12] Governments seem unable or unwilling to rein in banks, which are described by the *Financial Times'* Martin Wolf as a 'risk-loving industry guaranteed as a public utility'.[13] Increasingly reviled and mistrusted, financial institutions throughout the world are losing legitimacy.

*

To deal with domestic problems, developed nations are using a combination of low interest rates and increased money supply to devalue their currencies. The currency wars are part of a wider conflict between nations, under way since 2009.

Devaluation erodes the value of the sovereign bonds in which China, Japan, Germany and others have invested their savings, undermining global trust. Devaluation allows developed economies to capture a greater share of global trade, boosting their growth. But volatile capital movements and large currency fluctuations have the potential to destabilise smaller economies, derailing their development. As John Maynard Keynes argued, 'When the capital development of a country becomes a by-product of the activities of a casino, the job is likely to be ill done.'[14]

In 2014 Raghuram Rajan, head of India's central bank, warned of a breakdown in international coordination of monetary policy, claiming that developed economies were ignoring the impact of their policies on the rest of the world. Central bankers in the US, Europe and the UK denied any adverse side effects, claiming that a strong recovery in advanced economies was good for the world. In any case their mandates, the argument went, were domestic. Therefore, volatility in emerging markets was only relevant insofar as it affected their own economies.

There was disagreement between developed countries as well. When in 2013 the Bank of Japan and the European Central Bank began trying to weaken the yen and the euro in response to intensifying domestic economic difficulties, the US Fed expressed concern that the rapid rise of the US dollar was jeopardising an uneven US economic recovery. Switzerland, Denmark and Sweden imposed negative official interest rates to avoid large inflows of money seeking to escape weak currencies. Capital controls restricting movements of money were contemplated. It was similar to the 1930s, but instead of tariff barriers and trade wars, it was aggravated currency wars, low interest rates, QE and competitive devaluations.

German philosopher Immanuel Kant argued that the morality of an action can be judged by what would happen if it became a universal law; that is, if everybody acted in the same way. A calculated policy of engineered currency devaluations to gain trading advantages exacerbates the breakdown in international trust, which manifests itself in trade protectionism and disputes.

*

There is tension between developed and emerging countries over the operation of the IMF and the World Bank, wherein the US and Europe use their disproportionate voting power to set the agenda. Speaking at an IMF press conference, Brazil's finance minister highlighted the fact that the quotas for Argentina or South Africa were smaller than those for Luxembourg. Belgium enjoyed a share larger than that of Indonesia and around triple that of Nigeria. Spain's quota was larger than the combined vote of forty-four sub-Saharan African countries.[15]

This voting imbalance is a legacy of a time when the IMF was designed to aid ailing Third World countries, but the body's purpose has now changed. The developed world increasingly needs the savings of emerging nations to help solve current debt problems, such as those in Europe. When the IMF agreed to participate in the 2010 European bailout, China, Russia and Brazil sought evidence of Eurozone governance. It was ironic that a communist country, a formerly communist country, and one which had recently defaulted required proof of Western Europe's economic management credentials. The situation reflected increasing concern that countries where incomes per head are well below Western levels will incur large losses, to preserve the unsustainable economic arrangements of developed nations.

Emerging market countries, especially in Asia, considered the IMF conditions for the bailouts of Greece, Ireland and Portugal to be less onerous than those imposed on them in previous crises. These Asian countries did not receive generous financial support from other nations. During the 1997/98 Asian crisis, South Korea, Thailand and Indonesia suffered great hardship under draconian austerity regimes. In an act of patriotic sacrifice, ordinary Koreans donated gold, jewellery and other valuables to their government to ease financial pressure.[16]

In his resignation letter of July 2012, Peter Doyle, a senior IMF economist, excoriated the institution. He wrote of a European bias, arguing that the appointment of Christine Lagarde as president was 'tainted, as neither her gender, integrity, or élan can make up for the fundamental illegitimacy of the selection process'.[17] Denying emerging nations their legitimate role in international affairs undermines trust.

Resolving global problems like climate change and the conservation of resources, as well as economic management, requires international agreement based on mutual trust. But now international coordination resembles the Loch Ness monster, much discussed but rarely sighted.

*

The claim of central bankers and economists to vast powers on vital and complex matters, beyond the ability of citizens to understand, is now challenged.

Poor policies created an unbalanced economy and the conditions for financial collapse, rather than growth and prosperity. Policymakers did not anticipate problems or take the required preventive action. In the aftermath of the GFC, their inability to arrest decline and promote recovery has been evident, as have their lack of tools and the ineffectiveness of their dogma. But central bankers remain unchastened. In 2013 US congressman Frank Lucas asked Ben Bernanke how the Fed would determine when to reverse the policy of low interest rates and unprecedented liquidity, to avoid asset price bubbles and the risk of a new financial collapse. Displaying undiminished chutzpah, Dr Bernanke replied that the Fed would know.

Central bank forecasts of a return to good times have proved optimistic, necessitating frequent downwards revisions. The IMF launched a review of its forecasting performance – conducted by other economists. The ruminations of Indian central bank governor Raghuram Rajan rivalled former US Defense Secretary Donald Rumsfeld's known unknowns: 'Given that we gave it to you as a forecast, I can't forecast that we'll lower the forecast.'[18]

With their policy prescriptions unsuccessful, undaunted policymakers now propose new initiatives. One would involve helicopter drops of money, where the central bank prints large amounts and distributes it to the public to stimulate the economy. Another is for a nationwide treasure hunt for US$1 million caches hidden across America. Finders would be obliged to spend the money quickly. Consideration is being given to the idea of finite money and savings, which would expire if not spent by a certain date. Everyone would be forced to spend their savings to increase economic activity, or face the loss of these funds.

There are proposals for a debt jubilee, drawing on the Old Testament's Book of Deuteronomy. This entails forgiving existing debt and allowing governments, households and individuals to boost economic activity by spending the money currently directed to meeting interest and principal obligations. Given that one person's debt is another person's saving, a blanket debt jubilee on the scale required globally would cancel the liability of the borrower but also eliminate a large amount of savings, reducing consumption. The debt jubilee's veneer of morality and wealth redistribution is false. It rewards those who have taken out the largest loans, not the usual candidate of welfare.

Citigroup chief economist Willem Buiter described these policies as 'an intellectual potpourri of factoids, partial theories, empirical regularities without firm theoretical foundations, hunches, intuitions, and half-developed insights'.[19] Hedge fund manager Paul Singer argued that much of the economic improvement since the GFC was fake, based on 'fake growth, fake money, fake jobs, fake financial stability, fake inflation numbers and fake income growth'. He warned of a loss of trust, arguing that 'when confidence is lost, that loss can be severe, sudden and simultaneous across a number of markets and sectors'.[20]

*

Facing intractable problems and unpalatable choices after the GFC, politicians abnegated economic leadership. Unelected and largely unaccountable central bankers were left with the responsibility but not the power to deal with an increasingly difficult situation, a position described by the satirical British TV show *Yes, Prime Minister*'s Sir Humphrey Appleby as 'the prerogative of the eunuch throughout the ages'.[21] With their limited and ineffective policy options, central bankers resorted to 'forward guidance' – a tautology, as any guidance must be about future events. They would henceforth communicate commitments on future interest rates, liquidity provision or QE over a medium- to long-term horizon.

The US Fed committed to keeping rates low until the unemployment rate fell below 6 percent. In early 2014 it changed the unemployment target to a non-binding indicator. In May 2014 the employment goal was changed to cover the 'disadvantaged', including the long-term unemployed and workers forced to work part-time. The Bank of Japan and the European Central Bank targeted 2 percent inflation, despite the fact that actual inflation was near zero and proving unresponsive to traditional policies.

In March 2014, at her first press conference as Fed chair, Janet Yellen stated that the Fed would not increase interest rates for a 'considerable time'. When questioned about staff forecasts that showed rates rising earlier than expected, Yellen hedged: 'I really don't think it's appropriate to read very much into it.'[22] Further attempts at defining 'considerable' proved unhelpful. In December 2014 the Fed announced they would be 'patient', dropping the reference to 'considerable time', driving new semantic speculation. In February 2015 Yellen abandoned 'patient', simultaneously warning that this did not mean the Fed would be impatient.

Forward guidance from the other side of the Atlantic confirmed John Maynard Keynes's fear that 'confusion of thought and feeling leads to confusion of speech'.[23] On 4 July 2013 European Central Bank president Mario Draghi announced that 'key European Central Bank rates [will] remain at present or lower levels for an extended period of time'. On 5 July 2013 the governor of the Bank of Finland, Erkki Liikanen, stated: 'Everything depends on the development of the economy.' On 6 July 2013 European Central Bank board member Benoît Cœuré observed: '[forward guidance is] a change in communication but not in monetary policy strategy'. On 8 July 2013 Draghi provided clarification: 'We'll have to see what the market reaction has been, is and will be to this statement.' On 9 July 2013 European Central Bank board member Jörg Asmussen gave specific guidance: '[the period] is not six months, it's not twelve, it goes beyond'. The European Central Bank immediately issued a statement that Asmussen did not intend to give guidance on the exact length of time for which the bank expects to keep rates at record lows. On 11 July 2013 Bundesbank president Jens Weidmann resorted to classical allusion: 'It is not an absolute advanced commitment of the interest rate path. The European Central Bank Council has not, like Odysseus, simply tied itself to the mast.'

Mario Draghi's July 2012 statement that the European Central Bank would 'do whatever it takes' is credited with stabilising money markets and reducing borrowing costs of Eurozone countries without requiring any actual intervention. In October 2013 he was ready to consider all available instruments, a message repeated in November and again in December 2013. In January 2014 he stated that he would take further decisive action if required. In February and March 2014, despite the lack of actual initiatives, he again vowed to take further decisive action if required. In April and May 2014 the European Central Bank undertook to act swiftly if required. Forced finally to announce new measures in June 2014, Draghi finished with a rhetorical flourish: 'Are we finished? The answer is no.' By November 2014 he was recycling 2012: 'we must do what we must'.

In January 2015, announcing the Eurozone version of QE some six years after the GFC and five years into the European debt problems,

Draghi did not acknowledge any errors. Exactly a year earlier, at the Davos World Economic Forum, he had dismissed warnings of deflation and stated that QE was out of the question. The president now thought the program demonstrated his personal credibility and that of the European Central Bank. In March 2015, even before the program had actually commenced, Draghi pronounced it a complete success.

The increase in length and complexity of central bank statements has paralleled the rise in the size of their balance sheets. With fiscal policy constrained and monetary policy losing potency, forward guidance drew attention to the lack of options. The increasingly shrill utterances of central bankers sounded like the Wizard of Oz claiming superior, supernatural powers. But as in the film, the central bankers were revealing themselves as old men hidden behind drapes, pulling frantically at the levers to maintain an illusion. Leaked transcripts of interviews with former US Treasury Secretary Tim Geithner, not intended for publication, revealed that Mario Draghi had no actual plan, making it up as he went along.[24]

*

Financial repression is increasingly accompanied by political repression. Governments have systematically refused to disclose the severity of the crisis, avoided public scrutiny of their actions, and hidden the true cost of their policy measures. The official policy articulated by Jean-Claude Juncker, the head of the European Commission, is that when the situation becomes serious it is simply necessary to lie.[25]

Nowhere is the political repression more obvious than in Europe, where the dialogue has been Orwellian. In April 2011 Spain's finance minister, Elena Salgado, dismissed concerns about her country: 'I do not see any risk of contagion – we are totally out of this.'[26] In 2012 her successor, Luis de Guindos, was convinced 'that Spain will no longer be a problem, especially for the Spanish, but also for the European

Union'.[27] Prime Minister Mariano Rajoy attempted to maintain confidence a few days later: 'Spain is not going to be rescued. It's not possible to rescue Spain. There's no intention to, it's not necessary and therefore it's not going to be rescued.'[28] When eventually Spain did require support, the disambiguation reached a new level: 'What is being requested is financial assistance. It has nothing to do with a rescue.'[29]

With Greece, Portugal, Ireland, Spain and Cyprus all needing assistance, panic replaced denial. There was no willingness to deal with high debt levels that were incapable of being repaid, the lack of competitiveness of some Eurozone members, or the inflexible single currency and uniform interest rates across disparate economies. Creditors like Germany were unwilling to write off debt which would trigger a banking crisis. No one was willing to countenance a restructuring of the Eurozone or the euro, which had been designed without an exit mechanism. Lorenzo Bini Smaghi, an Italian European Central Bank executive board member, confessed that the euro project assumed there would be no crises.

Slow, tortuous processes yielded inadequate policy responses. The Stability and Growth Pact evoked a policy of austerity (reduction in budget deficits to 3 percent of GDP) and enforced debt reduction (to 60 percent of GDP). Actions by the European Central Bank decreased the interest rates of peripheral countries and drove a rally in stock markets, leading European leaders to declare mission accomplished. But there was no recovery in the real economy. Austerity failed to bring public finances and debt under control. Increases in taxes and cuts in government spending led to sharp contractions in economic activity, reducing government revenues and increasing welfare and support payments. Budget deficits, while smaller, persisted, and debt levels continued to rise.

The economies of Greece, Portugal, Ireland, Spain and Cyprus shrank, by up to 25 percent. Unemployment rose to around 20–25 percent, with youth unemployment reaching over 40 percent. Consumption fell, reflecting lower wages and cuts in transfer payments. Social exclusion rose and living conditions deteriorated, evidenced by the return of diseases like TB. In Spain, food banks were now responsible for feeding many of the unemployed and those whose incomes were insufficient to feed their families. Social workers lamented that their clients would remain with them for a long time to come.

With conditions not improving, nations pleaded exceptional circumstances, receiving more time to meet deficit and debt-reduction targets. Even these new reduced or deferred thresholds are unlikely to be met. Germany hypocritically threatened other Eurozone members with large fines. In 2003 France and Germany ran budget deficits in excess of 3 percent of their GDP, breaching EU treaties, but avoided sanctions by agreeing not to support fines on each other.

Other measures floundered on the lack of money and the complex chemistry. The European Stability Mechanism, the much vaunted bailout fund with a maximum lending capacity of €500 billion, relies on support from the very nations that might need to access it. A 2014 infrastructure fund was nothing more than vapourware, relying on €21 billion of EU money to be leveraged fifteen times with borrowings from private lenders. Measures to stabilise European banks were weakened by German opposition to dedicating financial resources to support deposit insurance and a centralised bank recapitalisation fund. Ultimately, it was a fantasy to believe that heavily indebted governments could bail out each other, a compromised banking system and their weak economies.

*

Policy failure was compounded by the manner of the decision-making. In Europe a self-serving political class and self-selecting mandarins promoted their agendas, outside of the democratic process and without electoral mandates. In February 2015 President François Hollande invoked a rarely used article in the French constitution to pass laws without a parliamentary vote. Facing a revolt from its own members, the government was unsure of its ability to command a majority to pass key reforms.

Commitments were repeatedly broken. In September 2012 Spanish Prime Minister Rajoy claimed that reality prevented him from keeping his electoral promises. This followed his claim the previous December that pension cuts were imposed by reality. He subsequently stated that reality required slower fiscal consolidation.

In the early days of the European crisis, important decisions were made privately by 'Merkozy' – the partnership of convenience between German Chancellor Angela Merkel and the then French president Nicolas Sarkozy. After Sarkozy was dethroned, major decisions were still made in private, but by 'Homer' – the German chancellor and the new French president, Hollande – until the two nations could not find common ground as France too encountered economic difficulties.

Finland was extended special terms to secure its part of commitments to the European bailout package. This followed an unsuccessful request, it was rumoured, for mortgages over some Greek islands. As one of the few AAA-rated countries remaining in the Eurozone, Finland's support for the bailout was seen as important.

In contrast, Greece had limited involvement in the design of its bailout package or the severe austerity measures dictated by the EU. Greek Prime Minister George Papandreou made an ill-fated attempt to stage a plebiscite on austerity policies, but this was dismissed by larger Eurozone states as 'disruptive'. Subsequently, the EU orchestrated the replacement of the Greek and Italian prime ministers with unelected technocrats palatable to Brussels – Mario Monti in Italy, and Lucas Papademos in Greece.

In his book *Stress Test: Reflections on Financial Crises,* Tim

Geithner describes being approached to withhold IMF approval for loans in order to force Italian Prime Minister Silvio Berlusconi to resign. The Italian leader was threatening to leave the common currency. As the European debt crisis unfolded in 2011, British member of the European Parliament Daniel Hannan noted that the true face of the European project was suddenly there for all to see.

In the 2013 Italian election, support for Prime Minister Monti (nicknamed Rigor Montis) was lacklustre. Italians joked that the election was contested by a former communist, a philanderer, a comedian and an economist (Monti). The punchline was that the economist finished last. A German newspaper headline proclaimed: 'Germany loses Italian Election'. Fearing the re-emergence of financial problems, an alarmed Germany and EU urged Italy to continue its austerity program and resist populism. These policies, which had reduced Italy's GDP below its 2001 level, were rejected by over 50 percent of Italian voters. As occurred in Greece after its 2012 elections, the EU and Germany sought to engineer a coalition between major parties committed to a continuation of approved policies.

In late 2014, polls showed that the opposition Syriza party was leading in Greece. Fearful of Syriza's anti-EU stance and its call for writing off Greek debt, Pierre Moscovici, the EU Commissioner for Economic and Financial Affairs, visited Athens. He declared support for Antonis Samaras, the beleaguered Greek prime minister who was willing to continue the EU-dictated policies, describing Syriza's position as suicidal. European Commission president Jean-Claude Juncker called for Greece to be led by 'known' faces. In early 2015 Syriza won government, defeating New Democracy and PASOK, the two major political parties that had ruled Greece since the restoration of democracy in 1974. German Finance Minister Wolfgang Schäuble stated that elections changed nothing, warning that things would become difficult if Greece took a different path.

The corrosive pattern was reminiscent of playwright Bertolt Brecht's observation on the suppression of workers' protests in East Berlin in 1953: 'the people / had lost the government's confidence ... would it not be simpler, / If the government simply dissolved the people / And elected another?'[30]

*

The scale of Europe's debt crisis, the inadequacy of financial resources available, and the political situation mean that resolution is difficult without greater integration. But this would require stronger, more creditworthy members to underwrite the borrowings of weaker nations. External balances and debt levels will necessitate a net wealth transfer from richer to poorer Eurozone members. But there is little appetite for such initiatives amongst stronger countries, especially Germany, whose citizens would have to pay for these measures.

Under integration, the EU would increase its power over member states, supervising national budgets, including individual nations' taxes, spending and policies, backed by financial sanctions. But there may be one rule for big nations and another for the rest. In 2014 France announced it would not meet mandated budget targets, despite earlier being given a two-year delay. With Gallic humility, French Prime Minister Manuel Valls argued that a big country must be respected and allowed to decide its budget. At about the same time the EU, led by Germany, was resisting Greek appeals for a relaxation of the austerity regime that was destroying the country. The European Central Bank, acting as Brussels and Berlin's enforcer, was restricting support for Greek banks, to maintain pressure on Athens to comply with its existing agreements.

The integration strategy also ignores the flaws and defects of the EU, its inherently unstable economic foundations as revealed by the economic crisis, its lack of transparency and its fragile electoral mandate, especially its lack of accountability to voters.

EU politicians ignore the potential loss of national sovereignty and the undemocratic process. They pursue a strategy of de facto integration by stealth, through centrally determined policies developed by trusted technocrats. The architect of the EU, Jean Monnet, is sometimes credited with having set out this covert approach: 'Europe's nations should be guided towards the superstate without their people understanding what is happening.'[31] Current European Commission president Jean-Claude Juncker provided details of the process of EU decision-making: 'If it's a Yes, we will say "on we go", and if it's a No we will say "we continue".'[32] The paradox is that the EU that was created 'as a way of avoiding a return to fascism in the post-war epoch has since mutated into a way of avoiding democracy itself'.[33]

In Germany, strong exports, low unemployment and pay rises made voters complacent. They were not informed of the risk of losses from the European bailouts. Guarantees and off-balance arrangements avoided immediate impact on German finances.

Their elected representatives seemed equally ignorant. After the Bundestag voted to approve the European bailouts, the majority of parliamentarians, when asked how much money Germany was guaranteeing and for whom, could not answer correctly. Some believed that only Greece had received money, whereas Ireland and Portugal had also received bailouts. Almost none knew the total amount of German guarantees. 'A few billion, I guess?' was a typical answer. The total committed was €211 billion, the largest single sum of money a German parliament had ever committed to any cause.

The size of these exposures is large, in relation to both Germany's GDP and savings. In addition, Germany has substantial levels of its own debt (around 81 percent of GDP). The increase in commitments or debt levels will absorb German savings, crippling an economy plagued by low growth, lack of investment and lacklustre productivity.

Germany's demographics, with an ageing population, compound its problems. But the country cannot easily disengage from Europe. It remains dependent on exports to other European countries, and risks losses on its financial exposure to Eurozone members, which may be as high as €1.5 trillion, or over 40 percent of GDP.

In the European endgame, ordinary Germans will have to pay threefold for the euro. They are still paying for the reunification of Germany. In the early 2000s they paid through reductions in real wages, unemployment and labour market reforms. Now, German taxpayers will have to pay for the bailouts that they were committed to without ever having directly understood or endorsed them.

*

Lack of trust manifests itself in various ways. There is growing interest in alternative money, such as the Bavarian chiemgauer, England's Lewes pound, and the BerkShares program in Massachusetts. Alternative currencies have limited acceptance within a small area and, sometimes, a finite expiry date. They are designed to encourage local business and emphasise community values. The rise of bitcoin, originally intended for anonymous payments for online purchases of illicit items, and of other digital or crypto-currencies reflects, in part, increased concern about the monetary system. But bitcoin is subject to price manipulation and fraud. When one bitcoin exchange collapsed, holders seeking to recover their investment discovered belatedly the rationale for state regulation of payment systems. Irrespective of whether alternative currencies succeed or fail, they are testament to a growing distrust of governments, central banks and the financial system, and represent a challenge to the authority and apparatus of the state.

To preserve the value of their savings, investors are switching from financial instruments to real assets – gold, commodities, farmland, fine arts and other collectibles.

In the US on Bank Transfer Day – an online phenomenon launched by an unhappy Bank of America client – disgruntled customers withdrew money from traditional banks and transferred it to not-for-profit community banks and mutual societies. Peer-to-peer lending, such as Prosper and Lending Club in the US, and Funding Circle in the UK, is part of this trend, matching savers and borrowers for small consumer and business loans. The use of crowdfunding – the practice of raising money from a large number of people, typically via the internet – to finance ventures is also part of it.

But a switch to alternative currencies, precious metals and non-financial investments undermines growth and economic activity. Savings are locked in unproductive investments or are unavailable to circulate freely. Bypassing traditional banks may lead to a contraction in the availability of credit globally. Investor protection in peer-to-peer lending, or crowdfunding, is unproven.

Loss of trust extends to dealings between central banks. In early 2013 the Bundesbank announced that it would move around 674 tonnes of its gold bullion from foreign central banks to Frankfurt. The move only affected about half of the Bundesbank's gold reserves, and officials stressed that there was no question of 'mistrust'. Bill Gross, a founder of investment firm Pimco, tweeted the obvious inference: 'Central banks don't trust each other?'

*

Lack of trust also drives political disengagement. Support for traditional parties is falling, as voters seek alternatives. These include the Tea Party wing of the US Republican Party, the United Kingdom Independence Party, Germany's AfD, France's Front National, Italy's Movimento 5 Stelle, Spain's Podemos and Greece's Syriza.

The rise of smaller parties increasingly necessitates governing coalitions. The process is complicated by the fact that many of these parties have no experience of governing. They also have complex and inconsistent ideologies. Policies vary significantly on central banking, the gold standard, the currency, taxes, austerity, the size and role of government, free trade, globalisation, immigration, religion, same-sex relationships, abortion, racism, discrimination, and the Jewish question. The alternative is deadlock, with bitter divisions over entrenched partisan positions. Political instability is rising, impeding progress on policy issues and increasing economic risks.

The May 2014 European Parliament elections saw many smaller parties gain a significant number of seats. In *la séisme* (the earthquake), as *Le Figaro* termed it, Marine Le Pen's Front National won in seventy-three electoral departments against President François Hollande's Socialists' two. With few exceptions, voters rejected austerity and debt reduction. President of the European Council, Herman Van Rompuy, rebutted criticism, differentiating between the elected parliament and those who make the real decisions.

Disregard for voters is widespread. In 2014 Matteo Renzi became Italy's third consecutive prime minister not elected by the population in a general election. Responding to the 2014 student protests, Hong Kong Chief Executive C.Y. Leung complained that an open political process would force politicians to take into account concerns of low-income earners. Laura Cha, a member of Hong Kong's policymaking Executive Council and of China's parliament, compared the protesters to slaves, to be emancipated slowly without compromising the economy.

CNBC TV pundit Rick Santelli sees voters being taken out of the game. Voter turnout and approval for elected representatives have fallen sharply in many countries. Loss of legitimacy of authority translates into growing suspicion of it, manifested as resistance to policies like compulsory schooling and vaccination programs, against scientific evidence. Ordinary people know that 'those who mind don't matter, and those who matter don't mind'.[34]

*

Breakdown in trust fuels social disorder. The global Occupy Wall Street movement, Spain's *Indignados*, Greek *Aganaktismenoi*, and protesters in Portugal, Ireland and Italy are symptomatic of growing discontent.

There are personal grievances: lost jobs, lack of unemployment benefits, pension cuts, mortgage foreclosures, homelessness, college fees or student loans. But there are also wider issues: the widening economic and social gap, the financialisation of the economy, allocation of the responsibility and burden of the GFC, disenfranchisement of voters, and inequality. The Guy Fawkes mask and the 'We are the 99 percent' chant, first heard in New York's Zuccotti Park, are emblems of a moral protest. The 1 percent saw it as violent revolution. An Occupy poster retorted: 'They don't call it class warfare until we fight back.'

The 1 percent argue that their wealth is the result of hard work. People are not of equal ability, they claim. One financier referred to those working for the minimum wage as mentally retarded. Canadian Broadcasting Corporation host Kevin O'Leary thought that it was fantastic that the world's eighty-five richest people had more assets than the poorest 3.5 billion. He saw it as motivating people to work hard and get rich.

Plutocrats defended their wealth by arguing that it financed philanthropy, supporting social and cultural projects. But the paradox of charity is that conspicuous generosity to the disadvantaged is financed at the expense of the same people it claims to help.

Philanthropy is opaque about the source of the money. Wealth may derive from exploitation, in jurisdictions with poor pay and working conditions, and inadequate environmental controls. The wealthy frequently minimise their tax obligations, preferring voluntary 'self-taxation' in the form of contributions to their preferred philanthropic causes. Warren Buffett was praised for leaving 85 percent of his multibillion-dollar fortune to charity, to be managed by his friend and fellow philanthropist Bill Gates. However, Buffett, who has spoken out in favour of higher taxes, used the US tax code to his advantage in a 2014 transaction to capture tax savings of around US$1 billion.

Few individuals or corporations really give away their money. They use tax-efficient trusts or foundations, with the donor retaining substantial control. Contributions are generally tax-deductible, or they protect wealth from death duties, inheritance or estate taxation. The trust or foundation also provides status for donors, as well as employment for them, their family and associates. Donations and good works confer business advantages, including post-retirement roles, which allow the maintenance of influential networks and dining places of honour in their social milieus.

Donors are free to channel funds to their chosen causes, some noble, some hubristic and some odd. Investment banker Ace Greenberg donated US$1 million to a hospital so that homeless men would have access to free Viagra. Philanthropy can undermine social policy, where it reflects the idiosyncratic views of the donor and the supplicant for funding rather than a rigorous analysis of issues or the best course of action. Such influence may be unhealthy in a democracy.

Sir Richard Branson, founder of Virgin, and George Soros, the billionaire hedge fund manager, highlight the contradictions of philanthropy. Branson vaunts his social conscience, but lives as a tax exile on Necker Island. Soros gained prominence on Black Wednesday, 16 September 1992, when his speculative bet on the fall of the pound sterling earned him around US$1.1 billion and cost UK taxpayers US$5 billion. Soros, through his foundation, supports free markets and democratic initiatives in emerging nations, particularly Eastern Europe. Slovenian philosopher Slavoj Žižek was not deceived: 'Half the day [Soros] engages in the most ruthless financial exploitations, ruining the lives of hundreds of thousands, even millions. The other half [of the day] he just gives part of it back.'[35]

The wealthy see themselves as victims of persecution. They argue that the attacks on them are politically motivated, play to populist sentiments, and encourage envy and jealousy. Venture capitalist Thomas Perkins drew parallels between America's class war and Nazi Germany's war on its 1 percent, the Jews.[36]

Zillionaire Nick Hanauer, whose family were forced to flee Nazi Germany, heard the sound of tumbrels and guillotines: 'The pitchforks are going to come for us. No society can sustain this kind of rising inequality. In fact, there is no example in human history where wealth accumulated like this and the pitchforks didn't eventually come out. You show me a highly unequal society, and I will show you a police state. Or an uprising. There are no counterexamples. None. It's not if, it's when.'[37]

*

Writing in March 1933 during the Great Depression, John Maynard Keynes reflected: 'We have reached a critical point ... We can ... see clearly the gulf to which our present path is leading. [If governments do not take action] we must expect the progressive breakdown of the existing structure of contract and instruments of indebtedness, accompanied by the utter discredit of orthodox leadership in finance and government, with what ultimate outcome we cannot predict.'[38]

The widening gap between the views and concerns of the people and the political and bureaucratic classes threatens the trust central to modern societies. Friedrich Nietzsche observed that, once compromised, trust is not easily restored: 'I'm not upset that you lied to me, I'm upset that from now on I can't believe you.'[39]

COLLATERAL DAMAGE

The Fallout
for Ordinary Lives

When asked how he went bankrupt, a character in Ernest Hemingway's novel *The Sun Also Rises* replies, 'Two ways. Gradually, then suddenly.'[1] The world faces financial, resource and environmental demands that it may not be able to meet. Most ordinary people face slow impoverishment. But the risk of a sudden collapse is ever-present.

Those preoccupied with work and families may sense important changes but not fully understand their implications. The studied complexity and obscurity of the language of economics and finance makes it incomprehensible to most people. This opacity is by design. In 1947 an American soldier in postwar Italy was disconcerted to find that Italians were more interested in politics than in the comparative merits of different consumer products. Increases in living standards and consumerism tend to make people focus on material prosperity, at the expense of engagement and activism that might be inimical to the existing political and economic order.[2]

For the moment, life everywhere continues, seemingly normally. In the words of Spanish philosopher José Ortega y Gasset: 'everyone lives as though his [or her] dreams of the future were already reality.'[3] But for many, the successful, prosperous and polished surface hides insecurities and concerns.

*

A job is the main thing that stands between most people and penury. But in recent years, employment opportunities, the rates of pay and working conditions have changed.

In the developed world, civilian employment has declined. In the US it has fallen to 59 percent of the total population, the same level as the late 1970s/early 1980s, and below the 2000 peak of over 64 percent. Similar or sharper declines are evident in many economies, although statistics do not record the full decline. The definition of unemployment generally excludes employees working part-time because full-time jobs are unavailable, and those discouraged people who are no longer seeking work. In the US true unemployment is probably around 12–15 percent of the workforce. There is also under-employment, with many graduates who are unable to find work consistent with their education working in low-paid, unskilled jobs.

In previous downturns, laid-off workers generally found new work relatively quickly. Following the GFC, the number of long-term unemployed (defined as more than six months) increased. In the US one-third of the long-term unemployed have been out of work for over two years. The trend is similar in Europe, Japan and other developed countries. The longer a worker is unemployed, the harder it becomes to find work. Older and less-skilled unemployed are unlikely to work again.

Wages have stagnated. US median earnings have not increased in real terms since the mid-1970s. Household income has fallen to the same level as in 1989. Average real Japanese and German household incomes have been stagnant for more than a decade. UK factory incomes are at or lower than the level of the late 1970s, after adjusting for inflation.

The decline in employment reflects reduced economic activity. Weak public finances have decreased government employment. Global supply chains and outsourcing have displaced expensive workers in developed countries. Initially, outsourcing and offshoring affected low-skilled manufacturing. Over time it has come to affect skilled professions. In February 2004 *Wired* magazine published a story about American software programmers protesting the export of their jobs, via websites like yourjobisgoingtoindia.com and nojobsfor-india.com.[4]

Technological advances have exacerbated declines in employment and incomes, eliminating certain tasks and deskilling some jobs. Computer software is replacing journalists, with news items being synthesised online without human intervention. Even traders in financial markets are being replaced by super-fast automated algorithms.

Communication technology now allows cheap, real-time transmissions of voice, and near-instantaneous transfers of vast amounts of data and increasingly high-definition images. This leads to the relocation of services such as engineering, architectural design, accounting, legal work, and even medical procedures. Analyses of X-rays, imaging results and cell samples can be performed more cheaply off-site, sometimes half a world away. In combination with remote command and control technology, originally developed for military drones, it is now possible to manage highly automated production lines and even large mines from distant sites. In time, some medical procedures, including operations, may be carried out using robotics controlled remotely.

Technology has also altered business models. Advertising that costs US$50 per thousand views drops to US$4 when delivered to a computer, or US$1 on a smart phone. Lower business revenues increase pressure to cut costs by reducing staff, wages or conditions. Blogging and websites with free access cannibalise traditional media, further reducing employment.

*

The modern workforce is increasingly stratified. There are well-paid jobs for a small portion with the requisite skills. The vast majority of new employment is in the low-paid service sector, such as retail, leisure, hospitality, security, aged care and healthcare.

The (sometimes) generous terms bargained for by unionised labour forces have been diluted. The established workforce may enjoy salaried employment, related benefits and protection from termination; new workers are increasingly employed casually or on fixed contracts, often of short duration. Effective earnings are lower because of reduced entitlements and benefits. Contract workers are not compensated for periods spent waiting for work, sick leave, training, or their tools of trade. There is reduced job and income security.

Youth unemployment remains high. Even where work can be found, starting incomes are around 10–12 percent lower than in 2007.

Exploitation is common. People live in fear of restructuring or termination of their employment, constantly competing to demonstrate their fitness for the job. Nichole Gracely, who has a Master's degree in American Studies, was one of Amazon's best order pickers. Dismissed in 2012 for protesting work practices and unemployed since then, she wrote that her worst days homeless and indigent were better than her best days working at the e-tailer.[5]

Even in the growing and profitable US technology sector, major firms have been accused of collusion to suppress pay levels. Abuse is greatest for foreign workers, such as the non-immigrant computer engineers with temporary H-1B visas, who are employed via recruiters known as body shops. A joint investigation by broadcaster NBC and The Center for Investigative Reporting found that firms abuse the program by bringing in technology graduates when there is no firm job and keeping them like slaves, hostaged until they find work. When working, they cannot change jobs, as employers can levy a punitive fee.

China frequently uses workers from home on foreign projects, to take advantage of lower costs and avoid the employment conditions of the host country. Conflicts, sometimes violent, with the local workforce are common.

Workers, irrespective of profession and skill, now face what John Maynard Keynes termed technological unemployment. The process was championed as reducing low-skilled monotonous jobs and increasing employment mobility, as well as providing greater employment and lifestyle choices. Economists lauded the new knowledge/ bioengineered/clean and green (delete as required) economy. The displaced workers would become highly educated and skilled, finding new, intellectually challenging and highly paid jobs. The more cautious argued that it was a case of TINA – there is no alternative.

English economic geographer John Lovering called it the 'transition fantasy of intellectuals and policy makers'.[6] Many 'demised' or 'involuntarily separated' employees (the Kafkaesque terms for losing your job) are unlikely to find new employment. It's doubtful that textile or assembly-line workers will reinvent themselves as knowledge workers, technologists, bioengineers, financiers or other professionals. Mobility of labour is restricted by skills and immigration opportunities, as well as family, social and financial commitments, such as home ownership.

Where transition is feasible, it requires adequately funded retraining facilities. The complexity and dynamism of the new economy means that employment opportunities for retrained people are not guaranteed. For those who do find jobs, the threat of underemployment or unemployment is constant, making it difficult to make long-term plans and achieve financial and personal security.

The economic argument in favour of flexible workforces does not factor in the inefficiency and high costs of constant re-education and retraining of workers with particular skills who may not want to change occupation. It does not include the health and societal costs of the discouraged and depressed. It does not acknowledge that cheaper goods and services can only be achieved by reducing the input cost, including reductions in employment or income levels to decrease labour costs.

Ironically, the middle and professional classes who once supported outsourcing and offshoring as a way of reducing union power and increasing access to cheaper goods and services, now face their own threat of displacement: 'When the Nazis came for the communists, I remained silent; I was not a communist. When they locked up the social democrats, I remained silent; I was not a social democrat. When they came for the trade unionists, I did not speak out; I was not a trade unionist. When they came for the Jews, I remained silent; I wasn't a Jew. When they came for me, there was no one left to speak out.'[7]

*

Technology and innovation are touted as sources of future employment. The sharing economy (also known as the peer economy, collaborative economy and gig economy) is based on the ubiquitous internet, improved broadband connectivity, smart phones and apps. Individuals with spare time, houses, rooms, cars and the like can use them as sources of work and income. The economy that benefits everyone focuses on transport (Uber, Lyft, Sidecar, GetTaxi, Hailo), short-term accommodation (Airbnb, HomeAway), small tasks (TaskRabbit, Fiverr), grocery-shopping services (Instacart), home-cooked meals (Feastly), on-demand delivery services (Postmates, Favor), pet transport (DogVacay, Rover), car rental (RelayRides, Getaround), boat rental (Boatbound) and tool rental (Zilok).

Its cheerleaders frame the sharing economy in lofty utopian terms: it's not business, but a social movement, transforming relationships between people in a new form of internet intimacy. Customers are not getting cheap services, but being helped by new, interesting friends. Providers are engaged in rich and diverse work, gaining valuable independence and flexibility. Lyft's slogan is 'Your Friend with a Car'. Airbnb and Feastly urge hosts and guests to share photos and communicate to build trust.

Some things remain the same. Researchers have found that, accounting for other variables, Airbnb guests pay black hosts less than they do white ones.[8]

The sharing economy, in reality, relies on disintermediating existing businesses and minimising regulatory costs. Amateur chauffeurs, chefs and personal assistants now perform, at a lower cost, work once undertaken by full-time professionals. Airbnb, Lyft and others do not always comply with regulations designed to ensure a minimum level of skill, standard of performance, safety and security, and insurance coverage. Taxi and hire-car drivers have protested about services that undercut their often regulated charges and livelihoods. There have been anecdotes about orgies in Airbnb-rented properties, and accidents or assaults involving ride-sharing drivers.

Accountability for these services relies on the parties to a transaction rating each other, ensuring that inadequate performance will preclude future participation. Like all online reviews and rating systems, this is not a substitute for independent evaluation and oversight. Unfair reviews, predicated on ulterior motives or malice, can exclude individuals from future work, 'deactivating' them. Like the scarlet letter in Nathaniel Hawthorne's novel, every evaluation has the potential to affect the rest of someone's life, without a reliable mechanism for redress.

Behind the 1960s peace, love and flowers of the sharing economy, it is Darwinian capitalism. Uber has obtained financing of more than us$1.5 billion, valuing the business at us$40 billion – a higher valuation than traditional car hire companies such as Hertz and Avis, and publicly listed transport companies such as Delta Air Lines, American Airlines and United Continental. Airbnb has a higher value than all but the biggest hotel chains. Given the high stakes, competition is fierce, unethical and unsavoury. Uber has admitted trying to disrupt Lyft's fundraising efforts. It does not welcome criticism, allegedly considering spending a million dollars to hire researchers to uncover information on the personal lives of reporters critical of its service in order to discredit them. TaskRabbit makes it difficult for the bunnies to communicate with each other, preventing them from organising or unionising.

In the latest technology gold rush, venture capital investors are speculating on businesses that effectively broker arrangements between customers and workers, betting that low prices will create mass markets for services once reserved for the wealthy. Central to the model is that new firms pay providers less and avoid expensive regulations.

The sharing economy is overrated. Like all businesses, the model requires consistently available product and service providers. Older peer-to-peer providers highlight the developmental arc. eBay evolved from a site where people occasionally sold unwanted items to a marketing channel for professional sellers. Peer-to-peer lending platforms were intended to be for individuals advancing money to other individuals and small businesses. Increasingly they attract institutional lenders and hedge funds, which use the sites to lend at attractive yields. Uber now acts more and more as a booking agent for professional taxis and hire cars. A small number of large property owners dominate Airbnb lettings. One reporter joked: 'who would want to stop a man with twelve apartments from making ends meet?'[9]

Peer-to-peer brokers reduce costs, decreasing the income of service providers. The sharing economy requires abundant cheap contract labourers to be available at the touch of a smart-phone screen. Full-time employees with normal benefits would make the model unworkable. Comparisons to Wikipedia and open-source software are misleading. In those cases, the individuals are employed elsewhere. They contribute their services free for the joy of participation and contribution, as well as recognition as a member of a community. The sharing economy exploits low-wage workers in a weak economic environment.

Despite improving economic statistics, the deterioration in real living conditions is evident. In 2013 US retailer Walmart hosted a Thanksgiving food drive for its workers. McDonald's helped its low-paid full-time workers to make a personal budget that assumed they worked a second job to make ends meet. Such a depressed labour market is essential to the sharing economy. Now paid less, forced to work part-time or be unemployed, individuals participate in the sharing economy to cover income shortfalls. Individuals renting out their houses, cars or labour make a fraction of what they would receive in traditional full-time jobs, without any employment benefits. In the sharing economy it is 'possible for a cash-flush tech start-up to have homeless workers'.[10]

Having ridden the globalisation wave with *The World is Flat*, *New York Times* columnist Thomas Friedman now endorses the sharing economy, celebrating new micro-entrepreneurs. It isn't entrepreneurship. Former US Labour Secretary Robert Reich termed it the 'share-the-scraps' economy. It harks back to earlier times when poor, uneducated workers, many of them immigrants, took on any work to survive. Today, a new underclass provides grist for the technology entrepreneurs and investors in the sharing economy. It is desperate piecework labour, the end of middle-class dreams.

*

Postwar society was built on good, well-paid jobs: 'The most important model that rolled off the Detroit assembly lines in the twentieth century was the middle class for blue-collar workers.'[11] Now the squeezed middle classes are members of the 'precariat' or the 'precarious proletariat'. The terms originally described Japanese workers without job security, who now make up over 30 percent of the country's workforce as companies cut labour costs. The phenomenon of short-term contract employment is global. Since 2009 the UK has enjoyed strong increases in employment but the type and quality of jobs have changed. Before 2007, self-employed workers accounted for 16 percent of new jobs created. By 2014 it was 45 percent. The threat of outsourcing and contracting creates Friedrich Engels' 'reserve army of labour', permanently limiting employment, wages and conditions. Stock speculator Jay Gould's view that you can hire one half of the working class to kill the other half was vindicated.

Many workers have been reduced to the nouveau poor. The US Fed's 2014 'Report on the Economic Well-Being of U.S. Households' found that only one-third of Americans aged 18–59 years had sufficient savings to cover three months of expenses; 52 percent of Americans could not produce US$400 on short notice without borrowing money or selling something; 45 percent saved none of their income. Around 46 million now qualify for food stamps, up from 17 million in 2000. It is English philosopher Thomas Hobbes's war of all against all, in which life for many workers becomes poorer and more precarious.

In the new 'eke-onomy', the precariat survive rather than prosper, in an essentially subsistence existence. Their life is like a modern version of the dance marathons popular during the Great Depression, when impoverished young couples competed for prize money, dancing sometimes for weeks until they dropped exhausted.

*

After rising steadily, home ownership levels, another contributor to improved living standards, stagnated or began to decline. In the US the home ownership rate fell from a peak of over 69 percent in 2006 to 65 percent in 2014, the same level as in the 1990s. In Italy and Spain it also fell significantly. In Canada, the UK and Australia it has remained relatively constant. The fall was most marked in people aged below forty-four years.

The decline in home ownership reflects high housing prices, soft economic conditions, weak income levels and rising job insecurity. In some countries it reflects a decline in the supply of housing finance, as banks with existing loans that may not be repaid, as well as capital shortfalls, reduce lending. Governments, for example in the UK, have been forced to initiate programs to increase the availability of housing finance. Where they are able to purchase, potential homebuyers are discouraged by the rising amount they have to borrow and the commitment of a high proportion of their income to meet repayments. The decline in home ownership and affordability is paradoxical, given government support for housing.

Originally, owning land or homes, the preserve of the wealthy, conferred the right to vote. Despite this no longer being the case, governments subsidise home ownership, believing that it creates a more stable society and greater political engagement. Most countries provide incentives for financial institutions to lend for housing. Mortgage-interest payments are sometimes tax-deductible. Capital gains from the sale of a residence attract no or low rates of tax. Concessions on property taxes, property transfer duties, or direct grants to assist in the purchase of homes are common.

Encouraged by government assistance and subsidies, there is over-investment in housing. Houses have become larger, with the average home doubling in size since the 1950s. In the developed world the affluent own holiday homes that stay empty for much of the year, while the less well-off make do with substandard accommodation or, in the case of the poor, no homes at all.

Overinvestment in housing is inefficient. Unlike businesses, houses, once constructed, produce limited income, profits, employment or investment. Overinvestment also reduces the mobility of workers, creating an inflexible labour force. The ability to follow employment opportunities is restricted by fluctuations in house prices, the time often needed to sell properties, and high transaction costs (buying and selling can cost 5–15 percent of value). Overinvestment also limits wage flexibility, as workers are constrained by their mortgage payments.

The link between higher rates of home ownership and the wealth of nations is tenuous. The US, UK and Australia have home ownership rates of around 65–70 percent. But French, German and Japanese rates are significantly lower. Russia, many Eastern European countries, China and Mexico have home-ownership rates of more than 80 percent.

*

The housing market is distorted by the fact that home ownership is no longer merely about secure shelter. The replacement in the 1980s of company- or government-funded retirement with self-funded arrangements has meant that houses are now the way for families to accumulate and store wealth. The shift confuses a simple consumption good with a financial asset or investment.

But a residence cannot be a financial asset as long as the owners require a place to live. A principal residence does not generate income, instead requiring cash to cover taxes, maintenance and other costs. A rise in a house's value does not provide income or cash flow to meet living expenses.

The key to home ownership as an investment relies on net equity – the difference between the value of a home and the outstanding debt – which increases as the mortgage is paid off or the value of the property increases. The ability to borrow against this net equity increasingly constitutes the core of household savings and wealth, and is used to finance consumption and eventually retirement. Treating their properties like Automatic Teller Machines, Americans extracted over US$4 trillion in home equity loans between 2000 and 2008. Alternatively, homeowners can sell their house and purchase something requiring a lower outlay, freeing up cash for their living expenses.

Many people also use borrowed money to purchase real estate to rent out, hoping to profit from both rental income and future property price rises. The income from property is rarely higher than that from other investments. Where borrowed money is used, the rent may not fully cover the interest cost and other outgoings, necessitating that purchasers have other sources of income, or increase their borrowing, to finance the investment. Reliance on ever-increasing property prices to provide a return, or repay the debt used to finance the property, is risky. Pundits with vested interests, and books and seminars on property ownership espouse the infallibility of housing as an investment, assuming irreversible and continual increases in prices.

Treating houses as a financial instrument results in undiversified investment portfolio, with savings concentrated in a single asset, and exposure to volatile prices. House prices can be affected by a confluence of adverse events – economic cycles, the availability of credit, and demographics, such as large cohorts of retirees needing to adjust their real estate holdings at the same time. Price fluctuations are exacerbated by the illiquidity of the asset.

Many economies now rely excessively on the housing market. It is less affected by globalisation and is essential to employment, income and economic activity. The rising paper wealth from higher house prices helps mask a lack of growth, a decline in income levels, or uncertain employment opportunities.

The policy is contradictory. If it succeeds, then higher house prices make housing unaffordable for large portions of the population. If it fails, an unwinding housing bubble is difficult to manage, as evidenced by the US, Ireland and Spain where house prices have fallen by up to 60 percent.

Economic activity slows as individuals and investors suffer large falls in wealth, exacerbated by the concentrated nature of property exposures. Where houses are used as collateral for borrowing, a fall in price can set off requirements to provide additional collateral, creating a liquidity crunch. Governments suffer revenue losses from lower property taxes; at the same time, expenditure may rise as homeowners who have lost their houses or whose properties have lost value are forced to turn to social services. Banks can find their solvency affected quickly by a fall in house prices because of their high exposure to mortgage loans or property as security. This is exaggerated by the leveraged nature of banks and, in many cases, their reliance on wholesale money markets for funding. The need for government support for financial institutions can compound the problem.

Policymakers have learnt little. Since 2009, government and central bank policies, especially low interest rates, in countries such as the US, UK, Canada, France, Germany, Australia, New Zealand and China have artificially boosted house prices without significantly increasing the construction of new houses. Facing low returns elsewhere and concerned about the safety of financial instruments, investors have aggressively purchased residential real estate to rent out, increasingly pricing new owner-occupiers out of the housing market.

A 2014 report by the McKinsey Global Institute highlighted the problem of housing affordability. It found that 330 million urban households around the world live in unsafe or inadequate housing, or are financially stressed by housing costs. The number is expected to rise to 440 million by 2025. The causes include property prices, land availability, development conditions and rent controls. Even in rich cities like New York and London, many low- and middle-income households cannot afford basic housing and spend a high percentage (30–50) of their income on rent or mortgage repayments. The lack of affordable housing constrains economic activity, and decreases productivity by reducing labour mobility and increasing transportation times and costs.

The availability of affordable, secure shelter is a basic right. Higher house prices, which exclude a portion of the population from home ownership, also reduce their ability to build up savings in the form of home equity, which would provide a buffer for employment uncertainty and future retirement income. But changes to housing policy are difficult, because existing home and property owners have a vested interest in higher prices and the continuation of present arrangements.

*

In the 1960s and 1970s social planners forecast a future involving less work and greater leisure time, filled with personal, social and cultural satisfaction. The Leisure Studies Association's 2007 conference asked: 'Whatever happened to the leisure society?' A reduction in working hours, and retirement at a reasonable age supported by adequate financial resources are now increasingly unattainable for most people.

Defined benefit pension schemes underwritten by governments and employers promised workers retirement income based on their final salaries, indexed to inflation. But few schemes were fully funded, and ageing populations, shrinking workforces, rising dependency ratios and increasing lifespans now make the plans unworkable.

Retirement schemes face other problems. The 2015 European Central Bank's QE program resulted in an 18 percent increase in EU corporate pension deficits. Pension schemes worldwide have been forced to make riskier investments to offset low interest rates, reducing the security of funds available to meet future obligations. In Greece a desperate government that was running out of money enacted legislation to access funds supposedly set aside for pensions, in order to keep the machinery of state operating. When companies fail, employees lose their retirement benefits. In 1974 the US established the Pension Benefit Guaranty Corporation to insure pension benefits. But premium levels were set at unrealistically low levels and the corporation's ability to meet all insured entitlements remains weak. In 2015 it reported that more than half the participants may have their benefits reduced if their plan becomes insolvent and they are forced to rely on government guarantees.

State and local governments and companies are renegotiating entitlements, increasing the retirement age, reducing or eliminating automatic cost-of-living adjustments, or decreasing benefit levels. If necessary they are using bankruptcy courts to facilitate the process. Without reform, they argue, pensions would devour budgets, like the Blob in the eponymous 1958 horror film.

Other than some legacy and government pension plans, workers now rely on defined contribution schemes, based on employee savings augmented by employer payments and investment earnings. Workers bear the risk of retirement income, being responsible for the level of savings, investment returns, increases in costs and their own longevity.

A 2014 global survey found that over two-thirds of working-age people worried about having enough money to live on or running out of money in retirement. But for 85 percent of working-age people, saving for retirement was not a priority because of mortgage or other debts, and incomes that were not rising as quickly as living expenses. A high portion of retirees surveyed had not prepared adequately for retirement, being unaware of the level of savings needed.[12]

Most ordinary people will now not be able to save enough for a satisfactory level of retirement. Assume two 25-year-old workers earning a combined income of US$80,000 plan to retire at sixty-five, with a life expectancy of eighty-five. In order to achieve the recommended level of retirement savings per couple in developed countries, they would need to set aside US$10,000 per annum (13 percent of pre-tax income). The savings together with investment returns would provide them with US$1.7 million at retirement (equivalent to US$750,000 in today's money), allowing them US$50,000 per annum to live on when they stop working. This assumes an inflation rate of 2 percent per annum, and investment returns of 3 percent per annum above inflation (5 percent in nominal terms).

In reality, retirement savings are well below these levels. American households have a median financial net worth of around US$11,000, excluding homes and cars. Households nearing retirement age (55–64 years) have around US$110,000. US households in the top 20 percent income bracket have retirement savings of around US$300,000, excluding government pension plans. Around half of US households don't have any retirement savings. In Australia, which has one of the world's better retirement systems, the average worker retires with US$180,000 if they are men, and US$100,000 if they are women.

Investment returns, fees and costs affect the adequacy of retirement savings. Returns are highly variable. An OECD study examined the hypothetical case of a worker saving 5 percent of their income, 60 percent of which is invested in shares and 40 percent in government bonds. The study found significant variability in the final amount of retirement savings, depending on timing. A Japanese worker would have received around 70 percent of final salary if they'd retired in the late 1980s, when the stock market peaked, and only around 10 percent if they'd retired in 2012. The amounts received by UK and US workers have also fallen significantly from the 50–60 percent level of final salary at the height of the dot-com boom in 2000. Fund manager GMO calculated that if a worker invests $1 in an asset with an average return of 5 percent per year, subject to an average annual variation of 14 percent, then the average retirement amount after forty years would be $11, while the median amount would be $7 and the most likely outcome just $3.40. The average is skewed by a few years of exceptionally high returns.

The ability to build adequate retirement savings is also affected by wage levels. Stagnant or falling real incomes; unemployment, especially for a significant period; increases in part-time work; uncertain and short-term employment contracts all decrease the capacity to contribute consistently. In some countries, such as the US, many low-wage or part-time jobs do not offer retirement plans.

Fiscal pressures that dictate reductions in public services such as health, education and childcare services also decrease the ability of workers to save for retirement, as households are forced to bear these expenses. The greatest effect of this is on low- and middle-income households, the major beneficiaries of welfare programs.

Savings are increasingly affected by pre-retirement withdrawals, necessitated by hardships such as unemployment or illness. Following the GFC, Americans made record premature withdrawals from retirement accounts.

Many retirees are likely to reach retirement with significant amounts of debt, especially mortgages. This reflects the high price of housing, low incomes, and innovations such as interest-only mortgages, which require no regular repayment of principal. A part of retirement savings will be needed to pay off this debt, reducing the amount available to finance post-employment life.

Increased life expectancy due to improvements in medical technology as well as sharp rises in healthcare and aged care costs will also pressure retirement finances.

A high proportion of households will run through retirement savings in their lifetimes, leaving them dependent on the state for financial support. But the poor shape of public finances means that access to pensions will be limited to only the neediest, and benefits will be at subsistence level. Some see the problem of inadequacy of retirement savings as a business opportunity. An Australian gaming group proposed a new lottery, known as Set for Life, to tap into customers' dreams of giving up working; the prize was A$20,000 a month for twenty years.

People will have to live for a shorter time, survive on less, save more or work longer. Unable to build adequate savings, and with an inadequate social safety net, retirement will become a luxury available to only a small part of the population. Many workers will have to work as long as they are physically capable or until death. Spanish pension reforms termed it 'active ageing'. Most will find kinship with singer Annie Lennox's song 'Cold', where she confessed that dying was easy but living scared her to death.

*

The existing economic model also creates intergenerational issues because of its reliance on deferring economic, resource and environmental adjustments into the future. In each area, short-term gains have been pursued at the expense of risks and costs that only emerge later, entailing a transfer of wealth from the future to the present.

In the period leading up to the GFC, risk, especially the ability of individuals and firms to repay borrowings, was underpriced. The true cost of polluting the environment and consuming non-renewable resources has also been ignored. There was significant privatisation of gains while losses were socialised. Financiers entered into increasingly destructive transactions, extracting large fees and leaving taxpayers to cover the cost of the economic damage. One regulator compared the banking industry to the auto industry – both produced pollutants: for cars it was exhaust fumes; for banks, systemic risk.[13]

Future generations will ultimately bear the cost of past and present decisions and inaction. Lack of economic growth will lead to declining living standards. At the same time, the financial burden of high levels of debt and entitlements will need to be met. The belief that growth and inflation will allow economies to recover and the debt burden to be reduced without default or bankruptcy is flawed: 'No amount of synthesized growth can evaporate global debt. Trying to sell creditors, debtors and taxpayers on the idea that it can be done is a futile and dangerous proposition ... There is debt that is owed and only money or assets-in-kind can satisfy it.'[14]

But policymakers still continue to avoid crucial decisions. Like Groucho Marx, they ask, 'Why should I care about future generations? What have they ever done for me?' The resulting generational wars will affect employment, housing, the availability of social services and future retirement benefits.

For all but a small group, employment opportunities will become more limited. The need for qualifications and the rising cost of tuition mean that the young will enter the workforce with significant student debt, unless their education has been paid for by families or scholarships. Seventy percent of US students now graduate with loans, up from 43 percent twenty years ago. The average student loan balance is US$33,000, double the level twenty years ago. The balance for doctors, engineers, lawyers and business graduates is much higher. Overall, US student loan balances are more than US$1.1 trillion, having almost quadrupled since 2003. This compares to increases of 65 percent in mortgage debt (to over US$8 trillion) and a decline in credit card debt of around 4 percent (to US$660 billion) over the same period.

Even with qualifications, there may be no jobs. Paid apprenticeships and training have been replaced by unpaid internships to gain work experience. The employment-to-population ratios for 25–34-year-olds globally has declined more than for older workers.

Youth unemployment is high throughout the world, with levels of up to 60 percent in some developed countries.

Young workers face increased competition from older workers, who are deferring retirement or re-entering the workforce because of inadequate retirement savings and low returns on investments. Competition has increased even for low-paying service jobs, in fast-food and similar industries, once dominated by young workers who typically progressed to better-paying jobs after finishing their training. Today, around one-third of fast-food workers are 25–54 years of age, many having lost higher-paying jobs. With many of those jobs lost permanently, and most new work being created in the low-paid service sector, this trend is likely to continue.

In developed countries a two-tier workforce has evolved. Older workers enjoy relatively good wages and conditions. New workers are employed casually or on contracts that can pay 30 percent less than traditional full-time wage levels, often with lower benefits. Between 2005 and 2012 the median annual income level for US graduates declined by 2 percent, while the student loan balance, adjusted for inflation, increased by 35 percent.

Levels of home ownership for the young have fallen sharply, driven by higher prices and low, variable incomes. For those entering the workforce, retirement is both temporally and economically distant. Low investment returns will make it difficult to save enough to retire at all. Younger generations will not receive the benefits of the very high returns of the last 20–30 years, which resulted from strong economic conditions.

Intergenerational conflict affects the economy. Weak employment markets and student debt burdens are delaying the formation of new households. This results in lower consumption and unbalanced housing markets, with the proportion of first-time buyers falling in most advanced economies. In turn, this drives lower growth, exacerbating the problems.

The young will pay twice. As dependency ratios increase, there will
be fewer tax-paying workers to finance rapidly increasing expenditure
on healthcare and aged care entitlements. Longevity will add to the
problem. Visiting Florida, known as the Seniors' State for its high
concentration of retirees, British author Martin Amis was struck by
how the elderly seemed to 'relish the challenge of something new,
especially when it concerns their physical survival'.[15] Faced with
limited social services, constrained by weak public finances, the young
will also need to allocate more of their reduced and uncertain income
to meet education, health and their own aged care expenses.

A 2010 study by US investment bank Morgan Stanley measured
the financial burden placed on future generations, focusing on existing
debt levels and future commitments, such as those for social services,
relative to actual and potential government revenues.[16] The analysis
calculated individual nations' net worth, measured as the difference
between the current value of future tax revenues and spending, taking
into account expected budget deficits and debt servicing costs. If the
difference is positive, then the country is solvent, with the government
able to provide promised services to citizens without increasing taxes
or failing to meet its obligations to creditors. If the difference is
negative, then the country is insolvent.

The study found that the US's net worth was negative 800 percent
of GDP; that is, its future tax revenues were below committed
obligations by an amount equivalent to eight times the value of all
the goods and services America produces in a single year. European
countries had net worth of around negative 250 percent (Italy) to
negative 1800 percent (Greece). Germany, France and the UK had net
worth of around negative 500, negative 600 and negative 1000 percent
of GDP. The public finances of many developed nations were found to
be overstretched, to the point where de facto insolvency is plausible.
The analysis in fact underestimated the shortfall, as it did not take

into account the cost of environmental damage or higher commodity prices as a result of resource shortages.

A separate 2011 study by two IMF economists on the burden for future generations used the concept of lifetime net tax benefit, or generational accounting. This measures the benefits received over a person's life by quantifying the difference between all taxes paid by that individual and all payments from the government that they have received and will receive.[17] The methodology assumes that taxes and benefits are unchanged for current generations for the rest of their lives. This study found that in the US the lifetime tax benefit was positive for all age groups above eighteen years, with the largest benefit accruing to those above fifty. These generations paid less in taxes than they received in benefits from the government. In contrast, the lifetime tax benefit for the very young and future generations is negative, meaning they will have to pay more in taxes than they will receive in benefits, to cover the shortfalls.[18]

This large financial burden on future generations will have to be met through higher taxes and lower levels of government services. The only alternative is to default on some or all of these obligations.

Between 1819 and 1823, Spanish artist Francisco Goya painted fourteen works known as the Black Paintings directly onto the walls of his house. The most dramatic is *Saturn Devouring His Son*, based on the Greek myth of the Titan Cronus (the Saturn in the title). Fearing he would be overthrown by one of his children, Cronus ate each child at birth. Art critic Robert Hughes noted the painting's depiction of the 'combination of uncontrollable appetite and overwhelming shame that comes with addiction'.[19] Today, the old are eating their children.

Present and past generations have failed to understand Edmund Burke's point that '[society is] . . . a partnership not only between those who are living, but between those who are living, those who are dead and those who are to be born'.[20]

*

In advanced economies, the majority of people face increasing difficulties in finding secure jobs, earning a reasonable wage, financing and
keeping adequate housing, and building up adequate savings for a life
after work. Future generations face diminished prospects, and will be
forced to bear the costs of the problems created by their predecessors.

In 2014 Dutch graphic design student Zilla van den Born's
bachelor's thesis on 'Fakebooking' garnered attention. Using photo-
editing software on social media, she faked a five-week trip to Laos,
Cambodia and Thailand, while spending the entire time at home
in Amsterdam. She deceived family, friends and even her academic
supervisor, who thought her thesis was on a different subject. Van den
Born wanted to illustrate that the virtual world we take to be real is in
fact manipulated. Today, ordinary people everywhere are fakebooking
their lives.

EPILOGUE

Final Orders

Memories of 2008 are fading. But as William Faulkner knew: 'The past is never dead. It's not even past.'[1] The GFC and the Great Recession continue to cast their shadow.

Much of the world still sees rising levels of economic activity and living standards as a given, confidently assuming an inevitable recovery. Shortly after his 2014 election, Indian Prime Minister Narendra Modi tweeted to his more than 8 million followers: 'good times are coming'. Governments everywhere perpetuate the myth, knowing that the great masses of people will more easily fall victim to a great lie than a small one.[2]

For most of human history, as Thomas Hobbes recognised, life has been 'solitary, poor, nasty, brutish, and short'.[3] The fortunate coincidence of factors that drove the unprecedented improvement in living standards following the Industrial Revolution, and especially in the period after World War II, may have been unique, a historical aberration. Now, different influences threaten to halt further increases, and even reverse the gains.

*

The GFC showed that perpetual growth and progress is an illusion. It exposed the high debt levels, credit-driven consumption, global imbalances, excessive financialisation, and unfinanced social entitlements that underpinned an unsustainable economic model. The crisis coincided with an emerging scarcity of energy, food and water, and increasing evidence of the impact of climate change. Excessive use of cheap resources and mispricing of environmental damage had boosted growth, raising living standards.

The problems exposed by the crisis remain. Fearing rejection by voters, and unwilling to challenge powerful lobby groups, risk-averse leaders have failed to make the necessary changes, instead deploying trusted instruments that were successful in reversing previous slowdowns. Public spending, financed by government debt or central banks, would boost demand. Interest rate cuts and liquidity injections into money markets would stabilise the financial system. Strong growth and increased inflation would correct the problems.

It was the grifter's long con, a confidence trick with a potentially large payoff but difficult to pull off. House prices and stock markets have risen, but growth, employment, income and investment have barely recovered to pre-crisis levels in most advanced economies.

Despite having fared better, the US and UK have levels of growth well below trend. Europe hovers on the edge of recession. Since 2008, Japan has experienced four recessions in six years. Emerging markets have not become the expected engine for global prosperity. While still high by developed country standards, growth in China and India has almost halved. Brazil and Russia are near or in recession. The slowdown in China affects other markets, all part of complex global supply chains. Higher demand for and prices of resources from China and India shielded Australia, Canada, South Africa and New Zealand from the impact of the GFC, but the slowdown in emerging markets is now reducing growth in these commodity-dependent economies. This feeble performance comes despite unprecedented efforts by governments and central banks to promote growth.

*

Growth based on the accumulation of new debt is difficult. Contrary to widely held beliefs, the world has not begun to reduce borrowing, and the global debt-to-GDP ratio is still growing, reaching new highs. A 2014 International Center for Monetary and Banking Studies conference report was titled 'Deleveraging? What Deleveraging?' Existing and projected levels of global public and private debt may now be too high for growth or austerity to deal with. Reduction of these levels of borrowings would require implausibly high economic growth, deep cuts in government spending or higher taxes, and very large asset sales.

Default, or debt restructuring with large-scale write-offs, especially of public debt, is economically and politically difficult. Significant writedowns would trigger major crises for banks and pension funds. The losses to savers would result in a sharp contraction of economic activity. National governments would need to inject capital into banks to maintain the integrity of the payment and financial system. Instead of being dealt with, the problem of unrecoverable debt is today disguised by lending more, low interest rates, and extending maturities to maintain the illusion of solvency. By mid-2015 Greece hovered on the edge of default, highlighting the unresolved problems of excessive debt and failed policies. It was a portent of the reckoning that awaits other countries.

Slower population increases, ageing workforces, lower rates of innovation, decreased productivity improvements, lower growth in global trade and cross-border capital movement, rising inequality, and a breakdown in trust also constrain growth.

There is risk of low inflation (dubbed lowflation) or deflation. Warnings about Weimar-era hyperinflation from gold bugs, who believe that the world should revert to backing currency with the precious metal, have proved incorrect. The gold price, a barometer of inflationary expectations, rose initially as large-scale central bank intervention stoked fears of rapid price increases. It peaked at around us$1800 per ounce in 2011 and subsequently fell by around 30 percent to us$1200. Lower commodity prices, currency devaluations, competition, industrial overcapacity, and changes in technology and business models are creating deflationary pressures globally.

Low economic growth rates and low inflation would not normally be an issue, helping resolve other pressing problems, such as carbon emissions and the availability of food and energy. But low growth, low inflation and high levels of debt are incompatible.

Geopolitical risks are rising, threatening to reverse the peace dividend that followed the end of the Cold War. In 2014 journalist Roger Cohen called it the great unravelling, a term that captures the increasing political powerlessness, absence of control, and difficulty in predicting the locus and evolution of current and future crises. The situation echoes the lead-up to World War I. British historian Sir Basil Liddell Hart, writing in the 1920s, described it as half a century of creating the conditions for conflict, which were then triggered by a series of errors and misunderstandings over a few days.[4]

*

The possibility of a historical shift does not inform current thinking. Policymakers interrogate their models and torture data, failing to grasp that 'many of the things you can count don't count [while] many of the things you can't count really count'.[5] Moribund growth, low inflation, persistent weakness in the financial system, and increasing stresses in emerging markets have not deterred policymakers from persisting with unsuccessful policies or implementing new, more novel ones rather than undertaking structural change.

In 2015 successive nations cut their official interest rates well below zero. In reality, negative rates are a sign of policy failure. They punish savers and investors, and are unlikely to be effective in boosting growth or inflation. Negative rates lead to socially and economically unproductive strategies.

A negative rate regime encourages taking money out of banks, hoarding cash, or purchasing assets like gold, property or even collectibles. Savers can withdraw funds in the form of a certified or banker's cheque made payable to the depositor, and then keep the cheque to avoid paying the bank to hold their money. These actions reduce bank deposits or make funding less stable, reducing the capacity to lend. People change their behaviour, wanting to make payments quickly, but to receive them in forms whereby collection of the funds can be deferred. Instead of electronic funds transfers, the preference shifts to cash or cheques that can be held back for collection. None of these actions or dubious innovations will assist the economy. In the 1990s zero rates and concern about banks made home safes, for the physical storage of money, one of the few growth industries in Japan.

Central bankers know, even if they are unwilling to publicly acknowledge it, that their tools are inadequate or exhausted, now possessing the potency of shamanic rain dances. More than two decades of trying similar measures in Japan highlight their ineffectiveness in avoiding stagnation.

Current policies also have unintended consequences. Lower interest rates decrease incentives to reduce debt and undertake the necessary but politically difficult reforms. In 2014 the Italian government proposed to use €10 billion of interest cost savings to increase spending.

Low rates create bubbles in financial assets and real estate. In 2014 and 2015 stock markets hit new highs almost daily. Bond yields fell to levels not seen since the seventeenth-century Dutch tulip bubble. The public flotation of new companies with no earnings is at the levels of the internet bubble of the late 1990s. Borrowing to buy shares has reached new heights. Companies continue to increase debt not to invest, but to buy back their own shares in record volumes. Corporate mergers and acquisition activity at exaggerated prices are commonplace. Poor-quality borrowers can obtain loans at very low rates, with minimal protection for lenders, as happened in the lead-up to the GFC.

One market observer joked that his only worry was that there was nothing to worry about. Reconciling the performance of financial markets with the continuing problems of the real economy requires perverse reasoning: 'I'm so Bearish, I'm Bullish ... Memo to self: always buy stocks & credit on a negative [growth number].'[6] Low interest rates, liquidity provided by central banks, and government support give the appearance of stability. Intervention by policymakers suppresses volatility, encouraging accumulation of leverage, financial excess and risky behaviour, creating the conditions for a new financial crisis.

In his December 2014 letter to investors in the Eclectica hedge fund, founder Hugh Hendry confessed that he had no choice but to behave as if the things he truly believed in were now irrelevant. He was buying risky assets at artificially high prices with his investors' money, knowing full well that those valuations could not be supported and that it would all end in tears. He marvelled at the human race and the financial markets' ability to suspend judgement so frequently and for such long periods. His views were shared by many financiers.

Hugh Hendry drew a parallel to the film *The Matrix*. Morpheus (Laurence Fishburne) offers Neo (Keanu Reeves) the choice of two pills: blue to forget about the Matrix and live in the world of illusion,

or red to live in the painful world of reality. Most of the world, especially policymakers, is taking the blue pills. But taking the red pills will
not help. Reality itself has become illusory in the euphoria of virtual
prosperity driven by the flood of cheap, easy money.

*

With the promise of improving income and living standards reced-
ing, politicians have been discombobulating. In 2013 the EU's
economic affairs commissioner, Olli Rehn, explained Europe's poor
economic performance in the following terms: 'we have disappointing hard data from the end of last year, some more encouraging
soft data in the recent past, and growing investor confidence in
the future'.[7] As Prime Minister Shinzō Abe's recovery program for
Japan floundered, Economy Minister Akira Amari told reporters
that disappointing economic numbers showed a robust recovery,
although the robustness was a bit weak. In early 2015 Jim Clifton,
chairman and CEO of Gallup, called the US unemployment statistics a lie.

Financial repression is used to deal with the economic problems. Manipulation is official policy. The approved narrative is of
improvement and a return to normality. Policymakers believe that 'the
receptivity of the masses is very limited, their intelligence is small, but
their power of forgetting is enormous ... all effective propaganda must
be limited to a very few points ... until the last member of the public
understands what you want him to understand'.[8]

Despite claims that everyone is in it together, ordinary people
know that they will have to ultimately pay the bill. But people choose
to believe the promises made, falling for a confidence trick that exploits
their greed, vanity and naivety.

Economic problems feed social and political discontent, opening the way for extremism. In the Great Depression the fear and

disaffection of ordinary people who had lost their jobs and savings gave rise to fascism. Writing of the period, historian A.J.P. Taylor noted: '[the] middle class, everywhere the pillar of stability and respectability ... was now utterly destroyed ... they became resentful ... violent and irresponsible ... ready to follow the first demagogic saviour ...'[9]

*

In the natural world, organisms respond to fecund conditions by over-reproducing and behaving in ways that can ultimately jeopardise their success. When conditions change, the population crashes in a process of natural regulation, sometimes resulting in extinction. The human race faces similar dangers.

Economic growth and prosperity were by-products of consumption, unsustainable resource exploitation and serious environmental damage. Societies and individuals cannot expect to maintain high living standards and survive without a radical transformation in practices and more frugal living, perhaps following the advice of nineteenth-century philosopher John Stuart Mill to '[seek] happiness by limiting ... desires, rather than in attempting to satisfy them'.

A *gedanken* or thought experiment, favoured by Albert Einstein, illustrates the required adjustments in living standards:

People work till they die or are incapable of labour, unless they have enough savings to finance their retirement. Taxes are set at a level sufficient to finance the public services and infrastructure deemed necessary by the citizens. All benefits and assistance from the state are subject to limits and rigorously means-tested.

High-density living becomes the norm, with restrictions on individual space. Compact living minimises environmental impact and reduces energy use, personal consumption and waste. Higher population densities mean location closer to workplaces and amenities, reducing the cost of infrastructure and allowing efficient public transport. This decreases the need for private car ownership, which would be highly restricted and punitively expensive.

Vegetarianism is mandatory. Around 9600 litres of water, over 5 kilograms of grain, 16 kilograms of topsoil, and the energy equivalent of 4 litres of petrol are required to produce 450 grams of beef. Animal production for human consumption does not significantly increase the available food protein: the biological value of protein in foods from animals is around 1.4 times that of foods from plants. Yet 70–80 percent of all farmland is devoted to the production of meat. Livestock also contributes 20 percent of greenhouse emissions, especially methane, whose effects on climate are twenty times greater than carbon dioxide over a hundred-year period.

Locavorism – eating only locally produced food in season, currently a fashionable, luxury choice – is widely implemented, minimising the energy utilised in transportation and storage and reducing the 30–40 percent of food currently lost in shipping to market. All water is recycled, with limits on its consumption. In the absence of proven contamination, bottled water is unavailable.

Air conditioning is banned, further reducing energy consumption and eliminating what British economist Gwyn Prins described as an 'addiction' to physical comfort and 'the most pervasive and least noticed epidemic in modern America'.[10]

Disposable items and redundant packaging are eradicated to reduce resource waste. The US alone uses more than 17 million barrels of oil a year to make polyethylene terephthalate (PET), primarily for plastic bottles and packaging. Around 8 million tonnes of plastic waste, which takes up to 500 years to biodegrade, enters the ocean, becoming a major ecological problem for marine life and the environment. Most of the rest ends up in landfill, polluting soil. Only 10 percent of PET waste is recycled globally.

Non-essential air travel is restricted. Civilian air travel contributes around 2 percent of all greenhouse emissions, an amount that is growing rapidly with the increased popularity of leisure travel, due to its declining cost.

Electricity consumption is rationed. The modern digital world requires power-consuming data centres and server cloud farms. A large amount of power is needed to keep machines in an available state, maintain operating temperatures, and provide redundancy and backup, with only a small portion being used to perform actual tasks.

Mandatory population control, a one-child policy, is enforced, reducing education and health costs and improving the quality of the workforce and productivity. Lifetime spending on healthcare and aged care is capped at a predetermined amount for every citizen.

Frugal living addresses economic and financial problems as well as conserving resources and environmental health, preserving both for future generations. Public finances become sustainable. The burden of healthcare and aged care is reduced due to extended working lives. With people forced to live together in larger family groupings or communities, they have to share to get by. Responsibility for the care of the sick and aged shifts back to households, reducing claims on public services. Housing becomes more affordable; the amount of debt needed to finance a home is lower. Reduced consumption allows pre-existing debt to be written off or gradually retired.

Voluntary euthanasia is permitted. Given the choices, those expecting a certain quality of life may avail themselves of this option early.

While frugal living would result in an immediate sharp contraction in economic activity, over time the economy will stabilise at lower levels of activity. John Stuart Mill anticipated this type of economy: 'The increase in wealth is not boundless. The end of growth leads to a stationary state. The stationary state of capital and wealth ... would be a very considerable improvement on our present condition.'[11]

These changes are not as radical as they appear. Much of humanity already lives like this, and the conditions described would be readily familiar to older generations.

The risk of not acting is significant. Economic activity is already stagnant. The threat of financial crises is increasing. Shortages of water and food loom. If greenhouse gas emissions continue unabated, then according to research published in the journal *Nature* a dramatic change in climate is inevitable, first affecting tropical countries around 2038. If emissions were to be stabilised in the coming decades, then the shift could be delayed by around 15–30 years depending on geography.

The measures, of course, have no chance of widespread adoption, at least until circumstances force change. As an old Chinese proverb states, 'To change from a thrifty lifestyle to one of luxury is easy, to shift from luxury back to thrift is hard.' On the question of living standards and lifestyle, many people are NIMBYs (not in my backyard), NIABYs (not in anyone's backyard), BANANAs (build absolutely nothing anymore near anyone), NOPEs (not on planet earth) or CAVE (citizens against virtually everything). Elected leaders are NIMTOs (not in my term of office). Philosopher David Hume knew that 'all plans of government, which suppose great reformation in the manners of mankind, are plainly imaginary'.[12]

The world seeks consolation in token gestures, such as Earth Hour, conceived by the World Wildlife Fund and an advertising agency and supported by celebrities. The symbolic turning off of lights for a single hour once a year is promoted as the largest mass participation event of its kind in the world. Critics allege that it does nothing to actually reduce emissions and may in fact increase them, due to complications related to rapidly lowering then increasing electricity output. The event does not factor in emissions from promoting and publicising the occasion, nor does it tackle the issues of overconsumption of scarce

resources and environmental damage. It is reminiscent of the observation by poet Sarojini Naidu that it cost a fortune to keep India's ascetic
leader Mahatma Gandhi in poverty.

In Greek mythology, two sea monsters, Scylla and Charybdis,
guarded the Strait of Messina, posing a grave threat to seafarers.
To avoid Scylla meant passing too close to Charybdis. Avoiding
Charybdis meant passing too close to Scylla. Odysseus, in Homer's
epic poem, is forced to choose which of these two monsters to confront while passing through the strait. Today, the world is trapped
between Scylla, existing policies that promise stagnation and slow
decline, and Charybdis, decisive action that leads to an immediate loss
in living standards.

*

In 2007, during the GFC, the economy of Iceland collapsed. The
stock market fell 77 percent. The currency also fell sharply. Banks
became insolvent, with depositors facing the loss of their savings.
With local interest rates at an asphyxiating 15.5 percent, ordinary
Icelanders had borrowed in low-interest currencies like Japanese yen,
Swiss francs or euros to buy houses and businesses. The repayments
on these borrowings now increased to unsustainable levels. More
than one-third of Icelanders contemplated emigration. Iceland was
even for sale on eBay.

In the lead-up to the crisis, Iceland had reinvented its economy
with debt and financial services. In 2003 the three largest Icelandic
banks had assets equal to the country's annual domestic production.
In the years that followed, the banks' assets grew to US$140 billion,
over eight times Iceland's GDP. The banks raised money overseas
and lent it to buy stocks and real estate. Between 2003 and 2007
the Icelandic stock market increased by around 900 percent, while
Reykjavík house prices tripled. Icelanders' wealth grew by around

three times, and Icelandic entrepreneurs fanned out across the globe, buying companies and making investments. Between 2002 and 2007 Icelanders increased their ownership of foreign assets by fifty times. The nation had absorbed the key lesson of the new economy: buy as many assets as possible with borrowed money because asset prices only rise.

But Iceland made a better recovery from the crisis than many other countries. It allowed its banks to fail, refusing to use taxpayers' money to support insolvent institutions. It protected local depositors but refused to pay out foreign lenders who had lent unwisely. Where mortgages were greater than the value of the house, the loan was written down to a level that could reasonably be repaid. The currency was allowed to devalue. Restrictions on capital outflows were implemented.

The measures were extremely painful. As much of Iceland's requirements must be imported, costs skyrocketed. Living standards fell sharply. A large amount of wealth was lost. Icelanders understood that the existing position was unsustainable. They set about returning the country's economy to its traditional base of agriculture, fishing, geothermal energy and tourism.

There was political change too. Icelanders mobilised in a series of grassroots protests, forcing the resignation of the government. The new parliament set about tackling problems with policies that sought to ensure the rebuilding costs would be shared equitably amongst Icelanders. It launched an enquiry into the crisis. The detailed, weighty report is an extraordinary document, designed to serve as a salutary warning to future generations of what can go wrong. In a process that has few parallels globally, senior business executives, bankers, politicians and policymakers were prosecuted and some convicted.

Iceland has not fully recovered from its problems, and will be burdened by the costs of the crisis for generations to come. It is a tiny nation with a population of around 300,000, and the economy is small. But it is endowed with abundant and well-managed natural resources, and its geographic position, harsh physical environment, severe weather and active volcanism force Icelanders to work together. The concept of the common good is strong. Iceland shows that where the will to acknowledge and confront problems exists, change is possible.

*

But for most large societies and institutions, the scale and complexity of the challenges have outpaced the ability to deal with them. The global economy has reached a point where the factors that drive growth are in decline, making it less responsive to traditional and unconventional economic policies. Head of the German Bundesbank, Jens Weidmann, argued that it is not possible to artificially increase growth for a sustained period of time: 'central banks do not have an Aladdin's Lamp that you just have to rub to make all wishes come true'.[13] Unwilling to admit failure, policymakers vacillate about the correct solution, or spend money on faux strategies unlikely to accomplish anything significant or lasting. They prefer to try to do the wrong thing righter, rather than doing the right thing wrong.[14]

Sustainable growth must come from the real economy. Current policies are financial in their focus. They encourage, in the words of IMF president Christine Lagarde, excessive financial risk-taking and not enough economic risk-taking. They do not directly create jobs, increase wages or encourage investment. They do not increase skills or productivity, which would enhance an economy's potential. The policies do not address the management of non-renewable natural resources or environmental damage.

The measures implemented to deal with the effects of the GFC delayed the precipitous decline in levels of economic activity and wealth that would otherwise have occurred. Spanish dictator General Franco distinguished between problems that time solved and those that it did not. The world continues the gamble that its problems are of the first type.

But authorities cannot defer reality forever. Kicking the can down the road only shifts the responsibility for dealing with it onto others, especially future generations. Postponing the inevitable ensures that the adjustment will be even more painful, as the problems will have gotten larger. A slow, controlled correction of the financial, economic, resource and environmental excesses now would be serious but manageable. If changes are not made, then the forced correction will be dramatic and violent, with unknown consequences.

The world is remarkably sanguine about a new major crisis. In an April 2015 *Wall Street Journal* opinion piece, former vice chairman of the US Fed Alan Blinder presented a novel argument as to why current policies posed little risk. In effect, he claimed that because none of the hypothesized financial hazards had yet surfaced, they weren't going to. It was akin to an 85-year-old arguing the case for immortality on the basis that he or she had survived to date. But then 'learning is not compulsory; neither is survival'.[15]

During the last half-century each successive economic crisis has increased in severity, requiring progressively larger measures to ameliorate its effects. Over time, the policies have distorted the economy. The effectiveness of existing instruments has diminished. With public finances weakened and interest rates at historic lows, there is little room for manoeuvre. A new crisis will be like a virulent infection attacking a body whose immune system is already compromised.

*

Large, complex systems operate at the boundary between order and disorder. They can appear to be stable, but a sudden or small change can initiate a phase transition, which triggers a massive failure. The addition of a single grain of sand can cause a large sand dune to collapse without warning. Today, the global economic and social system is on the edge of chaos.[16]

Change, Bertolt Brecht observed, is required 'because things are the way they are, things will not stay the way they are'.[17] But the world has postponed, indefinitely, dealing decisively with the challenges, choosing instead to risk stagnation or collapse. Anyone who questions the present course is held up to ridicule as a professional permanent pessimist, or worse. They are considered members of the 'reality-based community', which believes that solutions must be based on facts, rather than wishful thinking.[18]

The world firmly believes in the recovery of economic growth and prosperity, as well as imminent solutions to the problems of scarcity of non-renewable resources and irreversible environmental damage. But as philosopher Michel de Montaigne asked, 'How many things we regarded yesterday as articles of faith . . . seem to us only fables today?'[19]

Sooner or later everybody has to sit down to a banquet of consequences.[20]

POSTSCRIPT

The End of the Game

This postscript examines key events since 2015: the climate emergency, resources shortages, economic stagnation, the search for solutions and the political impasse. It analyses the pandemic, which brutally exposed fatal weaknesses in our systems. It looks at the alternatives that society must choose from on the difficult road ahead.

Unhinged

History, unlike time, is not linear. There are discontinuities; rapid, unexpected shifts. Approaching the 2020s, a succession of events threatened the world's equilibrium. Repeated episodes of pestilence, catastrophe, famine, war and social disorder tested the ability of human systems to cope. Journalistic clichés – 'uncharted waters' – or over-used adjectives – 'unprecedented', 'unimaginable' – do not adequately capture the scale of developments.

In March 2020 the world began to slowly shut down. In a few short weeks, countries progressively closed to combat the fast-spreading COVID-19 outbreak. Economic activity came to a near standstill. Lines of the newly unemployed circled city blocks outside government offices, waiting to register for welfare benefits. Prices of stocks, properties, currencies and commodities fell sharply, albeit from inflated levels.

The cover of the 21 March 2020 *Economist* magazine showed a picture of Earth from space with a 'Closed' sign hanging from it.

*

It isn't only the pandemic. There are other stresses, none of them new. Parts of various systems that the world relies on to survive are fall-ing apart or have been in crisis for a long time. Human beings have ignored the growing evidence of serious concerns for decades.

There is the climate emergency. The number of extreme weather events exacerbated if not caused by climate change is increasing. There are rising pressures on food and water stocks. There are over one hundred low-level wars and civil conflicts in Africa, the Middle East, Central Asia, Asia and South America. For populations in the advanced economies of North America, Europe or Oceania, these events are invisible or occasional and brief items in the news. For citizens in these advanced nations, refugees and illegal immigration are the only tangible interruption to their lives from these distant disturbances.

There are matters of wealth. Stagnant economic activity is reflected in moribund living standards for many. The global economy never recovered from the 2008 crisis. Unsustainable levels of debt still weigh heavily on activity. The impact of aging populations, trade wars and rising inequality has made for a weak recovery.

The cures have side effects. Low, zero or even negative interest rates, abundant money and government deficits did not create the hoped-for post-Global Financial Crisis (GFC) economic renaissance. At best, free money created an unstable stability.

The only real recovery was in the prices of financial assets. Share prices, in most countries, regained and passed their pre-2008 levels. In the US, the stock market more than tripled from its lowest point. The prices of houses and other investments increased.

These inflated prices do not represent fundamental factors. To paraphrase Oscar Wilde's observation on cynics, everybody now knows the price but not necessarily the value of anything. They are a by-product of central bank and government actions. The asset price boom benefitted the wealthy, who generally own more financial assets. It benefitted those who owned homes or had retirement savings invested in shares. It did not help others, heightening inequality. For large sections of society, the dreams of a better life are increasingly out of reach.

There are the inevitable political effects. Its most visible manifestations are the election of Donald Trump to the US presidency and Brexit, where the UK voted to leave the European Union.

There is also the rise of the far-right in many countries. Traditional socialism is fashionable amongst some. Jeremy Corbyn rose to the leadership of the UK's Labour Party on a platform that drew heavily on Cuba. Senator and serial presidential candidate Bernie Sanders sought to lead a revolutionary movement that would shift the US away from free markets and capitalism to a socialist state. Neither the septuagenarian nor many Americans seemed aware that the policies advocated are commonplace in most advanced capitalist nations.

The politics are familiar. People demand strong leadership. Populists rely on the seductive appeal of simple solutions and convenient scapegoats. With solutions proving elusive and disenchantment with the existing political system rising, protestors resort to civil unrest to seek change.

*

The 2020 global pandemic brought society's problems into even sharper focus. Concern about the virus will give way to concern about the consequences of the cure. The financial response will leave many countries mired in debt or debtsolated. The crisis will exacerbate inequality, with the less well off bearing a disproportionate share of the cost, again. As the pandemic wanes, new crises – for example, weather events – will compete for attention, resources, compassion and sympathy.

The pressures are related. Our approaches to deal with the problems are flawed.

In a system of shared and finite resources, individual users, acting independently and consistent only with their self-interest, will inevitably deplete or degrade available supplies to the detriment of everybody. This is the 'tragedy of the commons' postulated in 1833 by British economist William Forster Lloyd. It underlies the threat of collapse of various natural and societal systems from over-exploitation.

It explains current approaches to dealing with the issues. Solutions merely transfer the problem to another group within society or to other nations. Decisions are deferred, leaving the task for future generations.

Ignoring the global nature of the issues, humanity refuses to cooperate in managing the earth's available resources needed for human life to function prudently without collapse.

Events have now created a perfect storm of consequences that will not abate. Every action to deal with the issues has repercussions, some positive, some negative. There is nothing that does not impact someone or something. People need to be aware of the problems, possible solutions and the ramifications and corollaries of each. Societies need to confront hard truths and high costs of addressing the difficult challenges, mostly of our own making.

Humanity's current problems may not have the 'win-win', costless solutions beloved by everybody. Aleksandr Solzhenitsyn examined the contrasting societal arrangements of Western democracies and the old Soviet system. Where individuals possess different innate abilities, he noted that if people are free then they are not equal but if they are equal then they are not free.

People need to decide which things are more important. They need to decide how much they can live without, how much discomfort they are willing to accept and how it will be shared across societies and nations. There are no more easy solutions. If humans and our civilisation is going to survive, then we must act quickly. It is not an American, British, European, Japanese, Chinese, Indian or Australian planet. We have only one world.

A Russian folk tale portrays the delicate balance that exists within the cosmos. In it, Polaris (the North Star) is a mad dog tied to the Little Bear to keep it in check. If the chain ever breaks, then it would be the end of the world. The tie is near breaking point.

Eco-Anxieties

People focus on the immediate. Climate change is slow acting. Its effects are not always directly observable. With America in the middle of a cold snap, President Donald Trump joked that the country could use some global warming.

Today, the trends are unpromising. Extreme weather events are increasing in frequency.

Global temperatures are rising. 2019 was the second-warmest year on record, slightly behind 2016. The 2010s was the warmest decade on record globally. There were extraordinary heatwaves in many countries, creating public health and agricultural problems. Forecasts suggested that by 2030 up to 200 million Indians could face a 5 percent average annual probability of a heatwave not survivable for a healthy human in the shade. By 2050, 480 million people may be exposed to a 14 percent annual risk of lethal heatwaves.

However, it was the surge in extreme weather-fuelled natural disasters, such as stronger storms, fiercer wildfires, longer and more punishing droughts and floods, that affected people directly. No part of the globe was spared.

Hurricane *Dorian*, the second strongest Atlantic hurricane on record, ravaged the Bahamas, killing seventy and leaving 300 people missing. The damage represented over 25 percent of the island's US$12 billion GDP. The scale of the devastation if it had hit more-populated areas, such as Florida, would have been catastrophic.

Typhoon *Hagibis* was Japan's second most expensive typhoon. It killed ninety-eight people and caused over US$15 billion in damage, making it Earth's most expensive weather-related disaster of 2019. *Hagibis* came less than two months after Japan's seventh most expensive typhoon on record, Typhoon *Faxai*, which caused US$7 billion in damage. Cyclone *Idai*, which ravaged Mozambique, was the Southern Hemisphere's third deadliest tropical cyclone on record. Affecting one of the world's poorest countries, the full loss of life and livelihoods was difficult to measure. It left behind images of thousands of people marooned in an inland ocean up to 45 kilometres wide.

2019 was the wettest year in US history, resulting in losses of over US$15 billion. Only the great 1993 Midwest floods, which caused losses of US$37 billion (in 2019 dollars) was worse. India's wettest monsoon in twenty-five years brought disastrous flooding to India, causing at least 1750 known deaths, the deadliest weather-related disaster of 2019. It also caused US$10 billion in damage, making it the third most expensive flood in India's history, behind the US$17.6 billion in damage from the 2014 floods and the US$12.6 billion in damage from the 1993 floods.

Australia, Central America, Brazil and Chile experienced serious drought conditions. Laos, the Philippines, Thailand, Vietnam, Cambodia, Indonesia, Malaysia and Myanmar all experienced lower than usual rainfall. North Korea suffered its worst drought in thirty-seven years. The Panama Canal experienced its driest year. Victoria Falls, the powerful waterfall on the border of Zimbabwe and Zambia, was reduced to a weak stream by a multi-year drought. One of the longest droughts on record in California came to an end in 2019. It had lasted for 376 weeks from 20 December 2011 to 5 March 2019.

Wildfires burned in the Amazon, California and South-East Asia. In 2019/20, Australia experienced an apocalyptic fire season. The fires, the result of record heat and dry conditions, started in early spring, not summer as usual. Twenty-one people were killed, 15 million acres burned and 3500 structures were destroyed. There was even greater damage to the ecosystem, with an estimated 3 billion animals killed or displaced. Wildlife losses will ultimately be higher due to the destruction of habitat, with many unique species becoming extinct.

Climate change is clearly a factor in these events, especially in terms of the frequency, timing, duration and intensity. Some of the abnormally heavy rains of 2019 were thought to be due, in large part, to warm surface temperatures across the Arabian Sea, boosted by the strongest positive mode of a known weather pattern, the Indian Ocean Dipole (IOD), in sixty years. The unusual IOD in 2019 led to the most active tropical cyclone season in the region on record.

Alternate heavy rains and drought, due to weather pattern changes, increased the risk of even worse future wildfires. Australia's fires were not even the worst on record. On 7 February 2009, the Black Saturday fires killed 173 people. In 1974/75, approximately 15 percent of the entire Australian continent (289 million acres) burned. Heavy rains in the prior years led to unusually lush grasslands, which when dried out by summer heat allowed vast areas to burn.

*

There are other worrying trends. 2019 was the Arctic's second warmest year on record. The extent of sea ice at the end of that summer was the second lowest since satellite observations began in 1979. Only 2012 was lower. The thirteen lowest sea ice extents recorded have all occurred in the last thirteen years.

The long-feared acceleration of global warming due to thawing permafrost may have begun. Permafrost holds more than double the amount of carbon that is currently in the atmosphere in the form of heat-trapping gases like CO_2 and methane. The latter is roughly 30 times more potent than carbon dioxide. While it doesn't stay in the atmosphere as long as carbon dioxide, methane is more damaging to the climate because it absorbs heat more effectively initially after release. We must address both types of emissions if we want to reduce the impact of climate change. The estimated annual release rate in 2019 of 0.3–0.6 gigatons of carbon from permafrost constituted approximately 3–6 percent of the amount of carbon released by human combustion of fossil fuels. Without action on rising temperatures, it could be two to three times bigger by the end of the century.

The near-record melt rate of the Greenland ice sheet alone represented 20 percent of global sea level rise, contributing 0.7 millimetres – about 20 percent of the current 3.3-millimetre annual increase. Since 1992, the melting of the Greenland ice sheet has increased global sea levels by a centimetre. While the amount may seem tiny, every centimetre rise exposes around 6 million people to seasonal floods each year. Since 1992, overall sea levels have risen by around 8 centimetres.

The rate of sea level rise is now double the rate measured in the early 1990s and accelerating. Scientists project rises of around 60 to 90 centimetres by the end of the twenty-first century, although 200 to 270 centimetres is plausible. By the year 2050, 150 million people will be under the waterline during high tide and 300 million will live in zones with annual flooding. By the year 2100, in a high-emission scenario, the numbers would rise to 540 million and 640 million respectively. Seventy percent of these people will live in eight countries: China, Bangladesh, India, Indonesia, Thailand, Vietnam, Japan and the Philippines.

Nations will have to spend billions to prepare for coastal flooding. San Francisco is building barriers around its airport. In London, the height of the Thames Barrier will need to be increased. Indonesia is building sea walls to protect Jakarta and there are plans to relocate the entire capital city. The economic cost of these actions may be 4 percent of global GDP by 2100.

*

The 2018 United Nations Intergovernmental Panel on Climate Change (IPCC) report painted a bleak picture and highlighted the need for urgent action. Based on its survey of more than 6000 studies, the IPCC concluded that it is critical to keep global temperature rises to 1.5 degrees Celsius or less, 25 percent below the previous safe level of 2 degrees Celsius.

Even at 1.5 degrees Celsius, a large number of ecosystems will undergo major transformations – 6 percent of insect species, 8 percent of plants and 4 percent of vertebrates would lose more than half their habitat. The figures for 2 degrees Celsius are 18 percent, 16 percent and 8 percent, respectively. The IPCC found it almost certain that a rise of 2 degrees Celsius would wipe out more than 99 percent of corals. A rise of 1.5 degrees Celsius would leave only 10–30 percent alive. Even at the lower level, iconic ecosystems, like Australia's Great Barrier Reef, are likely to be irreparably damaged.

The 187 countries attending the Paris Climate Conference agreed to hold global temperature increases to within 2 degrees Celsius above pre-industrial levels and to pursue efforts to limit them to 1.5 degrees Celsius. But the proposed measures will not reduce emissions sufficiently to achieve the 2 degrees Celsius target. It is probable that temperature rises will be 2.7 to 3.5 degrees Celsius. The 1.5 degrees Celsius target would require the world to eliminate emissions and reduce existing atmospheric greenhouse gases.

The Paris Agreement became binding in November 2016 after fifty-five countries that produce at least 55 percent of the world's greenhouse gas emissions ratified it. As of November 2020, the countries that were not parties are the US, Turkey, Iran, Iraq, Angola, Libya, Yemen and South Sudan. Following the presidential elections, it is likely that America will rejoin the treaty.

The Agreement lacks effective sanctions or enforcement mechanisms. It relies on nations complying with unverifiable promises. The rules for accounting, reporting and reviewing actual emission reductions are vague. It is doubtful that high polluters such as China, the US, India, Canada, Russia, Indonesia and Australia, which generate more than half the world's greenhouse gas emissions, will voluntarily reduce their carbon pollution.

The threat from climate change is spiralling out of our control.

Victuals

Full supermarket shelves and the ready availability of once exotic foods do not suggest scarcity. Under the surface, things are different.

In recent years, while a few countries like the US, Canada and the Black Sea region of Russia and Ukraine recorded bumper harvests, food production almost everywhere else in the world has fallen. Australian grain production fell due to drought. Rice production across Asia fell due to erratic rains. Brazilian soybean and corn production were adversely affected by a lack of rainfall. There were significant local crop failures in East Africa.

In 2020, a plague of locusts, which in Arabic means 'teeth of the wind', spread rapidly, ravaging crops in Africa, the Middle East and Pakistan. If you survived COVID-19, then it was likely that Locust-20 would kill you. The plague, one of the worst in history, was the result of heavy rains on the Arabian Peninsula that created ideal conditions for the locusts to breed. Changes in weather patterns mean that such plagues are more likely in the future.

Tariff wars and hoarding complicate the problem. Facing anxiety over the availability of wheat supplies, Russia withheld stock from the global market. It allowed domestic bread prices to fall, but prices in the rest of the world rose. Food is now another weapon of war in geopolitical conflicts.

Aid organisations warn of humanitarian catastrophes as millions in poorer countries face hunger or severe food insecurity. Countries are reliant on global stockpiles to meet demand. In the Philippines, an inability to procure rice on the world market led to riots in Manila that were brutally suppressed by President Rodrigo Duterte. Food shortages and high prices created unrest in Indonesia, Myanmar and other places. In Egypt, which relies on imported wheat, reductions in government subsidies increased the cost of bread, triggering riots. Rising food prices and other grievances were behind the 2011 rebellion that led to the fall of the Mubarak regime. Desperate people fleeing starvation fuelled illegal immigration.

The UN Food and Agriculture Organization reports that the number of hungry and undernourished people is no longer falling but rising, reverting to levels of a decade ago. In 2018, 9.2 percent of the world population (or slightly more than 700 million people) were exposed to severe levels of food insecurity, mostly in Africa, Asia and South America. An additional 17.2 percent, 1.3 billion people, experienced moderate food insecurity, meaning they lack regular access to nutritious food. The combination of moderate and severe food insecurity totals 26.4 percent of the world population, about 2 billion people.

Hunger, as measured by undernourishment, is rising in many prosperous and middle-income countries. This is the effect of economic slowdowns and downturns, poverty, inequality and marginalisation.

At the same time, there is an epidemic of overweight and obese people. In addition, around one-third of all food produced, 1.6 billion tonnes worth around US$1.2 trillion, is wasted each year. Boston Consulting Group estimates that the annual loss will reach 2.1 billion tonnes and US$1.5 trillion by 2030.

*

Ready availability of clean water is a right in developed countries. Even there, consumers concerned about quality and safety choose to drink bottled water. Despite a lack of evidence that bottled water is safer, consumers are willing to pay thousands of times more than the cost of tap water. Discarded water bottles are a major source of plastic pollution.

There are now mineral water sommeliers. Martin Riese, whose website describes him as the world's foremost expert on water, launched his own brand of mineral water: Beverly Hills 90H2o. This is apparently the 'World's Best Still or Sparkling Water', although the basis of the claim is unclear. A bottle from the Luxury Collection, Diamond Edition costs $100,000. It has a white gold cap set with more than 850 white and black diamonds.

Many countries now face water shortages. As of 2019, seventeen countries covering around 1.7 billion people, over 70 percent of them in Asia – nearly a quarter of the world's population – experienced extremely high levels of water stress. If you include countries that face shortages for at least one month a year, that number almost doubles. They are not only in the developing world. Australia, Italy, Spain and America face severe water shortages.

Cape Town and Chennai, cities with populations of nearly 5 million and 7 million respectively, recently faced exhaustion of their water supply. Good winter rains in South Africa deferred Cape Town's day of reckoning. India's wettest monsoon in twenty-five years eased critical water shortages. It pushed back Day Zero, when over 100 million of India's 1.3 billion people were forecast to run out of water. Four years earlier, São Paulo in Brazil came close to running out of water, with reservoirs reduced to 5 percent of capacity.

Current demand for water is near the maximum that can be drawn without supplies being reduced below dangerous levels. Countries deemed to be at risk of water scarcity are withdrawing 80 percent of their available water supply every year to meet the needs of agriculture, industries and cities. During the Australian wildfires, the shortage of water due to drought impeded firefighting.

Global water demand has increased six-fold over the last century. It is expected to increase by up to 50 percent by 2050. Increasing population and more water-intensive lifestyles are driving the growing demand. Pollution of water sources and climate change increasingly affect supply. With a third of the world's biggest groundwater systems in danger of drying out and the numbers living under severe water stress climbing, a small change in conditions would exacerbate food insecurity, conflict, mass migration and financial instability.

China and India, between them, have about 36 percent of the world's people but only around 11 percent of its fresh water. A country with 1.4 billion people, China has the relative water resources of Somalia. Many Chinese rivers, lakes and aquifers are now unfit for human consumption. Mega dams, diversion schemes and the mining of Tibetan glaciers are designed to address water security. These projects are irreparably altering regional hydrology and destroying ecosystems. The risk of confrontation between China and downstream nations, such as India, Bangladesh and South-East Asian countries, is increasing.

In 2020 there was increasing rancour over Ethiopia's Grand Renaissance Dam on the Blue Nile. Filling the dam threatened areas on the Grand Nile River, including the Nile Valley, where up to 90 percent of Egyptians live. Ethiopia, Egypt and Sudan struggled to reach a negotiated settlement. An armed conflict could not be discounted.

Shortages of essential resources now increasingly limit humanity's options. The world is sliding towards a *Mad Max* future of armed groups fighting and dying to control the basic resources needed for survival.

Wages of War

Despite claims that the post-1989 world economy benefitted from a peace dividend, constant wars were needed to ensure peace. After the fall of the Berlin Wall, the global economy did gain from lower defence spending, the integration of former communist economies into the Western trading economy and improved security. It provided impetus to globalisation, which has reversed in recent years.

Now, there are new cold wars as the US, Russia and China compete on economic and military battlefields. Overlapping territorial claims simmer in the South China Sea and East Asia. North Korea's belligerence and growing nuclear capabilities remain a threat.

Hot wars continue. The Middle East has multiple regional conflicts in the aftermath of the failed Arab Spring and destabilising Western intervention in Afghanistan and Iraq after 9/11. Congo has experienced a series of rolling conflicts for a quarter of a century, causing over five million deaths, although the exact number remains disputed. Tribal wars in Africa's Horn and Great Rift Valley seem incapable of resolution.

Aided by great powers and regional actors, these wars take the form of sporadic fighting that results in limited direct military casualties. The major cost is mass civilian death through displacement, hunger and disease. In many cases, the combatants have lost sight of what they are even fighting about.

There are internal conflicts. Myanmar's army, backed by the Buddhist majority, attacked mainly Muslim Rohingya areas in the far west of the country in response to attacks on military outposts by a small guerrilla group. Aung San Suu Kyi, Myanmar's de facto leader, defended her country against charges of genocide before the International Court of Justice. She rejected allegations of mass shootings, throat-slittings, the tossing of babies into burning houses and women gang-raped or stabbed in the vagina. In awarding the Nobel Peace Prize to Aung San Suu Kyi in 1991, the committee had called her 'an important symbol in the struggle against oppression' and an inspiration to those 'striving to attain democracy, human rights and ethnic conciliation by peaceful means'.

Wars and conflicts are expensive. They require increased spending on defence and national security. There are direct costs, such as loss of life and destruction of property as well as the cost of waging war. There is also the indirect cost of disruptions, restrictions on normal commercial and personal life, and the loss of confidence, which impinges on economic activity. Even minor conflicts can disrupt critical resource supplies, like oil or crucial minerals, and trade routes.

The Syrian civil war illustrates the high humanitarian cost and the economic expense of dealing with wars. An estimated 6.5 million people have been displaced within Syria, while more than 3 million have fled to neighbouring countries. The Rohingya crisis led to an exodus of nearly a million refugees into neighbouring Bangladesh. War refugees and illegal immigration of innocent civilians flee-ing various conflicts around the world now affects North America, Europe and Australia.

In March 2019 an Australian, a member of the white suprema-cist alt-right, staged a terrorist attack on the Al Noor Mosque and Linwood Islamic Centre in Christchurch, New Zealand, during Friday prayer. The gunman, who live-streamed the first shooting on Facebook, killed over fifty people and injured about the same number. Elsewhere in the Middle East, Africa, North America, Europe and Australia, random acts of Islamic terrorism continue regularly. The war against terror did not eliminate but encouraged extremism.

Combating and controlling failed states requires the commitment of vast resources. Asymmetric warfare, cyber attacks or isolated terror-ist attacks impose high costs on economies. Some economists argue that this spending boosts economic activity. However, any rise is arti-ficial and temporary. In the nineteenth century, French economist Frédéric Bastiat explained that there is no benefit in the destruction of productive assets or expenditure on unproductive assets. The money expended could otherwise have been put to more productive uses, generating greater wealth.

From the Great Recession to the Great Stagnation

If climate concerns, resource security and conflict are remote and abstract for many, then economic concerns are immediate and visceral.

In most countries, the economy rebounded after the sharp 2008/09 global economic downturn – the Great Recession. The recovery, measured as real GDP or economic output per capita growth, was slow, uneven, weak and spasmodic. Countries with stronger pre-crisis positions and able to devalue their currencies were less affected. Many countries, like Italy and Spain, suffered long-term output losses of almost a fifth of their economy.

In economics, hysteresis refers to effects that persist after the initial causes are removed. Just as a heart attack victim may not recover full pulmonary function, crises usually cause long-lasting or permanent damage to economies. The dynamics of a large shock to the economic system are still not well understood. Studies show that the peak estimated output loss from a financial crisis may be almost 8 percent, with output losses of around 7 percent persisting at a ten-year horizon.

Central to hysteresis is the loss of wealth. In the GFC, the global losses were large, with the US alone losing around US$10 trillion in wealth, mainly falling values of houses and investments. Over the subsequent decade, rising share and house prices restored wealth, assuming you were not forced to sell your holdings. For the less wealthy, the losses are frequently irrecoverable.

The major problem is debt. In the years preceding the GFC, there was a significant accumulation of household debt. This reflected growing income inequality and wage stagnation. Households increased debt to maintain their desired living standard. The sharp decline in housing prices and the recession forced consumers to pay off loans. Over-indebted businesses did the same.

The diversion of income to repay debt reduced spending and investment. The rebound in the housing sector was well below prior recession recoveries because of the severity of the damage and reduced availability of credit. A decade after the crisis, millions of homeowners in the US and some badly affected countries still had mortgages that exceeded the value of their homes.

Governments propped up activity by running large budget deficits, which resulted in large rises in government debt. The deficits also reflected the cost of bailing out banks and the decline in tax revenues due to lower economic activity. The additional government spending was insufficient to offset private sector weakness.

In Europe, some countries embarked on ill-considered austerity programs, compounding the intensity and length of downturns. The after-effects of the Great Recession were one factor in Britain's decision to leave the European Union in 2016. Shortfalls in business investment and lower improvements in labour, capital and total factor productivity impeded growth.

Crises have persistent negative effects on the labour market. Ostensibly, employment recovered in most affected countries, but real unemployment is probably higher than official estimates. The measures of unemployment are increasingly meaningless. You are counted as working if you work for an hour a week or sell trinkets on eBay.

Statistics do not capture the millions who have left the workforce and lack any realistic prospects of getting work. There is a core of long-term unemployed whose depreciating job skills make it unlikely that they will ever be re-employed.

Underemployment, which considers people who wanted more hours or part-time workers seeking full-time work, remains stubbornly high. Many struggle to get jobs that pay as well as positions they enjoyed before the Great Recession. A high proportion of new jobs are casual, low paid and do not have benefits, such as leave, sick leave or, in some countries, healthcare. One estimate put the loss from the overall damage to labour markets at US$70,000 for every American.

For those with work, wage growth and job security are low. Deregulation of the labour market, weakening of union coverage and power and devolution of wage negotiation to enterprise or individual levels, combined with global competition, means that only those with highly sought-after skills are immune. The employment damage is widespread, but greatest amongst minority groups and immigrants.

Demographics is a factor in the growth slowdown. The aging population and lower fertility, in part driven by the 2008 crisis, reduces the size of the workforce. This is compounded by declines in net migration (immigration minus emigration) rates in advanced economies. In nations where output and employment losses from the crisis were large, income inequality increased, often reinforcing existing trends. This slowed growth as people with lower incomes have a higher marginal propensity to consume.

Hysteresis is also behavioural. Crises alter attitudes towards spending and saving. After the Great Depression, people became thriftier and more cautious, fearing a new dislocation that would threaten their survival.

*

Technology and deglobalisation affected the economic recovery.

Traditionally, innovation boosts growth by improving productivity and creating new industries that add large numbers of well-paid jobs. Today, technologies, which are tweaks on existing ideas rather than entirely new concepts, impact the economy differently.

The centrepiece of the age is the internet linking a plethora of personal communication devices, such as computers, tablets and smart phones. It is an evolution of the telegraph, the telephone, radio, the gramophone, cinema and TV, the library and the printing press. The internet combines a digital post office, shopping mall, library and newsstand, a music and video shop, an adult bookstore, casino and gaming arcade. While more efficient, it isn't radical.

Today, seven of the ten most valuable companies globally are 'platform' businesses. They create electronic marketplaces that allow people to buy and sell existing products or provide message boards for sharing information. Central to their success is the creation of digital communities, whose every click, every purchase and every interaction with others can be stored and studied. The resultant information can be used to target consumers to sell them stuff that they need or don't need. The data can be sold to people who seek to influence their behaviours.

These platforms – Facebook, Google, Amazon, Alibaba, Apple, Uber, Airbnb – take market share from existing businesses. In doing this, they create large profits for their shareholders but do not really contribute substantially to growth.

New technologies, such as robotics and artificial intelligence, seek to automate almost all economic activity and work. Automation and computerisation of tasks may eliminate up to 47 percent of total US employment over time. If this occurs, returns – that is, pay, benefits or other compensation – to a small number of skilled workers in the development and application of information and communications will remain high. It will result in large job losses in the middle and bottom of the income distribution curve. Some displaced workers may adapt but large numbers will be unemployed or only find jobs in low-wage sectors.

While the process is nascent, it is already having an impact in many professions, affecting the nature of work and levels of employment. Given that the global economy is reliant on consumption, the loss of jobs and income acts as a drag on activity levels.

*

Since the early 1980s, global trade and capital movements have been an important catalyst for growth. After 2008, there was a sharp drop in international trade. It recovered somewhat but had lost momentum and increasingly faces complex threats.

Trade volume expanded by about 1 percent in 2019, the weakest level since 2012, as America launched trade wars. Under President Trump, America turned its back on the rules-based international trade regime developed under the auspices of the World Trade Organization. He imposed tariffs initially on China but progressively on a wide range of trading partners including supposed allies. The US abandoned putative treaties or sought to renegotiate existing ones on terms consistent with the president's 'America First' policies. Underlying the shift were several concerns: the US trade deficit, intellectual property theft, China's relatively closed market and the need to honour election promises to boost American manufacturing.

In pursuit of this objective, America weaponised the US dollar using sanctions. Under the postwar Bretton Woods system, the US dollar functions as a reserve currency and major medium of payment in cross-border trade. While the US accounts for about 20 percent of the world's economic output, more than half of all global currency reserves and trade is denominated in dollars.

The Trump administration used descriptively titled legislation – the International Emergency Economic Powers Act, the Trading with the Enemy Act, the Patriot Act, Threats by Establishing Redlines Act and the Defending American Security from Kremlin Aggression Act – to exert unprecedented control over international economic activity. Sanctions target persons, entities, organisations, a regime or an entire country. Secondary curbs restrict foreign corporations, financial institutions and individuals from doing business with sanctioned entities. Any dollar payment flowing through a US bank or the American payments system provides the necessary nexus for the US to prosecute the offender or act against its American assets. This gives the US extraterritorial reach over non-Americans trading with or financing a sanctioned party. The mere threat of prosecution can destabilise finances, trade and currency markets, effectively disrupting the activities of non-Americans.

Trade had been mutually beneficial. In the past twenty years, trade helped China, a crucial driver of emerging markets, to grow from one-tenths to two-thirds the size of the US economy. Today, China's blacklisted Huawei Technologies Co. relies on chips designed in America while advanced economies benefit from its cheaper and often cutting-edge 5G technology. Three-quarters of the world's smart phones, mostly made in emerging markets and exported globally, use Google's Android mobile operating system.

Trade restrictions hurt everybody. President Trump claimed that China was paying the tariffs; billions were flowing into the American treasury coffers. In fact, the cost was being borne by US consumers. American restrictions hurt developing nations as well as advanced economies.

In a world of limited demand, irrespective of leadership or ideology, governments everywhere face a mounting anti-globalisation backlash. Nationalist agendas and a shift to autarky – closed economies – will persist. A return to strong growth in trade and cross-border capital flows seems unlikely.

Climate change and resource scarcity, as well as security concerns, affects growth. In 2019, damages from extreme weather events globally totalled in excess of US$40 billion. Climate was a major factor in at least fifteen events in 2019 that cost more than US$1 billion in damage, with over half of those costing more than US$10 billion each. Most of these losses were passed on to the general population in the form of larger insurance premiums.

Increasing food prices and the cost of aid to support populations suffering hunger and starvation also affect growth. Rising security and defence costs adds to the problem of public finances, which leads to increased debt, higher taxes or lost government services.

In the aftermath of the Great Recession, the global economy entered the Great Stagnation.

S.H.T.F.

For most, economic statistics about growth and employment are meaningless. Their focus is jobs, wages to pay for essentials and a bit more, the ability to buy homes, and to provide for children and retirement. The effect of the lacklustre economy on different strata of society varied.

Low-income groups found themselves trapped in the Shit Life Syndrome. Poorly educated and trained, they were forced to take low-wage, insecure, dead-end jobs. Many were too old, too sick, too inexperienced or trapped as carers for families. They relied on frequently inadequate state benefits. Low incomes led to bad diets, poor accommodation, and limited access to healthcare. They eked out bare existences, trapped in cycles of poverty.

Entire regions of countries were depressed. In a 2018 Orwell Prize-winning article, *Financial Times* reporter Sarah O'Connor depicted the Dickensian condition of Blackpool. She found that healthy, skilled people had left the town, leaving behind the unskilled, the unemployed and the unwell. Those that society left behind became concentrated in places like the seaside town in otherwise seemingly prosperous countries. The article was titled, 'Left behind: can anyone save the towns the economy forgot?'

Caseworkers were powerless to fix mental or physical health issues, inseparable from economic and emotional problems. Life expectancy and social wellbeing were in decline. Bombarded by glossy portrayals of out-of-reach lifestyles, many turned to alcohol, anti-depressants and opioids to cope with lives without prospects. Overwhelmed by financial or emotional pressures, many turned to violence, sometimes taking their own lives in what has become known as 'deaths of despair'.

The middle class, which had shrunk, faced different pressures. They struggled to maintain their tenuous hold on respectability, which could be compromised by a job loss, health or family issues. For the most part, they remained debt serfs, indebted successively by the cost of their education, houses and increasingly the cost of expected life-styles. Middle-class affability and confidence were mainly surface.

People in emerging markets were in similar positions. Belying self-serving statements about reductions in poverty, defined as earning less than US$1.90 per day, many slipped further into subsistence and lived on the edge of destitution. The middle class earned around US$3 to US$11 per day in lower-middle-income countries and three times that in upper-middle-income ones. Government services and welfare safety nets regarded as standard in advanced economies were rarely available. Like their First World counterparts, the middle class in developing economies hung on precariously.

The prospects for emerging markets have dimmed considerably since the heady days of the BRICS. In 2019, growth in developing countries fell to 3.7 percent, the slowest pace since 2009. Activity was affected by stagnant export demand from the developed world. Rising costs in many countries reduced competitiveness as industries relocated successively from China to Vietnam to Cambodia to Myanmar to Haiti. Skills and infrastructure shortages limited potential growth. Commodity exporters were affected by volatile prices, especially of oil. Endemic corruption and institutional weaknesses remained constant.

The emerging world has also become increasingly dependent on debt. This was a by-product of the post-2008 financial policies of developed countries. Abundant liquidity chasing higher returns poured into emerging markets. As a significant portion of emerging market borrowings were in foreign currency, usually US dollars, higher

American interest rates or a stronger dollar increased the financial pressure on debtor countries.

Trade conflicts hurt emerging countries. Sino-American trade tensions alone reduced the level of global GDP by 0.8 percent by 2020. This affected emerging countries' development paths. Lower income nations historically focused on export-oriented industries based around cheap labour costs, such as textiles and manufacturing. Now, weak demand and trade disputes limited this option, stunting their growth. Higher income developing countries faced technology transfer restrictions that constrained their growth.

Meanwhile, automation eroded the advantages of low-skilled, cheap labour and offshoring. Advanced economies encouraged companies to re-shore back to their home markets. The failure of Prime Minister Narendra Modi's Make in India strategy reflected the shift. India has failed to produce the 1 million new jobs per month needed to absorb new entrants into the workforce. Indian Railways recently received 23 million applications for 90,000 vacancies. Well-qualified applicants, some with advanced degrees, battled for often menial clerical positions. The slower growth created a dangerous feedback loop. Widespread dissatisfaction with economic conditions was the perfect breeding ground for civic unrest.

*

Boosted by rising asset prices and taking advantage of almost free money, the rich and ultra-rich prospered. The Credit Suisse Global Wealth Report recorded aggregate global wealth rose to US$360.6 trillion in 2019. Wealth was US$70,850 per adult, but half had a net worth below US$10,000. The richest 10 percent owned 82 percent of global wealth and the top 1 percent owned 45 percent.

A shift away from public markets gave the rich new opportunities for wealth accretion.

Increasingly, companies raised money, both equity and debt, privately. This allowed flexibility. It avoided onerous disclosure requirements designed to protect investors and overzealous scrutiny of their internal workings, especially remuneration of key employees. Family offices, rich individuals and funds catering to them enjoyed special access to these exclusive private opportunities.

Early investors in these private transactions were able to profit by marking up the value of investments before on-selling them to new investors who sought entry into the golden circle. Opaque models and secretive transactions, often between related parties, were used to set prices in a subjective process that lacked transparency and consistency. The share offerings of WeWork and Uber highlighted the often large disparity between valuations established in private transactions and eventual publicly traded prices.

Public markets were now simply designed to allow early investors to offload their holdings to a broader investor base to lock in gains. The moneyed always found ways to profit. John D. Rockefeller reputedly once claimed that he had ways of making money that no one knew about.

*

The interests of the wealthy and the poor had an unusual point of intersection – preparation for the end of days. Both groups did not like the direction of things.

Some from lower socio-economic backgrounds braced for S.H.T.F. (when the shit hits the fan). They worried about government intervention in their lives, the power of the elites, and out-of-control technology. This was the world of *Doomsday Preppers*, a reality show featuring bearded, self-sufficient Americans with the skills to live off the land. The focus was on everything needed to live off the grid, now or when the end of civilisation came. A large supporting industry provided supplies and equipment, as well as training courses in self-defence, firearms and farming. Yearning for a nostalgic, pastoral past, the survivalists were preparing for the world of Cormac McCarthy's *The Road*.

The rich were afraid of financial collapse and unrest. Fearing that paper money was becoming valueless, they purchased real assets – farmland, real estate, essential businesses, as well as gold and collectibles. Some ventured into crypto-currencies, like bitcoin, though few understood them.

These alternative currencies used blockchain, an encryption technology resistant to modification that can be used to store data safely. The information is held in open, distributed networks where any transaction or changes require the agreement of all participants. Institutions sanctioned by the state typically record ownership of assets like property and changes in holdings. Blockchain distributes that authority to participants in the network. Everybody must agree to your ownership of money or property and agree to any transfer. The sanction of governments or central banks is unnecessary.

In its first coming, bitcoin facilitated anonymous, illicit transactions on the dark web, especially the notorious Silk Road. Over time, as people questioned the economic future, bitcoin attracted wider interest as a hedge against instability. The rationale was that it existed outside the traditional financial system.

Other plutocrats, usually regular Burning Man attendees, sought safe havens as protection against any future collapse. New Zealand emerged as a favoured post-apocalypse refuge. It was a First World country with a population less than the city of New York and largely self-sufficient in energy, water and food. The government astutely sold citizenship rights for millions of dollars.

For everybody, the economic future was unusually uncertain.

Magical Economics

In the face of seemingly intractable problems, economic, technological and societal quackery promising simple, costless solutions took hold.

Policymakers embraced comedian Will Rogers' proposition that if stupidity got you into this mess then surely it could get you out. They bet on large-scale government spending, zero and even negative interest rates, unlimited funds and aerial money drops. They would restore growth and create inflation, a relatively painless way to lower high debt levels, a central cause of the last crisis.

Debt levels did not fall but increased in the aftermath of 2008, encouraged in part by low interest rates and abundant liquidity. Global debt as a percentage of GDP rose from around 250 percent in 2007 to 325 percent in 2019. Debt levels have tripled since 1999. All forms of borrowing increased – household, corporate and government. Public debt grew dramatically to finance rescue efforts after the Great Recession.

With growth and inflation sluggish, there were now limited options to reduce debt. Borrowers could divert income to pay off debt. That's easier said than done, given that very little of the debt assumed over the last decade was put to productive uses. As wages stagnated, households borrowed to finance consumption. Companies borrowed to finance share buybacks and acquisitions. Governments borrowed to finance current expenditure, rather than infrastructure or strategic investments. A sharp deleveraging now risked a recession, making repayment even more difficult. Shrinking the pile of public debt would require governments to raise taxes and cut spending, which would dampen economic activity.

The only other way to reduce debt levels was bankruptcy, write-offs or using negative nominal interest rates to reduce the face value of the debt. In all cases, investors, banks and depositors would lose savings and income. Financial institutions and pension funds may become insolvent. Retirement income and public services paid for by household taxes and contributions would not be delivered. In turn, this would reduce consumption, investment and the availability of credit. Depending on the size of the write-offs required, the economic and social losses could be considerable.

*

Not only did the policies not solve the economic problems, they created the conditions for future financial crises. Low rates and large amounts of cash swilling around set off the everything bubble, with prices of shares, especially in America, and real estate globally rising sharply.

Investment strategies became surreal. Investors purchased shares for income, the dividend, ignoring the risk of price falls. At the same time, they bought bonds that paid no or negative interest rates in the expectation of capital gains from even lower interest rates.

Advised by financial advisers and banks keen to earn sales commissions, investors took on more risk. Moving out of safe investments, they purchased corporate, high-yield and emerging-market debt, and made risky loans in support of private equity transactions. Securitisation and collateralised debt obligations, which were problematic in the 2008 crisis, re-emerged under new labels. Even subprime mortgages and auto loans were respectable again.

Investors bought ever longer fixed rate bonds, including century (100-year) bonds issued by Mexico, Argentina and the Brazilian state-owned oil company Petrobras. Investors even embraced hurricane, earthquake and pandemic risk in CAT or catastrophe bonds, where interest or principal is lost if a specified natural disaster occurs. One prospectus noted coyly that the issue had 'non-negligible risks to repayment'.

Lazy investors, unsure about which stock to buy, flocked to Exchange Traded Funds (ETFs), which created exposure to an index, effectively a basket of shares. The funds charged low and sometimes no fees. They promised investors ready access to their money. There was no guarantee that under stressed conditions the mechanism would work. Inclusion in popular share and bond indices meant that funds that tracked them became 'index tourists', forced to invest in these issues.

Investors sought to take advantage of the stability engineered by central bank intervention, selling insurance on price fluctuations of assets. They invested, via funds, in quantitative investment strategies, such as smart beta, factor investments, risk parity or volatility control. These funds were vulnerable to periods of high volatility.

Many strategies were momentum-driven and trend-following, forcing buying as prices rise and selling as they decline. This added to the price pressure, especially when markets became volatile.

Most strategies assumed securities could be readily traded. The problem was that automated trading dominated activity, being responsible for about 80 percent of total activity. They used algorithms calibrated to past data, weighted heavily to recent artificially benign market conditions. In times of stress, algorithmic traders stopped trading, magnifying shocks. The smartest people in the room seemed not to grasp that no investment product can be more liquid than its underlying asset, which frequently ceased to trade during dislocations.

Many investors and funds borrowed money to enhance returns. These leveraged investors would be forced to sell liquid assets in a major correction, regardless of the price outlook, in order to raise funds for margin calls or redemptions. No one knew how these investments would fare in volatile, falling and illiquid markets. In early 2018, a relatively minor dislocation in volatility markets spread rapidly to other assets, resulting in global losses of around US$5 trillion, providing warnings of the real risk.

*

John Kenneth Galbraith in *The Great Crash, 1929* describes 'bezzle'. This is theft where there is a lengthy interval between the crime and its discovery. Unaware of the loss, the owner continues to feel richer. A common feature of the new investments was high current returns, which did not compensate for the real risk that would only emerge much later. Fearing depreciation of the purchasing power of their savings, investors invested in different flavours of bezzle.

Argentina's century bond spoke to the times. Since gaining independence from Spain in 1816, the Latin American nation has defaulted on its debt no less than nine times, most recently in 2001. In June 2017, in a remarkable rehabilitation, Argentina issued US dollar-denominated bonds maturing in 100 years to raise US$2.75 billion at a cost of 7.9 percent. Ignoring risk and history, enthusiastic investors, hungry for the high returns, oversubscribed the issue many times over.

By 2019 the bonds had lost half their value, as Argentina ran into familiar problems. By mid-2020, the combination of another economic crisis and the pandemic pushed the country towards default yet again. The country would not be in a position to make any interest or principal payments on its borrowings for years. The bond now trades at twenty to thirty cents in the dollar, leaving investors with a capital loss of over 70 percent.

There are different ways to lose money. During a period of rising prices, you lose by not buying. When markets turn and prices fall, you lose by having bought during the rally. One way or another, investors were exposed.

*

Belatedly, central bankers, at least in the US, tried to normalise interest rates to rein in the excesses. Beginning in late 2015, the US Federal Reserve moved their target interest rates from 0–0.25 percent to 2.5 percent in increments of 0.25 percent and began to turn off the money spigot. The move was carefully calibrated to avoid the disastrous taper tantrum when Chairman Bernanke had attempted the same thing in 2013. It ended the same way, eventually.

In December 2018, financial factors – falling equity markets, rising borrowing costs, increased volatility – and a perceived weakening of economic activity, primarily in Europe and China, forced a retracement. Central banks collectively injected as much as US$500 billion of liquidity to stabilise economic conditions. The US Federal Reserve put interest rate increases on hold and contemplated a halt to its balance sheet reduction plan. Other central banks took similar actions, fuelling a new phase of the bubble as markets careened from December's indiscriminate selling to January's indiscriminate buying.

Walter Bagehot's oft-cited rule was that central banks should act only as lenders of last resort in times of financial crisis. Now, central bankers were lenders of first resort, expected to step in at any sign of problems. They found themselves boxed into a situation where they could not normalise policy and must maintain low rates and abundant liquidity, lest they destabilise fragile asset markets and spur low growth and disinflation. This was quantitative easing infinity (QE infinity). Central banks were, as was now fashionable to state, the only game in town. In fact, the game was lost.

*

For the real economy, this meant Japanification: chronic stagnation, characterised by anaemic economic growth and feeble inflation or even deflation. It meant an economy that was on permanent life-support, reliant on low interest rates and regular infusions of government and central bank money. It meant a world where central banks bought government bonds, corporate debt and shares to keep prices from falling.

It was a world of lost decades and generations. In Japan, it created a strange sub-culture of herbivores or grass-eaters – men who lived alone and rarely went out, had no interest in getting married or find-ing a girlfriend and acted out their life independently of other people.

For the financial markets, it meant that notions of value were irrel-evant. Rising prices that drove fictitious paper wealth revolved around the actions of central banks. Bad news was good news. Slower eco-nomic growth and poor performance of the real economy created expectations of more central bank money, lower rates and government spending. Like Pavlov's dog, financial markets instinctively salivated at the slightest hint of intervention.

Policymakers sought to project a sense of control, insisting that there was more they could do to revive growth and inflation. They sounded like Monty Python's Black Knight, the limbless, mortally wounded war-rior who threatens to bleed on his victorious opponent. The truth was that governments and central banks had very few weapons left. They had probably lost any chance of restoring the economy's health.

Bernanke's successor, Janet Yellen, thought that central bankers had done a good job. They had . . . in ensuring stagnation, creating asset price bubbles, allowing an epic build-up of debt, crucifying sav-ers, bailing out banks and inefficient businesses, and entrenching inequality. Vitas Vasiliauskas, a member of the European Central Bank Governing Council, thought central bankers were 'magic people'. One businessman probably captured the truth: '[Central banks are like] an ant on a log who's been given a steering wheel going down a river . . . The log is just taking him down river.'

Techno-Optimism

Just as to someone with a hammer everything looks like a nail, tech-nologists had technological solutions for everything. Evgeny Morozov, a Belarusian intellectual who studies political and social implica-tions of technology, sarcastically titled his book, *To Save Everything, Click Here*.

Intellectual overreach was founded on financial success and astronomical share market valuations of the FAANGs (an acronym consisting of the five prominent American technology companies: Facebook, Amazon, Apple, Netflix and Google – now known as Alphabet). Not satisfied with their Croesus-like wealth, technologists had opinions on everything and wanted to run the world. Noam Cohen, an American journalist, called them 'the Know-It-Alls'.

In a poorly disguised reconnaissance trip for a possible presidential tilt, Facebook founder Mark Zuckerberg discovered that America was deeply polarised, unequal and suffering from an opioid crisis. Subsequently, in a public letter to his daughter, Zuckerberg and his wife set out their banal and myopic world view. Everything would be solved by technological progress and connectivity. Access to the internet would facilitate education, health, financial services and employment, even if you didn't live in a good economy. Technology would advance human potential and promote equality. It was simple!

Many technologists used their wealth to promote conservative libertarian agendas. They proposed floating sea-steading communities beyond the reach of nation states. Rejecting normal taxation, they wanted charitable donations from their monopoly profits to finance governments. It would be an opt-in society run by technocrats.

It wasn't a matter of differing education backgrounds or the different cultures between science and humanities identified by C. P. Snow in his 1959 lecture 'The Two Cultures'. It was John Kenneth Galbraith's observation that association with large sums of money created an illusion of intelligence, which was just that – an illusion.

*

While Apple at least made some things, many of the FAANGs were not technology companies. Amazon sold things but was evolving into a virtual marketplace catering to third parties. Facebook and Google were little more than advertising platforms. Extracted user information and data trails were sold to advertisers for targeting potential clients. Shoshana Zuboff, an American author and scholar, termed it 'surveillance capitalism'. Human experience was now raw data recorded, analysed and translated into behavioural information that sought to predict commercial decisions and wider choices.

The technologists wanted a world where a device linked to the internet and the cloud intermediates every human or commercial interaction. The bait was that the highly addictive services were free. Everybody ignored the axiom of the digital age: if it's free, you're the product. The providers monitored the behaviour of users electronically and even physically in astonishing detail, frequently without their explicit consent. The companies fostered user ignorance to disguise their true modus operandi. The people that controlled the devices and access wielded enormous power. Everybody and everything were their hostage.

Due to its novelty, the companies operated in an area that was poorly regulated. For example, Google sought to digitise and store every book ever printed, ignoring intellectual property. It did not seek permission from anyone to photograph every street and house on the planet. Facebook's beacons reported user activities and published them to others' news feeds without consent. Even where users specifically denied consent, the companies used secret techniques to extract or infer data. The technologists worked on the principle that rather than ask for permission in advance they would apologise if queried.

The businesses were inherently anti-competitive. Power became concentrated in the feudal internet, dominated by a few, mainly American, companies. This was driven by network effects, economies of scale and first-mover advantages. It was enforced by litigation, acquisition of competitors and ruthless restricting of competition.

In recent years, Google alone has paid the European Union around €8.2 billion (US$9.3 billion) in antitrust fines.

Over time, the advertising platforms became tools of influence. The ability to deliver ideological and political messages to targeted segments of the population were crucial in the Brexit referendum and 2016 US election outcome. The influencers were not necessarily politicians. Evidence that Russia used these pathways to seek to influence American politics heightened concern. Fake news and propaganda on social media now created asymmetries of knowledge that affected how liberal democracies functioned.

With the darker aspects of the internet apparent, governments legislated for consumer protection and privacy. In 2019 Facebook was fined US$5 billion by the US Federal Trade Commission for violating consumers' privacy rights. The settlement required the company to update and adopt new privacy and security measures. The industry unsurprisingly resisted regulation, asserting that the complexity of their businesses demanded self-regulation. Privacy rules and restrictions on sharing information as well as controlling content posed a serious threat to the industry's structure and profitability.

Despite lofty aspirations to transform the world into a better place, technology giants increasingly resembled John D. Rockefeller's Standard Oil Company and Trust, which controlled almost all oil production, processing, marketing and transportation in the US. Focused on the future and poor students of history, the technologists seemed unaware that governments regulated and ultimately engineered the break-up of Standard Oil.

*

Real scientists embraced technological solutionism, keen to solve the problems of the age, especially climate change and clean energy. A key requirement was that the answer should not necessitate any substantive change in human behaviour and assumptions. They proposed solutions that would not be out of place in Jules Verne's science fiction.

Solar radiation management would limit temperature increases by deflecting sunlight, through injection of particles into the atmosphere, suspending giant mirrors in space or, more modestly, painting surfaces white. The technology was unproven. It was based on idealised scenarios different from real-world applications. In any case, solar radiation management could only mask global warming temporarily. It risked interfering with weather systems, altering the global hydrological cycle, such as monsoons. It did not halt, reverse or address problems of ocean acidification from CO_2 emissions.

Carbon capture was fashionable. Bioengineering or sequestration techniques would absorb and store CO_2 in underground reservoirs or in solids. The required scale was greater than that of the current international oil industry. The technology was not mature, at least on an industrial scale. Even with scale, the economics were unattractive unless the sequestered carbon could be used, for example, to maintain reservoir pressure in producing oil and gas fields or trapping in solids usable as building materials.

*

While increasing scale and technical advancements have reduced costs, renewables suffer from limitations and drawbacks. Problems of intermittency, storage, geographical location and lower energy and power density pose important challenges.

A key concept in energy economics is EROEI, energy returned on energy invested. It is the ratio of the amount of usable energy (the exergy) delivered to the amount used to obtain that resource. When the EROEI is less than or equal to one, that energy source becomes a net energy sink, not a source of energy.

The EROEI of our most important fuels is declining as cheap and easy to extract sources are exhausted. Most renewable and non-conventional energy alternatives have substantially lower EROEI values than traditional, conventional fossil fuels. It takes a lot of time to generate enough power from solar or wind to equal the energy in a barrel of oil. Once all the energy inputs required to manufacture, generate and distribute are considered, the emission reduction potential of renewables is lower than assumed.

Renewables create unexpected problems. The core of turbine blades needed for wind energy uses strong and light balsawood, better known for its use in model aircraft, table tennis bats and surfboards. Rising demand created shortages, prompting additional land clearing for new plantations in Ecuador, Indonesia and Papua New Guinea. The wind turbine blades, which are built to withstand hurricane-force winds, cannot be easily crushed, recycled or repurposed. In the US and Europe, there are around 12,000 blades that must be disposed of annually, usually in landfill. As installations increase, the problem will increase.

Batteries are essential to the storage of renewable energy. They are central to electric vehicles. But batteries are frustratingly inefficient. Petrol has six times more joules of energy per kilogram than the best batteries currently. This constrains grid-scale storage and the range of electric vehicles. The costs are high. Batteries use lithium, cobalt and rare earths. Demand for lithium is damaging rare and fragile ecosystems in the High Andes of South America. Demand for cobalt and rare earths is fuelling highly risky mining operations in many countries and financing brutal wars.

The scientific quest is driven by a refusal to reduce energy consumption. Modern energy-intensive lifestyles are sacrosanct. Individual transport in a petrol, diesel or electric vehicle is now an inalienable right that is spreading globally. Air-conditioned comfort is essential. The new digital economy and even the mining of bitcoins consumes ever-increasing amounts of electricity. Worldwide energy demand is increasing by 2–3 percent annually and is expected to increase by around 50 percent by 2040, led by Asian demand. Instead of questioning the insatiable demands, the focus is on finding new sources or switching to renewables.

The real energy debate requires working out what energy sources are available, calculating their sustainability and then shaping energy demand around these constraints. This requires sacrifices to constrain demand. Unfortunately, a society preoccupied with individuality and convinced that technology can solve all problems finds these choices unpalatable.

*

Full life-cycle analysis of the consequences of inventions and technologies, including side effects, is rarely done. Investors and early exploiters of the internal combustion engine and the attendant use of fossil fuels never attempted to understand the impact of CO_2 emissions, preferring to focus on the revolutionary advantages of the technology.

Chernobyl and Fukushima illustrate the often disastrous and long-lived side effects of errors. Technology is often the problem, not the solution.

Technological and scientific hubris is commonplace. It is driven by a fundamental need to avoid confronting the limits of progress and costs of adjustments that would be necessary in the absence of this faith. Increasingly, it approximates a starving man hallucinating about banquets.

In 2020 the medieval strategies underlying the health response to the COVID-19 virus highlighted the limitations of modern technology. Social and national isolation, originally devised by Italian city-states in the fourteenth century, was the first line of defence.

The word 'quarantine' is Italian, referring to the forty-day period Venice required ships to wait before they could enter the port. Luxurious cruise liners with infected passengers drifting at sea resembled the death ships of yore. Individuals followed Florence Nightingale's advice of frequent hand washing and hygiene for health.

With smart-phone-based apps proving deficient, authorities conducted laborious interviews and recorded details of individuals in public places using pen and paper to enable track and trace needed for infection control.

Virtue Signalling

In the presence of growing problems and the absence of easy answers, ordinary people, at least the minority who were engaged, embraced non-solutions. They engaged in virtue signalling, adopting superficial actions, such as waste recycling, or supporting movements promoting change.

The consume-and-discard model that underlies economic growth has created massive waste by-products. Households and commercial businesses generate over 2 billion tonnes of waste annually. Industries generate even more. Advanced countries produce around 35 percent of this waste despite having only 16 percent of the world's population. As living standards grow and Western habits take hold, waste from the developing world, a significant proportion in Asia and Africa, will increase rapidly.

This waste is in danger of burying some cities under garbage. Most of it goes to landfill, open dumps or is incinerated. Toxic run-off pollutes the soil, waterways and ultimately the watertable. It generates air pollution that results in acute respiratory infections. Greenhouse gases resulting from chemical reactions may account for up to 10 percent of emissions by 2025.

Some of the waste makes its way into the world's oceans. There may be around 80,000 tonnes of plastic in the Great Pacific Garbage Patch, an Alaska-sized ocean gyre in the ocean's north where currents channel floating debris. There will soon be more plastic in the world's oceans than fish biomass.

E-waste, some of it highly toxic metals, is increasing. According to the United Nations, discarded electronic equipment, such as TVs, mobile phones, computers, printers, batteries and peripherals that power the digital economy, reached around 54 million tonnes in 2019. This is equivalent in size to 350 *Queen Mary 2* cruise ships.

*

In advanced countries, waste management increasingly focuses on recycling. Households and businesses are required to place their discarded refuse in neatly marked containers to facilitate reuse. The slickly marketed initiatives are sold as helping 'save the planet'. The idea is that items are recycled, with valuable materials being extracted from the waste streams and reused. Reducing the amount of waste allows investment in better managed landfills or low-polluting incinerators. Unfortunately, recycling is far from a solution.

In developed countries, not everything is recycled. In the developing world, 50 percent or less of waste is collected, let alone recycled. In low-income countries, it is estimated that perhaps 90 percent of all waste is placed in open dumps. Recycling is complex, and improper separation of waste by households and businesses renders a large proportion incapable of processing and reuse. Simply placing the wrong items in the relevant containers can contaminate the process or make it uneconomic to recycle.

Advanced economies rely on developing countries to recycle their waste. Working in unsafe conditions, low-paid workers separate and reprocess materials for reuse in a form of waste imperialism. China dominates this trade in waste, especially in plastics and scrap metal, such as copper needed to wire cities or in the electronics industry. It has a large requirement for cheap resources for its rapidly growing economy. It complements its trade flows. Container vessels that ferry Chinese products to developed markets turn around and backhaul recyclable waste on the return leg at low prices.

Under this model, China imported, mainly from advanced countries, in excess of half of the world's used plastic, paper and cardboard, representing around 32 million tonnes per year. These imports totalled around US$24 billion per year, a quarter of the total global trade. Over the last quarter of a century, China took 106 million tonnes of plastic alone for recycling.

In 2017 China banned the import of twenty-four kinds of solid waste from foreign countries, including plastics, paper products and textiles. The ban reflected Chinese concern for its own environment, which was becoming a concern for its increasingly prosperous citizens. Other less-developed countries followed, banning imports of waste for reprocessing. Western nations found themselves with tonnes of unwanted rubbish.

*

In order to lower environmental footprints, consumers need to change habits to decouple waste from rising living standards. This requires reusing items and abandoning single-use material. The 'take, make, dispose' model has to be replaced by a circular society of 'reduce, reuse, recycle'.

It is not easy to change consumer behaviour. The ban on single-use plastic bags resulted in forgetful customers purchasing stronger, thicker plastic multi-use bags at supermarkets on each visit. When discarded, these bags are slower to degrade than single-use ones.

Bringing bottles to the supermarket to buy milk, spooning nuts into existing jars, or vegetables not wrapped in plastic, seem simply a step too far for consumers.

The economics of the circular economy are complex. Recycled and virgin materials compete. Recycling would reduce industrial production of new raw materials, decreasing economic growth. It might suppress commodity prices, which many emerging countries are dependent upon.

There are barriers to long-term investment in recycling. While costs of collection, transport and processing of scrap are relatively fixed, commodity prices are volatile. When raw material prices fall, recyclers can quickly become uncompetitive. Needing reliable and stable supply of inputs, businesses may be reluctant to buy from recyclers who cannot guarantee long-term supply.

While metals, glass and paper are extensively recovered, only around 10 percent of plastics, a major pollutant, are recycled. This is because polymers derived from oil are cheap to make while expensive to extract from waste. E-waste contains large amounts of copper, gold and other precious metals. Despite its high value, only around one sixth of this is recycled. The remainder, valued at about US$57 billion, is not reclaimed.

Recycling signals consumer virtues and their eco-friendly credentials, but it cannot solve the underlying issue of excessive and rapidly increasing waste generation.

*

Even without the prophylactic rules required by the pandemic, most people live in bubbles. In a clash between beliefs and self-interest, the latter dominates. Solutions must respect their priorities and convenience. They confine activism to supporting just causes or influencers, usually through monetary contributions. Greta Thunberg was perfect for the concerned to signal their social awareness. If she had not existed, then she would have had to be manufactured.

The 16-year-old started by spending her school days outside the Swedish parliament, calling for stronger action on climate change. Over time, she was joined by other students who began to undertake similar protests in their own communities. This culminated in an organised school climate strike movement: *Fridays for Future*.

Using social media and support from youth activists, Thunberg built a profile that attracted attention from the press. This drew international attention to climate change and the Swedish teenager. Her growing profile and support created momentum, culminating in a series of appearances, speeches and meetings. These included the 2018 United Nations Climate Change Conference; the British, European and French parliaments; the Vatican; and the Davos World Economic Forum, which she headlined with US President Donald Trump.

Thunberg's position is not original. She believes that global warming is an existential crisis. Caused by the current and previous generations, she argues, correctly, it will have a disproportionate effect on the young and future generations. Thunberg argues that the world is not acting quickly enough, and the commitments made at the Paris Agreement are insufficient.

Her graphic imagery – 'our house is on fire' – and dramatic, blunt language – 'how dare you' – made her irresistible to the media. Thunberg's approach is simplistic. Beyond the outrage, there is no coherent plan for decarbonising the world. Real change requires new laws, incentives and enforcement mechanisms to persuade businesses and individuals to alter practices.

Some world leaders who ignored similar advice from scientists meekly listened to Thunberg. Others were critical. Some thought she was causing unnecessary anxiety to the young and damaging their education by encouraging them to demonstrate in the streets rather than concentrating on school. Ingrained attitudes towards women and children underlay some male leaders' reactions to the young, courageous Swede.

Russian President Vladimir Putin provided the most objective critique. Thunberg was kind and sincere. Her efforts were drawing attention to an important issue. She did not understand the complexity of rearranging the energy sources for a power-addicted world. Reining in emissions had to be reconciled with the needs of many Africans, Asians and Latinos who aspire to the living standards of Sweden. President Putin feared that Thunberg was being manipulated to serve the interests of others.

Greta Thunberg is now one of the planet's most famous people and a world opinion leader. Supporting her is an easy path to virtue signalling for a world unwilling to make major sacrifices.

Kakistocracy

There is a defined relationship between individuals and the state and its institutions. While the details have been fiercely debated through the ages, security is its foundation. The state guarantees a citizen's safety in exchange for adherence to laws and contributions, such as service or taxes. Protection, property rights, access to justice, varying degrees of political participation and the ability to pursue personal and commercial activities are extensions of this relationship.

Over time, with the evolution of the state, individual rights and welfare, this social compact has become more expansive. People expect education and training to equip them for work. They require stable employment, a safe working environment, fair wages and benefits, for example, paid holidays and sick leave, and career progression. In time, task satisfaction and work flexibility also became important. Citizens demanded access to basic and discretionary goods and services of quality at affordable prices. They expected increased choice. Individuals required income levels that allowed adequate saving for retirement, stable and secure investments and reasonable returns on wealth.

Over time, these entitlements became the guaranteed minimum in advanced economies. As economic growth slowed, governments found it increasingly difficult to meet these expectations, feeding social disquiet. Accustomed to the relative stability and bounty of the postwar period, people valued predictability and certainty. After 2008, the rise in uncertainty created social instability, which manifested itself in politics.

*

Prime Minister David Cameron called the referendum on the UK's membership of the European Union to resolve internal Tory tensions and protect the party from being outflanked by the anti-Europe United Kingdom Independence Party led by Nigel Farage. The plebiscite inadvertently let loose two disparate forces. It provided Boris Johnson with the opportunity to pursue the prime ministership, a role that he believed was his birthright. It gave expression to known class, wealth, education and geographic tensions within Britain.

The educated, well-paid, upwardly mobile or wealthy, especially in south-east England, favoured remaining in the European Union. Those lacking the skills and education required for social mobility were anti-European. Many were trapped in dead-end lives. Vote Leave played to their grievances. The leavers were seduced by promises of sovereignty, taking back control and the restoration of national pride. They wanted to believe in the fantasy that everything could be fixed by a no vote. Leavers were not interested in the economic consequences or the practicalities. The remainers, 'remoaners' to opponents, were equally uninterested in the real concerns and the problems of the leavers.

Donald Trump's successful campaign for the US presidency relied on the support of people like the leavers. He cleverly targeted the weak and unrecognised – the forgotten people, Richard Nixon's silent majority. He focused on white identity politics, repeating simple, divisive and politically incorrect themes: protectionism, isolationism, opposition to immigration.

He positioned himself as an anti-politician politician who could take the country back from out-of-touch elites and political lackeys. It was a clever ploy against his opponent, Hillary Clinton, who was burdened by her history and the legacy of her husband's presidency.

Like Boris Johnson, Trump tapped into the anger of disaffected parts of the population, who shared his pessimism and hostility to immigrants and free trade. Both cultivated the false status of an outsider to increase their appeal. Johnson's studied disorder and Trump's natural incoherence enhanced their appeal. Voters embraced them as their own. In fact, they were uninterested in their supporters but wanted to be 'world kings', Johnson's childhood ambition.

The UK and America were not unique. In Europe, especially the formerly socialist Eastern Bloc, nationalist leaders and movements gained prominence. Similar trends were evident in Asia and Latin America. The ascendancy of Matteo Salvini (Italy), Viktor Orbán (Hungary), Recep Tayyip Erdoğan (Turkey), Narendra Modi (India), Rodrigo Duterte (the Philippines) and Jair Bolsonaro (Brazil) were all premised on analogous forces. Craving clarity, nation after nation voted in strong leaders promising solutions and a return to certainty. Even when the leaders or movements, such as France's National Front (rebranded as Rassemblement National or National Rally in 2018) and Germany's Alternative for Germany (AfD), did not gain power, they shaped the political agenda.

*

Many people care less about who is running the country than who coaches their favourite sporting team. While that remains largely true, some now sought change.

The new populism and politics of rage were grounded in the marginalisation of entire parts of advanced countries. Economic weakness devastated many industrial regions and towns. Unable to compete with lower-cost firms in developing countries, workers lost jobs, especially in manufacturing, and slid down the social ladder. The affected were anti-globalisation, anti-trade, anti-immigration and anti-technology, believing these forces to be the cause of their misfortune. Often socially conservative, they felt that their culture, values, faith and identity were threatened. Amid a growing economic and social divide, they believed that political and institutional elites did not accurately represent their needs and preferences.

In the postwar period, most advanced economies drifted into a two-party or similar arrangement, with power being traded over time. The conservative side or centre-right represented free markets, business, personal and property rights and freedom. They sought a culture of success and trickle-down wealth. The progressive or centre-left believed in greater government intervention. They were wary of business, favoured redistribution through taxes and supported state-funded education, healthcare and welfare safety nets.

The original constituency of progressive forces was the working class. As living standards rose, their focus shifted to other issues: racial and sexual equality, minorities, culture and the environment. Blue collar, non-college-educated and rural voters were unenthusiastic about the virtuous politics of better-off, liberal urbanites. Support for the centre-left fell.

In any case, there was little difference between the policies of the two sides. The centre-right borrowed from centre-left to soften its free-market policies. The centre-left borrowed from the centre-right to ensure the creation of wealth to redistribute or finance social agendas. The lack of political choice meant rule by indistinguishable, alternating oligarchies. This made the political structure vulnerable.

Over the last two decades, electoral dynamics have shifted. The differences exposed by Brexit transcended traditional class, professional, geographical or the right-versus-left differences. Society split between who voted to remain and who voted to leave. Conservatives and Labour Party supporters voted to leave. Older voters backed Brexit. The young voted overwhelmingly to stay. Newer migrants supported leaving the European Union because they were curiously anti-immigration – subsequent arrivals absorbed scarce resources or threatened their own advancement. Trump's supporters spanned traditional Republicans, normally Democratic voters trapped in disadvantage in the Rust Belt, rural voters, Hispanics and Asian Americans.

Existing forces sought to counter populism with the perennial antidote of money. Underlying the political battles were the unseen forces of campaign and party funding. In pay-to-play politics, vested interests sought to influence policies and results by directing money to favoured candidates. Hidden behind a bewildering array of think tanks and policy institutes, which were thinly veiled propaganda machines, businesses and the moneyed wanted their fingers on the electoral scale.

It was not new. Traditionally, the system relied on countervailing forces, the idea of power within a polity having several centres that usefully balance and oppose each other. Business and the wealthy were opposed by organised labour. The decline of unions, resulting from the change in the structure of the economy and labour markets, meant that the precarious equilibrium was no longer in place.

*

The politicians themselves were, overall, unimpressive. Douglas Adams warned that people who want to rule people are, ipso facto, those least suited to the task. The modest pay, constant public scrutiny of personal lives and the needs of fundraising to finance election campaigns discouraged many able, high-calibre political aspirants. With rare exceptions, there was a minimal grasp of history or tradition. They lacked a clear ideology or principles, following fashion rather than conviction. They legislated and made policy without understanding the content or grasping the true economic, social or even political effect. Delusions of adequacy and a certain lowlife cunning sustained them.

They were mainly professional politicians who moved through university debating societies, think tanks or party policy positions, roles as advisors or assistants to elected officials. Many were related to office-bearers or belonged to prominent political dynasties. Most lacked real-world experience in business or professions. David Halberstam in *The Best and the Brightest* wrote that Vice-President Lyndon Johnson, upon reviewing the resumés of the Kennedy cabinet, remarked that he would have felt a whole lot better if even one had ever run for something practical, like the office of sheriff. There was also inbreeding. A revolving door process meant that ousted politicians parked themselves in congenial policy institutes, foundations, lobby groups or law firms, awaiting a change in government and their turn in office.

The inadequacy of incumbents was evident in the quality of decision-making. Successive generations of politicians practised 'cakeism' – the notion that it is possible to govern without making hard choices. Prime Minister Boris Johnson famously summarised his approach to cake as pro having it and pro eating it too. Its companion was 'boosterism' – unfinanced spending sprees to buy elections.

*

John Kenneth Galbraith believed that true leadership required the willingness to confront unequivocally the major anxieties and issues of the time. Based on that standard, today's politicians are not leaders. With an eye to popularity, governing required sophisticated analysis of public opinion to ensure that you led from behind.

Major political parties governed with caution, a lack of inspiration and a dominant focus on their own and their party's agendas over broader interests. The priority was to maintain the appearance of normality, to engender confidence. The economy was strong. All that it needed was a little bit more debt, a little bit more printed money, a little lower interest rates, a little lower currency. Technology and the market would solve the problems of growth, resources and poverty, as well as male pattern baldness and double chins. Another summit would fix climate change. They supported every side in controversial social matters or avoided the issue altogether for fear of causing offence.

The political centre unsurprisingly collapsed, with its share of the overall vote steadily declining. Parties to the right and left of the traditional rivals prospered. Usually led by skilful demagogues, they tapped into the consuming resentments of the disadvantaged and disenfranchised. They played to the demand for immediate and radical change of a system that had failed these sections of the community.

Politics, as historian Henry Adams understood it, is the organisation of hatreds. People do not vote for people they like or whose ideas they embrace but against candidates they dislike. Politicians directed the anger towards any available targets – the elites, immigrants, the European Union, other countries. Technology allowed them to cheaply get their message to the target audience.

The political process lost cogency and civility. Objectives and the national interest were subsumed into spectacle. Performance superseded substance. President Trump's success owed much to his status as a recognisable TV reality show celebrity. Boris Johnson used a media career and his carefully calculated tonsure and dishevelment to build a political brand.

Tweetable slogans replaced policy. Leaders triangulated, selecting positions that maximised popularity and support. They used
wedge politics to divide opponents and the electorate, polarising
opinion along racial, regional or other demographic lines for political
advantage.

At election time, politicians sought to bribe the electorate using
Roman poet Juvenal's 'bread and circuses' strategy. Bread was tax cuts,
welfare benefits and food stamps. The circus was continuously streamed
news, terrorist and war dramas, celebrity and pornography to flat-
screen televisions, computer screens and mobile phones. Elections and
partisan political coverage were part of the circus. Joseph Goebbels
and Edward Bernays showed that with correct programming and
favourable circumstances the population would embrace anything.

*

Political leaders change. The pendulum swings between different ideas
and forces. Hopes of improvement persist.

In November 2020, Donald Trump was defeated after an unpleasant and ill-tempered campaign. He lost the popular vote by around
6 million, but the Electoral College's bias towards rural voters made
the race close in key states.

Stalin recognised that what counts is not the people who vote but
those who count the votes. As the results went against him, the president's reaction was predictable.

Even by Trumpian standards, the lies were astonishing. Against
a background of American flags, he claimed victory. A sad group of
people were perpetrating a fraud on the public to prevent him winning. The vote should be stopped because his lead in crucial states was
insurmountable. It was unclear whether Trump was talking about voting (which had ceased) or counting (which was continuing and always
took time, sometimes several days).

Trump and his supporters did not seem to grasp that a halt in the count would hand the election to his opponent. Clarification followed. Vote counting should stop in states where the president was in the lead, although a substantial volume of postal votes expected to favour the challenger remained untallied. Where Trump was behind, voting should continue, presumably until he led, and then stop.

Worried about his prospects, Trump had repeatedly cast unsubstantiated doubts on mail-in postal ballots in the lead-up to the election. He now alleged vote tampering without offering evidence. If not declared the victor, then Trump would go to the Supreme Court, where he had appointed three justices and there was a conservative majority. In reality, the available legal avenues were limited and unlikely to affect the outcome.

It was a messaging exercise to flummox the public. Trump timed his press conference to coincide with the TV networks' evening newscasts to maximise his audience. Tellingly, many broadcasters broke away well before the president had finished. Anchors rushed to correct his falsehoods. Even Fox News, traditionally ardent Trump cheerleaders, warned viewers of the absence of evidence of electoral fraud.

The claims were psychological. Narcissists cannot accept a challenge to their superiority. Losing is a catastrophic threat to their ego. It was inconceivable that he, Trump, could lose. The president needed to persuade supporters that he had not lost. He was the victim of a coup d'état by the deep state. There were practical concerns. Removal from office would deprive Trump of immunity in various court proceedings.

One news broadcaster likened the president's behaviour to recklessly throwing a lighted match into a flammable situation. On cue, as counting dragged on, pro- and anti-Trump demonstrations protested on the streets against and for vote counting to continue in critical swing states that would determine the outcome. The possibility of violent confrontations was real. There was fear that the armed militias, encouraged by President Trump to 'stand by', would take matters into their own hands.

When Biden claimed victory, Trump refused to concede, reiterating allegations of a fake result and forthcoming legal challenges. He lashed out at the media who had called the election for his opponent. Acolytes cravenly defended the president, displaying, in the words of one veteran journalist, a Tonto-like independence from the Lone Ranger. At a hastily convened press conference in Philadelphia at a landscaping business located between a crematorium and a sex shop, former New York City mayor Rudy Giuliani made baseless claims about voter fraud. Self-absorbed as always, Trump was happy to destroy America to save it.

Whatever the result, a disputed election undermined the validity of the system and institutions. Legal proceedings could create a constitutional crisis. It risked damaging the standing of the courts. If the president won via the Electoral College without an overall majority of the vote, it would be the second time he and the third time a Republican had done so in four elections since 2000. Fomenting doubts about the balloting damaged faith in elections and democratic processes.

Suggestions that Trump might not leave the White House if he lost did not eventuate, although there was no gracious transition. Until Biden's formal inauguration, he continued to obstruct actions to bring the pandemic under control, wage vendettas against his opponents and hand out pardons and last-minute favours to allies.

There was speculation about Trump's future. He had suggested that he might leave America if he lost to 'Sleepy Joe', his derogatory title for Biden. The defeated president might create Trump TV, starring himself. Twitter provided a continuing platform for his diatribes. His ability to influence the news cycle remained. Even as defeat loomed, the focus was not on President-elect Biden but on

Donald Trump. Younger than Biden, a comeback in 2024 could not be ruled out, either as a Republican or head of his own party. Trump family members may seek future high public office.

*

The mystery was how the contest could have been close. Polls had suggested a clear-cut victory for Joe Biden and the Democratic Party for months.

Star pollsters, who had relied on data-intensive analysis, offered excuses. There were sampling difficulties, error margins, low response rates and closet Trump voters. The same defences had been offered in 2016 when the polls had also been wrong. One TV personality suggested pollsters seek more gainful employment, such as construction or labouring work.

Whining pundits puzzled as to how the Democratic Party could fail to secure a convincing victory. One humourist suggested that a new political contest was needed so that the Democrats could find a way to lose that as well.

President Trump's period in office was turbulent. He was unpopular. The House of Representatives had brought impeachment proceedings against him. The president had mishandled a public health crisis. Other than avoiding a new foreign shooting war, he had fulfilled few of his 2016 campaign pledges. He fomented racism, misogyny and homophobia. He promoted conspiracy theories, such as Democrats being devil-worshipping paedophiles. He referred to the vice-presidential candidate Kamala Harris as 'nasty' and a 'monster'.

At the Democratic convention, Biden drew on Irish poet Seamus Heaney. The message was one of miraculous hope and justice despite history's record of hopelessness. Biden evoked the need for cures and healing. But hope does not guarantee outcomes. Trump's opponent could not persuade around half of the voters. The 2020 election merely confirmed that America's divisions were too entrenched to overcome.

The electorate is evenly split, each side fired by a bitter, hateful energy. The circles of their lives and beliefs barely touch let alone overlap. Each side defines itself primarily as a negation of the other. They yell past each other. It is pure oppositional politics. Elections cannot resolve such differences.

Biden, like most recent elected US presidents, is unlikely to consistently command the support of both houses of the legislature. The scope to implement effective economic, social and public health policies is limited. Divisive issues like environment, international relations, race, minority rights and inequality are impossible to address. The result is terminal gridlock. America may be ungovernable. Presidents are now mere caretakers of a nation where half the citizenry questions his or her legitimacy.

*

The differences between the opposing groups are not ideological or centred on policy matters.

Conservatives, their fates inextricably tied to Trump, have moved away from free markets, trade, open borders and prudent finances. In its place, there is a grab bag of perceived vote-winners targeting economically distressed white males and evangelicals – isolationism, deglobalisation, protectionism, state subsidies, tax cuts, stacking courts with sympathetic judges, opposition to abortion or gender rights, cronyism and nativism. In the aftermath of 2020, one Republican politician proclaimed, without irony, that the party of business and wealth was now the party of the American working classes.

Progressive forces believed that ABT (anyone but Trump) would be sufficient in 2020. There were tired Democratic programs with nods to climate change and culture wars to appease the radical wing of the party. Internal differences over core principles and disunity were glossed over. After the election, one Democrat argued that it had become a party of urban coastal elites, concerned with policing cultural issues – a party that no longer represented the working class. The criticism was rejected but deep fault lines simmered.

The Democratic Party did not acknowledge the fragmentation of their base. The defection of traditional supporters over decades was treated as an aberration. In 2020, some white blue-collar workers did return to the fold. Minorities, especially African Americans and Hispanic voters, were important in Biden eking out his victory. But they voted for the former vice-president without enthusiasm. Perhaps they had grown tired of the chaos or feared for their survival.

Personality cults and identity were to the fore. Trump was a combination of Alfred Jarry's grotesque *Ubu Roi* and reincarnated scientology founder L. Ron Hubbard. It was historian Richard Hofstadter's paranoid style of politics – a mix of excited exaggeration, suspicion, victimhood and absorption with conspiracy.

Whatever his failings, the president had a sure grasp of his supporters' key touchpoints. He played up his business credentials, claiming to have built the greatest economy in the history of the US. The pandemic-induced recession wasn't his fault. He could make the economy great again.

In the closing stages of the campaign, he skilfully courted black and Hispanic voters. His victory in Florida owed much to Cuban and Venezuelan exiles. Trump convinced them that the Democrats would turn America into a socialist state. They forgave his demonisation of all Mexicans as rapists and murderers and plans for a border wall to keep out brown people. His contempt and crudity, rejecting politically correct language, resonated with followers.

In Soho, a team of artists fashioned a 30-metre (100-foot), colour-coded mural out of 20,000 false and misleading statements by the president, documented and fact-checked by *The Washington Post*. The lies did not affect his popularity. If Trump claimed that the earth was flat, then his supporters would believe it. An earlier version of the installation was defaced by the president's followers, who daubed slogans over it, including 'Vote Trump or Die'.

In losing, Trump got more votes than in 2016 – in fact, the second-highest total received. His support among minorities was high for the Grand Old Party. Democrats did not improve their Congressional position. Without the pandemic, the president would probably have been re-elected.

The refusal to accept the result and fostering the myth of being cheated forced Republicans to defend him. It entrenched his power over supporters and the party. Despite having sought high office for personal glorification, Trump had remade the party of Abraham Lincoln and conservative politics for the foreseeable future.

The president's defeat did not mean that the factors behind his rise had disappeared. Half the electorate, over 70 million votes, did not repudiate Donald Trump's populist platform. The divisions – urban against rural, cosmopolitan against insular, educated against uneducated, black and coloured against white, religious against secular – will play out in a long civil war, the intensity and format of which remain uncertain.

*

What holds for the US holds true elsewhere. The essential tendencies favour illiberal rule, jingoism, xenophobia and tribal, racial or religious chauvinism.

America's failure to reject Trump decisively will encourage populist nationalists everywhere. Consistent support for the president suggests that opposition to multilateralism, globalisation, immigration, elites, experts and institutions remains electorally popular. Coincidentally, as the 2020 US election played out, Nigel Farage, a prominent figure in the Brexit Leave campaign, announced his political comeback.

Trump and the 2020 election damaged democracy. China's President Xi could not have found a better argument favouring the stability of one-party rule. In Russia, one Kremlin official urged his countrymen to grab some popcorn and watch the US tear itself apart. In theocratic Iran, leaders belittled the spectacle.

The US political trajectory fatally weakened the prospects of international cooperation. Trump's bullying, transactional America First and Alone approach to foreign affairs will make other nations wary of alliances. The fear is that any change under a Biden presidency could be reversed again by a future administration. It made dealing with issues requiring coordinated global action, such as a worldwide health emergency or climate change, difficult.

The problem is that societies are irreconcilably divided over essential issues. They are burdened by inescapable legacies and matters over which they have little control. Politicians have limited scope to change direction meaningfully. Populist opponents stalk them unceasingly.

The deterioration of the political process parallels the decline in economic, environmental and resource outlook. The mental and rhetorical sparring of modern politics cannot address the urgent problems. As time goes on and the failure becomes palpable, a drift into intolerant nationalism and gangster capitalism is inevitable. Authoritarian leaders control the courts, curtail civil liberties, turn the media into mouthpieces and use state companies to further political aims. Any criticism is, of course, 'fake news'.

A world of increasing complexity, unfathomable linkages and rapid change combined with demands for simple explanations and painless answers doom political systems to impotence. Speaking about Indian Prime Minister Jawaharlal Nehru, cartoonist R. K. Laxman summed up this propensity more than half a century ago. In the beginning,

Nehru had a solution to every difficulty, whereas by the end he faced difficulties with every solution.

Gatekeepers or Cheerleaders

Institutional failures exacerbated the difficulties of a fractured political process.

Government appointments have politicised bureaucracies once tasked with providing impartial, non-partisan advice. Led by ministers and cabinet members who owe their position less to expertise than to political affiliation, they now were sycophants, cheerleading for political agendas. Resistance or attempts to perform their true function were grounds for dismissal or being sidelined. Public service increasingly attracted short-termers who saw it as a stepping stone to lucrative opportunities in the private sector or political office.

In developed nations, this left the way open for lobbyists and powerful alliances to determine policies and draft legislation. It benefitted their constituencies but left large costs to be borne by the rest of the population. Over time such groups accumulated power, burdening and ultimately paralysing the system. It was a kakistocracy, government by the least suitable or competent citizens of a state. In emerging nations, there was no need for pretence that the political system or public service was anything other than a mechanism of organised looting.

Such corruption is not new. Those with money, power or both have routinely sought to advance their own interests, using bribes, kickbacks and other corrupt practices. Increasingly, corruption has become institutionalised as national strategy. The US, Europe and others have joined traditional offenders like authoritarian regimes and tin-pot Third World dictators in using these practices as an instrument of policy. Incentives to obtain commercial contracts, votes at the UN or other international forums, and influence elections in foreign countries have become commonplace. Weaponised corruption now extends beyond national borders and is an integral part of government, statecraft and diplomacy.

*

Traditional controls and balances were now weaker.

The judiciary tried to check the excesses of governments. However, their independence was compromised by political appointments, particularly in the US. Increasingly, decisions reflected the ideological leanings of individual judges. Under President Donald Trump there was increasing politicisation of the Justice Department, with prosecutors being dismissed over several investigations of the president's allies or interests. Many involved the US Attorney's Office for the Southern District of New York known for prosecuting high-profile white-collar criminals, large US financial institutions and international corruption. Where the US led, other nations followed.

The high cost of legal proceedings meant that ordinary litigants found it difficult to enforce their rights or challenge decisions. Governments and large businesses used delaying tactics to make the expense beyond all but the best resourced and wealthy. They required lodgement of large sums as surety against their legal expenses to deter potential litigants.

Police and law enforcement were perceived to be biased. After the crash of 1929, the head of the New York Stock Exchange was convicted and jailed. In the 1980s the US savings and loans crisis saw over one thousand people, including senior bankers, prosecuted. After the dot.com bust, top executives from WorldCom, Enron, Qwest and Tyco, amongst others, went to prison. After 2008, with the notable exception of Iceland, few – if any – bankers and corporate officers were held accountable for their failures. It was elite malfeasance: selective pardons, cover-ups and falsehoods. Ordinary people resented the lack of accountability.

In May 2020 the killing of George Floyd by police officers in Minneapolis, captured graphically on film, unleashed sometimes violent protests in the US. The disturbances, perhaps the worst since the civil rights era, exposed the persistent, in-built prejudice against minorities.

George Floyd's death was not an isolated incident, as the #blacklivesmatter movement had highlighted. Historically charged statements by President Trump, such as 'when the looting starts, the shooting starts' and threats to greet protesters 'with the most vicious dogs' harkened back to America's deeply racist past. With an election looming in November 2020 and behind in the polls, the president blamed far-left anarchists and resorted to the law-and-order rhetoric reminiscent of Richard Nixon's 1968 campaign.

The problem was not confined to the US. In Great Britain, Europe and Australia, racial profiling of Muslims, indigenous peoples, immigrants and refugees by police forces was deeply ingrained. In Australia, which boasted of its tolerance and multiculturalism, the Aboriginal community was around 3 percent of the population but nearly 28 percent of those incarcerated. Young Aboriginal people constituted over 50 percent of imprisoned youth. These statistics were worse than comparable numbers for African Americans. There was a 'legitimation crisis', in the words of the German sociologist Jürgen Habermas: loss of faith in institutions, processes and those in charge.

*

The press, especially investigative journalists, once spoke truth to power. Now, they provided, for the most part, infotainment. As Oscar Wilde once noted, the public have an insatiable curiosity for everything except what is worth knowing. Journalists now rushed to supply this demand.

The decline was driven by financial weakness. A business model based on hard copy and advertising revenues was undermined by digital

competitors. Mainstream firms lost advertisers to online channels better able to target potential customers. The proliferation of free news
and media undermined existing mediums. Cost cutting meant cutting
corners.

What remained of the quality press dumbed down coverage to
compete for attention. Factual reporting gave way to sensationalism
and opinion pieces from columnists who claimed instant expertise
on everything. Opining was cheaper than reporting and appealed to
advertisers able to tailor ads to more specific audiences. Embedded in
politics and business, fearing loss of revenue and privileged access to
decision-makers, reporters, for the most part, uncritically transmitted
the official view. Regurgitation of press releases and self-serving interviews became the norm. The deaf transcribed the speech of the dumb
who conveyed the eye-witness accounts of the blind.

The void was filled by social media focused on aggregating information rather than original reporting or research. The emphasis was
on items that would trend or go viral, boosting advertising revenue
rather than accuracy or fact. Legalised lying, which is what H. G.
Wells termed advertising, now financed news where truth was scant.

With limited regulation or oversight, social media created its own
reality. Sociologist Niklas Luhmann identified the difference between
the imagined reality of social media (*Medienwirklichkeit*) and the reality of life (*Lebenswirklichkeit*). Philosopher Walter Benjamin once
puzzled that every morning brought the news of the globe, and yet
people remained uninformed about newsworthy matters. There was
now no ambiguity. There was more news in menus than in most media
stories.

The promise of the internet was utopian. It was built on naivety.
The contradictions were many. While it was capable of exposing people
to the widest range of thought, in practice it did exactly the opposite. People isolated themselves in tribal groups, closing themselves

off from views other than their own. Disinformation masqueraded as truth. Free speech was a weapon to subdue and silence enemies. Social bonds were created to promote antisocial activities. It connected people only to divide people, pitting groups against each other. Instead of greater understanding, it promoted hate and anger. It was George Orwell's 'doublethink', but at warp speed.

*

Expertise and critical thought, a potential bulwark against power, was weaker. This reflected professional changes. In the humanities, there were endless debates couched in esoteric and impenetrable language. The arguments were difficult to decipher, making engagement impossible. Excessive empiricism confused rather than elucidated.

Declines in real terms in university and research funding forced changes. In STEM studies, there was increasing reliance on corporate investment or sponsorship. This accentuated applied research rather than basic, pure theoretical work required for true innovation. Research shifted to safer proposals likely to receive funding rather than uncertain but potentially ground-breaking areas. Crucial fundamental knowledge was now neglected in favour of ideas that could be commercialised rapidly. Academic excellence was subsumed into private wealth creation and consumerism.

Experts needed to build media profiles to ensure research funding. Many universities now have sophisticated public relations departments focused on obtaining media coverage for academics to place them in the centre of any debate. Researchers embraced an illiterate celebrity culture of vacuous opinion pieces and soundbites. Thoughtful and complex critical thinking was replaced by mechanistic formulas and recipes.

There was anti-intellectualism. Social media made everyone an expert in everything. It spread damaging and often fatal beliefs, such as campaigns against vaccinations, grounded in faith but unsupported by scientific evidence. During the Brexit debates, Michael Gove, one of the Leave campaign's leaders, rejected concerns about the economic impact of exiting the European Union stating, 'People in this country have had enough of experts.'

Even faith was mired in doubt. There were the usual doctrinal debates about abortion, contraception, LGBTQI rights, same-sex marriage, women's ordination and adaptation to modern society. Many churches found themselves caught up in allegations of sexual abuse of minors and attempts to cover up criminal acts. It was familiar. Writing in the eleventh century, Peter Damian observed that, 'The Church was sunk in moral squalor . . . Bishoprics were bought and sold . . . a corrupt and venal papacy was despised . . .' In a thoroughly modern touch, many churches used bankers to remove their assets out of the reach of potential claimants.

The 2020 pandemic would show that our systems are fragile and ineffective. It would show that the failing political and institutional arrangements of most advanced economies were now incapable of resolving the multiple emergencies that they face.

The Perfect Disruptor

In early 2020, a new viral disease, originally reported in China's Hubei province, evolved rapidly into a global pandemic. COVID-19 was a coronavirus, a group of diseases that includes the common cold and influenza. By November 2020, cumulative cases were in excess of 60 million and the number of deaths exceeded 1.4 million. In reality, both the number of infections and deaths attributable to the virus were much greater. There were few signs that the pandemic was slowing or under control in most countires.

The pandemic was unsurprising. There had been outbreaks of other coronaviruses, such as SARS and MERS, as well as H5N1 avian influenza, Ebola, swine fever and zika. Health professionals repeatedly warned of the possibility. In his 2015 TED Talk, Bill Gates advocated greater preparedness. In October 2019 the Johns Hopkins Center for Health Security conducted a high-level pandemic exercise.

Just as economists assumed that the economic cycle had been tamed, scientists believed that medical advances had eliminated pandemics. In 1948 US Secretary of State George Marshall confidently predicted the eradication of all infectious diseases. The US Surgeon General, William H. Stewart, told Congress in 1969 that it was time 'to close the books on infectious diseases' and 'declare the war against pestilence won'. In advanced societies, success against polio, typhoid, cholera and measles encouraged confidence. Even after the emergence of SARS in 2003, governments failed to invest in a broad-based vaccine for coronaviruses, refusing to take the threat seriously.

*

COVID-19 was an enigmatic pathogen, which, while frequently not serious, could unpredictably turn deadly. Reported effects ranged from mild symptoms (cough and shortness of breath) to severe illness (pneumonia and death). Around 20 percent of those infected showed no symptoms. But asymptomatic transmission was possible; that is, COVID-19 could be contagious even where carriers did not show symptoms. With increased research, the clinical characteristics of the virus proved complex and sinister. Unlike similar respiratory pathogens, COVID-19 seemed to cause damage to organs other than the lungs, including impairment to heart, liver, kidney and brain functions. In some cases, it triggered autoimmune diseases, caused blood clots or oxygen deprivation. Even where an infected patient recovered there were continuing, sometimes long-term effects, which came to be known as long COVID.

It was contagious. Infection by some viruses, such as Ebola and HIV, requires prolonged exposure or contact with infected blood or body fluids. This means they pose little risk to travellers or the general public who have not cared for or been in close contact with an infected person. In contrast, COVID-19 transmission was thought to be mainly person-to-person, usually by contact between people within about two metres. Transmission was mainly through contact with respiratory droplets produced when an infected person coughed or sneezed. After initially downplaying the risk of airborne transmission, which makes the disease more contagious, by July 2020 scientists could not rule out the possibility, citing evidence that exhaled aerosols spread the infection. Other possible methods of transmission included contact with infected surfaces or objects. The period that the virus survived outside the human body was unclear. There were cases where infection might have taken place as a result of contact with objects contaminated hours or days previously.

*

Epidemics are shaped by a virus's reproductive rate, the number of new cases that are likely to be infected by a carrier. A high reproductive rate, or R, creates sustained transmission. For COVID-19, R was estimated initially at between 2 and 2.5. The second factor is serial time, how quickly a virus multiplies. Assuming a reproductive rate of 2.3 and a serial interval of seven days, the virus would infect around 300,000 cases in one week. If the serial interval is six days, the number of cases is 1.5 million. The first million COVID-19 infections took three months, the second took just eight days.

Soon everyone was an expert on R, with the term leaping into public discourse. The problem was, as infectious disease specialists warned, that it was simplistic and one factor in the spread of the disease. Transmission depended on many factors, including new infection trends, geographic dispersion of infections, deaths, hospital admissions, the overall numbers within a population that currently had the disease or have already had it, and the effect of super-spreaders – carriers who infected large numbers. It was an average that masked significant local variations. All that did not stop it from becoming a central focus of policy. The mantra was, 'Get R below 1'.

Morbidity was marked in older patients or those with pre-existing conditions, such as compromised immune systems or respiratory issues. Others at high risk were health workers and carers. Death rates were thought to be around 0.5-1.0 percent, although there were significant variations between countries. This was around five to ten times the fatality rate of seasonal flu, which was under 0.10 percent. Other coronaviruses such as SARS and MERS had fatality rates of around 10 percent and over 30 percent, respectively. Ebola killed over 40 percent of infected patients.

Mortality rates can only be definitively established after the fact, by taking the dead and testing a large random sample for the pathogen. Calculations are liable to two errors; the numerator – the number of the dead – is affected by incorrect cause of death and the denominator – the number infected – is affected by the accuracy of identifying infection.

A significant percentage of COVID-19 patients required hospitalisation, with some needing intensive care, including mechanical ventilation support. The typical period in intensive care was long, sometimes as much as twenty days. Without appropriate care, the infection risked becoming severe, and sometimes fatal. To put COVID-19 into perspective, influenza was responsible for around 500,000 deaths annually, two-thirds among people 65 years or older. Malaria killed a similar number, mostly in Africa and India.

The problem was that there were few definitive facts. It was mostly informed extrapolation from what was known about similar viruses and evolving research. There was opinion and speculation. COVID-19 was perfect for the zeitgeist.

*

Controlling the spread of the virus was difficult. There are few therapies for viruses generally, other than treating the symptoms. The primary defence is the body's immune response. As a new virus, there was no general immunity to the disease. Until a vaccine is available and vaccinations completed, the only way to prevent illness is to prevent infection.

The public health approach coalesced around two possible strategies. The first was Darwinian, to allow the infection to spread, creating immunity within the population. This is herd immunity, where the spread of a contagious disease within a population slows because a sufficiently high proportion of individuals, usually around 60 percent, are immune to the disease.

The second came to be known as 'flattening the curve', where regimes are implemented to defer or reduce the rates of infection. In the case of COVID-19, this meant progressively stricter controls to avoid exposure, such as social distancing, various degrees of isolation or quarantine and bans on movement and travel. In its most stringent form, this meant strict shelter-at-home orders and closure of internal and international borders.

Public policy was influenced by a study by London's Imperial College that forecast up to 2.2 million and 0.5 million deaths in the US and UK respectively without any action. The projections showed demand for hospital and intensive care units outstripping availability, exacerbating the toll.

The models were sensitive to small changes in assumptions about reproduction rate, serial time, progress of the disease and the impact of the measures taken to control transmission. Studies of previous epidemics show the difficulty of assessing the effectiveness of strategies, even after more definitive evidence is available. Interestingly, the Imperial College model had earlier concluded that simple prophylactic measures, such as washing hands, would be enough. Nevertheless, the study became the political script.

Governments took measures to flatten the curve. It had to do with refusing to admit that health systems were inadequate. The electoral risks of voters being denied essential care and dying was a strong motivator. Politicians needed to avoid the damaging spectre of patients waiting for beds in hospital corridors, temporary beds in car parks and dead bodies piling up in streets.

Although a pandemic would always test capabilities severely, a combination of austerity, privatisation and poor policy had left health systems unprepared. In many countries, the number of intensive care places had fallen over time. In the US, the number, measured against population, had almost halved over the last several decades. While he garnered praise for his handling of the crisis, New York's Governor Andrew Cuomo had previously reduced the number of beds and closed hospitals, especially in rural areas. The strategy was an admission that nations did not have the resources or structures to implement alternatives, such as rapid testing of a large portion of the population, isolation of identified cases and contact tracing.

There was shrewd political calculation underlying the choice. After the 2008 crisis, politicians passed the poisoned chalice of dealing with the crisis to central bankers. They would take credit if the strategies worked. If policies failed, then politicians would blame the economic advisors. Following the same logic, they skilfully delegated responsibility for the COVID-19 crisis to medical experts. Whatever their public health credentials, the doctors and scientists, like the central bankers, were naive.

*

Flattening the curve was a flawed strategy. Depending on the existing reservoir of infected carriers in a population, trying to slow the rate of infection by literally shutting down activity would prolong the pandemic. It was not clear whether the number of infections or deaths would be lower. It was unclear whether alternatives such as protecting the old and the frail only would also have similar outcomes. The object of rationing of scarce resources was questionable as shortages of beds, doctors and equipment, such as test kits, personal protective equipment (PPE), ventilators and drugs emerged quickly anyway. Scenes from hospitals in Italy, Spain, France and New York suggested health systems on the verge of breakdown.

It was difficult to establish whether the curve was flattening. Measures of progress, such as infection and mortality rates, were inaccurate. For example, the number of new cases was highly dependent on the level of testing and where it was carried out. The flattening of the death rates was probably due to the most vulnerable dying first as much as the lockdown.

The measures did not allow build-up of immunity within populations. Everything was predicated on the availability of a vaccine. The most optimistic forecast was twelve to eighteen months, shorter than the four to five years – or even longer – historically needed to develop vaccines.

There is no guarantee that an effective vaccine will be found. There is none for the common cold. The influenza vaccine has around 60–70 percent effectiveness in preventing or reducing the symptoms of the disease.

If found, production of the vaccine in the quantities needed would be a logistical challenge. Necessary vaccination programs would require time, money and skilled resources. Opposition to vaccination from vocal minorities suggested that coverage of entire populations would prove difficult.

The durability of acquired immunity from infection or a vaccine was uncertain. One early UK study suggested that people who have recovered from COVID-19 could lose their immunity to the disease within months. The virus could reinfect people year after year, like the cold or flu. If protection was short term, then a regular program of vaccinations, as with the influenza virus, would be needed. All this assumed crucially that there was one or several closely related strains of COVID-19. If the virus mutated, then creating a successful vaccine would be more difficult.

The Hammer and the Dance

With few alternatives, governments were forced to adopt a stop-go approach – the hammer and the dance. Strict restrictions with controls being relaxed when cases decrease and then reimposed if they rise. This would allow the health system to be scaled up to meet demand and the development of more effective testing and contact tracing protocols.

The policy largely ignored other interests. The mandated shutdowns created large economic costs in the form of unemployment, business failures and a financial crisis. The Imperial College study acknowledged that the social and economic costs would be substantial and fall disproportionately on lower income groups. In older times, highwaymen demanded 'your money or your life'. In the COVID-19 pandemic, it was a case of 'your health or your wealth', and perhaps both.

Governments throughout the world instituted a variety of lockdowns. In developed countries, the measures helped reduce infection numbers and deaths, easing the pressure on health resources. In developing countries, especially South America and South Asia, progress in controlling the virus was more variable.

Eager to restart economies, many governments eased restrictions at the first signs of progress, often against the advice of epidemiologists.

In September 2020, infections started to rise again, especially in the US and Europe. Shortly thereafter, there were record new infections, straining health facilities again. Death rates were lower, reflecting improved diagnoses, better therapies and different demographics of those infected. Nevertheless, there were fears of a repeat of the 1918 Spanish flu episode, where deaths in the second wave were five times greater than those in the first.

The reasons for the surge were the 3Cs: closed spaces, crowded places and close contact. Resumption of travel spread the virus. In the initial outbreak, many European chains of transmission originated in Alpine ski resorts. New outbreaks were traced to people from around the continent holidaying in Spain and other Mediterranean resorts.

Testing capacity was inadequate. Turnaround of test results was too slow for effective infection control. Medical resources and supplies remained in short supply. Track-and-trace systems, even if effective, were quickly overwhelmed. They did not work across jurisdictions – not helpful in cross-border transmissions. The lack of consistent policies and coordination among European countries and between American states hindered the ability to control the spread.

As infection levels rose, grim-faced European leaders reimposed progressively tighter lockdowns. Some American states reintroduced restrictions. Others chose the economy and livelihoods over public health concerns. Facing economic oblivion, developing countries could not afford new restrictions irrespective of the consequences.

China, Australia, New Zealand and several Asian nations succeeded in bringing infection numbers under control. This required draconian lockdowns, near universal use of face masks and restrictions on movement and travel. It needed a culture of compliance and prioritising the collective good, which many Asian countries in particular accepted. Some countries were unwilling to impose the necessary strictures. Individual rights and freedoms were paramount. Their less onerous measures proved inadequate.

Even where successfully implemented, the containment strategy is fragile. Hotspots and flare-ups can occur. Unless all countries have the disease under control, national or even state borders must remain closed as free movement risks new infection waves.

Like anti-personnel mines, COVID-19 did not kill large numbers but tied up vast resources in supporting its victims. Controlling the virus required measures that strangled human and economic activity.

*

Science is not perfect. Scientists are not always right. In the late 1990s, doctors began over-prescribing painkillers, creating America's opioid crisis. By April 2020, Professor Neil Ferguson, the lead researcher of the Imperial College study, admitted that they had no clear exit strategy.

Matters did not improve when Professor Ferguson, nicknamed 'Professor Lockdown', was forced to resign from the UK government's Scientific Advisory Group for Emergencies (the amusing acronym of which is SAGE). His married lover had visited him at home in contravention of lockdown rules. Government and scientific authority on maintaining strict social distancing suffered a serious setback.

From an epidemiological point, the pandemic will end when the proportion of society immune to COVID-19 is sufficient to prevent widespread, ongoing transmission, most likely via a vaccine. This would allow resumption of social and economic life without fear of infection and the resulting death or long-term health consequences. Partial reopening before the epidemiological end of the pandemic was possible. It required controlling the spread among high-risk populations, rapid and accurate testing, strict quarantine of the infected and improved treatments.

In the short-run, the most probable scenario was a patchwork quilt reopening – some relaxation of national lockdowns but continuance of restrictions on certain activities and total or partial border closures. Periodic reintroductions of strict controls if there are new outbreaks or new viruses could not be discounted. Without a vaccine, treatment, suppression or the disappearance of the virus, a cycle of 'lock, unlock, lock, repeat' was likely.

The chance that the public health crisis and restrictions could continue for some time was significant. There was increasing despondency as people desperately sought a return to normality, to restart and rebuild lives.

Profound Uncertainty

In type and magnitude, the 2020 crisis was unlike anything experienced since World War II. Recent crises, except for the 1970s oil shocks, were primarily financial. This crisis combined public health, economic and financial elements, each costly.

The health costs included direct expenditures on resources, treatment and, perhaps ultimately, vaccines and vaccination programs. The cost of an intensive care unit is in the order of US$5000 per day per patient. Assuming 1000 admissions and a twenty-day duration, the cost is US$100 million. There were economic and financial costs as a result of the shutdowns. Then, there were the costs of supporting the economy and society through the crisis and beyond.

Economic activity slowed sharply. Global trade plummeted by up to 32 percent, a larger contraction than the 12 percent in 2009. Businesses faced often precipitous declines in revenue, earnings and cashflows. The services sector was worst affected. Travel, tourism and anything involving direct contact were affected by restrictions on movement and social distancing. Retailers of discretionary items, restaurants and entertainment closed or were forced to switch to takeaway or online sales.

Non-essential construction work was adversely affected by containment policies or reductions in investment and funding. The effect on manufacturing was smaller but some sectors, such as automobiles and aerospace, were hampered by the lack of sales or difficulties in obtaining necessary inputs from suppliers in other countries.

Initially, food retailers and producers benefitted, although stockpiling eventually slowed. Over time, the food supply chain suffered from a combination of infected workers, shortages of immigrant labourers and transport constraints.

Ultimately, movement restrictions, diversion of resources to fight the virus and demand constrained by falling income would affect even sectors considered insulated, such as staples, utilities, telecommunications, online media and even the health sector. Investors assumed technology companies would be protected from the downturn. They misunderstood that Facebook and Google were marketing vehicles, whose viability and growth depends on ad spending, which had fallen sharply.

The business slowdown fed unemployment. The International Labour Organization forecast that global working hours would decline by the equivalent of over 300 million full-time jobs, which represents over 10 percent of the workforce. Among the most vulnerable in the labour market, almost 1.6 billion informal economy workers were expected to be significantly impacted. As the pandemic's effects spread across the US, the total number of jobs lost by July 2020 was over 30 million. Jobs created over two decades had been destroyed, some of them probably permanently.

No one could really tell how bad things were because the data and collection processes were inadequate to cope with things like workers furloughed or stood down, government support schemes and the large numbers of people who simply left the workforce because they knew there was no work available. But it was clear that conditions were bad, far exceeding the declines after 2008.

The loss of household income set off a deadly feedback loop as reduced consumption drove lower business revenues, forcing businesses to downsize and eventually shut down, creating even more unemployment. It was the same across the world.

Given that advanced economies are structured around consumption, which frequently makes up around 50–70 percent of activity, output declines of 50–100 percent translated into a contraction of around 20–25 percent. The impact on growth was estimated at around 0.50–0.75 percent per week. The overall damage depended on the length of the disruption.

The bland numbers did not register the human effects. In June 2020, using an international poverty line of US$5.50 per day in income, the World Bank estimated that anywhere up to 220 million would be pushed into poverty by COVID-19. Major charities were more pessimistic, predicting that as many as 420 million people would slip into poverty, with many falling into extreme indigence. Decades of effort to alleviate poverty were being reversed in the greatest decline in income in nearly a century.

An entire system predicated on the intricate division of tasks between people, producers and consumers, and connections between cities and rural communities and nations, was fracturing. The outlook was one of profound uncertainty.

*

The reaction of the financial markets was predictable. There was an initial period of calm. As the impact of the public health measures become apparent, asset prices fell. Global stock markets lost approximately one-third of their value. Bond markets grappled with contradictory forces: the safety offered by government securities, increased central bank buying, lower target interest rates, liquidity infusions, increased issuance and the possibility of higher inflation.

Commodity prices fell. Traditional safe havens, such as the US dollar and gold, attracted buyers. Borrowing costs increased sharply. Volatility spiked. Share prices, interest rates, commodities and currencies moved by record amounts daily.

Feedback processes that drive asset prices began to work in reverse. Prices adjusted to the economic slowdown. They were forced to reflect lower corporate earnings, reduced rental income from properties, and reductions in dividends and buybacks, driven by the lack of profits or regulatory prohibitions.

Leveraged investors – hedge funds, private investors and entrepreneurs who had borrowed against assets – faced margin calls. Many funds suspended redemptions as they could not sell illiquid investments. Investors' access to cash was limited. Attempts to hedge against further falls added to pressure on values and liquidity, transmitting the stresses across asset classes and markets. With each iteration, the process accelerated. Declining investment income and the inability to realise investments decreased household cash resources and constrained spending.

Banks initially benefitted from higher trading income and companies rushing to secure emergency funding. This was short-lived as volatility declined and activity slowed. As the crisis intensified, borrowers – households, businesses, investors – initially breached loan conditions and eventually defaulted or entered debt restructurings. Forced sales of collateral weighed on asset prices. Reduced savings affected the banks' access to deposits.

Rising bad debts reduced the banks' willingness to lend. Where funds were available, borrowings costs were much higher. The credit-dependent real economy and investment markets were increasingly affected. Recapitalisation might necessitate converting hybrid instruments issued by banks into equity or writing down capital values of bail-in bonds, adding to pressure on investors.

The shape of the ensuing financial crisis was familiar. It was a rerun of past episodes, like 2008. But this repeat would hold some surprises.

Drowning in Oil

There was a parallel crisis in the oil markets. The price for crude oil fell by around 60 percent from the levels at the start of 2020.

Against a background of weakening oil demand as economic activity collapsed, the Organization of the Petroleum Exporting Countries (OPEC) announced plans for production cuts of 1.5 million barrels a day. While not technically a member, Russia had over recent years coordinated its output with the oil cartel. Now, Russia refused to comply with the planned cuts that were designed to support the old price of around $50–60 a barrel. With around half a trillion dollars in foreign currency reserves and a budget surplus, Russia seemed sanguine with a lower oil price of $25–30 for the next six to ten years.

The Russian refusal triggered a contretemps with Saudi Arabia's Crown Prince Mohammed bin Salman (MBS). Saudi Arabia retaliated by increasing output to over 12 million barrels per day, an increase of 25 percent, and offered discounts to buyers. Russia responded by raising its production by 500,000 barrels a day to around 11 million barrels. Oil prices went into freefall, recording some of the largest daily moves in history.

The underlying agendas were complex. MBS was involved in an internal power struggle to succeed King Salman. The Crown Prince was deeply damaged by his mistakes: the ill-conceived military intervention in Yemen, proxy conflicts against Iran, the alleged complicity in Jamal Khashoggi's murder and the shakedown of several rich Saudi businessmen. There was the ill-conceived and expensive Saudi Vision 2030 plan to reduce the Kingdom's dependence on oil and diversify its economy into health, education, infrastructure, recreation and tourism. MBS believed that Saudi Arabia had a narrow window to monetise its large oil reserves before demand for fossil fuels collapsed. He sought to capture market share irrespective of price. The decision was curious given that the profligate Kingdom needed a price of around $80 to cover public spending.

Russia did not trust the Saudis. President Vladimir Putin believed that Saudi activities in oil markets in the 1980s played a role in the collapse of the Soviet Union. Russia wanted to damage the US shale oil industry and retaliate against American sanctions and interference in its energy deals with Europe. In the strange nature of the oil markets, the Saudis were happy to check the growth of the US shale industry that it had tried unsuccessfully to destroy in 2014 by flooding the market with oil.

*

In the last decade, the US rapidly increased energy production through the growth of the shale sector. After the 2014 oil price falls, shale oil and gas producers had increased efficiency and reduced costs, but their recovery required the Saudi–Russia oil alliance to stay in place. Since 2016 the oil price had remained at a level that allowed the fracking industry to survive.

Even before the price falls the shale oil and gas industry was struggling due to systemic weaknesses. Few firms were profitable. The industry spent over a quarter trillion dollars of cash more than it had generated over the last decade. In recent years, major resource firms wrote down their shale oil investments. Chevron wrote off US$11 billion, mainly related to its Appalachian-region shale gas acreage.

The business model required constant cash injections to maintain output. The shale oil industry is financed by banks and public markets that have lent large amounts to small companies to finance fracking shale formations when oil prices are high. It was a gigantic money pit sustained by debt. The major beneficiaries were bankers who earned fees on financings.

The financial toll from lower oil prices from an expected 30 percent fall in demand from the COVID-19 crisis and increased supply was severe. Oil importing countries benefitted from lower prices. However, fuel cost savings are unlikely to translate into more spending because of the restriction from COVID-19. Nations dependent on oil exports revenue are especially vulnerable if prices remain depressed. If oil prices stay low, investment will drop sharply, perhaps by as much as 70 percent. With lower earnings, oil companies will have to cut shareholder payouts.

In the US, any benefit for consumers from lower petrol prices will be offset by the damage to the shale oil industry, which is profitable at $100 a barrel, probably breaks even at $50 and is insolvent at $25.

Once hedges that guarantee a higher price expire, shale oil and gas producers will struggle to cover the costs of production. Production cuts and lay-offs will be the first step. The industry must repay around US$200 billion in debt by 2025, including US$40 billion in 2020. As the credit ratings of producers fall to high-yield or junk categories, their ability to refinance existing debt when it is due for repayment is questionable. By July 2020 many shale oil and gas firms had filed for bankruptcy protection. More failures seemed likely.

The problems affect major oil producing regions where the entire economy is dependent on fracking. US energy independence and rising exports will reverse. Lower oil prices will also hurt the Saudi and Russian economies. If the COVID-19 crisis persists and producers do not cut back production, then there will be no winners.

*

Concerned about the rising fallout, President Trump tweeted that Saudi Arabia and Russia were in discussions on how to curb production by 15 million barrels a day. The claims were denied by both parties. Subsequently, an OPEC meeting was scheduled. Russia suggested that an agreement was possible but would require restrictions on US production and other American concessions, highlighting the complex politics.

The US government threatened to impose tariffs on Saudi and Russian oil exports to North America to protect domestic producers. The White House suggested the possibility of restricting arms sales to Saudi Arabia if it did not cut its output to boost prices. The motivation was political. The falls undermined the Trump administration's strategy of US energy independence and domination. The US shale oil and gas industry, directly or indirectly, employs 6 million workers in electorally significant states such as Texas, Oklahoma, North Dakota, Louisiana and Colorado.

In early April 2020, OPEC and Russia agreed to cut oil production by around 10 million barrels a day. There were suggested reductions in production by non-OPEC members US and Canada of 5 million barrels. The G20 endorsed the agreement, although the US indicated that it could not force cuts due to antitrust laws. The cuts were lower than the stated figure and, in any case, insufficient given that demand had fallen by around 30 million barrels a day as a result of the COVID-19 crisis. There were doubts on compliance with and the sustainability of the agreement. Oil prices did not rise but fell.

On 20 April 2020, US oil prices went negative for the first time. It traded at negative US$37.63, compared to US$18.27 the previous trading day – an astonishing 300 percent fall. The price reflected a record 1 billion barrels of oil in inventory, a shortage of additional storage facilities and the cost of reducing production. Producers paid buyers to take oil off their hands. The price recovered to positive levels the next day. Over time, oil prices rose to around US$40 per barrel, reflecting stabilisation of demand and optimism about a global economic recovery. By July 2020 oil producers were contemplating reversing production cuts and boosting supply.

Low oil prices compounded the economic and financial problems caused by the pandemic.

Drowning Not Waving

Emerging markets, which could not cope with routine healthcare needs, lacked the resources to deal with the pandemic. While home to around half the global population, healthcare spending in emerging markets at 5–6 percent of GDP was less than half the 14 percent in developed economies. On a per capita basis, emerging market spending is around 5 percent of that of richer nations.

Controlling the spread of COVID-19 was difficult given high population densities, especially in slums and informal settlements. The general health of the population was poorer. They had pre-existing conditions, including respiratory diseases from poor air quality, tuberculosis or HIV. Prophylactic measures, such as better hygiene, quarantine, social distance and mobility restrictions, were impracticable. In India, Prime Minister Narendra Modi imposed a shelter-in-place order and encouraged hand washing, but large numbers of Indians lacked proper housing and access to clean, running water.

A large portion of the population in emerging nations were at risk of infection and death. Around 5–6 percent of India's population died in the Spanish flu pandemic.

The economic impact was significant. In many countries the informal economy, with its micro-businesses and traders, is large. It could not function under lockdowns, eliminating livelihoods and incomes of many poor people. Export demand fell sharply with the slowdown in advanced economies. Tourism collapsed. Falls in commodities prices, especially oil and metals, and lower volumes reduced income.

Many developing countries rely on remittances from nationals working overseas. The cashflow, around US$500 billion per annum, exceeds all foreign direct investment and aid to emerging markets. Remittances contribute significantly to growth, savings and financing of the balance of payments. The Philippines receives around US$34 billion a year, reducing the country's current account deficit from 10 percent to around 1.5 percent of GDP. In the pandemic, remittances decreased as richer countries scaled back. Foreign workers were mainly employed in badly affected sectors, such as hospitality, domestic work and construction.

Debt compounded the pressure. Over the past ten years, official debt for the thirty largest emerging markets increased to over $70 trillion, a rise of 168 percent. Falling income, higher interest costs and capital flight – nearly $100 billion of foreign capital was withdrawn in March 2020 – made borrowings difficult to service and refinance. As a significant proportion of the debt was in foreign currency, falls in emerging market currencies added to problems.

*

Slowing growth, a deteriorating balance of payments and lack of capital inflows constrained the response to the health crisis and support for the economy. Absence of financial and social infrastructure made it difficult to get assistance to those in need in any case. In Peru, the government found it hard to distribute a payment of 380 soles (US$108) to families. In some Latin American countries, drug gangs that ruled the favelas filled the vacuum, enforcing social distancing and providing financial assistance. They followed the lead of the mafia, which played a similar role in poorer parts of Italy.

In Brazil, President Bolsonaro dismissed the virus as a sniffle and the concerned as cowards. In July 2020 the Brazilian president was diagnosed with COVID-19. He claimed that the symptoms were mild, and he expected to make a full and quick recovery.

Understandably, the health and economic focus was national,

but the effects of the pandemic on emerging markets fed back into advanced economies. Unless all countries make uniform progress in bringing the virus under control, borders cannot be reopened and freedom of travel restored. Trade, travel and tourism would be impaired.

Failing emerging markets, which contributed around 60–70 percent to global growth since 2008, would feed weaknesses in advanced economies. The health crisis would interrupt supplies, especially of essential food products and raw materials. Markets for exports of finished goods from advanced economies would contract. As the major creditors of emerging markets, investors in richer countries risked loss of income and capital as borrowers defaulted or restructured debt.

In the worst case, advanced economies would have to deal with illegal immigration or drug trafficking and terrorism originating from these failed nations.

Break Glass Only in Case of Emergency

Governments and central banks struggled to deal with the crisis. They settled on familiar stimulus packages and accommodative monetary policies.

Health services to deal with the pandemic were expanded. There was support for the unemployed, lengthening and expanding coverage as well as increasing benefits. There were helicopter drops of cash to lower income families. Governments supported businesses affected by the shutdowns through payments designed to ensure continued employment of staff. Loans and government guarantees were designed to ensure small and large businesses did not fail. Governments legislated to defer taxes as well as rent, mortgage and debt payments to stave off eviction or failure. They even relaxed prohibitions on businesses trading when insolvent, quickly christened the 'honest idiot' exemption.

Central banks lowered rates, providing ready access to money. They purchased securities. Quantitative easing programs were expanded beyond government bonds and mortgage-backed securities to corporate debt, even that issued by low-quality, non-investment-grade issuers. The US Federal Reserve provided US dollars to other central banks to ease a perceived shortage.

By end of June 2020 governments had committed more than US$20 trillion, or around 24 percent of global GDP, split approximately equally between fiscal and monetary support, to fight the coronavirus pandemic. The packages were large, frequently 10–30 percent of GDP. The US package alone was around US$9.5 trillion, or 44 percent of GDP. Europe and Japan each allocated around 30 percent of GDP in assistance. Developing countries could only afford lower levels of assistance. Overall, measured as a percentage of GDP, the support was over six times the levels after the 2008 crisis.

Just as control of COVID-19 required slowing transmission, policymakers wanted to interrupt the pernicious financial feedback loops that the pandemic had set in motion. Employee income support schemes and rent and mortgage deferrals targeted households. As demand was muted by lockdowns, grants, rent and payment suspensions and loans sought to support businesses. Central banks propped up prices of houses and investments. They facilitated trading as financial markets seized up. They provided funds to banks as well as relaxing capital and accounting rules for impaired assets.

With half the world's population under some form of stay-at-home order by end of March 2020, it was unclear whether the intervention could both halt the pandemic and prevent a financial crisis. Printing money was not the same as printing jobs.

*

No two crises are the same. Responses are different. The problems with the proposed solutions, however, remain unchanged.

Agencies and banks tasked with administering the hastily created programs struggled with implementation. Eligibility criteria and details needed repeated clarification. Unintended consequences abounded. Many affected groups and businesses didn't qualify while many that did not need assistance were included. In the US, the government sent $1.4 billion in stimulus to dead people. Websites crashed. Call centres were overwhelmed. With delays and backlogs growing, assistance was slow. Supporting documentation needed to qualify was difficult to obtain. For many, applying for aid was now their full-time job.

The effectiveness of the response was uncertain. The one-time direct payments and unemployment benefits were modest relative to living expenses. They had a time limit.

Familiar prejudices emerged. Conservatives expressed concern about the expansion of welfare safety nets and its effects on incentives to work. Channelling Marie Antoinette's 'let them eat brioche' moment, Ivanka Trump, America's self-styled First Daughter, lectured the nation's 30 million unemployed to find something new to do. The president's daughter, who openly flaunted her wealth, privilege, inheritance and unelected influence, was, with her husband, Jared Kushner, amongst Donald Trump's closest advisors.

Discussing long queues at welfare offices, an Australian minister told a talk-show host that the whole thing was heartbreaking because 'decent people' found themselves in difficult circumstances through no fault of their own. The implication that previous recipients of assistance were undeserving was unmistakeable. For the better off, it was an unexpected fall in standing.

*

With around two-thirds of assistance being concessional loans, it was unclear how increasing borrowing helped already indebted businesses and individuals. Deferred rents and mortgage payments still needed to be made. For many it delayed the inevitable. Banks charged with making the loans worried that they would be left with bad loans if they failed to comply with ambiguous criteria or the advance was not forgiven where funds were not used as specified by the programs.

Measures to suspend rents and loan repayments were reminiscent of the 2008–09 US mortgage modification program, designed to save millions of people from foreclosure. It failed, being characterised by ongoing chaos and lax enforcement of the rules.

There were wasteful overlaps and redundancies. If the income support and unemployment safety net were adequate, then why was separate support for businesses needed? If there was assistance for employees and business as well as additional loans and government loan guarantees, then why were rent and debt suspensions necessary? The deferral of repayments created problems for banks, which then needed additional support. If there were general funds for business and loan support schemes, then why were separate packages for individual industries being provided? How could hedge funds claim benefits that were intended for small businesses? It was chaotic and panicked policymaking.

The COVID-19 shutdown created a simultaneous demand-and-supply shock. Businesses were faced with falling revenues and working capital problems. Massive fiscal and monetary stimulus may not be the correct response. Even if it was, there was no guarantee that the measures would create demand. When governments previously mailed additional funds to households, the money was generally saved or used to pay down debt. This time, the lockdowns made it difficult to spend the money in any case.

The bigger problem was that the world had not recovered from 2008. The actions over the last decade had reduced the ability of authorities to respond.

Loss of tax revenues, rising health expenditure and the cost of supporting the economy necessitated increases in government debt.

Additional borrowing could offset the efforts to reduce rates. It placed pressure on the currency, making it difficult for capital-importing countries to attract external investors, especially with low or negative rates. Alternative financing, through debt monetisation, also risked debasing the currency.

It was uncertain whether lowering already low rates would off-set declines in economic activity in a falling income, overly indebted world or support asset prices. More quantitative easing may be inef-fective, as it was reaching its limits.

In seeking to arrest the crisis, advanced country governments were assuming large liabilities. Given the state of public finances, it was unlikely that governments, especially heavily indebted ones, would be able to sustain the level of support required if the lockdown continued for any length of time.

Governments were looking to their treasuries and central banks to respond to the fallout from a public health problem. People joked that in case of an alien invasion, the first thing that policymakers would do is cut interest rates. No policymaker or politician would admit that cheap money could not save a failing economy. A new coat of paint would not save a condemned building.

*

Unlike 2008, when support measures were criticised for favouring banks and businesses, assistance this time supposedly targeted the general population. But the mistakes of the past were repeated. The fear was that, like last time, large corporations would recover but most ordinary people would see their living standards deteriorate.

There was substantial aid for large companies. In the US, the total was over US$500 billion, and it could be leveraged up by the Federal Reserve, which could lend ten times that to corporations. The con-ditions attached to the assistance were weak. The money could only support domestic operations. Dividends and share buybacks were prohibited, but they would have been suspended in any case on financial grounds. Restrictions on executive compensation required limited sacrifices being based on 2019 levels when they were frequently near or at all-time highs. It was unclear whether assistance from the US Federal Reserve was even subject to these conditions.

Banks stood to make billions in fees and interest from some programs. If 2008 was a guide, then it was unlikely that banks would provide debt relief or expand lending as required. Oversight was weak. Corporate beneficiaries only needed to produce good-faith certification of adherence to conditions. In the US, the treasury secretary could waive any conditions it deemed necessary to protect the interests of the federal government.

Everywhere, politically connected insiders benefitted from government assistance. Think tanks and foundations devoted to smaller government, libertarian values and opposed to welfare availed themselves of available funds.

The Ayn Rand Institute saw no breach of integrity in accepting government money. The justification was that the government bore significant blame for the problems because of the mandatory lockdowns. In a blog entitled 'To Take Or Not To Take', the institute stated it would accept any relief money on offer because it constituted partial restitution for government-inflicted losses. It was their duty to accept relief because it would be unjust for pro-capitalists to step aside and leave the funds to those indifferent or actively hostile to capitalism. The escapist from Leninism, Alissa Zinovievna Rosenbaum aka Ayn Rand, would have been proud of the sophistry underlying this rarefied defence.

*

Europe was severely affected by COVID-19 and faced a deep downturn. Negotiations of assistance packages raised familiar tensions.

Weaker and more indebted countries, still struggling from the effects of the European debt crisis, needed urgent funds for public health and the economy.

The European Central Bank ramped up purchase of government bonds and corporate debt and moved to support the fragile banking sector. President Christine Lagarde's comment that it wasn't the central bank's job to narrow the differences in borrowing costs between different Eurozone countries proved inflammatory.

The European Union, eventually, announced a €750 billion fund to aid member nations. It was opposed by the more frugal nations, led by the Netherlands. They insisted that most of the money should take the form of loans, not outright grants, and conditions must be placed on any assistance. Weaker nations, led by Italy, complained about a lack of solidarity and European Union support. They rejected any conditionality. The proposal itself remained vague. There were questions about how the sums were to be raised.

Familiar divisions remerged. The weaker countries tried to resurrect proposals for a Eurobond, now rebranded 'Corona bonds', which would be supported jointly and severally by all member countries. Stronger countries, especially Germany, would de facto underwrite European Union borrowings and provide cheaper financing for weaker members. Such debt mutualisation was duly rejected. Racked by political divisions and trapped between being a trading block and a unified political entity, the typical European nothing-burger emerged.

To compound matters, the German Constitutional Court questioned the European Central Bank's program of purchases of government and corporate debt. Responding to a petition from about 1750 complainants, led by German economists and law professors, the court ordered the German government and parliament to ensure the European Central Bank carried out a 'proportionality assessment' of its vast purchases of government debt to ensure their economic and fiscal policy effects did not outweigh its policy objectives. If this was not completed within three months, it threatened to block new bond buying.

The German government, central bank and the European Central Bank assured everyone that it could show that the purchases were proportional and appropriate. However, future challenges from disgruntled Germans could not be ruled out.

*

Throughout the world, the desperate attempt to combat the economic fallout distorted incentives. Central bank buying of corporate and junk bonds created moral hazard. Investors who had knowingly purchased risky securities for higher returns were being bailed out. Central bank purchases of corporate debt helped private equity funds, whose managers and owners would not even be subject to any remuneration restrictions. The purchases provided backdoor assistance for beleaguered energy producers of up to US$44 billion because they were among the largest issuers of junk bonds.

As well as using their political power to ensure financial survival, energy producers used the crisis to roll back safety and environmental regulations, some designed to reduce emissions. At the same time, pollution from the energy and petrochemical industry was aggravating the effects of COVID-19 infections. For affected people, long-term exposure to toxic chemicals that damaged the lungs increased the risk of pulmonary problems if they were infected by the virus.

Accelerants

The coronavirus was simply the match that started the conflagration. Shortfalls in revenue and cashflows, caused by the partial or total shutdowns, exposed vulnerabilities of a structurally unsound economic and financial system.

Buffers against potential shocks were minimal. Governments and central banks had steadily eroded their war chests and ammunition, leaving them with limited ability to deal with a major dislocation. Corporations convinced themselves that they could raise cheap capital at will and reduced shareholders' funds, buying back their own shares or paying large dividends financed by borrowings.

Households reduced savings and borrowed to fund consumption and purchase houses. In the case of the economically disadvantaged, this was compounded by low wage growth, lack of employment security and inequality. In the US, the Federal Reserve found that many would struggle to raise US$400 in an emergency. In Australia, the Grattan Institute found that 10 percent of households have less than A$90 (US$63) for emergencies. Around 50 percent have less than A$7000 (US$4900).

The lack of preparedness was not universal. After the European debt crisis, Germany was heavily criticised for its conservative attitudes to debt and spending. In a better position now, Germany expanded the Kurzarbeit scheme (where the state partly covers the lost wages of workers who have their hours cut), extended various loan guarantees and even earmarked funds for direct investment in companies. The package totalled around €750 billion, with the potential for increases. With surplus intensive care facilities, the country was able to manage the health crisis better.

*

There were financial weaknesses. A fall in revenue may be manageable without debt. Unfortunately, borrowings were unsustainably high. Businesses and households, with declining or no income and high levels of borrowing, now struggled to meet large financial commitments. Payment holidays from lenders and government could keep delinquency at bay while the measures were continued. But the debt crisis had been delayed, not averted.

Policymakers artificially boosted the values of financial assets. Toxic layers of debt were heavily exposed to significant revenue downturns. Weaknesses of the banking system were ignored. Regulatory rollbacks and tolerance for large dividends and capital buybacks under lobbying pressure undermined steps to strengthen bank capital and liquidity. In Europe and many emerging markets, non-performing loans were not appropriately recognised. The interconnectedness of the financial system and growth of the shadow banking sector was not checked.

In the search for returns, investors purchased riskier and less liquid securities. Redemption terms offered by investment funds, which allowed investors to withdraw money at short notice, were inconsistent with their holdings of securities that were not easy to sell. There was substantial investment in unlisted securities, which are difficult to value. The inability to trade even modest parcels of many securities or redeem investments was always going to create problems in any financial disturbance.

All this was compounded by hubris. The global economic and financial system was predicated on perfection. It is no surprise that the COVID-19 shock created problems. If it wasn't the virus, it would have been something else.

*

The crisis exposed weaknesses in the structure of economies.

As in the 2011 Thai floods and Fukushima disaster, the COVID-19 crisis disrupted production and transport links. Global supply chains made manufacturing vulnerable to even small breakdowns. Dependence upon imports of intermediate components and finished goods risked shortages. The public health response was hampered in many countries by reliance on medical items, often small and inexpensive, sourced from China.

Beyond supply chains, restrictions on movement and the closure of borders affected immigration. The US and Australia rely on immigrants for growth. Immigration is an essential source of labour for many countries. Agriculture in the US, Europe and Australia depends on itinerant foreign seasonal workers. Technology firms rely on skilled workers from India and China. Countries and industries reliant on foreign students and general or medical tourism suffered steep drops in revenues, threatening their survival.

Adopted to save costs, just-in-time practices, low inventories, frequent deliveries and logistical integration are difficult to re-engineer quickly. Minor interruptions can halt production. The practice even extended to critical healthcare, which assumed the ability to scale up, at short notice, to meet surge capacity. This underestimated the time and cost of acquiring resources and staff in an emergency.

Outsourcing of services has similar risks. Call centres, sometimes for essential services, were forced to close or operate at reduced capacity due to lockdowns in developing countries.

*

The economic structure is now weighted in favour of consumption of personal services, entertainment, arts, sport, travel and tourism, which are vulnerable to social distancing and limits on movement. Even online services use content whose production requires close personal contact.

Services are non-storable. They exhibit infinite wastage; if not consumed when available, the supply is lost forever. If a restaurant is closed for a month, then it is difficult to make up lost revenue through increased future sales. In contrast, if demand for manufactured goods cannot be met now and the buyers are willing to wait, they can be supplied later. Income losses in services through disruption are permanent, creating greater problems for businesses where they must

suspend operations. Advanced economies' shift to services from manufacturing and production made them vulnerable to shocks.

Around 40 percent of the workforce in the US, UK, Australia and
New Zealand are now casual or contractors. Of the around 30 million small businesses in America, 80 percent or 24 million are sole
proprietorships, such as hairdressers, personal trainers, Uber drivers, or pieceworkers in the gig economy. Lacking protections, such as
sick leave or holidays, they are vulnerable to any inability to work. In
some countries, if you are casual or lose your job, then you may lose
health insurance coverage. Casual employees, contractors or the self-
employed typically lack capital or cash reserves and access to finance.
They cannot survive shocks, even if short-lived. In a crisis, it is difficult
to channel assistance to these groups.

Since the 1980s, many essential services, such as health, telecommu-
nication, utilities and emergency care have been transferred to private
ownership. In a crisis, responsibility of private firms to shareholders, sometimes foreign, may conflict with national interests. Markets
don't always work in crises. Problems in procuring and distributing
ventilators, PPE and even basic medical consumables, highlighted
the problem. Countries and even states or municipalities engaged
in wasteful bidding wars against each other for essential equipment
and supplies. Arguably, in dealing with the COVID-19 crisis, China
could act quickly and decisively because the bulk of the economy is
government-owned or controlled.

*

Policymakers described their approach to the COVID-19 crisis as
placing the economy in hibernation or an induced coma. Animals that
hibernate need to have reserves to survive winter. If they do not have
enough fat, then they die. In an induced coma, the body shuts down
and needs progressively more assistance to function. A patient's life

expectancy drops dramatically once placed in an induced coma, often from dangerous secondary infections. The restoration of normal function after the pandemic was always going to be the true measure of the success of the strategy.

As after 2008, the post-pandemic recovery will be affected by hysteresis. The destruction of wealth, legacy of debt and employment effects would limit recovery. The effect on businesses, especially small- and medium-sized enterprises, is a major concern.

Most smaller businesses lack reserves to meet expenses for more than a month or, at most, a quarter. Many affected businesses will close and never reopen. Invested capital will be lost. Customers may shift to other providers. Failures destroy intellectual property embedded in networks of customers, staff, suppliers and processes. Reversing this loss takes time.

Businesses that continue to operate will radically restructure operations, for example, reducing their scale. Numerous airlines, such as British Airways, Lufthansa, Emirates and the major US carriers, announced shutdowns of parts of the business. They decommissioned large numbers of aircraft, effectively reducing future capacity and routes. These decisions will flow back along supply chains. Operations will not return to pre-crisis levels for years.

Many tourism and hospitality businesses, including airlines, will be burdened by crisis liabilities. In order to conserve cash, they did not refund cancelled bookings but provided vouchers for future use. When operations resume, they will incur the costs of meeting these obligations without fresh revenue.

Changes in consumer demand may affect the level of activity generally and certain businesses specifically. Business travel may be substantially replaced by teleconferencing. Growth in working remotely, online shopping and entertainment may change demand for real estate. Fear of being trapped in floating plague ships or disease-prone petri dishes may make cruising less attractive. People may be reluctant to travel overseas, fearing future lockdowns, difficulties in returning home, loss of pre-payments and unavailability of insurance coverage.

Behavioural changes will be significant. Fear of acquiring diseases from contact with people may speed up automation, threatening jobs. Scarring from the crisis will affect family or household formation and fertility, which will alter demographics and accelerate the effects of an aging population. Like the Great Depression and the GFC in 2008, people's willingness to consume or go into debt may be affected for a generation or more.

History suggests that increased state involvement will be difficult to reverse. Essential or strategically important services may be placed under some form of government control. Bailouts may reduce competition and create industrial zombies, christened 'the walking debt', as governments seek to preserve firms and employment. Widespread income support may alter incentives to work.

*

Kenichi Ohmae's 1990 book *The Borderless World* was globalisation's blueprint. But COVID-19 and pre-existing post-2008 pressures favour national identity, deglobalisation, protectionism and stringent restrictions on immigration. It favours borders. While the most extreme barriers to travel may be lifted eventually, it is unlikely that a full restoration will occur. Fearful of foreign dependence and focused on self-sufficiency, nations will accelerate the drift towards autarky. They may restrict exports of strategic or essential products and reduce reliance on imports or lengthy international chains of supply. Foreign ownership and free capital movements face greater barriers.

Local production will be more expensive, sub-optimal in scale, inefficient and require redundant capacity. Developing nations that compete within the international supply chain purely on cheap labour will lose their advantage and will need to adjust. The alternative is operating with larger inventories; just in case rather than just in time.

Switzerland, on a per capita basis, was the worst-hit state in Europe because of its proximity to Northern Italy, the initial locus of the European outbreak. The country imports 40–50 percent of its food. Despite a lockdown, supply chain disruption was minimal because the country had strategic stockpiles of three to six months' worth of essential foodstuffs and goods within the country's borders. But maintenance of buffer stocks is expensive.

These changes will affect growth and shift resource allocation within economies, limiting the pace and quantum of any recovery. Governments can minimise some elements of hysteresis, for example, by facilitating investment and offering retraining facilities. However, many of the effects are outside their control. Over time, the combination of bankruptcies, restructuring, downsizing, and structural and behavioural changes will remorselessly bleed out jobs and economic capacity.

Neither a Borrower Nor a Lender Be

Energy sources based around fossil fuels, especially coal and petroleum, powered the rise of modern industrial civilisation. Since the 1980s, debt has fuelled economies. Now, as after 2008, the world turned once again to even more borrowing. The disease was the cure. A major legacy of the pandemic will be a significant increase in already high global debt levels. In OECD countries alone, debt levels are expected to increase by $17 trillion, rising from 109 percent to more than 137 percent of GDP. In the US, government debt was forecast to rise by the end of 2020 to around $27 trillion – a debt-to-GDP ratio of 135 percent.

Public sector debt increases reflect higher healthcare spending, actions to alleviate the economic effects of the crisis, and emergency loans as well as loss of tax revenues. Households and businesses also substantially increased borrowings to cover income shortfalls. If the recovery is slower than expected then the rise in borrowings will be greater.

The debt incurred supplemented lost cashflow or facilitated business survival. Borrowings were not invested in productive activities that could generate future earnings to pay back interest and principal. Government would face constraints in raising revenues through higher taxes to decrease public debt levels because of fears of a drop in already weak economic activity. With the outlook one of lacklustre growth and low inflation, the options to reduce debt were increasingly limited.

One complication was that growth and debt were now inextricably linked in a fatal embrace. Increasing amounts of debt were needed to generate growth. In an unsustainable relationship, debt was increasing at a faster rate than growth. This meant that bringing borrowing under control would reduce growth, setting off a disastrous negative spiral. Currency devaluations, another option, were difficult in a world where every nation wanted to lower the value of its currency to increase export competitiveness as well as reduce debt burdens.

*

The historical precedents are not encouraging. Between 1914 and 1939, World War I, postwar rebuilding and the Great Depression damaged public finances. Immediately after the Great War, UK debt rose to 140 percent of GDP. Attempts to reduce debt through austerity failed. Debt rose to 170 percent of GDP as economic growth fell with 1928 output below that of 1918. Bearing its war losses and reparations, Germany experienced hyperinflation and the destruction of its currency, which reduced its debt burden by 129 percent of GDP. In the 1930s, countries making up nearly half of global GDP defaulted or entered debt restructuring. The social and economic costs were severe.

After World War II, some countries defaulted or experienced hyperinflation. Others used financial repression, such as negative real rates, controlled lending and deposit rates, capital controls and forcing institutions and households to finance the government at below-market rates to manage debt. Real interest rates in advanced economies were negative roughly half the time between 1945 and 1980. These actions and strong growth driven by postwar reconstruction helped reduce debt levels.

Given the limited options, the current debt burden will be managed, in the short run, using zero or negative interest rates to make borrowing bearable. Debt will be consolidated onto the government balance sheet. In the current crisis, governments globally have acted as lenders to businesses and individuals. Some loans will be of necessity converted into grants. Student loans or some delinquent mortgages may be assumed by government or written-off. In the absence of growth or inflation, default, either explicit or in the form of debasement of the currency to wipe out the obligations, may be unavoidable.

Debt is analogous to the effect of ice on flight. Planes are designed to cope with modest icing on the wings. However, large build-ups cause a loss of lift, resulting progressively in erratic flight, loss of altitude and ultimately a crash. Global debt levels now resemble a large build-up of ice on the wings of the global economy and threaten a catastrophic final chapter.

Visits from Alien Economists

Since 2008 the world economy has been trapped in a protracted semi-slump managed by ever lower rates, repeated bouts of quantitative easing and bursts of fiscal stimulus. The economic effects of the pandemic, especially the growing debt overhang, encouraged the search for creative solutions. This was MMT (Modern Monetary Theory).

Critics noted that the arrangement was not modern, not monetary and not a theory. They unkindly pointed out that the acronym might just stand for magic money tree.

The central elements are straightforward. A state, proponents argued, does not finance its spending out of taxes or borrowing but by creating money. Nations cannot go bankrupt when they can print their currency. Therefore, there is no real financial constraint on the amount a government can spend. Under MMT, a country with its own currency does not have to worry about accumulating too much debt and can run deficits at almost whatever level deemed necessary. It can always print more money to pay interest and principal. It is a sophisticated version of the 'deficits don't matter' argument propounded by former US Vice-President Dick Cheney.

MMT draws on several strands of economics: Abba Lerner's functional finance; Wynne Godley's sectoral balances; Hyman Minsky's financial instability hypothesis; Neo-Chartalist relationships between the banking system, the central bank and treasury; and Keynes's advocacy of government use of budgets to achieve macroeconomic outcomes.

The theory is associated with Bernie Sanders's unsuccessful 2016 and 2020 campaigns for the Democratic Party's presidential nomination. MMT underlay the funding of ambitious policies, such as free universal health care, employment guarantees, free public university education and employee business ownership.

The attraction of the argument is obvious. MMT appeals to governments as an easy way to deal with high debt levels and large deficits.

*

For MMT economists, unemployment means that demand is inadequate. Governments should spend to move the economy to full employment. This is the natural rate of employment because there is always some unemployment as workers change jobs or leave the workforce. The job guarantee requires everyone who is willing to work to have one. This is a moral imperative.

An alternative to the job guarantee is universal basic income (UBI), a concept first suggested by Sir Thomas More in his sixteenth-century work *Utopia*. It was championed more recently by free-market economists, such as Friedrich Hayek and Milton Friedman.

UBI provides every individual an unconditional flat-rate payment irrespective of circumstances. It would address the poverty traps inherent in traditional welfare systems, the declining share of income going to labour and increasing threats to employment from automation. UBI may increase the efficiency of government assistance programs by minimising bureaucracy, the administrative costs of delivery and drainage of resources through political exploitation or benefit fraud.

The traditional objection to UBI is its direct monetary cost and the financing of payments. In the US, US$1000 per month per person would equate to a total cost of around $4 trillion per year, approximately the size of the pre-pandemic federal budget. The Organization for Economic Co-operation and Development found that income tax would have to increase by almost 30 percent to fund a modest UBI. MMT removes this financing barrier.

Some MMT advocates reject the idea of UBI. They see the job guarantee, where only those who work get paid, as superior because of economic and social factors.

*

MMT poses several questions. Governments creating and spending money do not directly affect the real, productive sector that produces actual goods and services. It is unclear how the jobs are to be created. It is unclear whether the deficit spending needs to be productive. Ultimately, all activities must earn a financial or social rate of return in excess of cost.

MMT advocates argue that useful, well-compensated work will be available. Details are sketchy. Government taxes can be used to control behaviours and direct production. Centrally planned economies point to difficulties. Stories of simultaneous abundance and shortages of specific goods from maladministration are legendary.

Critics point to the risk of inflation from excess government spending. Large deficits financed by money creation exceeding economic production changes can lead to hyperinflation, as in the Weimar Republic or in Zimbabwe. MMT economists acknowledge the risk but only where the economy is at full employment or there is no excess capacity. Where that is the case, the government could raise taxes or reduce spending to ease inflationary pressures.

There are related operational challenges. In addition to creating the right jobs, it would be necessary to calculate and set the natural rate of employment or the UBI level and structure. Unemployment is difficult to define and measure, as the pandemic illustrated. Measures used to set policy, such as NAIRU (the non-accelerating inflation rate of unemployment), the Phillips curve (the relationship between inflation and unemployment) or money supply statistics, are complex to calculate in practice. The effects of actions are unpredictable in quantum and timing. These details must work if MMT is to be effective.

By definition, the idea only applies to states able to issue their own fiat currencies. It could not be applied to the European Union, where individual nations have ceded currency sovereignty to the European Central Bank. It is also unavailable to private businesses or households. This means that the sovereign may need to assume all private debt, especially in case of a crisis, to assure debt sustainability.

A major concern is where a country borrows in its own currency from overseas investors. Modern central banks can theoretically issue unlimited amounts of money. But there are practical constraints. Investors must have confidence in the government, monetary authorities and in the stability of the exchange rate. Excess deficits and money printing may cause financial markets to lose confidence and force a devaluation, even rendering the currency worthless or unacceptable. Businesses may not be able to import goods at affordable cost or service foreign currency denominated debt. The exchange rate is a serious constraint on MMT.

Policymakers may be unable to control the process once set in motion. Where supply constraints are reached, excessive deficit-financed spending would result in inflation and a currency correction. Lags in the availability of data, which may be ambiguous, make management difficult. In fairness, this is a problem affecting all economic policy.

*

Proponents are coy about the administration of MMT. They argue against unelected central bankers having too much power. They prefer elected politicians to be responsible for economic management.

Critics argue that elected representatives are poorly equipped to establish when the economy is at full capacity or the deficit level required. Political rather than economic considerations and cronyism may drive decisions. Deadlock would be problematic. The US Congress last completed all budgetary bills on time over two decades ago. As a result of the frequent gridlock, congressional budgets now require appropriations and continuing resolutions simply to keep America operating.

There are considerable risks. Banker Mayer Amschel Rothschild supposedly stated, 'Permit me to issue and control the money of a nation, and I care not who makes its laws!' MMT would confer great power that could be misused.

*

The pandemic created a unique opportunity to advance MMT agendas. It offered theoretical cover for governments to avoid dealing with the seemingly insoluble problem of mounting debt levels. The promise of something for nothing is always alluring.

Little about MMT is new. Most of the tenets are well known. Government expenditure to stimulate economic activity and create employment has been part of the policy tool set since the 1930s. The idea that a country can print its own currency has been accepted since the 1970s. Central bank financed government spending via quantitative easing has been used extensively, especially since 2008. MMT does not address key structural issues, such as excessive debt, sectoral and cross-border imbalances, industrial structure, trade policy, wage levels and demographics. Adoption would mean the economy becomes dependent on government intervention to sustain activity.

The approach is lazy. It neatly avoids having to deal with messy and controversial matters, such as the appropriate distribution of income and wealth or systemic inequalities. It ignores how wealth is created. It wants to wish away resource scarcity, environmental and growth constraints, as well as the economic inter-relationships between countries.

MMT, irrespective of whether it funds a job guarantee or UBI, might create unease amongst citizens. Instead of spending the money made available, they may question a world where governments print money and give it away. It might undermine the economic and societal system, perhaps irreparably. If printing money was all it took to ensure prosperity for all, then it is surprising that it hadn't been enthusiastically embraced earlier.

Like Keynesian, Monetarist or Marxist economics, the theory is a political program. A terminally ill person, desperate to live, is always tempted by an experimental drug or a mystic faith-healer's unproven cure. In another chapter of magical economics, MMT offers a facile solution to public finance problems. A world of unlimited borrowing and continuous budget deficits is too good to be true. The problem of over-indebtedness is unavoidable. It will eventually have to be confronted.

Buy the F**king Dip

After the initial, violent gyrations, by mid-April 2020 financial markets had recovered most of the losses. It was the blink-and-you'll-miss-it crash. Share prices rebounded from their lows by around 20 percent in many markets in a matter of weeks – a higher return than that investor received in many full years. The prices of riskier bonds as well as some commodities also recovered. Property values, other than luxury real estate, remained largely unchanged. FOMO (fear of missing out) replaced FOGO (fear of getting out).

Professional investors assumed that the problem was temporary – a rapid economic recovery would ensue; any decline would be made up in later 'catch-up' growth; central banks would successfully cushion any fallout as they had done since the 1980s. The prevailing view was that the serial bubble needs to continue to sustain the global financial system and avoid a complete rupture.

Part of the recovery was bizarrely led by gamblers. Unable to bet on professional sports as fixtures had been cancelled, they flocked instead to the stock market, opening accounts at online brokerages and fuelling the rally. Dave Portnoy, a boisterous sports blogger, emerged as the face of the movement. With *Star Wars* and *Top Gun*-themed videos and missives to his 1.5 million Twitter followers crowing about his abilities, the self-proclaimed supreme leader of the retail traders became a familiar face on financial media.

Portnoy had two rules for share trading; 'stocks only go up' and 'when in doubt whether to buy or sell, see Rule One'. He was captured on film selecting stocks to purchase by picking Scrabble letters from a bag. The model had the benefit of being simpler than the quantitative or analytical ones favoured by professional money managers.

Immediate success as stocks rallied sharply fed their mys-
tique and egos. Much of their success revolved around low-value
stocks of failed companies. Shares in bankrupt Hertz, the car hire
company, rallied 1500 percent. JC Penney, the bankrupt retailer,
rose more than 500 percent. Hertz even tried to take advantage
of rising prices by undertaking a stock offering until the regulators intervened. The speculative boom was nicknamed the 'flight to
crap' to distinguish it from the more normal 'flight to quality' seen
during crises.

*

The investment culture was reminiscent of the day traders during
the height of the 1990s' dot.com boom. They railed against people
who begrudged their success, especially fund managers, Wall Street
pin-stripe suits and Warren Buffett. The retail investors had little
real impact because the size of their purchases was small. The price
increases reflected massive concerted central bank intervention.

Despite the rally, markets remained fragile. Only a small portion
of stock markets recovered, with most stocks still below their pre-
pandemic levels. The rises in stock prices were dominated by the
big tech firms, FAAMG: Facebook, Amazon, Apple, Microsoft and
Google (Alphabet) or, if you subscribed to a different sect, FANGAM:
the previous firms plus Netflix, which had replaced the FAANG.

The retail traders were driving the excesses, with sometimes tragic
consequences. A twenty-year-old committed suicide after losing
nearly three-quarters of a million dollars. In fact, he may not really
have lost that amount as the negative balance was temporary, pend-
ing settlement of transactions. His suicide note questioned how a
young person with no income was able to get so much trading leeway.
Central bank money now allowed small amounts to be leveraged up to
trade stocks in casino-like markets.

*

The disconnections were widespread, and not only in shares. Companies were able to raise record sums from lenders in a dash for cash. Global issuance of debt in the first few months of 2020 equalled the total amount raised in 2019 as businesses shored up their financial position to ride out the economic slowdown. While this survival strategy made sense for companies, investor willingness to provide funds was less easily understandable.

Investors purchased debt at low returns, fearful that interest rates would fall further and become negative. Given portfolios are tied to indices of securities, fund managers were forced to buy as investors gave them money to invest preferring debt to other investments. They looked to the 'other side of the valley', assuming normality would return sooner rather than later.

Investors seemed oblivious to the fact that the borrowings were substituting for lost revenues and not funding productive new investments. They also ignored the effect of these borrowings on corporate credit worthiness. Deferred repayments, new debt and lower earnings would increase the debt-to-equity ratio of already highly leveraged firms. In effect, the cheap new borrowing merely put off the day of reckoning for many businesses, even those that were financially viable before the pandemic.

Lenders would generally not look favourably at any loan request designed to fund current expenditures reliant on uncertain or, in some cases, non-existent future revenue for repayment. Yet, in many cases, that is what lenders were now doing in the new crowdfunding, go-fund-me markets. Perhaps they were basing their optimism on the fact that central banks, which were now actively purchasing corporate debt, would have no choice but to buy all the outstanding corporate debt in case of problems.

*

It was the culmination of a process that had taken place over more than a decade. Central banks and governments had manipulated prices and fabricated valuations through low interest rates, abundant money and encouragement of more and more borrowing. The policies had been in place for so long that everyone accepted them as conventional, even though the basic pricing and market mechanism was broken.

The actions had not boosted the real economy, investment, jobs or incomes. It had merely forced the prices of financial assets, especially real estate and stocks, higher. They had ignored the effects of these policies on inequality and society, which underlay division, unrest and populism. The only ones who couldn't see that were those whose salaries and wealth depended on the forever bubble. Participants, especially in financial markets, were in the grip of a collective hallucination, which they continued to participate in, believing that there was no alternative (TINA).

*

Assuming a quick end to the pandemic, investors forecast a 'V, U or W' shaped recovery and swift return to economic normality. Valuation models assumed a short, say, three- or six-month, disturbance, which equated to a minor interruption in normal cashflows over, say, a ten-year investment horizon. Earnings and dividends were forecast to decrease by 25–50 percent in 2020 but then return to normal. To suggest a bathtub or L-shaped outlook was considered unduly pessimistic.

The initial price falls, around 20–30 percent, were rationalised as a necessary correction. Buying dips had been an extremely successful investment strategy over the past decade, but if the lockdowns continued then large sectors of the economy faced negligible revenue, losses and insolvencies. Significant rises in bad debts were not incorporated in valuations. Without income, dividends or rent, risky assets, such as stocks, residential or commercial real estate, or infrastructure, are worth much less. Investors failed to grasp that for most businesses the focus was now survival. They confused solvency and the effects of artificial injections of central bank liquidity. Investors ignored the risk of social unrest and political fractures.

Weaknesses in economic structure exposed by COVID-19 and the effects of hysteresis meant that any recovery would be weak. There would be permanent scarring. Economic activity may stabilise at levels substantially below normal levels. The post COVID-19 economy may be 'the 90 percent economy', 'the empty chair economy', or 'the zombie recovery'. The chances were that the global economy would find itself in an in-between world, sustained by government support but unable to maintain normal activity by itself. Forecasts and asset values did not countenance this possibility.

Writing about the 1929 US stock market crash, John Kenneth Galbraith noted that during speculative frenzies investors ignore reality and find excuses to embrace fantasies. So, while the real economy died, Wall Street recorded one of its greatest rallies. Ironically, recoveries in equity, credit and commodity markets left them more exposed to a longer-than-expected crisis and any attendant deep downturn and slow recovery. Financial prices were now priced for vaccination as well as perfection. By the end of 2020, with a rapid end to the pandemic not in sight, a new letter 'K' entered the recovery lexicon. Some parts of the economy would do well, while others lagged.

*

Economic and financial relationships are imprecise. Human behaviour is unpredictable. There are unknowable second, third order – and even higher order – effects. But in financial markets, the most difficult thing is to admit that you don't know. To navigate this world, investors place their faith in a plethora of largely occult theories and models that do not always hold, making them sometimes useful but always dangerous.

Investors have a near infinite capacity for rationalisation. In the run-up to the November 2020 US election, they bet heavily on the blue wave – a Democratic series of victories in the presidency, Senate and House of Representatives. The so-called reflation trade assumed substantial government spending and rising inflation. This, in turn, would result in higher interest rates on long-term government debt and a weaker US dollar driving the stock market lower. Actual events did not follow expectations, share prices rose sharply and interest rates fell.

Before the election, the consensus was that a contested presidential election and divided control of the executive and legislative arms were bad outcomes. The hastily constructed new story was that they were good. Taxes and regulations were unlikely to change. The government would struggle to aid economic recovery. The US Federal Reserve would have to step in. Rates would be lower for longer. More money would be provided. All this would boost asset prices.

In negotiating the pandemic, investors became absorbed by false narratives. Attractive stock valuations based on measures such as price/earnings ratios presumed profits. If you assumed sharp falls in earnings, then the recent recovery in prices meant that valuations were near or above their all-time highs of February 2020. If you assumed that stock price should track earnings, then a substantial fall in profits would correspond to a large fall in share prices, not the modest recent declines.

Parallels were drawn with the 2001 September 11 terrorist attacks, which disrupted the real economy, affecting airlines, tourism and hospitality. The comparison was unhelpful as economic activity resumed quickly – it was localised not global, and stock markets were much lower because of the earlier 2000 dot.com crash. The scope for central bank action was also greater then because interest rates were higher and balance sheets were less stretched.

Investors did not notice that policymakers were running on fumes, increasingly at the limits of their legal powers and resources. Their actions were mitigation, designed to prevent a deeper downturn, rather than reflate the economy or price. In any case, further actions to support financial assets could have perverse outcomes.

If the lockdown continued and current initiatives proved ineffective, then government's final option would be to take over large parts of economic activity, entailing partial or total nationalisation, and rewriting economic relationships. Conventional free markets would mutate into something closer to Soviet-style command economies, altering values of financial assets. In post-revolutionary Russia and China, there was no market for financial assets, little ability to extract income and constraints on private ownership.

Markets were experiencing what pilots call a black hole illusion. When flying at night, a featureless terrain can mislead flyers into thinking they are higher than the true altitude, causing them to fly dangerously low and crash when trying to land. Markets were blind to the consequences of the world that may emerge if the COVID-19 crisis was not short-lived.

Washing Hands While Singing 'Happy Birthday' (Twice)

With few exceptions, politicians and business leaders were dilatory in dealing with the COVID-19 crisis. Complacent governments initially did not act quickly enough. Some leaders advised that washing hands while singing 'Happy Birthday' twice would suffice. Once the seriousness became apparent, they overreacted, and finally moved to denial, brazenly toughing it out as solutions proved elusive.

They were poor at balancing competing interests. Churchillian speeches could not mask the lack of preparedness, the paucity of the initial response or the callous calculation underlying the inevitable capitulation. The principal metaphor was war, except most countries were better prepared for that contingency.

US President Trump led the world in serial poor decision-making. Having earlier dismantled the Center for Disease Control's pandemic unit, he denied the severity of the crisis, refused to take recommended measures or use government emergency powers to secure needed medical equipment and supplies. When action commenced, it was chaotic. What action there was turned out, frequently, to be chaotic. The script was Lenin's: first action, then see what happens.

*

With a few notable exceptions, there was little leadership. Messages to the population were frequently mixed and contradictory. In many countries, politicians clashed with public health officials providing unwelcome advice or challenging their comforting prognosis. Intellectual convolutions abounded. Rising numbers of infected reflected more testing, not the lack of control over the disease. Uninformed suggestions – the use of ultra-violet light inside the body and ingesting anti-bacterial liquids – diverted resources from real tasks.

Partisan divisions were never far away. Politicians even clashed with members of their own tribe. The wearing of masks and restrictions on mobility becoming watermark issues of ideological purity. Each side threw red meat to its supporters, even if it meant death and suffering for many citizens.

Unable to bring the virus under control, President Trump, facing an imminent election and behind in the polls, decided to ignore the epidemic. He wanted a rapid wind-back of restrictions to get the economy back on track to boost his prospects. Humorists awaited a presidential executive order, Trump's preferred style of governing, banning COVID-19 and placing sanctions on anyone who was infected. When challenged about his handling of the crisis, Brazilian President Jair Bolsonaro, an acolyte of the American president, told reporters, 'So what? . . . I'm sorry. What do you want me to do?'

Umair Haque, a London-based consultant, asserted, in the context of the opioid crisis, that America was the world's first rich failed state. Many other advanced economies, such as Britain, were not far behind. Ordinary citizens, especially in the worst affected countries, found themselves trapped in a horror movie of illness, death, overburdened hospitals and makeshift morgues against a soundtrack of wailing ambulance sirens.

*

The global scope of the crisis required international cooperation. Instead, squabbles broke out. The United Nations was indecisive. A Security Council motion was delayed over China's objection to any reference to the 'Wuhan flu'.

Many countries, including the US and European Union, restricted exports of medical supplies. The US used threats and emergency powers to force vital supplies to be redirected to America, leading to accusations from Germany of piracy. The US drew the ire of other nations for buying up much of the global supply of the drug Remdesivir, which initially seemed useful in reducing the hospitalisation period of COVID-19 patients. Wealthier and more powerful nations tried to tie up supplies of vaccines or treatment, if and when available, exclusively for their citizens.

Food security for poorer countries was an increasing concern. Supply chains were affected by the closing of plants after workers were infected with coronavirus, transport interruptions and shortages of migrant labour. Some countries suspended food exports. In addition to access, the pandemic left many without necessary income to buy food. The G20 agriculture ministers issued a lame statement agreeing to guard against unjustified restrictive measures and called for cooperation and innovative responses.

At the same time, in scenes reminiscent of the Great Depression, food producers in many countries were dumping milk and destroying crops, ploughing them into unharvested fields. The farmers had lost customers as restaurants, hotels and schools shut. Redirecting their produce to grocery stores proved difficult because of the differing demands of commercial food operations, grocery chains and households.

Developing countries, particularly oil exporters and those dependent on tourism and remittances, needed money. More than 100 of the International Monetary Fund's 189 member countries asked for aid – the greatest number ever. The Fund doubled its available rapid-financing lending to US$100 billion. The World Bank committed US$160 billion to budget support and health infrastructure. Bilateral lenders were asked to suspend debt payments for the poorest nations. The International Monetary Fund estimated that the support needed was US$2.5 trillion. Despite the obvious self-interest, advanced economies were uninterested in assisting, citing the strains on finances that moreover would not be electorally popular.

President Trump insisted on referring to COVID-19 as the 'Chinese Flu'. Erick Erickson, a conservative evangelical radio host and Trump supporter, called it the 'Kung Flu'. The president cancelled American funding for the World Health Organization. The UN agency was apparently biased towards China and had minimised the threat harming America. The World Health Organization had warned all countries about the risks as early as 10 January 2020 and urged precautions, which President Trump had ignored.

The fracturing of international cooperation in dealing with the pandemic was dangerous. It did not augur well for dealing with global issues such as the climate emergency.

*

The political calculus was obvious. With so many unknowns, politicians initially hoped that the crisis would burn out. Once the virus had become a pandemic, inaction was impossible – the stench of large numbers of fatalities would ensure electoral death. However, they faced conflicting advice and no obvious course of action. If the measures worked then they could claim credit. If the measures failed, then it would be justified on the basis that the actions prevented an unknown and unquantified worse outcome. Action was the best political course.

However, the measures threatened mass unemployment and economic collapse. For politicians, it was the worst of times – dying voters and a struggling economy. Politicians feared that they would be judged to have failed.

Governments and politicians use crises to expand power. In many countries, politicians now enacted states of emergency and concentrated authority. Draconian laws suppressed freedom of expression in the interest of eliminating the spread of false information about the pandemic. Several cleverly blamed elites or foreign nationals. COVID-19 provided unquestioned justification for aspiring strongmen to consolidate control.

Viktor Orbán, Hungary's prime minister, was once greeted publicly by European Union president Jean-Claude Juncker as 'dictator'. He enacted a law that allowed him to rule by decree, ostensibly until the coronavirus crisis was over. He was now *The Mikado*'s Pooh-Bah: the lord high everything else, first lord of the treasury, lord chief justice, commander-in-chief, lord high admiral, master of the buckhounds, groom of the back stairs, archbishop of Titipu and lord mayor, both acting and elect, all rolled into one. The Hungarian was not alone, with many other leaders following his example.

Expanded surveillance, defended on the grounds of public health, could be used to control populations and enshrine authoritarian governments. It was the world of *The Minority Report*, based on a Philip K. Dick science-fiction story. Criminal acts could be detected before they are committed. Future culprits can be named, arrested and found guilty of 'pre-crime' on the word of a team of soothsayers. It was viral authoritarianism.

Hamsterkauf

For ordinary citizens, it was *hamsterkauf* – German for 'panic buying'. Stockpiling emptied the shelves and empty shelves promoted more buying, in a desperate cycle. Supermarkets everywhere were now meeting the demand from two countries, not one.

Fearing complete lockdown, households hoarded a bewildering array of items. Irrespective of their utility, masks, gloves, sanitisers and painkillers were stockpiled. Eggs, pasta, rice, breakfast cereals, baked beans and other easy-to-cook foodstuffs were in high demand. Despite the glut of TV celebrity cooking shows and *MasterChef* contests, the population's culinary skills were rudimentary. The demand for alcohol was understandable.

The hoarding of toilet paper would have interested Sigmund Freud. As COVID-19 did not have any major gastrointestinal symptoms, the logic was unclear. Shortages led to learned online debates about alternatives. Interest in bidets and posh Japanese toilets that washed, dried and buffed surged.

The predominant factor was fear. In advanced countries, people were disconnected from risk. Relative peace and plenty encouraged an erroneous sense of security. Everything – cooking, crossing a street, driving, travel – involves risk. It is impossible to eliminate.

People had forgotten that uncertainty is central to existence. They had become removed from the inevitability of death. Medical science encouraged the belief that we can protect against illnesses and defer death, perhaps for ever. Lack of direct experience of war or even industrial accidents shielded most from serious trauma or fatalities. Advances in healthcare and pharmacology, especially antibiotics and vaccines, reduced child mortality and increased longevity. As recently as 1950, US life expectancy was sixty-eight years against seventy-nine years currently. The improvement was even more marked in other countries where average life expectancies were well above eighty years.

*

COVID-19 revived concerns about hardship and mortality. The anxiety was most marked in the better off and rich. They assumed that wealth insulated them from most of life's vicissitudes. They understood certain things – relationship mishaps, divorces, malignant children, occasional investment reversals and routine diseases, for which they could buy the best care. But there was little even the most prepared could do about the pandemic. It was impossible to have a fully-equipped home hospital. The gap between expectations and events was incomprehensible. Bad shit like this only happened to the poor!

The well-off from developed countries found themselves confined to homes, hotel rooms or army barracks. Some found themselves marooned at sea or in foreign countries, begging their governments to be evacuated or having to pay large sums for rescues. Previously indifferent or hostile to refugees, illegal immigrants and the indigent, they now claimed ill-treatment or violations of their civil rights. The *schadenfreude* was tempered by the fact that the position for the wretched was worse. Packed in camps with limited health facilities, they waited for the pandemic.

The COVID-19 lockdown coincided with the release of Irish film-maker Lorcan Finnegan's *Vivarium*, a satire of suburban domesticity. The plot revolves around an ordinary young couple trapped in a housing estate, whose only other inhabitant is a baby they are forced to raise. For many, the film was their new reality – the creepy horror of being in lockdown with immediate family. Blaise Pascal's observation that the sole cause of man's unhappiness is that he cannot stay quietly in his room was never more true.

*

There was optimism that the pandemic may lead to the revival of community and civil society. The media focused on positive messages: hope in darkness, we're all in this together. Saccharine sweet, uplifting stories of kindness to strangers and inspirational images of people in isolation proliferated. Each uplifting story denied thousands and millions of unsung individual acts of heroism. The collective experience was erased in efforts to induce dopamine-laced cheap grace. With the world caught in the middle of a pandemic, economic crash, geopolitical tensions and the accelerating surveillance state, journalists decided on promulgating positive ideas. The underlying causes that necessitated desperate heroism were ignored.

In the short run, people were supportive and understanding. As the economic consequences manifested themselves, people's interests diverged, revealing deep divisions. The emphasis shifted to preservation of oligarchy and existing interests.

*

The end-of-the-world bacchanal gave way to *The Lord of the Flies*. Panic buying, the reckless refusal to maintain physical distance, the looting of medical supplies, familiar prejudices and the scam artists appeared.

Individuals who had recovered from COVID-19 hid the fact to avoid discrimination from employers and landlords. In some countries, the Chinese were assaulted as the source of the pandemic. In China, black African students found themselves discriminated against. In India, police were attacked, with one officer having his hand cut off while trying to enforce the lockdown. A French bus driver died from an attack by passengers after he asked them to wear face masks aboard his vehicle. In America, a man in a supermarket drew a handgun when refused admission without a face covering. In many countries, health workers were persecuted by people fearing that they were COVID-19 carriers.

In the US, there were physical confrontations as libertarians sought to have the lockdown lifted. The demonstrators, some brandishing automatic weapons, protested the economic cost and asserted their civil liberties. President Trump, fearing that a downturn would damage his 'greatest economy ever' and, more importantly, his re-election prospects, encouraged the protests. In a series of all-caps tweets, Trump declared, 'LIBERATE MICHIGAN!' and 'LIBERATE MINNESOTA!' – two states whose Democratic governors had imposed strict restrictions.

Abandoning any semblance of bipartisanship, President Trump sought to divide the country by playing to his political base. It was not a new strategy. In 2017, at a rally in Charlottesville, Virginia, a self-identified white supremacist, James Alex Fields Jr., deliberately rammed his car into a crowd of counter-protesters, killing Heather Heyer. President Trump referred to 'very fine people on both sides', equating neo-Nazis and those who were protesting against them.

*

The middle class and the affluent were used to normalcy and abundance. The pandemic exposed primal anxieties. Under stress, humans reverted to baser animal instincts. Survival became the limits of their ambition. The starving stole from the starving. The weak destroyed those who were weaker. You accepted that another's suffering and death is the price of living.

The trajectory, whether the better-off and privileged understood it or not, was the natural consequence of a deeply exploitative system that had benefitted them. History shows that it typically ends in an 'eating-the-rich' moment. The willingness of greedy or ignorant human beings to harm themselves and others is not always avoidable. The fear was that things could become much worse. As the threat of social unrest and violence escalated, the wealthy retained security services. The problem was that they could not be certain that their protectors would not turn on them.

A Future More Uncertain

By November 2020, several vaccines under development had progressed. Lavishly funded by desperate governments, a few showed promise in trials and looked likely to be rolled out. However, challenges remained.

Facilities need to be scaled up to make sufficient doses to vaccinate several billion people. Making a few thousand doses for a clinical trial is vastly different to large-scale production, especially as some vaccines used new technologies. Manufacture required establishing suitable supply chains and the availability of raw materials, biological and chemical agents.

There were other bottlenecks. Without the necessary vials and syringes, whose supply would need to be increased, vaccines would be useless. Distribution and delivery was complex. Some of the candidates had short shelf-lives or needed to be stored at extremely cold temperatures, -70 degrees Celsius. Cold chain delivery was not easy in advanced economies, let alone in less-developed parts of the globe. Trained resources were needed to administer the vaccine.

The difficulties with large-scale testing and case tracking suggest that a mass vaccination program will not be simple or quick. The global eradication effort for smallpox entailed a strategy to achieve 80 percent vaccine coverage in each country. Subsequent case-finding and vaccination of all known and possible contacts was used to contain outbreaks. The campaign ran from 1966 to 1977.

A vaccine may not end the pandemic. The world will be divided into countries with and those without vaccines because of differences in population size, health infrastructure and financial resources. A return to the pre-pandemic status quo will take time because full lifting of lockdowns and reopening borders require vaccination of a significant proportion of the global population. A vaccine might be light at the end of the tunnel, but the remaining distance to be travelled is considerable.

Scientists cautioned that COVID-19 or its variants might not be able to be eradicated globally. Without universal vaccination, the virus can dictate the duration and arc of the pandemic. It might continue until the last susceptible individual is affected. Like a fire, it will only end when all the fuel has been consumed. For the time being, humans may have to live with the virus as a part of everyday life. COVID-19 was nature's perfect response to assertions of human exceptionalism.

As they awaited the vaccine, governments struggled to balance the public health concerns of a relaxation of controls too quickly and overly restrictive constraints that would cause irreparable economic damage. Politically, reimposing lockdowns or maintaining them for long periods was difficult. Without rigorous police enforcement, people might not comply. Images of people defying social distancing, refusing to wear masks and generally not following prudent practices highlighted the tensions and difficulty in obtaining cooperation.

The controversy over the wearing of masks was not new. In the 1918 influenza pandemic, the authorities encouraged their use but faced opposition. Just as in 2020, resisters, especially in the US, saw the face coverings as government overreach. An Anti-Mask League emerged. Branded 'muzzles' or 'germ shields', opponents argued that they did not want to be seen with a porcine snout. Symbols of resistance included making holes to allow for smoking or fastening masks to dogs. Little, it seems, has changed. Only now, the images of defiance are disseminated by Instagram or TikTok.

There was always going to be a cost – deaths, serious illnesses with potential long-term health effects, mass unemployment, the destruction of livelihoods and the breakdown of economies. It would create social problems, such as addiction, domestic violence, loneliness and isolation. All treatments have negative side effects. The attempts to control COVID-19 were no different.

*

Even if the pandemic was resolved, the problems were not going to go away. COVID-19 was just one disease amongst many. It would mutate. In fact, vaccines invited mutation. There were other coronaviruses. Influenza seemed to be getting worse each year.

Epidemics were going to become more routine. In June 2020 Singapore reported record numbers of dengue fever, also known as 'break-bone fever' because of the joint pain that is one of its symptoms. The female Aedes mosquito, whose bite transmits the disease, is common in South-East Asia. It thrives in stagnant water in and around dwellings. Scientists speculated that the lockdowns created an environment where mosquitoes are interacting more with the population because of COVID-19 movement restrictions. Climate change would contribute to the spread of dengue fever and other diseases, many of which were poorly understood and lacked treatments.

There was the growing problem of antibiotic resistance that could turn currently treatable diseases into potentially fatal conditions. A simple cut if infected could prove lethal. Routine surgical procedures might become intolerably dangerous. Unless new therapies could be developed, anti-microbial resistance, according to the UN, may kill 10 million people a year by 2050, up from 700,000 currently, costing US$100 trillion. The favoured answer was research into new antibiotics. The real problem – inappropriate prescription for trivial conditions and excessive use in cruel and overcrowded factory farming – was ignored.

The public health response to pandemics and diseases is expensive. Limited available resources have to be allocated between competing claims. The lockdown and funding the COVID-19 fight diverted resources and attention away from regular vaccinations and other illnesses.

*

Disease was just one issue. Extreme weather events driven by climate change were ever-present. As the pandemic reigned, storms, tornados and floods claimed lives and damaged properties. The US West Coast experienced the biggest wildfires in history, necessitating mass evacuations. A larger than usual number of severe tropical storms hit the US Atlantic and Gulf coasts, leaving a trail of extensive damage. Heavy monsoon rains and storms left parts of South Asia flooded. Parts of Australia that had been severely damaged by earlier fires experienced heavy rains and flash flooding. Climate change contributed to the fires and storms. The pandemic complicated the emergency response.

The Arctic experienced record temperatures, above 38 degrees Celsius (100 degrees Fahrenheit). In the Antarctic, scientists focused on the Thwaites Glacier, which acts as a dam holding back other glaciers in West Antarctica. As Thwaites collapses, it will affect contiguous ice sheets, causing large amounts of ice to drain into the ocean. As it melts, these alone could raise sea levels by an additional 65 centimetres. This would lead to a rise in sea levels of up to 3 metres – double the predictions of existing models without Thwaites. The melting of the 'doomsday glacier' would be severe for most coastal cities.

A large part of the warming processes, like the disappearance of summer Arctic sea ice, melting permafrost and the disappearance of Antarctic ice sheets, is already locked in. They are probably impossible to halt or reverse. All science can do now is study them.

Food and water security were deteriorating. Only one-third of the world's population can feed itself using staple crops grown within a 100-kilometre (60-mile) radius. Instead, they rely on imports increasingly vulnerable to crises. If governments move to improve their food sovereignty by limiting exports in the aftermath of the pandemic, then many countries will face increased food insecurity.

There were other natural risks. Volcanic eruptions were a known hazard. Even a small asteroid hit posed danger. A coronal mass ejection from the Sun – in effect, a discharge of vast amounts of charged particles – could damage electrical and communication networks. This could leave large parts of the world without electricity or communication for unknown periods ranging from hours to months.

Governments could not shield the population from every one of these threats. Society would now lurch from problem to problem, crisis to crisis.

*

COVID-19 was a window into some of the interconnections between human activity and the risks. The pathogen, like SARS and Ebola, had crossed boundaries through zoonosis, where viral mutations infect humans through the mingling of people and animals. It was related to human exploitation of natural resources. Deforestation to accommodate ever-growing populations or to access resources brought humans into contact with wild animals. Overfishing in African waters by foreign fleets led Africans to turn to bushmeat for protein. In some places, rising living standards created demand for exotic wild animals, considered delicacies.

Economics dictated the concentration of people in large, densely populated cities. Combined with the appetite for leisure travel, it helped contagious pathogens spread rapidly. Natural barriers, such as bodies of water, mountain ranges or deserts, no longer prevented the spread of many diseases.

Banning the trade in wildlife and wet markets will not be enough. The major problem is industrial animal agriculture feeding growing populations. In many developing countries, there are high concentrations of livestock mixing with wild animals. Poor food safety and inadequate hygiene is common. Animal faecal matter can enter groundwater where the watertable is near the surface. This is an ideal location for pathogens to cross species boundaries.

Seeing themselves as above nature, humans believed that they could manipulate the planet for their own purposes. This arrogance exposed the species to threats of climate change, loss of biodiversity and the emergence of entirely new pathogens.

*

One benefit of the COVID-19 pandemic, people asserted, was a fall in carbon emissions. It was illusory. Atmospheric carbon dioxide reached more than 417 parts per million on average during May 2020 at the Mauna Loa Observatory in Hawaii – a new record.

A massive amount of plastic waste, in the form of discarded masks, gloves and disposable supplies, piled up as waste processing and recycling facilities reduced or stopped treatment. Predictably, emissions bounced back where normal activity resumed. By July, air pollution levels had rebounded sharply in a number of leading cities, driven by an increase in traffic and congestion. Due to fear of infection and the difficulty of maintaining social distancing on public transport, the use of cars increased, adding to emissions.

In the long run, COVID-19 was disastrous for the climate. The environment rapidly receded from the list of major concerns for individuals, replaced by healthcare, unemployment and the economy. Leaders would be reluctant to impose curbs that would impede economic recovery and restoration of living standards. Many countries aggressively rolled back environmental protections to fast-track job-creating new projects. Governments, their treasuries exhausted from spending to support the economy, would lack the money to finance initiatives to fight the climate emergency. By June 2020, with economic pressures undermining clean energy initiatives, China approved new coal power plants at the fastest rate since 2015.

It was also a disaster for the planet's remaining natural ecosystems. Lack of tourists and loss of livelihoods meant increasing encroachment of humans into protected areas. Hunger and the need for income led to increases in hunting for bushmeat and poaching. Local populations had no incentives to protect the few vulnerable pockets of remaining habitat. Soon, nothing will remain.

The pious polemic, espoused by idealists, of a reset in behaviours proved reliably incorrect. Habits did not change. As lockdowns eased, people flocked to post-lockdown beach outings, picnics and parties. Half a million people descended on UK's Bournemouth beach on a hot day, ignoring all health recommendations, leaving behind fifty tonnes of rubbish for sanitation workers and volunteers to pick up. There were similar scenes in the US, Europe and Australia. People reverted to normal, assuming unnamed others would clean up the mess. Exhortations for cooperation, responsibility and accountability were nonsense.

The Road to Nowhere

The various problems facing humanity are similar. In each case, society borrows from and pushes problems into the future.

Although difficult to reverse, the effects of climate change are not immediately obvious. Underpriced, finite resources are wantonly utilised without proper concern about conservation for future use. The effects of low investment in public health and ignoring deadly pathogens create long-term risks. Economic growth and wealth are based on borrowed money. Debt allows society to borrow from tomorrow, accelerating spending as borrowed funds are used to purchase something today against the uncertain promise of paying it back in the future. Inequality creates social problems that only appear later.

Current growth, short-term profits and higher living standards for some are pursued at the expense of costs that are not evident immediately but will emerge later. The problems often manifest themselves beyond individual life spans. The lack of immediate effects creates a false sense of security. It enables us to ignore the problems.

Deeper, lasting solutions, especially when they entail cost, are eschewed in favour of temporary patches.

In Stanford University's marshmallow experiment, young children were offered the choice between one marshmallow now or two marshmallows a few minutes later. Most chose one now. Repetition of the study found that the subjects found it difficult to defer appetites when the reward items were directly in front of them. The world's approach to its problems, including the pandemic, reflects the logic of immediate gratification.

The basic strategy is to 'extend and pretend' or 'kick the can down the road'. It is to shift the responsibility onto others, especially future generations. It postpones the inevitable. The strategy assumes there is time. The world, like Dickens's Mr Micawber, waits for something to turn up. In a Faustian bargain, having mortgaged the future for present prosperity, the world has remortgaged it again for a precarious and short-lived stability.

But time has run out. The pandemic showed that the human race may have spun out the clock as long as it can. Events – climate change, pathogens, economic failure – are driven by compound growth. Pressures are now growing at an exponential pace. The rate of change will overwhelm attempts at containment and mitigation. It is the 'Parable of the Wise and the Foolish Builders' in the Gospel of Matthew: 'He was like a foolish man who built his house upon the sand; and the rain fell, and the floods came, the winds blew and beat against that house ... and great was the fall thereof.'

*

Fundamental adjustments, now much larger and more painful due to earlier delays, are needed. Living standards and expectations need to be lowered. Resource intensity, especially energy usage, must decrease. Lowering debt and consumption will reduce growth but ensure sustainability.

Various inequalities need to be addressed. Inequality within societies is a barrier to solving many problems. Low incomes inhibit sustainability as they emphasise cheap but often wasteful solutions. Fast food is cheaper than fresh food, but it's imprudent and based on poor agricultural, distribution and packaging practices. It leaves a legacy of expensive health externalities that burden the entire community.

The pandemic highlighted the problems of inequality. The scarcity of public health resources disproportionately affected disadvantaged groups without private medical care. Rural communities were severely under-resourced in comparison to urban centres. Indigenous tribes in countries like Brazil were badly affected. In America, blacks and Latinos were many times more likely to die than whites from the virus.

People from lower socio-economic circumstances worked in low-paid industries, like domestic help, retail, delivery services, food processing such as meatworks, aged care and healthcare. They were more likely to use public transport. They were more exposed to the risk of infection from COVID-19. Many were pieceworkers who faced penury if they stopped working or called in sick, forcing them to continue to work and increasing the risk to them and their communities. The race riots following the police killing of George Floyd were, in part, fuelled by the anger of minority communities about the health and economic inequities exposed by the virus.

The disadvantaged lack access to important resources. The smart phone system, proposed by Apple and Google, for tracking contact with infected people would be unavailable to as many as 2 billion phone owners around the world, many poorer and older people who are among the most vulnerable to COVID-19. Lower-income families lacked access to digital facilities. Unable to attend school during the lockdown, their children encountered educational disadvantages, leaving them further behind their wealthier counterparts.

Income determined the fortunes of people in the pandemic. Those with money and influence could social distance more easily. Help took care of external chores where they might be exposed to the risk of infection. Private tutors ensured their children would not be deprived of schooling. Chefs brought fine dining into their homes. Some plutocrats purchased private islands to self-isolate. Private jets (PJs to the initiated) overcame the problems of travel on limited scheduled flights. Quarantine restrictions were waived for the wealthy, allowing them to isolate in their luxury homes rather than in premises allocated by the authorities. The monied complained that political correctness meant they couldn't complain about their deprivation. For the rich, everything, including the pandemic, was different.

Gender equality is essential. In the developing world, education and empowerment of women is a highly effective way of improving living standards and sustainability. This is primarily the result of tapping neglected human resources as well as delayed child-bearing and lower numbers of children.

The economic fallout of the pandemic was especially damaging to women. One study found that women make up 39 percent of global employment but accounted for 54 percent of overall job losses. Women are heavily dependent on jobs in sectors most affected by the shutdowns, such as hospitality, and in part-time positions. For women, the virus also significantly increased the burden of unpaid care. If this gender-regressive trend continues, there will be up to a US$1 trillion loss in global GDP by 2030. Despite this, policies targeted assistance to traditionally male-dominated sectors, such as construction and infrastructure.

Equality between generations must be established. The young were disproportionately affected by the 2008 crisis. The pandemic resulted, according to the International Labour Organization estimates, in more than one in six young people losing their jobs. Those that were still employed had their working hours cut by over 20 percent. This boosted already high youth unemployment and under-employment rates.

The young faced many of the same labour market problems as women. Lacking experience and tenure, the young are also more susceptible to losing their jobs and having their hours reduced in downturns. Young women were more adversely affected than young men. Without a strong entry into the workforce, the young are at risk of long-term financial disadvantage and potential welfare dependence.

In 2017 Australian property developer Tim Gurner rejected the notion that economic hardship was disadvantaging Millennials. He argued that it was a flamboyant, spendthrift lifestyle. Despite the attractiveness of the argument amongst older generations, there is little evidence to support the 'avocado toast fallacy'. The young were sacrificed to safeguard the old, in terms of health and wealth.

Many current practices and solutions shift the cost and risk into the future. Allocating resources and wealth equitably across generations is essential to equity and sustainability. The citizenry must embrace an old Greek proverb: 'A society grows great when the old plant trees whose shade they know they shall never sit in.'

Inequality between nations must be corrected. Developing countries should not have to bear a disproportionate share of the cost of corrective actions to reduce climate change when the major part of the responsibility lies with advanced economies and their centuries of pollution.

The wider consequences of inequality quickly became evident in dealing with the virus. The disadvantaged worked jobs where the risk of COVID-19 infection was high, lacked savings to isolate even when ill, lived in frequently overcrowded or unhygienic conditions and had poorer health, increasing susceptibility to the virus. Outbreaks amongst these groups posed a serious threat to the broader population. This forced hard lockdowns and more stringent restrictions for longer periods, delaying reopenings and affecting entire societies. Inadequate health services in poor, emerging nations fed back into advanced economies through international supply chains. High rates of infection and risk of contagion forced continued travel restrictions, prolonging the crisis.

Finally, perhaps most importantly, the population of the planet must be stabilised and then reduced, because it lies at the core of many current challenges. The earth simply does not have the carrying capacity for the current and projected population, especially if the entire planet aspires to the high living standards of developed economies.

The antinatalist philosopher David Benatar argues that it would be better for human beings to stop having children, on compassionate grounds. While blithely wishing to spare their future children suffering, people avoid the reality that, given the current state of things, the only guaranteed way to achieve this is by not bringing children into existence in the first place. In *The Fixed Period*, Anthony Trollope proposed euthanasia as a radical solution to the problem of the aged. In the mythical country of Britannula, all Britannulans are obliged by law to retire from their worldly affairs at sixty-seven years and begin a year of preparation for death.

*

Opponents of this approach to degrowth offer three main critiques: it is unjust, it marks the end of progress, and it is unnecessary.

The burden of the adjustment would fall on the better off and advanced nations. It is not clear why this is unjust given that those nations use a disproportionate share of resources and their wealth is, in part, based on the exploitation of nature, resources and people in poorer countries, especially during the colonial period.

Progress is narrowly based on economic and health parameters. Increasingly, improvement is excessive consumption of unnecessary items and economic activity of little obvious benefit to human well-being. The benefits are not evenly shared and are unsustainable.

Action is not only necessary, it is urgent. The alternative is social breakdown and environmental collapse.

Countries as disparate as the US, UK, France, Spain, Hong Kong, China, Lebanon, Ecuador, Argentina, Brazil and Chile have experienced serious civil disorder in recent years. There are commonalities: inequality, corruption, civic freedoms and the right to self-determination. There is dissatisfaction with austerity, rollback of government services and failures to address environmental change. A Chilean woman spoke for many: 'You politicians, did this really have to happen so that you stop robbing money from the people?'

The prospects for peaceful reform and change are low. Changing a system that refuses to acknowledge that it is the problem is difficult.

It is even more so when those who benefit from its inequities must correct the failings. The alternative is revolution or tyranny. Nonviolence only works, as black civil activist Stokely Carmichael once noted, if your opponent has a conscience.

In the absence of fundamental changes, state violence is inevitably met with counter-violence. Brutal crackdowns on the grounds of law and order feed lawlessness and disorder. Tear gas, water cannons, baton charges, rubber bullets and eventually live rounds turn streets into battlegrounds. Ill treatment of protestors by police or the military set off new protests. The risk of tyranny and breakdown escalates. It is the *Hunger Games*: 'If we burn, you burn with us.'

*

Crucially, changes are needed to live within planetary boundaries. Basic ecology dictates biodiversity, interconnectedness and the need to exist with finite resources. The lessons from nature are salutary. If in contradiction to the basic rules one species expands beyond available resources, it must monopolise what is there or prey on other species. This reduces biodiversity. Given the interdependences of species, the overpopulation and damage to the ecosystem is corrected by the decline or extinction of the offending group.

Patagonia in South America illustrates these rules. It is a world of miniatures. Everything is small, such as the pudú, the world's smallest deer. This is designed to accommodate a world of resource scarcity. Small minimises resource needs. Human society has chosen a different path, growing steadily larger, requiring more and more resources. Today, we probably need two or three earths to sustain the needs of human society.

A quasi-religious belief in modern technology cannot vanquish scarcity and overturn the fundamental laws of science. Our species, despite its overweening arrogance, is a passenger along for the ride. If humanity cannot or will not make the required changes, then those changes will be forced on us. An advanced technological civilisation has now found itself humbled by a primitive organism. Society suffered a fearful end of self-confidence. More patient than humans, COVID-19 determined the sequence and pace of events. Nature was always going to have the final say.

*

Disregard for truth, denial and a refusal to acknowledge limits to individual freedoms are at the heart of the unwillingness to act. Individuals were once entitled to their own opinion, but not their own *facts*. Now, you are entitled to both.

During COVID-19, a 1920 letter, supposedly from F. Scott Fitzgerald while under quarantine during the Spanish flu outbreak, was shared on Instagram and Twitter, quickly going viral. Its sentimental tone, images and flourish offered hope. It was, in fact, a parody, written by Nick Farriella, for the humour website McSweeney's. Wisdom and memes shared should carry the health warning: 'Dubious origin, probably fake, but worth sharing.'

Some fake news or misinformation was harmful. Untruths about borders closing or unverified treatments for the virus multiplied as quickly as the coronavirus. Treatments included drinking bleach, snorting cocaine, smoking and consuming alcohol as well as diet supplements and a special toothpaste, available at an exorbitant price online. Hindu groups, affiliated with Prime Minister Narendra Modi's BJP, promoted yoga and drinking cow urine to ward off coronavirus and cure illnesses like cancer.

The US president promoted an antimalarial drug, hydroxychloroquine, as a 'game-changer' cure. There was no evidence that it was effective. It had potentially serious side effects. Demand for the drug created shortages, affecting patients with lupus, arthritis and other conditions, who genuinely needed the medicine.

Celebrities got tests suspiciously early, released patronising videos and dished out dubious health advice. J. K. Rowling, whose medical qualifications were hitherto unknown, used social media to promote breathing techniques and controlled coughing, which had helped her coronavirus-like respiratory symptoms. There was no confirmation that she had ever been infected.

Even before a vaccine for COVID-19 had been found, the internet was full of misinformation. Well versed in manipulating the media and exploiting the weaknesses of social media platforms, the anti-vaccine community were already engaged in a war against vaccinations.

In his 2020 St Patrick's Day address, Irish Taoiseach Leo Varadkar warned people to get information from official, trusted sources rather than from social media. Misinformation, speculation and conspiracy theories were doing as much harm as the virus, creating a 'contagion of fear'. The pleas fell on deaf ears in an era when the fanciful was routinely accepted. It was a matter of faith, belief and a person's political leanings rather than evidence.

Truth is now variable; facts are no longer objective. Reality is orthodoxy decided by a select group to suit their shifting agenda. It is dictated to others who must adhere to its tenets. To disagree with this consensus risks ostracism, being bullied, termination of employment or worse. Wrongthink has supplanted Groupthink.

In 2004, Karl Rove, advisor to President George W. Bush, thought that the world worked differently now. A statement's truth is based on intuition or perceptions of some individuals, not on discernible reality, evidence or logic.

The claim that a lot of people are saying something establishes legitimacy. Even if something is not true, if someone on TV says it there must be something there. If it doesn't fit your frame of reference, then it is fake. An indifference to truth and falsity is widespread.

Truth has been replaced by what comedian Stephen Colbert termed 'truthiness'. These are things that are not true. They are things one *wishes* were true. Our desperate needs, our unrealistic expectations, mean that we can no longer distinguish between what is real and what is not.

Assertions of individuals' rights now mask self-interest and a culture of narcissism. Freedom is the right to do anything with the environment, society and the economy. In America, many considered the right to own assault weapons more vital than the threat of gun violence. During the pandemic, the individual freedom to eat out, go to a bar, visit a spa or have your nails done was more important than the need to protect the community from infection.

People have turned denial into an art form. You cannot take necessary corrective measures because others may not do the same. People are willing to allow problems to get so bad that it was pointless to do anything or it was simply too late. People rationalise everything endlessly. They believe that to question the status quo is to risk everything – their jobs, their wealth, their daily lives, their future. In the words of Aleksandr Solzhenitsyn, the 'permanent lie [has become] the only safe form of existence'.

*

Nobody exemplified disregard for the truth or denial better than US President Donald Trump.

He wasted time playing down the seriousness of the COVID-19 crisis, asserting that it would simply disappear, like a miracle, and have little impact on the US. Forced to act by the health crisis spiralling out of control, he claimed previously unknown medical expertise, stating that he had always known that it was an epidemic. Against a backdrop of urgent pleas from governors and mayors for medical supplies and lockdowns, the president announced plans to reopen the economy by Easter.

On 5 May 2020 President Trump's economic advisors projected that there would be no more COVID-19 deaths, starting 16 May. Contemporaneously, the Centers for Disease Control and Prevention released new internal projections suggesting that US deaths would rise by the beginning of June, weeks after states had begun reopening their economies. The startling White House forecast was based on fitting a curve using a cubic polynomial to the data. The released curve was manipulated, as it would otherwise have shown negative deaths. People would start rising from their graves.

There was daily rambling, lengthy press conferences that allowed the president to put himself at the centre of attention. They became showcases designed to advance his re-election campaign. Trump ignored questions that showed him in an unfavourable light. He launched into lengthy exegeses of his own superiority to fawning queries from hand-selected reporters. He rated his handling of the crisis as ten out of ten. His team had done 'amazing', 'incredible' work, opinions shared by no one outside his supporters.

After repeatedly ignoring medical recommendations, the president and several associates became infected with COVID-19. He recklessly undertook high-risk activities while still infectious, unnecessarily endangering people around him. Upon release from hospital, he appeared on the White House balcony in a scene that echoed Evita Perón, to proclaim his divinely ordained return.

After receiving medical care that few Americans could afford, he claimed that COVID-19 was inconsequential. The mainstream media were using it to damage him. He repeated earlier claims that it would disappear. A vaccine or cure would be available by the election date for everybody. As he continued to lie about the pandemic, US infections exceeded 120,000 per day and total deaths approached a quarter of a million people – one of the worst performances in advanced economies.

President Trump's rise to office was built on his ability to convince the required number of the voting public of his wealth and acumen, even if these did not quite match the facts. He shaped a public image of his stable genius, superior intellect and triumphs with women. Underlying this were his selling skills and modest reality show success, where he played a brilliant businessman. The president's signature style was 'kayfabe', as professional wrestlers call their scripted reality where the audience accepts the authenticity of what is obviously staged. Trump grasped that politics is not a contest of ideas. It is soap opera, like professional wrestling.

President Trump tried to shape events in terms of his own alternate reality, even when they were at odds with the facts. In the words of Rudy Giuliani, his personal lawyer, the truth wasn't truth. The president, as one commentator put it, did not even know what it is to know.

Trump's defeat was cast in the same fictional terms as his time in office. A reality TV presidency had been cancelled after a four-year run. Tens of thousands of tweets dismissed the president in the language of his show *The Apprentice*: 'You're fired!' As networks called the election for his Democratic opponent, Trump was quixotically playing golf, a pastime where he allegedly cheated and sabotaged other players.

President Trump's narcissistic personality, need for adulation, disregard for facts, denial of unpleasant truths and lack of empathy is well known. The problem is that in dealing with the challenges facing mankind, there is something of those same elements in everybody. Favouring self-interest and the refusal to face up to reality are widespread. Modern society is more like Trump than we would like to admit. He is the ideal leader for a world that has evolved into a Disney-like Fantasyland.

A Date with the Finite

Everything is finite. There are limits to everything. Humans, the product of 4 billion years of evolution, are not nature's zenith. When the sun collapses 6 billion years from now, destroying the earth, it is unlikely that humanity will still exist. Civilisations have much shorter life spans. Ambitious empires that ignore the boundaries within which they operate are always at risk of demise.

History shows that declines are driven by a combination of resource depletion, environmental damage and declines in the ability to create wealth. Financial factors include poor public finances, debasement of currencies and financial trickery. Working becomes degrading. Unproductive complexity rises. Inequality and oligarchy proliferate. Decision-making becomes sclerotic. Governments and institutions are corrupted. There is complacency. Sensing the imminent end, people loot what is there. Society becomes vulnerable to shocks such as war, natural disasters, famine and plagues.

In the 1970s, a model developed by the Massachusetts Institute of Technology predicted civilisation's collapse by 2040 based on pollution levels, population growth, availability of natural resources and the overall quality of life. The forecast is on track. Modern civilisation is doomed by its fundamental structure and nature. The strains on the ecological carrying capacity and the economic stratification of society are fatal. Technology improves the efficiency of resource use, but it also raises consumption and resource extraction. Its benefits are outweighed by over-burdening of the system, making collapse even more likely.

Today, people's sense of security does not spring from conviction – it is based on habit. George Eliot argued that belief that something will never happen is based on the length of time that things have continued in their agreeable state. Unfortunately, the elapse of time makes the event more likely. Eliot used the analogy of ageing: the older a man gets, the more difficult it is for him to believe in his own death.

Today, the game is reaching its final phase. The pandemic is a trial, the first of many to follow. The real tests, particularly the problems of climate change and scarcity of vital resources, lie ahead. Without drastic action, humanity faces a series of insurmountable challenges.

In an interview in 2009, American biologist E. O. Wilson thought the problem was that human beings sought to confront the task with Paleolithic emotions, medieval institutions and faith in god-like technology. Solving the multiple crises confronting society required intelligence but, perhaps more importantly, honesty and humility. He thought we were on thin ground.

History suggests the prospects of society adopting the necessary corrective measures are low. At best, there will be adaptation to living under deteriorating physical conditions and constraints. It might already be too late, even for that.

NOTES

Prologue

1   Ayn Rand, 'The Objectivist Ethics', a paper delivered at the University of Wisconsin Symposium on 'Ethics in Our Time' in Madison, Wisconsin, 9 February 1961.

2   C.S. Lewis, *Mere Christianity*, Book 1, 'Right and Wrong As a Clue to the Meaning of the Universe', Part V, 'We Have Cause to Be Uneasy', 1943.

Great Expectations

1   Harold Macmillan, speech at Bedford, England, 20 July 1957. Quoted in 'More production "the only answer" to inflation', *The Times*, 22 July 1957.

2   Sloan Wilson, *The Man in the Gray Flannel Suit*, Da Capo Press, 1955, p. 3.

3   Willy Brandt, 'The Dream of European Unity', *Awake! Magazine*, 22 December 1991.

4   Robert Lucas, 'Macroeconomic priorities', *American Economic Review*, vol. 93, no. 1 (2003), pp. 1–14.

5   Peter Schwartz and Peter Leyden, 'The Long Boom: A History of the Future, 1980–2020', *Wired*, July 1997. http://archive.wired.com/wired/archive/5.07/longboom.html

6   Alan Greenspan, *The Age of Turbulence: Adventures in a New World*, Allen Lane, 2007, p. 230.

7   Joe Nocera, 'As credit crisis spiralled, alarm led to action', *New York Times*, 1 October 2008.

8   See 'Bernanke: Why are we still listening to this guy?', www.youtube.com/watch?v=HQ79Pt2GNJo.

Borrowed Times

1   See George Soros, 'Worst financial crisis in 60 years marks end of an era', *Financial Times*, 23 January 2008.

2   Richard Dobbs, Susan Lund, Jonathan Woetzel and Mina Mutafchieva, *Debt and (not much) deleveraging*, McKinsey Global Institute, 2015.

3   See Henry Hazlitt, *Economics in One Lesson*, 1946, p. 17. http://mises.org/books/economics_in_one_lesson_hazlitt.pdf

4   A phrase coined by Lord Adair Turner, a former UK regulator; see Gillian Tett, 'West's debt explosion is real story behind Fed QE dance', *Financial Times,* 20 September 2013.

5   See Piergiorgio Alessandri and Andrew G. Haldane, 'Banking on the State', speech based on a presentation delivered at the Federal Reserve Bank of Chicago twelfth annual International Banking Conference on 'The International Financial Crisis: Have the Rules of Finance Changed?', 25 September 2009. www.bankofengland.co.uk/archive/Documents/historicpubs/speeches/2009/speech409.pdf

6   Peter Drucker, 'The Mirage of Pensions', *Harper's Monthly*, February 1950.

7   Jagadeesh Gokhale, *Measuring the Unfunded Obligations of European Countries*, National Centre for Policy Studies, Policy Report Number 319, January 2009.

8   See Quentin Peel, 'Merkel warns on cost of welfare', *Financial Times*, 16 December 2012.

9   See AFP, 'Impact of US financial crisis will be felt around world: Chinese PM', 28 September 2008.

10   See Martin Wolf, 'Reform of British banking needs to go further', *Financial Times*, 20 June 2013.

11   A phrase coined by Andrew Haldane of the Bank of England.

12   See Simon Schama, *The American Future: A History from the Founding Fathers to Barack Obama*, 2010, p. 311.

13   See 'Jean-Claude Juncker Interview: The Demons Haven't Been Banished', *Der Spiegel*, 11 March 2013. www.spiegel.de/international/europe/spiegel-interview-with-luxembourg-prime-minister-juncker-a-888021.html

Escape Velocity

1   Edward P. Lazear, *Economic Imperialism*, Hoover Institution and Graduate School of Business, Stanford University, May 1999. http://faculty-gsb.stanford.edu/lazear/personal/pdfs/economic%20imperialism.pdf

2   John Maynard Keynes, *General Theory Of Employment, Interest And Money*, Atlantic Publishers & Distributors, (1936) 2006, p. 272.

3   Raghuram Rajan, 'The Paranoid Style in Economics', *Project Syndicate*, 8 August 2013. www.project-syndicate.org/commentary/the-declining-quality-of-public-economic-debate-by-raghuram-rajan

4   G.K. Chesterton, *Orthodoxy*, Chapter VI, 1908. http://en.wikiquote.org/wiki/G._K._Chesterton

5   Carmen M. Reinhart and Kenneth Rogoff, *This Time is Different: Eight Centuries of Financial Folly*, Princeton University Press, 2009.

6   See Patrick Bernau, '"Eine Hexenjagd" – Keneth Rogoff über seinen Excel-Fehler',

Fazit, 22 October 2013. http://blogs.faz.net/fazit/2013/10/22/kenneth-rogoff-
ueber-excel-fehler-hexenjagd-2818/

7   Frederic Mishkin, 'The economist's reply to the "Inside Job"', *Financial Times,* 8
    October 2010.

8   Quoted in Robert John, 'Behind the Balfour Declaration: Britain's Great War
    Pledge to Lord Rothschild', *The Journal of Historical Review*, vol. 6, no. 4 (Win-
    ter 1985-6), pp. 389–450.

9   See Neil Irwin, 'With consumers slow to spend, businesses are slow to hire', *Wash-
    ington Post,* 21 August 2010.

10 Tim Duy, 'Yes, I am Optimistic', 30 November 2014. *http://economistsview.typepad.
    com/timduy/2014/11/yes-i-am-optimistic-1.html*

11 Wynne Godley, 'Macroeconomics Without Equilibrium or Disequilibrium', The
    Jerome Levy Economics Institute, Working Paper No. 205, August 1997. www.
    levyinstitute.org/pubs/wp205.pdf

12 Olivier Blanchard, 'Monetary Policy Will Never Be the Same', *IMF Direct*, 19
    November 2013. http://blog-imfdirect.imf.org/2013/11/19/monetary-policy-will-
    never-be-the-same/

13 Fyodor Dostoyevsky, trans. Constance Garnett, *The Brothers Karamazov*, Book VI,
    Chapter III: 'Conversations and Exhortations of Father Zossima; of Prayer, of
    Love, and of Contact with other Worlds', (1879) 2009. http://www.gutenberg.
    org/files/28054/28054-h/28054-h.html#toc85

14 Molière, *Le Malade Imaginaire*, 1673, Act III, sc. iii.

15 See Eshe Nelson and Sharon Chen, 'Hair-of-Dog Policy Risks U.K. Housing
    Boom Repeat, Turner Says', *Bloomberg*, 28 October 2013. www.bloomberg.com/
    news/articles/2013-10-28/hair-of-dog-policy-risks-u-k-housing-boom-repeat-
    turner-says

16 Milton and Rose Friedman, *Tyranny of the Status Quo*, Houghton Mifflin Harcourt,
    1984, p. 115.

17 See Chris Giles, 'King warns BoE action reaching limit', *Financial Times*, 24 Octo-
    ber 2012.

18 Jeff Frank, letter to the editor, '"Bold move" will be to withdraw the money later',
    Financial Times, 26 January 2015.

19 Simon Kennedy and Jennifer Ryan, 'Carney Says Policy Must Achieve "Escape
    Velocity"', *Bloomberg*, 28 January 2013. www.bloomberg.com/news/arti-
    cles/2013-01-26/carney-says-flexible-central-banks-not-maxed-out-on-policy

20 See Michael Pascoe, 'The RBA guide to housing prices', *Yahoo7 Finance*, 23
    January 2013. http://au.pfinance.yahoo.com/our-experts/michael-pascoe/arti-
    cle/-/15932231/the-rba-guide-to-housing-prices/

21 See 'William White: Central Banking ... Not a Science', www.youtube.com/
    watch?v=tCx-lKdRrPs.

22 A.P. Chekhov, trans. Julius West, *The Cherry Orchard*, (1904) 1916. www.eldritch-
    press.org/ac/chorch.htm

23 Russell Brand, 'For Amy', 24 July 2011. www.russellbrand.com/for-amy/

The End of Growth

1   Arthur Miller, 'The Year it Came Apart', *New York Magazine*, vol. 8, no. 1 (30 December 1974 – 6 January 1975), p. 30.
2   See Reuters, 'China's GDP is "man-made", unreliable: top leader', 6 December 2010. www.reuters.com/article/2010/12/06/us-china-economy-wikileaks-idUS-TRE6B527D20101206
3   Robert F. Kennedy, remarks at the University of Kansas, Lawrence, Kansas, 18 March 1968. www.jfklibrary.org/Research/Research-Aids/Ready-Reference/RFK-Speeches/Remarks-of-Robert-F-Kennedy-at-the-University-of-Kansas-March-18-1968.aspx
4   Henry C. Wallich, 'Zero Growth', *Newsweek*, 24 January 1972.
5   J.R. McNeill, *Something New Under The Sun: An Environmental History of the Twentieth Century World*, W.W. Norton & Company, 2000, pp. 5–7.
6   Robert J. Gordon, 'Is US Economic Growth Over? Faltering Innovation Confronts The Six Headwinds', Centre for Economic Policy Research, *Policy Insight*, no. 63 (September 2012).
7   Justin McCurry, 'Let elderly people "hurry up and die", says Japanese minister', *The Guardian*, 22 January 2013.
8   Richard Dobbs, Jaana Remes and Jonathan Woetzel, 'Where to look for global growth: Productivity gains could make the difference in an aging world', *McKinsey Quarterly*, January 2015.
9   Robert J. Gordon, 'Is US Economic Growth Over? Faltering Innovation Confronts The Six Headwinds', Centre for Economic Policy Research, *Policy Insight*, no. 63 (September 2012).
10   Robert Salow, 'We'd Better Watch Out', *New York Times Book Review*, 12 July 1987.
11   See Founders Fund, 'What happened to the future?' www.foundersfund.com/the-future
12   Andy Xie, 'Mirage of the "new economy"', *Marketwatch*, 26 March 2014. www.marketwatch.com/story/mirage-of-the-new-economy-2014-03-26
13   Suzanne Woolley, 'Amazon May Have Just Created a Weapon of Mass Consumption', *Financial Times*, 21 June 2014.
14   Jill Lepore, 'The Disruption Machine: What the gospel of innovation gets wrong', *New Yorker*, 23 June 2014. www.newyorker.com/reporting/2014/06/23/140623fa_fact_lepore?currentPage=all
15   Alfred North Whitehead, *Science and the Modern World*, Macmillan, 1925, p. 96.
16   Jonathan Huebner, 'A possible declining trend for worldwide innovation', *Technological Forecasting & Social Change*, vol. 72, no. 8 (2005), pp. 980–986.
17   Mentioned in a conference about automation held by the UAW–CIO union in November 1954. http://quoteinvestigator.com/2011/11/16/robots-buy-cars/
18   John Steinbeck, *The Grapes of Wrath*, Penguin, (1939) 1992, p. 44.

Running on Empty

1   John Hicks, *Value and Capital*, 2nd edition, Clarendon, 1946.

2   Edward Abbey, *Desert Solitaire: A Season in the Wilderness*, Touchstone, 1990, p. 113.
3   Graham Turner, 'A Comparison of *The Limits to Growth* with Thirty Years of Reality', *Socio-Economics and the Environment in Discussion (SEED)*, CSIRO Working Paper Series 2008–09, June 2008.
4   Joseph Tainter, *The Collapse of Complex Societies*, Cambridge University Press, 2003.
5   Andrew Sheng, 'Too Big to Fail, Too Big to Jail', presentation at INET session on Sovereignty and LCFIs, Bretton Woods, New Hampshire, 9 April 2011. www.youtube.com/watch?v=TdVc4oMc9cQ
6   Jeremy Grantham, 'Welcome To Dystopia! Entering a Long-Term and Politically Dangerous Food Crisis', GMO *Quarterly Letter*, July 2012.
7   Roger Revelle and Hans E. Suess, 'Carbon Dioxide Exchange between Atmosphere and Ocean and the Question of an Increase of Atmospheric CO_2 During the Past Decades', *Tellus*, vol. 9, no. 1 (February 1957), pp. 18–27.
8   Joseph Conrad, letter to the owner and crew of the sailing ship *Tusitala*, 2 June 1923. http://joan-druett.blogspot.com.au/2011/05/joseph-conrad-letter-on-auction-block.html.
9   E. F. Schumacher, originated from a conference in Germany in 1954. Quoted in Ramchandra Guha, *Environmentalism: A Global History*, Longman, 2000, pp. 66–67.
10   Jared Diamond, *Collapse: How Societies Choose to Fail or Succeed*, Penguin, 2006, p. 313.

Circling the Wagons

1   John Maynard Keynes, *The Economic Consequences of the Peace*, Harcourt, Brace, and Howe, (1919) 1920. www.econlib.org/library/YPDBooks/Keynes/kynsCP2.html
2   Susan Lund et al., 'Financial Globalization: Retreat Or Reset', McKinsey Global Institute, March 2013; James Manyika et al., 'Global Flows in a Digital Age: How Trade, Finance, People, And Data Connect The World Economy', McKinsey Global Institute, April 2014.
3   See 'Tiger Management Founder Julian Robertson Speaks with Kelly Evans on CNBC's "Closing Bell"', 12 June 2014. www.cnbc.com/id/101754198
4   Pascal Lamy, speech to the Federation of Indian Chambers of Commerce and Industry (FICCI), New Delhi, 3 September 2009. www.wto.org/english/news_e/sppl_e/sppl33_e.htm
5   Felipe Larrain, 'QE takes a toll on emerging economies', *Financial Times*, 4 February 2013.
6   'Mario Draghi says talk of currency war "excessive"', *Daily Telegraph* (UK), 18 February 2013.
7   See Linette Lopez, 'You F---ing Americans. Who Are You To Tell Us, The Rest Of The World, That We're Not Going To Deal With Iranians', *Business Insider*, 7 August 2012. www.businessinsider.com.au/standard-chartered-complaint-quote-you-fcking-americans-2012-8

8   William G. Hyland, speech at Washington University, St. Louis, Missouri, 15 May
      1987. www.nytimes.com/1987/05/17/us/commencements-washington-university.
      html

9   Christopher Hibbert, *The Dragon Wakes: China and the West 1793–1911*, Penguin,
      1984, p. 32.

10   Michael Greenberg, *British Trade And The Opening Of China 1800–1842*, Cambridge
      University Press, 1969, p. 5.

11   See Tracy Withers, 'English Says N.Z. Won't Enter Currency War Zone With
      Peashooter', *Bloomberg*, 13 February 2013. www.bloomberg.com/news/2013-02-
      12/english-says-n-z-won-t-enter-currency-war-zone-with-peashooter.html

12   The phrase was used by US Secretary of State Madeleine Albright on NBC's *Today
      Show*, 19 February 1998.

13   The phrase 'entangling alliances' was used by US President Thomas Jefferson in his
      4 March 1801 inaugural address, and 'in search of monsters to destroy' by US
      Secretary of State John Quincy Adams in an address on 4 July 1821.

14   Winston Churchill, speech at Westminster College, Fulton, Missouri, 5 March
      1946. www.fordham.edu/halsall/mod/churchill-iron.asp

BRIC(S) to BIITS

1   Alfred Russell Wallace, *The Wonderful Century; Its Successes and Its Failures*, Swan
      Sonnenschein & Co., 1898. http://wallace-online.org/content/frameset?pagese-
      q=397&itemID=S726&viewtype=side

2   Karl Marx, 'The Future Results of British Rule in India', *New-York Daily Tribune*, 8
      August 1853.

3   See Michael F. Bishop, 'The Lion at Twilight', *National Review*, 21 July 2014.
      https://nationalreview.com/nrd/articles/381881/lion-twilight

4   Peter Whitfield, *Travel: A Literary History*, Bodleian Library, University of Oxford,
      2011, p. 46.

5   Jawaharlal Nehru, speech on the Granting of Indian Independence, New Delhi, 14
      August 1947. www.fordham.edu/halsall/mod/1947nehru1.html

6   Attributed variously to German Chancellor Helmut Schmidt, British Prime Min-
      ister Margaret Thatcher and journalist Xan Smiley.

7   The actual quote is from Victor Hugo, *Histoire d'un Crime* (*History of a Crime*),
      written 1852, first published 1877. It is usually translated as: 'One resists the inva-
      sion of armies; one does not resist the invasion of ideas.'

8   David Rothkopf, 'The BRICs and What the BRICs Would Be Without China …',
      Foreign Policy, 15 June 2009. http://foreignpolicy.com/2009/06/15/the-brics-and-
      what-the-brics-would-be-without-china/

9   '"China's spirit", a "Great Wall" at heart built to ward off global crisis', *People's
      Daily*, 30 July 2009. http://en.people.cn/90001/90780/91342/6714668.html

10   See Brett Logiurato, 'John McCain: Russia is a "Gas Station Masquerading as a
      Country"', *Business Insider*, 17 March 2014. www.businessinsider.com.au/mccain-
      russia-putin-gas-sanctions-ukraine-crimea-referendum-2014-3 .

11 Henry Kissinger, quoted in *The New York Times Magazine*, 1 June 1969.

12 Rudiger Dornbusch, interview for *Frontline Special*, 'Murder, Money, and Mexico', PBS, 1997. www.pbs.org/wgbh/pages/frontline/shows/mexico/interviews/dornbusch.html .

13 See Tom Donilon, 'We're Number 1 (and We're Going to Stay That Way): Why the Prophets of American Doom Are Wrong', *Foreign Policy*, 3 July 2014. http://foreignpolicy.com/2014/07/03/were-no-1-and-were-going-to-stay-that-way/

14 Michael Beckley, 'China's Century? Why America's Edge Will Endure', *International Security*, vol. 36, no. 3 (Winter 2011/12), pp. 41–78.

Economic Apartheid

1 Bill and Melinda Gates, 'Three Myths on the World's Poor', *Wall Street Journal* , 17 January 2014. www.wsj.com/articles/SB10001424052702304149404579324530112590864

2 These figures are from the World Bank's GINI index database. Care should be taken in interpreting the estimates as they are the latest available but not necessarily from the same year.

3 See 'Top 10 Tax Dodgers', *Time*, http://content.time.com/time/specials/packages/article/0,28804,1891335_1891333_1891317,00.html

4 Branko Milanović, 'Global Income Inequality by the Numbers: in History and Now: An Overview', World Bank Policy Research Working Paper 6259, November 2012. http://elibrary.worldbank.org/doi/pdf/10.1596/1813-9450-6259

5 'Full Transcript of the Mitt Romney Secret Video', *Mother Jones*, 19 September 2012. www.motherjones.com/politics/2012/09/full-transcript-mitt-romney-secret-video

6 Ben S. Bernanke, 'What the Fed Did and Why: Supporting the Recovery and Sustaining Price Stability', *Washington Post*, 4 November 2010. www.washingtonpost.com/wp-dyn/content/article/2010/11/03/AR2010110307372.html

7 The term 'human shields' was suggested by Steve Randy Waldman, 'Some thoughts on QE', 2 November 2014. www.interfluidity.com/v2/5773.html

8 See United Kingdom's *Budget 2012: thirtieth report of session 2010–12*, vol. 1, p. 26; oral evidence to the Treasury select committee, Bank of England February 2012 Inflation Report, HC (2010–12) 1867, Q 84.

9 Oscar Wilde, *The Soul of Man under Socialism*, 1891. www.gutenberg.org/files/1017/1017-h/1017-h.htm.

10 George Orwell, 'Marrakech', in *Essays*, Everyman's Library, (1939) 2002, pp. 121–122.

11 Chrystia Freeland, *Sale of the Century: Russia's Wild Ride from Communism to Capitalism*, Crown Business, 2000, p. 14.

12 George Orwell, 'Rudyard Kipling', in *Essays*, Everyman's Library, (1942) 2002, p. 400.

13 The term 'economic apartheid' was first suggested by Simon Kuper, 'Economic Apartheid, Just Less Black And White', *Financial Times*, 25 April 2014.

14 David Cameron, 'The Big Society', Sixth Annual Hugo Young Memorial Lecture, London, 10 November 2009. www.theguardian.com/politics/video/2009/nov/10/david-cameron-hugo-young-lecture

15 Thomas Gray, 'Elegy written in a Country Churchyard', in Arthur Quiller-Couch (ed.), *The Oxford Book of English Verse: 1250–1900*, Oxford University Press, (1751) 1919. www.bartleby.com/101/453.html

16 Robert Shrimsley, 'The Nine Stages of the Piketty Bubble', *Financial Times*, 30 April 2014.

17 Pope Francis, 'Evangelii Gaudium', 24 November 2013. http://w2.vatican.va/content/francesco/en/apost_exhortations/documents/papa-francesco_esortazione-ap_20131124_evangelii-gaudium.html

18 See Benedict Mander and John Paul Rathbone, 'Chile: Limits to Growth', *Financial Times*, 1 July 2014.

The End of Trust

1 Konrad Heiden, trans. Ralph Mannheim, *Der Fuehrer: Hitler's Rise to Power*, Houghton Mifflin, 1944, excerpted in Fritz Ringer, *The German Inflation of 1923*, Oxford University Press, 1969, p. 170.

2 See Michael Mackenzie, Dan McCrum and Stephen Foley, 'Bond Markets: A False Sense of Security', *Financial Times*, 18 November 2012.

3 See Ralph Atkins and Martin Sandbu, 'FT interview transcript: Jens Weidmann', *Financial Times*, 13 November 2011.

4 See Ben McLannahan, 'Japan Bonds Swing Wildly After BoJ Move', *Financial Times*, 5 April 2013.

5 John Maynard Keynes, quoted in Robert Sidelsky, *John Maynard Keynes: The Economist As Saviour 1920-1937*, Macmillan, 1992, p. 62.

6 Greg Smith, 'Why I Am Leaving Goldman Sachs', *New York Times*, 14 March 2012.

7 Upton Sinclair, *I, Candidate for Governor: And How I Got Licked*, University of California Press, (1935) 1994, p. 109.

8 'Wall Street and the Financial Crisis: The Role Of Investment Banks', Senate Hearing 111-674, vol. 4, 27 April 2010. www.gpo.gov/fdsys/pkg/CHRG-111shrg57322/html/CHRG-111shrg57322.htm

9 Matt Taibbi, 'The Great American Bubble Machine', *Rolling Stone*, 5 April 2010.

10 Liam Vaughan and Jesse Westbrook, 'Barclays Big-Boy Breaches Mean Libor Fixes Not Enough', *Bloomberg*, 29 June 2012. www.bloomberg.com/news/articles/2012-06-29/barclays-big-boy-breaches-mean-libor-fixes-not-enough

11 Martin Arnold, 'HSBC shares drop after full-year profits fall', *Financial Times*, 23 February 2015

12 Ferdinand Pecora, *Wall Street under Oath*, Simon & Schuster, 1939, p. 130. http://books.google.com.au/books?id=i2AUAQAAMAAJ&dq=Wall%20Street%20Under%20Oath

13   Martin Wolf, 'Why banking is an accident waiting to happen', *Financial Times*,
      27 November 2007. www.ft.com/intl/cms/s/0/3da550e8-9d0e-11dc-af03-
      0000779fd2ac.html#axzz3ZxuzhRuO

14   John Maynard Keynes, *General Theory of Employment, Interest and Money*, Macmil-
      lan, 1936, Chapter 12, Part VI.

15   'Statement by Mr Guideo Mantega, Minister of Finance of Brazil', International
      Monetary and Financial Committee, Twenty-Fifth Meeting, 21 April 2012.
      www.imf.org/External/spring/2012/imfc/statement/eng/bra.pdf

16   Jin Liqun and Keyu Jin, 'Europe should stop arguing and look to Asia', *Financial
      Times*, 7 June 2012.

17   AAP, '"Ashamed" IMF economist Peter Doyle quits organisation', *news.com.
      au*, 21 July 2012. www.news.com.au/world/ashamed-imf-economist-quits-
      organisation/story-fndir2ev-1226431366257

18   Victor Mallet, 'Indian Growth: Rose Tinted', *Financial Times*,
      17 December 2012.

19   Willem Buiter, 'The Unfortunate Uselessness of Most "State of the Art"
      Academic Monetary Economics', *Vox*, 6 March 2009. www.voxeu.org/article/
      macroeconomics-crisis-irrelevance

20   Mark Melin, 'Paul Singer Blasts "Krugmanization" of Economics', *ValueWalk*, 3
      November 2014. www.valuewalk.com/2014/11/paul-singer-paul-krugman/

21   Jonathan Lynn and Anthony Jay, *Yes, Prime Minister: The Diaries of the Rt Hon.
      James Hacker, MP*, BBC Books, 1987, p. 218.

22   'Transcript of Chair Yellen's Press Conference', Federal Reserve, 19 March 2014.
      www.federalreserve.gov/mediacenter/files/FOMCpresconf20140319.pdf

23   John Maynard Keynes, *The End of Laissez-Faire*, Hogarth Press, 1926. This
      essay, published as a pamphlet in July 1926, was based on the Sidney Ball
      Lecture given by Keynes at Oxford in November 1924 and on a lecture given
      by him at the University of Berlin in June 1926. www.panarchy.org/keynes/
      laissezfaire.1926.html

24   Peter Spiegel, 'Draghi's ECB Management: The Leaked Geithner Files', *Financial
      Times*, 11 November 2014.

25   Bruno Waterfield, 'Jean-Claude Juncker Profile: "When It Becomes Serious, You
      Have To Lie"', *Daily Telegraph* (UK), 12 November 2014.

26   James G. Neuger and Mark Deen, 'Portugal Told to Make Deeper Deficit Cuts to
      Gain $116 Billion EU Bailout', *Bloomberg*, 10 April 2011. www.bloomberg.com/
      news/2011-04-08/portugal-may-be-forced-to-make-deeper-cuts-than-ones-re-
      jected-by-lawmakers.html

27   Miles Johnson, 'Spain unveils new austerity measures', *Financial Times*, 30 March
      2012.

28   Louise Armitstead, 'Spanish Bailout "Impossible" For Eurozone, Says Prime Min-
      ister Mariano Rajoy', *Daily Telegraph* (UK), 12 April 2012.

29   Peter Spiegel and Victor Mallet, 'Spain Seeks Eurozone Bailout', *Financial Times*,
      10 June 2012.

30   Bertolt Brecht, *The Solution*, as translated in George Tabori, *Brecht on Brecht: An Improvisation*, French, (1953) 1967, p. 17.

31   This quote is commonly attributed to Jean Monnet, a letter to a friend, 30 April 1952. www.rense.com/general87/nationstates.htm. However, there are suggestions that the statement was not made by Monnet but by Adrian Hilton in his book *The Principality and Power of Europe*.

32   David Rennie, 'Keep Up The Pressure For A No Vote, Left Warned', *Daily Telegraph* (UK), 26 May 2005.

33   Peter Oborne, 'Europe Is Slowly Strangling the Life Out Of National Democracy', *Daily Telegraph* (UK), 1 January 2014.

34   The quote is attributed to a variety of people but most often associated with financier Bernard Baruch. http://quoteinvestigator.com/2012/12/04/those-who-mind/.

35   Slavoj Žižek, 'The Reality of the Virtual'. www.izlese.org/slavoj-a-34-ia-34-ek-the-reality-of-the-virtual-1-7.html

36   Tom Perkins, 'Letter: Progressive Kristallnacht Coming?', *Wall Street Journal*, 24 January 2014. www.wsj.com/articles/SB10001424052702304549504579316913982034286

37   Nick Hanauer, 'The Pitchforks Are Coming . . . For Us Plutocrats', *Politico*, July/August 2014. www.politico.com/magazine/story/2014/06/the-pitchforks-are-coming-for-us-plutocrats-108014.html#ixzz3IuF76580

38   John Maynard Keynes, *The Means to Prosperity*, Macmillan, 1933, p. 37. www.gutenberg.ca/ebooks/keynes-means/keynes-means-00-h.html

39   This is actually a popular derivation of a quote from Nietzsche's *Beyond Good and Evil*, Aphorism 183: 'Not that you lied to me but that I no longer believe you has shaken me.'

Collateral Damage

1   Ernest Hemingway, *The Sun Also Rises*, Arrow, (1926) 2004, p. 119.

2   Marshall McLuhan, 'American Advertising', *Horizon*, 93–94 (1947), pp. 132–141. www.unz.org/Pub/Horizon-1947oct-00132

3   Quoted in Kevin Foster, 'A Country Dying on its Feet: Naipaul, Argentina, and Britain', *Modern Fiction Studies*, vol. 48 (Spring 2002), pp. 169–193. http://muse.jhu.edu/journals/mfs/summary/v048/48.1foster.html

4   Daniel H. Pink, 'The New Face of the Silicon Age', *Wired*, February 2004. http://archive.wired.com/wired/archive/12.02/india.html.

5   Nichole Gracely, 'Being Homeless Is Better Than Working For Amazon', *The Guardian*, 29 November 2014. www.theguardian.com/money/2014/nov/28/being-homeless-is-better-than-working-for-amazon

6   John Lovering, 'Creating Discourses Rather Than Jobs: the Crisis in the Cities and the Transition Fantasies of Intellectuals and Policy Makers', in Patsy Healey (ed.), *Managing Cities: The New Urban Context*, John Wiley, 1995.

7   There are many different version of this statement. The origins have been traced to a speech given by Martin Niemoller, the Lutheran pastor and victim of Nazi persecution, on 6 January 1946 to the representatives of the Confessing Church in Frankfurt.

8   Cited in Jason Tanz, 'How Airbnb and Lyft Finally Got Americans to Trust Each Other', *Wired*, 23 April 2014. www.wired.com/2014/04/trust-in-the-share-economy

9   William Alden, 'The Business Tycoons of Airbnb', *The New York Times Magazine*, 30 November 2014. www.nytimes.com/2014/11/30/magazine/the-business-tycoons-of-airbnb.html

10 Kevin Roose, 'Does Silicon Valley Have a Contract-Worker Problem?', *New York Magazine*, 18 September 2014. http://nymag.com/daily/intelligencer/2014/09/silicon-valleys-contract-worker-problem.html

11 Harley Shaken, a labour economist at the University of California at Berkeley, quoted in Louis Uchitelle, 'The wage that meant middle class', *New York Times*, 20 April 2008.

12 *The Future of Retirement (2015) – Global Report*, HSBC Holdings plc

13 Andrew Haldane, 'The $100 billion question', Speech at the Institute of Regulation & Risk, North Asia (IRRNA) in Hong Kong, 30 March 2010. www.bankofengland.co.uk/archive/Documents/historicpubs/news/2010/036.pdf

14 Paul Brodsky, 'Plastics', 14 November 2011. www.ritholtz.com/blog/2011/11/plastics/

15 Martin Amis, 'Martin Amis on God, Money, and What's Wrong with the GOP', *Newsweek*, 10 September 2012. www.newsweek.com/martin-amis-god-money-and-whats-wrong-gop-64629

16 Arnaud Marès, 'Ask Not *Whether* Governments Will Default, but *How*', Morgan Stanley, 26 August 2010. http://economics.uwo.ca/fubar_docs/july_dec10/morganstanleyreport_sept10.pdf

17 Alan J. Auerbach, Jagadeesh Gokhale and Laurence J. Kotlikoff, 'Generational Accounting: A Meaningful Way to Evaluate Fiscal Policy', *Journal of Economic Perspectives*, vol. 8, no. 1 (Winter 1994), pp. 73–94.

18 Nicoletta Batini and Giovanni Callegari, 'Balancing the Burden' , *Finance and Development*, June 2011, pp. 19–21.

19 Robert Hughes, *Goya*, Alfred A. Knopf, 2003, p. 383.

20 Edmund Burke, *Reflections on the Revolution In France*, Liberty Fund, 1790. www.econlib.org/library/LFBooks/Burke/brkSWv2c0.html

Epilogue

1   William Faulkner, *Requiem for a Nun*, Random House, 1950, Act I, sc. 3.

2   Adolf Hitler, trans. James Murphy, *Mein Kampf*, (1925) 1939, vol. I, Chapter X. http://gutenberg.net.au/ebooks02/0200601.txt .

3   Thomas Hobbes, *Leviathan*, 1651, Chapter XIII.

4   B.H. Liddell Hart, *A History of the First World War*, Macmillan, 1970, p. 1.

5 Often attributed to Albert Einstein, the statement derives from William Bruce Cameron, *Informal Sociology: A Casual Introduction to Sociological Thinking*, Random House, 1963, p. 13. http://quoteinvestigator.com/2010/05/26/every-thing-counts-einstein/

6 See Wolf Richter, 'If This Ends Badly, How Will Such Reports Be Read, In Hindsight. Mad?', *Wolf Street*, 8 July 2014. http://wolfstreet.com/2014/07/08/bofa-conundrum-im-so-bearish-im-bullish/

7 See Peter Spiegel, 'EU forecasts paint grim economic picture', *Financial Times*, 22 February 2013.

8 Adolf Hitler, trans. James Murphy, *Mein Kampf*, (1925) 1939, vol. I, Chapter VI. http://gutenberg.net.au/ebooks02/0200601.txt

9 A.J.P. Taylor, *The Course of German History: A Survey of the Development of German History since 1815*, Routledge, 1945, p. 228.

10 Gwyn Prins, 'On Condis and Coolth', *Energy and Buildings*, vol. 18, issues 3–4 (1992). Quoted in Stan Cox, *Losing Our Cool: Uncomfortable Truths about Our Air-Conditioned World (and Finding New Ways to Get Through Summer)*, The New Press, 2010, p. xii.

11 John Stuart Mill, 'Of the Stationary State', in *Principles of Political Economy: With Some of Their Applications to Social Philosophy*, J.W. Parker, 1848, Book IV, Chapter VI. www.econlib.org/library/Mill/mlP61.html

12 David Hume, *Idea of a Perfect Commonwealth*, 1754. www.constitution.org/dh/perf-comw.txt

13 See Reuters, 'Central Banks Can't Raise Growth Potential, Says European Central Bank's Weidmann', 28 November 2014.

14 Russell Ackoff, *A Lifetime of Systems Thinking*, Leverage Points, 1999, p. 115.

15 This is the common version of a statement by W. Edward Deming, quoted in Frank Voehl, *Deming: The Way We Knew Him*, St. Lucie, 1995, p. 125. The real quote is: 'Learning is not compulsory; it's voluntary. Improvement is not compulsory; it's voluntary. But to survive, we must learn.'

16 Christopher G. Langton, 'Computation at the Edge of Chaos', *Phyisca D*, vol. 42 (1990), pp. 12–37.

17 Bertolt Brecht, quoted in John Cook, *The Book of Positive Quotations*, Fairview Press, 2007, p. 390.

18 The phrase is attributed to President George W. Bush's adviser Karl Rove; Ron Suskind, 'Faith, Certainty and the Presidency of George W. Bush', *The New York Times Magazine*, 17 October 2004.

19 Michel de Montaigne, trans. John Florio, 'It Is Folly to Refer Truth or Falsehood to Our Sufficiency', in Robert Andrews (ed.), *The Columbia Dictionary of Quotations*, Columbia University Press, 1993.

20 The statement attributed to Robert Louis Stevenson is based on his essay 'Old Mortality': '. . . shadowing the complexity of that game of consequences to which we all sit down . . .'

ACKNOWLEDGEMENTS

I would like to thank Ben Ball, Publishing Director at Penguin Australia for his brave and enthusiastic support for the book from inception.

A special thanks to my editor, Meredith Rose, who worked with me patiently and very closely in improving the book without ever losing its essence. I would like also to thank the skilled and diligent team at Penguin, including Rebecca Bauert who carefully helped sort out the proofs and correct my errors, John Canty (designer), Johannes Jakob and Imogen Dewey (editorial assistance), Tracey Jarrett (production controller) and Jeanne Rudd (who prepared the index).

I would like to thank Brandon VanOver, Commissioning Editor, for his enthusiastic support for this revised edition. I would also like to thank Patrick Mangan, Nerrilee Weir and Emily Cook for their help with the project.

The epigraph by George F. Kennan is from his book *American Diplomacy 1900–1950*, University of Chicago Press, 1951, p. 66. The second epigraph is attributed to George Orwell but there is no evidence that he said or wrote it; see quoteinvestigator. com/2013/02/24/truth-revolutionary. Grateful acknowledgement is made to the following for permission to reproduce copyrighted material: an extract (on page 7) from *Mere Christianity* by C.S. Lewis © copyright CS Lewis Pte Ltd 1942, 1943, 1944, 1952. Reproduced by permission of The CS Lewis Company Ltd. Extracts (on pages 221–22, 224) from George Orwell: *Essays by George Orwell* with an introduction by Bernard Crick. First published as *The Collected Essays: Journalism and Letters of George Orwell* volumes 1–4, Martin Secker & Warburg 1968. This edition Penguin Books 2000, copyright © George Orwell and the Estate of Sonia Brownell Orwell, 1984. Introduction copyright © Bernard Crick, 1994, copyright © 1950 by Houghton Mifflin Harcourt

Publishing Company, copyright © renewed 1978 by Sonia Brownell. Reproduced by permission of Penguin Books Ltd; Bill Hamilton as the Literary Executor of the Estate of the Late Sonia Brownell Orwell and Houghton Mifflin Harcourt Publishing Company. All rights reserved.

SELECTED FURTHER READING

The list below sets out suggestions for further reading on different aspects of the matters covered in *A Banquet of Consequences*. The list is not comprehensive and reflects the author's biases and prejudices.

Economic History

Piers Brendon, *The Dark Valley: A Panorama of the 1930s*, Pimlico, 2000.

John Brooks, *The Go-Go Years: The Drama and Crashing Finale of Wall Street's Bullish 60s*, John Wiley, 1998.

John Cassidy, *dot.con*, Perennial, 2002.

Adam Ferguson, *When Money Dies: The Nightmare of the Weimar Hyper-Inflation*, Old Street Publishing, 2010.

Niall Ferguson, *The Ascent of Money*, Allen Lane, 2008.

Julie Froud, Sukhdev Johal, Adam Leaver and Karel Williams, *Financialization and Strategy: Narrative and Numbers*, Routledge, 2006.

John Kenneth Galbraith, *The Great Crash, 1929*, Penguin, 1975.

——*The Age of Uncertainty*, Houghton Mifflin, 1977.

——*The Affluent Society*, Mariner, 1998.

Jon Gertner, *The Idea Factory: Bell Labs and The Great Age of American Innovation*, Penguin, 2012.

Michael A. Hiltzik, *Dealers of Lightning: Xerox PARC and the Dawn of the Computer Age*, Harper Business, 1991.

Tony Judt, *Postwar: A History of Europe Since 1945*, Vintage, 2005.

Charles P. Kindleberger, *Manias, Panics and Crashes: A History of Financial Crisis*, Basic Books, 1978.

Luuk van Middelaar, *The Passage to Europe: How a Continent Became a Union*, Yale University Press, 2013.

Lawrence E. Mitchell, *The Speculation Economy: How Finance Triumphed Over Industry*, Berrett-Koehler Publishing, 2007.

Jürgen Osterhammel, *The Transformation of the World: A Global History of the Nineteenth Century*, Princeton University Press, 2014.

R. Taggart Murphy, *Japan and the Shackles of the Past*, Oxford University Press, 2014.

Adam Tooze, *Crashed: How A Decade of Financial Crisis Changed the World*, Allen Lane, 2018.

Richard Vague, *A Brief History of Doom: Two Hundred Years of Financial Crises*, University of Pennsylvania Press, 2019.

Christopher Wood, *The Bubble Economy: Japan's Extraordinary Speculative Boom of the '80s and the Dramatic Bust of the '90s*, Solstice Publishing, 2006.

The Global Financial Crisis

John Authers, *The Fearful Rise of Markets: A Short View of Global Bubbles and Synchronised Meltdowns*, FT Prentice Hall, 2010.

William D. Cohan, *House of Cards: How Wall Street's Gamblers Broke Capitalism*, Allen Lane, 2009.

Satyajit Das, *Traders Guns and Money: Knowns and Unknowns in the Dazzling World of Financial Derivatives*, FT Prentice Hall, 2006.

——*Extreme Money: The Masters of the Universe and the Cult of Risk*, Penguin Books Australia, 2014.

Andrew Gamble, *The Spectre at the Feast: Capitalist Crisis and the Politics of Recession*, Palgrave MacMillan, 2009.

Simon Johnson and James Kwak, *13 Bankers: The Wall Street Takeover and the Next Financial Meltdown*, Pantheon Books, 2010.

Ásgeir Jónsson, *Why Iceland?: How One of The World's Smallest Countries Became The Meltdown's Biggest Casualty*, McGraw Hill, 2009.

Randall Lane, *The Zeroes: My Misadventures in the Decade Wall Street Went Insane*, Portfolio, 2010.

Michael Lewis, *The Big Short: Inside the Doomsday Machine*, Allen Lane, 2010.

Jason Manolopoulos, *Greece's 'Odious' Debt: The Looting of the Hellenic Republic by the Euro, the Political Elite and the Investment Community*, Anthem, 2011.

Ashoka Mody, *Euro Tragedy: A Drama in Nine Acts*, Oxford University Press, 2018.

Charles Morris, *The Two Trillion Dollar Meltdown: Easy Money, High Rollers and the Great Credit Crash*, Public Affairs, 2008.

Yves Smith, *ECONned: How Unenlightened Self Interest Undermined Democracy and Corrupted Capitalism*, Palgrave Macmillan, 2010.

Andrew Ross Sorkin, *Too Big to Fail: Inside the Battle to Save Wall Street*, Allen Lane, 2009.

Gillian Tett, *Fool's Gold: How Unrestrained Greed Corrupted a Dream, Shattered Global Markets and Unleashed a Catastrophe*, Little Brown, 2009.

Economic Policy and Central Banking

Liaquat Ahamed, *Lords of Finance: The Bankers Who Broke the World*, Penguin, 2009.

Peter L. Bernstein, *Against The Gods: The Remarkable Story of Risk*, John Wiley, 1996.

Luigi Buttiglione, Philip R. Lane, Lucrezia Reichlin and Vincent Reinhart, *Deleveraging, What Deleveraging? The 16th Geneva Report on the World Economy*, International Center For Monetary and Banking Studies, 2014.

John Cassidy, *How Markets Fail: The Logic of Economic Calamities*, Allen Lane, 2009.

Edward Chancellor, *Devil Take The Hindmost*, Plume Books, 2000.

Richard Dobbs, Susan Lund, Jonathan Woetzel and Mina Mutafchieva, *Debt and (not much) deleveraging*, McKinsey Global Institute, 2015.

Richard Dobbs, Susan Lund, Tim Koller and Ari Shwayder, *QE and ultra-low interest rates: Distributional effects and risks*, McKinsey Global Institute, 2013.

Barry Eichengreen, *Exorbitant Privilege: The Rise and Fall of the Dollar*, Oxford University Press, 2011.

Alan Greenspan, *The Age of Turbulence: Adventures in a New World*, Allen Lane, 2007.

William Grieder, *Secret of the Temple: How the Federal Reserve Runs the Country*, Simon & Schuster, 1987.

John Kay, *The Truth About Markets: Why Some Nations are Rich But Most Remain Poor*, Penguin, 2004.

Vivek Kaul, *Easy Money: Evolution of the Global Financial System to the Great Bubble Burst*, Sage Publications, 2014.

——*Easy Money: The Greatest Ponzi Scheme Ever and How It Is Set to Destroy the Global Financial System*, Sage Publications, 2014.

Stephen D. King, *When The Money Runs Out: The End of Western Affluence*, Yale University Press, 2013.

Charles MacKay, *Extraordinary Popular Delusions and the Madness of Crowds* and Joseph de la Vega, *Confusión de Confusiones*, John Wiley, 1996.

Graeme Maxton, *The End of Progress: How Modern Economics Has Failed Us*, John Wiley, 2011.

Johan van Overtveldt, *The Chicago School: How the University of Chicago Assembled the Thinkers Who Revolutionised Economics and Business*, Agate Books, 2007.

John Quiggin, *Zombie Economics: How Dead Ideas Still Walk Among Us*, Princeton University Press, 2010.

Raghuram G. Rajan, *Fault Lines: How Hidden Fractures Still Threaten the World Economy*, Princeton University Press, 2010.

David Roche and Bob McKee, *New Monetarism: New Edition*, An Independent Strategy Publication, 2008.

——*Democrisis: Democracy caused the debt crisis. Will it survive it?* An Independent Strategy Publication, 2012.

Robert Skidelsky, *John Maynard Keynes 1883–1946: Economist, Philosopher, Statesman*, Penguin, 2003.

Benn Steil, *The Battle of Bretton Woods: John Maynard Keynes, Harry Dexter White, and the Making of a New World Order*, Princeton University Press, 2013.

David Wessel, *In Fed We Trust: Ben Bernanke's War on the Great Panic*, Scribe Publications, 2010.

Martin Wolf, *The Shifts and the Shocks: What We've Learned—and Have Still to Learn—from the Financial Crisis*, Penguin, 2014.
Daniel Yergin and Joseph Stanislaw, *The Commanding Heights: The Battle for the World Economy*, Touchstone Books, 2002.

Growth
Robert J. Gordon, *The Rise and Fall of American Growth: The U.S. Standard of Living since the Civil War*, Princeton University Press, 2016.
Vaclav Smil, *Growth: From Microorganisms to Megacities*, MIT Press, 2019.

Technology
Naom Cohen, *The Know It Alls: The Rise of Silicon Valley as a Political Powerhouse and Social Wrecking Ball*, Oneworld, 2017.
Brian Merchant, *The One Device: The Secret History of the iPhone*, Corgi Books, 2017.
Evgeny Morozov, *To Save Everything, Click Here: The Folly of Technological Solutionsim*, Public Affairs, 2013.
Margaret O'Mara, *The Code: Silicon Valley and the Remaking of America*, Penguin Random House, 2019.
Shoshana Zuboff, *The Age of Surveillance Capitalism: The Fight for a Human Future at the New Frontier of Power*, Profile Books, 2019.

Globalisation & Emerging Markets
William J. Bernstein, *A Splendid Exchange: How Trade Shaped the World*, Grove Press, 2008.
Jonathan Fenby, *Tiger Head, Snake Tails: China Today, How It Got There and Where It Is Heading*, Simon & Schuster, 2012.
Thomas Friedman, *The World Is Flat: The Globalised World of the Twenty-First Century*, Penguin, 2006.
Chrystia Freeland, *Sale of the Century: The Inside Story of the Second Russian Revolution*, Abacus, 2000.
Ramachandra Guha, *India After Gandhi: The History of the World's Largest Democracy*, Harper Perennial, 2003.
Henry Kissinger, *On China*, Penguin, 2011.
Hamish MacDonald, *Mahabharata in Polyester: The Making of the World's Richest Brothers and Their Feud*, New South Wales University Press, 2010.
Richard McGregor, *The Party: The Secret World of China's Communist Rulers*, Allen Lane, 2010.
Michael Pettis, *Restructuring the Chinese Economy: Economic Distortions and the Next Decade of Chinese Growth*, Carnegie Endowment for International Peace, 2013.
Victor C. Shih, *Factions and Finance in China*, Cambridge University Press, 2008.
Joseph E. Stiglitz, *Globalisation and its Discontents*, Penguin, 2002.
Carl E. Walter and Fraser J.T. Howie, *Red Capitalism: The Fragile Financial Foundation of China's Extraordinary Rise*, John Wiley, 2010.

Demographics & Retirement Savings

Robin Blackburn, *Banking on Death*, Verso, 2002.

Roger Lowenstein, *While America Aged: How Pension Debts Ruined General Motors, Stopped the NYC Subways, Bankrupted San Diego and Loom as the Next Financial Crisis*, Penguin, 2008.

George Magnus, *The Age of Aging: How Demographics are Changing the Global Economy and Our World*, John Wiley, 2009.

Non-Renewable Resources and Environmental Damage

David Attenborough, *A Life on Our Planet*, Penguin Random House, 2020.

Robert Bryce, *Power Hungry: The Myths of 'Green' Energy and the Real Fuels of the Future*, Public Affairs, 2010.

McKenzie Funk, *Windfall: The Booming Business of Global Warming*, Portfolio, 2014.

Elizabeth Kolbert, *Field Notes from a Catastrophe: Man, Nature, and Climate Change*, Bloomsbury, 2006.

J.R.McNeill, *Something New Under the Sun: An Environmental History of the Twentieth-Century World*, W.W. Norton & Company, 2000.

Peter Maass, *Crude World: The Violent Twilight of Oil*, Allen Lane, 2009.

Oliver Morton, *The Planet Remade: How Geoengineering Could Change the World*, Granta, 2016.

Guillaume Pitron (translated by Bianca Jacobsohn), *The Rare Metals of War: The Dark Side of Clean Energy and Digital Technologies*, Scribe, 2020.

Craig Roach, *Simply Electrifying: The Technology that Transformed the World, from Benjamin Franklin to Elon Musk*, BenBella Books, 2017.

Vaclav Smil, *Energy Transitions: History, Requirements, Prospects*, Praeger, 2010.

Steven Solomon, *Water: The Epic Struggle for Wealth, Power, and Civilisation*, Harper Perennial, 2010.

Nicholas Stern, *The Economics of Climate Change: The Stern Review*, Cambridge University Press, 2007.

David Wallace-Wells, *The Uninhabitable Earth: A Story of the Future*, Allen Lane, 2019.

Alan Weisman, *The World Without Us*, Picador, 2007.

Daniel Yergin, *The Prize: The Epic Quest for Oil, Money & Power*, Touchstone Books, 1991.

——*The Quest: Energy, Security, and the Remaking of the Modern World*, Penguin, 2011.

Inequality & Trust

Geoffrey Hosking, *Trust: A History*, Oxford University Press, 2014.

Thomas Piketty, *Capital in the Twenty-First Century*, Belknap Press, 2014.

Richard Wilkinson and Kate Pickett, *The Spirit Level: Why Greater Equality Makes Societies Stronger*, Bloomsbury Press, 2011.

Pandemic

John M. Barry, *The Great Influenza: The Epic Story of the Deadliest Plague in History*, Penguin Random House, 2006.

Laurie Garrett. *The Coming Plague: Newly Emerging Diseases in a World Out of Balance*, Penguin Random House, 1995.

Mark Honigsbaum, *The Pandemic Century: A History of Global Contagion from the Spanish Flu to Covid-19*, Penguin Random House, 2019

Debora MacKenzie, *Covid-19: The Pandemic that Never Should Have Happened, and How to Stop the Next One*, Hachette, 2020.

David Quammen, *Spillover: Animal Infections and the Next Human Pandemic*, Vintage Books, 2012.

Frank M. Snowden, *Epidemics and Society: From the Black Death to the Present*, Yale University Press, 2020.

INDEX